"Triana offers a highly informative, well-written, and well-organized book that will be useful to students, researchers, and practitioners interested in diversity and inclusion issues. One of the strengths of this book is its presentation of examples and case studies from a wide range of international settings, making it a valuable resource for those who study and work outside of North America."

Raymond Trau, *RMIT University, Australia*

"Triana has written an excellent resource for advanced students and teachers of diversity in organizations. She provides thorough coverage of the topic and interweaves the latest research findings with compelling illustrations from the real world and thought-provoking discussion questions. Diversity continues to be a hot topic and Triana provides a text which both educates and engages the reader."

Adrienne Colella, *Tulane University, USA*

"This book provides a clear discussion of how to approach and think about diversity in the workplace. It includes a review of the issues relating to historically disadvantaged groups in the United States, discusses the literature on how diversity can affect team and organizational performance, describes the policy landscape, and gives concrete suggestions for policies that will increase inclusion and collaboration. It is useful reading for anyone who wants to be more aware of the challenges created by diversity within an organization and wishes to build diverse teams that lead to better decision-making and stronger performance."

Rebecca M. Blank, *University of Wisconsin–Madison, USA*

"Taking a global view, this comprehensive and engaging new book gives an excellent overview of the various facets of diversity and the challenges associated with managing diversity in organizations. Providing key term definitions, lively cases, and easy to understand theory, it is a must read for students, scholars, and practitioners alike."

Tanja Rabl, *University of Kaiserslautern, Germany*

"If you're looking to understand why and how business should care for diversity, this is a must-read. By articulating both the benefits and challenges of diversity, this book provides rich theoretical explanations and useful practical implications. Global views are particularly invaluable as workplaces become increasingly diverse around the world."

Kwanghyun "Harry" Kim, *Korea University, South Korea*

Managing Diversity in Organizations

This book equips students with a thorough understanding of the advantages and challenges presented by workplace diversity, suggesting techniques to manage diversity effectively and maximize its benefits. Readers will learn to work with diverse groups to create a productive organization in which everyone feels included.

The author offers a comprehensive survey of demographic groups and an analysis of their history, allowing students to develop a deep understanding of the dimensions of diversity. From this foundation, students are taught to manage diversity effectively on the basis of race, sex, LGBTQIA, religion, age, ability, national origin, and intersectionality in organizations and to understand the issues various groups face, including discrimination. Opening with current case studies and discussion questions to enhance comprehension, the chapters provide practical insight into subconscious/implicit bias, team diversity, and diversity management in the United States and abroad. "Global View" examples further highlight how diversity management unfolds around the world.

Offering a fresh look at workplace diversity, this book will serve students of diversity, human resource management, and organizational studies. A companion website featuring an instructor's manual, PowerPoint slides, and test banks provides additional support for students and instructors.

María del Carmen Triana is an associate professor at the University of Wisconsin–Madison, USA.

Managing Diversity in Organizations

A Global Perspective

MARÍA TRIANA

Routledge
Taylor & Francis Group

NEW YORK AND LONDON

First published 2017
by Routledge
711 Third Avenue, New York, NY 10017

and by Routledge
2 Park Square, Milton Park, Abingdon, Oxon OX14 4RN

Routledge is an imprint of the Taylor & Francis Group, an informa business

© 2017 Taylor & Francis

The right of MTriana, LLC to be identified as author of this work has been asserted by M. Triana in accordance with sections 77 and 78 of the Copyright, Designs and Patents Act 1988.

Library of Congress Cataloging-in-Publication Data
Names: Triana, María del Carmen, author.
Title: Managing diversity in organizations : a global perspective /
    María del Carmen Triana.
Description: 1 Edition. | New York : Routledge, 2017.
Identifiers: LCCN 2016059463 | ISBN 9781138917019 (hbk) |
    ISBN 9781138917026 (pbk) | ISBN 9781315689289 (ebk)
Subjects: LCSH: Diversity in the workplace. | Sex discrimination in
    employment. | Minorities—Employment. | Personnel management.
Classification: LCC HF5549.5.M5 T735 2017 | DDC 658.3008—dc23
LC record available at https://lccn.loc.gov/2016059463

ISBN: 978-1-138-91701-9 (hbk)
ISBN: 978-1-138-91702-6 (pbk)
ISBN: 978-1-315-68928-9 (ebk)

Typeset in Minion
by Apex CoVantage, LLC

Visit the companion website: www.routledge.com/cw/triana

Contents

Tables and Figures

Tables

Figures

Acknowledgments

I am grateful to the diverse team of people who contributed to this book by reviewing chapters, providing feedback, or giving me ideas for the content of the text. Specifically, I would like to thank Alejandro, Binnu, Chris, David, Dora, Dora Maria, Gabe, Fatima, Ilona, Joseph, Lenore, Manuel, Olga, Pradeep, Roque, Sharon, and Vinod.

one
Introduction to Diversity

Opening Case

The San Antonio Spurs: A Diverse National Basketball Association (NBA) Championship Winning Team

Some have referred to the San Antonio Spurs as "The United Nations of Hoops" (Salzbrener, 2014). In June of 2014, the Spurs won their fifth NBA championship in 16 seasons. Tim Duncan, the oldest of the star players on the team at the time (at age 38), had been playing basketball for the Spurs about as long as the youngest player on the Spurs has been alive. The Spurs players also come from all parts of the world. According to the NBA, there were 92 international players in the NBA for the 2013–2014 season across 30 teams, for an expected average of three international players per team. There were 10 international players on the Spurs, more than half the team, which makes the Spurs one of (if not) the most diverse teams in the NBA (NBA, 2013). The men on this team represent the United States, France, Argentina, Italy, Brazil, Australia, Canada, and the U.S. Virgin Islands (Cacciola, 2014). They speak many different languages, come from completely different cultures, and vary dramatically in age and appearance. Yet they play basketball very well and very reliably year after year, making plays that require tacit coordination and execution in a split second. Sportscasters have joked that the only thing the Spurs players have in common is how different they are. How do they handle diversity in the process of being so successful?

Aside from having an excellent coach and players with a great level of ability who complement each others' skills very well, the San Antonio Spurs appear to have a culture that accepts diversity. They are the first NBA team to have a woman assistant coach, Becky Hammon (National Basketball Association, 2014). They also seem to use the players' international diversity to their advantage. For example, they use their knowledge of language to help reinforce plays and tactics on the basketball court. Tony Parker and Boris Diaw are both French and sometimes speak to each other in French during the game when they need to convey something quickly. The two Australians on the team, Patty Mills and Aron Baynes, have their own dialect. Also, Manu Ginobili of Argentina speaks three different languages, Spanish, Italian, and English. He speaks in Spanish to his teammate Tiago Splitter, in Italian to the Italian teammate, Marco Belinelli, and in English with everyone else (Cacciola, 2014). According to Belinelli, "When me and Manu speak Italian on court, we try to use that as an advantage" (Cacciola, 2014). Therefore, they have found a way to take a situation that might normally present language barriers and have turned it into a tactical advantage (Rice, 2014).

It is also notable that their coach seems quite open to diversity and respectful of the multicultural background of his team (Salzbrenner, 2014). The coach, Gregg Popovich, had a Serbian father and a Croatian mother and takes pleasure in learning about his players' backgrounds. In fact, when they go on the road trips, the team visits museums together. According to a quote from Popovich, "I think it's just a respect for letting them know you understand they are from another place. We all grew up differently." Popovich majored in Soviet studies while at the Air Force Academy and is known for being able to converse a little bit in different languages with various players (Cacciola, 2014).

This is an example of how diversity can be an advantage in teams if it is managed properly (Salzbrenner, 2014). The subgroups within the team that form based on nationality and language are used up to the point where they provide camaraderie and a tactical advantage. Beyond that, the players carefully note that they speak English most of the time because they do not want the majority of the team to feel excluded (Cacciola, 2014). Further, by having a coach who sets a tone of inclusion and valuing their multiculturalism, diversity becomes a strength and its challenges are mitigated (Rice, 2014).

Discussion Questions:

1. In what ways do you think the diversity of the Spurs could be an advantage?
2. In what ways do you think the diversity of the Spurs could present challenges?
3. If you were coaching the Spurs, what types of things would you do to mitigate the potential challenges and increase the team's advantage associated with diversity?

Learning Objectives

After reading this chapter, you should be able to:

- Define diversity
- Discuss different types of diversity
- Understand the arguments behind the business case for diversity
- Articulate both the advantages and the challenges of diversity

This chapter defines diversity and explains that diversity comes in many different forms. Then, research findings on the advantages of diversity and the business case for diversity as well as the challenges of diversity are presented. Suggestions for managing diversity based on best-known methods from diversity research are discussed. Finally, the chapter concludes with a short statement about the organization of the subsequent chapters in the book.

What Is Diversity?

Organizations worldwide are becoming more diverse. By 2050 there will be no majority racial/ethnic group in the United States (Cárdenas, Ajinkya, & Léger, 2011). In Europe, the European Union has facilitated commerce and employment across national boundaries. Globalization, immigration, and expatriate assignments across many parts of the world including Asia, the Middle East, Latin America, and Africa have also contributed to the diversity of organizations today. As workplaces become increasingly diverse, it is increasingly likely that subordinates and supervisors will come from different demographic backgrounds or religions, hold different cultural values about the nature of work and their roles at work, and have differences along several other dimensions (Jun & Gentry, 2005; Taras, Steel, & Kirkman, 2012). This diversity presents great opportunity for organizations to innovate and to improve their performance both domestically and abroad, and it also presents the challenge of managing diversity well in order to obtain the benefits of a diverse workforce.

Diversity is defined as "the distribution of differences among the members of a unit with respect to a common attribute X" (Harrison & Klein, 2007, p. 1200). Others have defined diversity as a group characteristic that reflects the degree to which there are objective and/or subjective differences among group members (van Knippenberg & Schippers, 2007). Quite simply, diversity can be any difference between the members of a group on any given dimension. Diversity can be real, or it can be perceived by the members of the team. Examples of attributes on which teams can be diverse include sex, race, age, personality traits, attitudes, values, religion, skin color, hair color, education, sexual orientation, functional area, and organizational tenure to name a few.

Diversity is a unit-level construct. Therefore, we refer to a team as being diverse but not an individual. Team diversity has been studied at the **dyadic** level (typically between supervisors and subordinates), team level, and organizational level.

Team-level diversity has been a popular research topic over the past few decades given the overwhelming use of work teams in organizations and the global nature of today's workforce (Jackson, May, & Whitney, 1995; Milliken & Martins, 1996). Recently, much research on team diversity has been devoted to understanding the reasons why there are so many inconsistent results in the study of team diversity (van Knippenberg & Schippers, 2007; Webber & Donahue, 2001).

Different Types of Diversity

Attributes that make up a team's diversity can be classified into what is called **surface-level** and **deep-level** diversity (Harrison, Price, & Bell, 1998; Jackson et al., 1995). Surface-level diversity refers to characteristics that are noticeable when you look at someone "on the surface." This includes things like sex, race, age, and weight. Deep-level diversity refers to attributes that are not immediately observable such as attitudes, values, and personality. Pelled and colleagues (Pelled, 1996; Pelled, Eisenhardt, & Xin, 1999) categorized diversity attributes as being **highly job-related** (e.g., knowledge, experience) or **less job-related** (e.g., sex, race) to the task that is to be performed by the team.

Harrison and Klein (2007) proposed that there are three distinct types of diversity: **separation**, **variety**, and **disparity**. Diversity as separation refers to differences on a particular attribute such as attitudes, beliefs, and values. Examples of separation diversity would include cultural values, job attitudes, and political beliefs. Diversity as variety refers to differences in knowledge, life experience, and information among team members. Examples include different professional backgrounds, functional areas, and expertise. Finally, diversity as disparity refers to differences in status or power. This could reflect the concentration of resources including status, pay, and the prestige of assignments among team members. Separation in a team will likely increase conflict, but it should also produce better decisions due to the increase in knowledge from various perspectives. Variety should also help teams because it represents expertise and information, but it is potentially linked to a longer decision-making process and conflict due to the volume of information being considered. Disparity diversity is probably the most damaging in most contexts because it can create a situation where some team members feel more valued than others, possibly causing the rest of the team members to become dissatisfied, withdraw from work, or compete for resources, all of which can damage camaraderie.

More recently, researchers have begun to examine multiple forms of diversity that can create divisions within a team, known as **faultlines**. Faultlines are hypothetical dividing lines which divide a group into subgroups based on the alignment of team members' attributes (Lau & Murnighan, 1998). For example, if a team of six people is comprised of three men and three women, that team would have a faultline on gender because half are obviously men and the other half are women. Faultlines research presumes that group members act in ways consistent with their subgroups, based on the alignment of individual characteristics (Bez-rukova, Jehn, Zanutto, & Thatcher, 2009; Lau & Murnighan, 2005; Williams & O'Reilly, 1998). Therefore, while traditional diversity measures examine the effects of group-level attributes in teams (i.e., overall level of gender diversity in a team), faultlines explain how the alignment of attributes within the group can create subgroup-level dynamics (Lau & Murnighan, 1998).

Why Is Diversity Obvious to People?

In order to understand why diversity matters and why it affects teams and organizations, it is necessary to study the major diversity theories that explain diversity in teams. **Relational demography theory** (Pfeffer, 1983) represents some of the earliest work in the team diversity literature which examined the basic characteristics of teams (e.g., tenure, age, gender, race). Continuing this line of work, others have explored diversity within dyadic relationships (typically supervisor–subordinate; Tsui, Egan, & O'Reilly, 1992). Relational demography researchers suggest that people compare their own demographic characteristics with those of their teammates to determine whether they are similar or different; those demographic similarities or differences then affect team communication, team processes, and team dynamics (Riordan, 2000; Tsui et al., 1992; Tsui & O'Reilly, 1989).

Some of the most influential theories in the study of team diversity are the **social categorization theories** and the **value in diversity hypothesis**. Social categorization theories are based on the ideas of **social identity** and **self-categorization** (Hogg & Terry, 2000; Tajfel, 1978; Tajfel & Turner, 1986; Turner, 1985, 1987). **Self-categorization** theory maintains that people categorize themselves and others into **in-group** (those who are similar to them) and **out-group** (those who are different from them) membership based on surface-level characteristics (e.g., age, sex, and race; Harrison, Price, & Bell, 1998). These categories then determine social inclusion/exclusion of others. This is an important factor in team dynamics because **social identity theory** shows that we derive part of our self-esteem from our identity groups (Hogg & Terry, 2000). Therefore, we tend to ascribe positive characteristics to those in our in-group and negative characteristics to those in our out-group. Self-categorization theory has been termed the "pessimistic" view of diversity (Mannix & Neale, 2005, p. 34) because demographic differences often have negative effects on group processes and outcomes (Horwitz & Horwitz, 2007; Webber & Donahue, 2001; Williams & O'Reilly, 1998).

This reasoning is also consistent with the **similarity-attraction hypothesis** (Byrne, 1971) which predicts that diverse teams will be less productive than homogenous teams because homogenous teams share similar attributes and are more attracted to working with one another. Mutual attraction can help make team processes such as communication more efficient, and team members may cooperate more with members of their in-group than with members of the out-group (van Knippenberg, De Dreu, & Homan, 2004) because of **intergroup bias**.

The Business Case for Diversity

The **value in diversity hypothesis** (Cox & Blake, 1991; Cox, Lobel, & McLeod, 1991) has been called the "optimistic" view of diversity (Mannix & Neale, 2005, p. 33). It proposes many ways in which diversity can create value for teams and how that value could overshadow any negative effects of team diversity, providing a competitive advantage (Cox & Blake, 1991; Cox et al., 1991). The **creativity argument** is one of these ways.

The creativity argument suggests that a diversity of opinions in a decision-making process should de-emphasize conforming to norms of the past and should spur creativity (Cox & Blake, 1991, p. 47). The value in diversity hypothesis also proposes a **problem-solving argument** explaining that diverse teams should produce better decisions via a wider range of perspectives considered and a more thorough analysis of issues (Cox & Blake, 1991, p. 47). The value in diversity hypothesis also presents a **cost argument**, which means that as organizations become more diverse, those that are able to integrate diversity more smoothly will realize cost advantages. The **resource-acquisition argument** proposes that companies with a good reputation for being inclusive and integrating diversity well will win the competition for the best talent. The **marketing argument** suggests that diverse companies with a wealth of cultural information among employees will be able to better market their products in foreign markets as well as to domestic subgroups of the population. Finally, the **system flexibility argument** states that companies adopting a multicultural approach to managing diversity will be less rigid and more fluid, which will allow them to better respond to environmental change (Cox & Blake, 1991, p. 47).

Another major perspective describing the advantages of diversity is the **information-processing perspective** (Galbraith, 1974; Sanders & Carpenter, 1998; Tihanyi & Thomas, 2005). This perspective argues that any time there is task uncertainty, there is a greater amount of information which must be processed to accomplish a task and obtain good performance (Galbraith, 1974; Sanders & Carpenter, 1998; Tihanyi & Thomas, 2005). Particularly when organizations enter new markets and conduct business abroad, having diverse employees who understand those markets will provide knowledge about local laws, norms, and culture which are important to the firm's success. A diverse workforce can help an organization meet information-processing demands and yield a competitive advantage by providing appropriate perspectives on cultural, institutional, and competitive environments (Lawrence & Lorsch, 1967).

When conducting business in an international setting, having a diverse board of directors and/or firm executives with expertise related to the regions in which a firm does business will be critical to firm performance. Sanders and Carpenter (1998) report that since internationalization increases the complexity of a company and its information-processing demands, firms can meet these information-processing demands through their governance structure. Firm internationalization is positively related to the size of a board of directors (Sanders & Carpenter, 1998), which implies firms can handle the complexity of international operations by adding members with knowledge of institutional, cultural, and competitive environments pertaining to the regions in question. Gómez-Mejía and Palich (1997) also described that when firms conduct business abroad they are exposed to unfamiliar environmental conditions, and having resources to help the firm make decisions will help counteract any performance losses brought about by a lack of understanding the environment. Hutzschenreuter, Voll, and Verbeke (2011) further found that the larger the cultural distance between the home country and an international venture, the slower the international expansion. Because cultural distance is associated with complexity, companies must adjust their coordination to match the culture in the new market (Gómez-Mejía & Palich, 1997; Hutzschenreuter et al., 2011). In sum, the information-processing perspective explains why diverse employees including the board of directors and executives can help companies navigate the cultural complexities they encounter in foreign countries and, therefore, perform better.

A prominent example of a company that has successfully drawn on its employees' diversity to obtain a competitive advantage is IDEO, a Silicon Valley–based organization that specializes in the process of innovation. IDEO deliberately forms diverse teams whereby team members bring diverse educational, functional, and demographic backgrounds to the team. Such diversity allows IDEO to generate many rich ideas and perspectives during team processes, thereby generating a richer pool of ideas and solutions from which to innovate. This has allowed IDEO to be a leader in the creativity and innovation space for decades. For a documentary (produced by Nightline, 1999) about the creative process that made IDEO famous, see the following link: https://www.youtube.com/watch?v=taJOV-YCieI. For information about the company today, see www.ideo.com.

The Positive and Negative Effects of Diversity

Diversity researchers sometimes describe diversity as a double-edged sword because diversity can be both helpful and challenging for organizations and teams (Mannix & Neale, 2005; Milliken & Martins, 1996). For example, studies examining the relationship between diversity on boards of directors and firm outcomes are inconsistent, with some positive effects (Carter, Simkins, & Simpson, 2003; Erhardt, Werbel, & Shrader, 2003; Galbreath, 2011; Mahadeo, Soobaroyen, & Hanuman, 2012; Miller & Triana, 2009; Torchia, Calabrò, & Huse, 2011), some negative effects (Shrader, Blackburn, & Iles, 1997), and some non-significant effects (Dwyer, Richard, & Chadwick, 2003; Miller & Triana, 2009). Several theories of diversity have been put forth to explain why sometimes diversity helps teams and other times it does not.

Findings Supporting the Optimistic View of Diversity

Consistent with the value in diversity hypothesis, which discusses ways in which diversity is helpful to organizations and teams because it creates a pool of information (Cox & Blake, 1991; Cox et al., 1991), several studies show that diversity helps team performance. A team with a greater variety of information, experiences, and perspectives is more likely to have a larger pool of task-relevant information than a team with less information and fewer experiences and perspectives (Milliken & Martins, 1996). Diverse groups that can exchange, discuss, and integrate the task-relevant information are more likely to reap the rewards of these informational resources (van Knippenberg et al., 2004). Diverse teams operating under these conditions are more likely to reach higher quality and more creative and innovative outcomes (van Knippenberg & Schippers, 2007). In a **meta-analysis** (a study that statistically aggregates the results of many other studies), Horwitz and Horwitz (2007) found that task-related diversity was positively related to both quality and quantity of team performance; the effects were small in magnitude but positive. Demographic diversity, however, showed a near zero relationship with team performance. Therefore, task-relevant information seems more directly helpful to teams in most instances than demographic diversity. In instances where the task at hand requires knowledge of another culture or demographic group, then demographic diversity would be task-relevant information and should help the team succeed.

Research also shows that team diversity may be helpful to teams on many different outcome variables, not just team performance. For example, diverse teams produce more creative solutions than do homogenous teams (Jackson, 1992; Triandis, Hall, & Ewen, 1965). Especially on complicated or difficult tasks, having a diversity of knowledge and perspectives seems important to enhance the alternatives discussed and the quality of decisions made.

Research also shows that team diversity on the board of directors may help performance at the organizational level. The board of directors is a team because its members are interdependent and share a common goal of successful organizational performance (Forbes & Milliken, 1999; Kozlowski & Bell, 2003). Several studies find a positive relationship between demographic diversity on boards of directors and firm performance (Bilimoria, 2006; Burke, 2000; Carter et al., 2003; Erhardt et al., 2003). For example, gender diversity may help a firm through the expertise, resources, and perspectives of women directors (Bilimoria & Wheeler, 2000; Hillman, Shropshire, & Cannella, 2007; Miller & Triana, 2009). Torchia et al. (2011) showed that having three or more women on boards positively influenced firm innovation through board strategic tasks. Miller and Triana (2009) found a positive relationship between board racial diversity and each of firm innovation, firm reputation, and firm performance. Richard, Murthi, and Ismail (2007) found that organizational racial diversity was positively related to long-term firm performance.

Along these lines, diverse boards of directors have been linked to firm innovation (Miller & Triana, 2009; Torchia et al., 2011). A diverse team with differing perspectives should produce a broader range of ideas which spur innovation (Amason & Sapienza, 1997; Milliken & Vollrath, 1991; Schweiger, Sandberg, & Ragan, 1996). Conflict resulting from diverse perspectives might also be good in some instances if it leads to devil's advocacy (Schulz-Hardt, Jochims, & Frey, 2002), and informational differences across subgroups can lead to increased monitoring (Tuggle, Schnatterly, & Johnson, 2010), higher vigilance (Ormiston & Wong, 2012), and lower collusion (Jehn & Bezrukova, 2012) among individuals. These things could all be good for boards of directors if their governance capability increases because they do a better job of monitoring the activities of the executives to ensure shareholder interests are met.

Global View: Diversity Efforts at Multinational Companies

A very interesting article was recently published in the *Economist* (2014) on how multinational companies are making substantial efforts to be more connected to and know more about other parts of the world. Here are some examples cited in that article:

- Proctor & Gamble relocated a global cosmetics unit from Cincinnati to Singapore.
- General Electric Health Care moved the headquarters of an X-ray business from Wisconsin to Beijing.
- Daimler-Benz has decided that half of its participants in a company leadership program should come from outside Germany (*Economist*, 2014).

In a different article, Hong and Doz (2013) describe multiculturalism efforts by L'Oréal, the global French cosmetics company based in Paris. "It has built a portfolio of brands from many cultures—French, of course (L'Oréal Paris, Garnier, Lancôme), but also American (Maybelline, Kiehl's, SoftSheen-Carson), British (The Body Shop), Italian (Giorgio Armani), and Japanese (Shu Uemura). The company now has offices in more than 130 countries, and in 2012 over half its sales came from new markets outside Europe and North America, mostly in emerging economies" (Hong & Doz, 2013). According to Jean-Paul Agon, Chairman and CEO of L'Oreal, "A diversified workforce in every function and on all levels strengthens our creativity and our understanding of consumers and it enables us to develop and market products that are relevant" (Agon, 2017). This is another example of how a large multinational company is using diversity to its advantage.

Findings Supporting the Pessimistic View of Diversity

Supporting the pessimistic view of diversity, other research studies suggest that diversity can lead to less cooperation, coordination, and cohesion among team members, which ultimately reduces team performance (Milliken & Martins, 1996). If diversity increases the volume of information and perspectives discussed in a team, it also comes at a cost because it may impede group decision-making (Miller, Burke, & Glick, 1998) due to difficulty reaching consensus (Goodstein, Gautam, & Boecker, 1994) or increased conflict (Jehn, Chadwick, & Thatcher, 1997). Social categorization may lead to lengthy or inefficient processes in teams due to difficulty in communicating, trouble coordinating, a lack of cohesion, or increased levels of conflict (Horwitz & Horwitz, 2007; Jehn et al., 1997; Pelled, 1996; Webber & Donahue, 2001; Williams & O'Reilly, 1998). In a review of team diversity, Van Knippenberg and Schippers (2007) concluded that a number of studies present results consistent with social categorization theory, but few studies have tested or revealed the reasons why demographic team diversity is often negatively related to team performance. They suggested that more research is necessary to uncover the variables that may explain this process.

At the organizational level, some studies report negative or no effects of diversity on firm performance. Miller et al. (1998) reported that cognitive diversity among executives inhibited rather than promoted long-term planning. The authors surmised that because diversity produces differing opinions, executives were more likely to have trouble agreeing on a course of action, which would inhibit their ability to make changes at the firm level. This finding is consistent with reviews of team diversity research showing that surface-level diversity, including gender diversity, can reduce cohesion and cooperation in a team and lead to conflict that may impact team decision-making (Webber & Donahue, 2001; Williams & O'Reilly, 1998). Adams and Ferreira (2009) found that while having women directors improved monitoring, the effect of board gender diversity on firm performance was negative. Dobbin and Jung (2011) found that board gender diversity was negatively associated with future stock price because the investors responded negatively to the appointment of women to boards. Shrader et al. (1997) also found a negative relationship between the percentage of women on boards and firm performance. Other researchers have reported no relationship between board demographic diversity and firm performance. For instance, Richard (2000) found no relationship between firm racial diversity and firm performance. Richard, Barnett, Dwyer, and Chadwick (2004) found a negative relationship and no relationship between racial diversity in management and firm productivity and return on equity (respectively). Bezrukova et al. (2009) found a small negative effect (not statistically significant) between demographic faultlines and both perceived team performance and team discretionary awards. Dwyer et al. (2003), Dimovski and Brooks (2006), Miller and Triana (2009), and Richard et al. (2004) reported no significant relationship between board gender diversity and firm performance. In sum, consistent with research describing the double-edged nature of diversity, some studies find that diversity helps while others find that it does not (e.g., Mannix & Neale, 2005).

Global View: England

Inevitably, one issue that frequently arises as organizations become more diverse is that of representation of the minority group both in desirable organizational positions and in positions of power in organizations. As members of minority groups become part of organizations, people will inevitably notice if those minority members seem to be occupationally segregated into certain positions, often lower-level positions, whereas members of the majority group tend to occupy the higher-level positions. In England, the Sports People's Think Tank is asking why there are so few Black and ethnic minority coaches and suggesting a target of 20% minority coaches (*BBC News*, 2014a).

BBC News recently reported that there are 19 Black and racial/ethnic minority coaches out of 552 top coaching jobs within England (Conway, 2014). This report, which was created by Sports Persons' Think Tank, found that while at least 25% of players are Black or racial ethnic minorities, only 3.4% of the top coaching jobs are held by minorities. This has prompted people to say that institutional discrimination appears to be present in these English sports leagues and to question whether England should adopt something similar to the Rooney Rule adopted in the United States in 2002 for the same reason. The Rooney Rule requires that when a head coach or general manager position comes open, the team must interview at least one person who is a racial or ethnic minority for that position (Conway, 2014).

Racial and ethnic minorities are not the only ones who have had difficulty making inroads in some organizations. Women also face challenges. Also from England, the *BBC News* reported that a male official from the Northumberland County Football Association told a female referee that "a woman's place is in the kitchen and not on a football field" (*BBC News*, 2014b). Afterwards, this official apologized and said it has been a joke for 20 years that a woman's place is in the home (*BBC News*, 2014b). Others did not find this joke as amusing as he did. For the record, the official policy of the Northumberland County Football Association on discrimination is as follows:

> The Northumberland FA, in all its activities, will not discriminate, nor treat anyone less favourably, on grounds of gender, sexual orientation, marital status, race, nationality, ethnic origin, religion or belief, ability or disability. The Northumberland FA will ensure that it treats people fairly and with respect and will provide access and opportunities for all members of the community to take part in, and enjoy, its activities.
>
> (*BBC News*, 2014b)

Best Practices for Managing Diversity

Research shows that for diversity management practices to be successful, they need to have the support of top management and managers need to be held responsible for diversity outcomes (Cox, 1994; Kalev, Dobbin, & Kelly, 2006; Kossek & Zonia, 1993). Team members also need to be of a mind-set that diversity can be an opportunity rather than a threat. Problems are more likely to arise in diverse teams when the team members have a low value of diversity (van Dick, van Knippenberg, Hägele, Guillaume, & Brodbeck, 2008).

The way in which the organization's leadership approaches diversity is also important. Diversity practices that endorse multiculturalism, which acknowledges differences between different groups, have a more positive impact on social interactions than a colorblind approach, which attempts to ignore differences between groups (Vorauer, Gagnon, & Sasaki, 2009). The problem with the colorblind approach is that it encourages people to prevent problems by ignoring their differences and trying to avoid discussions that could offend others. However, this may inadvertently result in people becoming apprehensive and reducing communication between groups, which may lead to poor team dynamics. While emphasizing the similarities between team members could increase harmony in the team, it also discourages individuals from analyzing issues from multiple perspectives and engaging in deeper and more complex discussions (Todd, Hanko, Galinsky, & Mussweiler, 2010). Instead, a more robust approach to diversity management could be to have a zero-tolerance policy for discriminatory or exclusive behavior combined with a mentality that multiculturalism is an advantage to an organization and differences are to be embraced and respected. Diversity management will be discussed in more detail in Chapter 15 (Diversity Management).

Global View: New Zealand

We can also see examples from around the world about why diversity management is important.

In New Zealand, the New Zealand Institute of Management and the Government's Office of Ethnic Affairs have united in an initiative to help businesses "meet new world employment, management, marketplace and growth strategies" (Birchfield, 2013). In an effort to help the businesses of New Zealand think more internationally and succeed in business ventures abroad, the government is delivering "public and in-company ethnic diversity programmes to businesses and other organizations" (Birchfield, 2013). The Institute of Management New Zealand (2017) currently offers a course called Managing for Diversity which teaches students how to avoid unconscious bias and reap the benefits of workplace diversity.

The Roadmap for the Chapters That Follow

This book is organized into four sections. Section 1 is an overview on diversity, the study of diversity, and legislation. This section will provide a summary of the major diversity theories used in diversity research to understand organizational diversity as well as legislation in the United States and abroad. Section 2 is about the major types of human differences that result in diversity. This includes race/ethnicity, gender, sexual orientation, religion, age, disability, national origin and immigration, and other types of diversity such as weight, appearance, pregnancy, family responsibility, and genetics. Section 3 will cover how differences unfold for individuals and teams. This will include a chapter on the intersectionality of different types of diversity as well as a chapter on team diversity. Finally, Section 4 covers diversity management challenges and successes. This section will include chapters on subconscious/implicit bias and diversity management and concluding comments for the book.

Closing Case

Black Pete: A Diversity Conflict in Amsterdam

Black Pete is a controversial character in Amsterdam. He is a historical figure and sidekick to Santa Claus, but he also portrays a negative image of Blacks. The Mayor of Amsterdam has stated that Black Pete will change appearance over the next few years to become less offensive (Schuetze, 2014).

Black Pete is always represented by White citizens wearing dark makeup with red painted lips and an Afro hairdo. Many in the Netherlands, a predominantly White country, enjoy this festive tradition. They say that St. Nick's helper is an inoffensive fictitious character and that no offense is intended (*USA Today*, 2014). However, those against the idea argue that Black Pete perpetuates racist stereotypes against Blacks. Protesters have been going to Amsterdam City Hall to complain about Black Pete. One Black man who filed a formal complaint said he grew up as the only Black person in his class and remembers being taunted and asked if he could do tricks (Sterling, 2013). He said others are afraid to speak out against Black Pete for fear of being ridiculed or losing their jobs (Sterling, 2013).

According to the court, "Black Pete's appearance in combination with the fact that he is often portrayed as dumb and servile makes it a negative stereotype of Black people" (*USA Today*, 2014). A recent article related to human rights reported that the Dutch in command of the festival frequently act in opposition and with "irritation and dismissal" when the topic of racism is raised, even though work discrimination is documented in the country (*USA Today*, 2014). The Amsterdam District Court asked the city to re-evaluate its decision to grant permission for a part of the festival where many children attend "the arrival of St. Nicholas, or Sinterklaas" (*USA Today*, 2014).

Discussion Questions:

1. Do you agree with the Amsterdam citizens who say that Black Pete is a fictitious character and that no offense is intended? Why? Why not?
2. It seems that the festival is liked by most people because it has been a tradition for many years. Can you think of some changes the Dutch can make in order to keep their tradition from offending others?

References

Adams, R. B., & Ferreira, D. (2009). Women in the boardroom and their impact on governance and performance. *Journal of Financial Economics*, *94*, 291–309.

Agon, J-P. (2017). L'Oreal Diversity and Inclusion. Retrieved from http://www.lorealusa.com/group/diversity-and-inclusion

Amason, A. C., & Sapienza, H. J. (1997). The effects of top management team size and interaction norms on cognitive and affective conflict. *Journal of Management*, *23*(4), 495–516.

BBC News. (2014a, November 11). Black and ethnic minority coaches: Think tank sets 20% target. *BBC Sport*. Retrieved from http://www.bbc.com/sport/football/29996225

BBC News. (2014b, November 20). "Kitchen" insult appeal dismissed. *BBC Sport*. Retrieved from http://www.bbc.com/sport/0/football/30130219

Bezrukova, K., Jehn, K., Zanutto, E., & Thatcher, S. (2009). Do workgroup faultlines help or hurt? A moderated model of faultlines, team identification, and group performance. *Organization Science*, *20*(1), 35–50.

Bilimoria, D. (2006). The relationship between women corporate directors and women corporate officers. *Journal of Managerial Issues*, *18*(1), 47–61.

Bilimoria, D., & Wheeler, J. V. (2000). Women corporate directors: Current research and future directions. In R. J. Burke & M. C. Mattis (Eds.), *Women in management: Current research issues* (pp. 138–163). London: Sage.

Birchfield, R. (2013). A diversity of attractions. *New Zealand Management*, *60*(4), 18–19.

Burke, R. J. (2000). Women on Canadian corporate boards of directors: Still a long way to go. In R. J. Burke & M. C. Mattis (Eds.), *Women on corporate boards of directors: International challenges and opportunities* (pp. 97–110). Dordrecht: Kluwer Academic Publishers.

Byrne, D. (1971). *The attraction paradigm*. New York: Academic Press.

Cacciola, S. (2014, June 15). The United Nations of the hardwood: San Antonio Spurs use language barriers to their advantage. Retrieved from http://www.nytimes.com/2014/06/16/sports/basketball/san-antonio-spurs-use-language-barriers-to-their-advantage.html?_r=0

Cárdenas, V., Ajinkya, J., & Léger, D. G. (2011, October). Progress 2050: New ideas for a diverse America. Center for American Progress. Retrieved from https://cdn.americanprogress.org/wp-content/uploads/issues/2011/10/pdf/progress_2050.pdf

Carter, D. A., Simkins, B. J., & Simpson, W. G. (2003). Corporate governance, board diversity, and firm value. *Financial Review, 38*, 33–53.

Conway, R. (2014, November 10). Black and ethnic minority coaches not getting top jobs, study shows. *BBC News*, Sport Football. Retrieved from http://www.bbc.com/sport/0/football/29976832

Cox, T. H., Jr. (1994). *Cultural diversity in organizations: Theory, research and practice*. San Francisco, CA: Berrett-Koehler.

Cox, T. H., & Blake, S. (1991). Managing cultural diversity: Implications for organizational competitiveness. *Academy of Management Executive, 5*, 45–56.

Cox, T. H., Lobel, S. A., & McLeod, P. L. (1991). Effects of ethnic group cultural differences on cooperative and competitive behavior on a group task. *Academy of Management Journal, 34*(4), 827–847.

Dimovski, W., & Brooks, R. (2006). The gender composition of boards after an IPO. *Corporate Governance, 6*, 11–17.

Dobbin, F., & Jung, J. (2011). Corporate board gender diversity and stock performance: The competence gap or institutional investor bias? *North Carolina Law Review, 89*, 809–838.

Dwyer, S., Richard, O. C., & Chadwick, K. (2003). Gender diversity in management and firm performance: The influence of growth orientation and organizational culture. *Journal of Business Research, 56*(12), 1009–1019.

Economist. (2014, May 10). Bumpkin Bosses. Retrieved from http://www.economist.com/news/business/21601889-leaders-western-companies-are-less-globally-minded-they-think-they-are-bumpkin-bosses

Erhardt, N. L., Werbel, J. D., & Shrader, C. B. (2003). Board of director diversity and firm financial performance. *Corporate Governance: An International Review, 11*(2), 102–111.

Forbes, D. P., & Milliken, F. J. (1999). Cognition and corporate governance: Understanding boards of directors as strategic decision-making groups. *Academy of Management Review, 24*(3), 489–505.

Galbreath, J. (2011). Are there gender-related influences on corporate sustainability? A study of women on boards of directors. *Journal of Management & Organizations, 17*, 17–38.

Galbraith, J. R. (1974). Organizational design: An information processing view. *Interfaces, 4*(3), 28–36.

Gómez-Mejía, L. R., & Palich, L. E. (1997). Cultural diversity and the performance of multinational firms. *Journal of International Business Studies, 28*(2), 309–336.

Goodstein, J., Gautam, K., & Boecker, W. (1994). The effects of board size and diversity on strategic change. *Strategic Management Journal, 15*, 241–250.

Harrison, D. A., & Klein, K. J. (2007). What's the difference? Diversity constructs as separation, variety, and disparity in organization. *Academy of Management Review, 32*, 1199–1228.

Harrison, D. A., Price, K. H., & Bell, M. P. (1998). Beyond relational demography: Time and the effects of surface- and deep-level diversity on group cohesion. *Academy of Management Journal, 41*, 96–107.

Hillman, A. J., Shropshire, C., & Cannella, A. A. (2007). Organizational predictors of women on corporate boards. *Academy of Management Journal, 50*(4), 941–952.

Hogg, M., & Terry, D. J. (2000). Social identity and self-categorization processes in organizational contexts. *Academy of Management Review, 25*, 121–140.

Hong, H., & Doz, Y. (2013). L'Oréal masters multiculturalism. *Harvard Business Review, 91*, 114–119.

Horwitz, S. K., & Horwitz, I. B. (2007). The effects of team diversity on team outcomes: A meta-analytic review of team demography. *Journal of Management, 33*, 987–1015.

Hutzschenreuter, T., Voll, J. C., & Verbeke, A. (2011). The impact of added cultural distance and cultural diversity on international expansion patterns: A Penrosean perspective. *Journal of Management Studies, 48,* 305–329.

Institute of Management New Zealand. (2017). 2017 Training Directory. Retrieved from http://imnz.net.nz/

Jackson, S. E. (1992). Team composition in organizational settings: Issues in managing an increasingly diverse work force. In S. Worchel, W. Wood, & J. A. Simpson (Eds.), *Group process and productivity* (pp. 138–173). Newbury Park, CA: Sage.

Jackson, S. E., May, K. E., & Whitney, K. (1995). Understanding the dynamics of diversity in decision-making teams. In R. Guzzo, E. Salas, & Associates (Eds.), *Team effectiveness and decision making in organizations* (pp. 204–261). San Francisco, CA: Jossey Bass Publishers.

Jehn, K. A., & Bezrukova, K. (2012). The faultline activation process and the effects of activated faultlines on coalition formation, conflict, and group outcomes. *Organizational Behavior and Human Decision Processes, 112*(1), 24–42.

Jehn, K. A., Chadwick, C., & Thatcher, S. (1997). To agree or not to agree: The effects of value congruence, individual demographic dissimilarity, and conflict in workgroup outcomes. *International Journal of Conflict Management, 8,* 287–305.

Jun, S., & Gentry, J. W. (2005). An exploratory investigation of the relative importance of cultural similarity and personal fit in the selection and performance of expatriates. *Journal of World Business, 40,* 1–8.

Kalev, A., Dobbin, F., & Kelly, E. (2006). Best practices or best guesses? Assessing the efficacy of corporate affirmative action and diversity policies. *American Sociological Review, 71,* 589–617. doi:10.1177/000312240607100404.

Kossek, E. E., & Zonia, S. C. (1993). Assessing diversity climate: A field study of reactions to employer efforts to promote diversity. *Journal of Organizational Behavior, 14,* 61–81.

Kozlowski, S. W. J., & Bell, B. S. (2003). Work groups and teams in organizations. In W. C. Borman, D. R. Ilgen, & R. Klimoski (Eds.), *Handbook of industrial and organizational psychology* (Vol. 12, pp. 333–375). New York: Wiley.

Lau, D. C., & Murnighan, J. K. (1998). Demographic diversity and faultlines: The compositional dynamics of organizational groups. *Academy of Management Review, 23*(2), 325–340.

Lau, D. C., & Murnighan, J. K. (2005). Interactions within groups and subgroups: The effects of demographic faultlines. *Academy of Management Journal, 48*(4), 645–659.

Lawrence, P. R., & Lorsch, J. W. (1967). Differentiation and integration in complex organizations. *Administrative Science Quarterly, 12,* 1–47.

Mahadeo, J. D., Soobaroyen, T., & Hanuman, V. O. (2012). Board composition and financial performance: Uncovering the effects of diversity in an emerging economy. *Journal of Business Ethics, 105,* 375–388.

Mannix, E., & Neale, M. A. (2005). What differences make a difference? The promise and reality of diverse teams in organizations. *Psychological Science in the Public Interest, 6*(2), 31–55.

Miller, C. C., Burke, L. M., & Glick, W. H. (1998). Cognitive diversity among upper-echelon executives: Implications for strategic decision processes. *Strategic Management Journal, 19*(1), 39–58.

Miller, T., & Triana, M. (2009). Demographic diversity in the boardroom: Mediators of the board diversity-firm performance relationship. *Journal of Management Studies, 46*(5), 755–786.

Milliken, F. J., & Martins, L. L. (1996). Searching for common threads: Understanding the multiple effects of diversity in organizational groups. *Academy of Management Review, 21*(2), 402–433.

Milliken, F. J., & Vollrath, D. (1991). Strategic decision-making tasks and group effectiveness: Insights from theory and research on small groups. *Human Relations, 44*, 1229–1253.

National Basketball Association (NBA). (2013, October 29). NBA tips off 2013–2014 season with record international player presence. Retrieved from http://www.nba.com/global/nba_tips_off_201314_season_with_record_international_presence_2013_10_29.html

National Basketball Association (NBA). (2014, August 5). Spurs name Becky Hammon assistant coach. Retrieved from http://www.nba.com/spurs/spurs-name-becky-hammon-assistant-coach

Nightline. (1999, July 13). IDEO shopping cart project. Retrieved from https://www.youtube.com/watch?v=taJOV-YCieI

Ormiston, M. E., & Wong, E. M. (2012). The gleam of the double-edged sword: The benefits of subgroups for organizational ethics. *Psychological Science, 23*(4), 400–403.

Pelled, L. H. (1996). Demographic diversity, conflict, and work group outcomes: An intervening process theory. *Organization Science, 7*, 615–631.

Pelled, L. H., Eisenhardt, K. M., & Xin, K. R. (1999). Exploring the black box: An analysis of work group diversity, conflict, and performance. *Administrative Science Quarterly, 44*, 1–28.

Pfeffer, J. (1983). Organizational demography. In B. M. Staw & L. L. Cummings (Eds.), *Research in organizational behavior* (Vol. 5, pp. 299–357). Greenwich, CT: JAI Press.

Richard, O. C. (2000). Racial diversity, business strategy, and firm performance: A resource-based view. *Academy of Management Journal, 43*(2), 164–177.

Richard, O. C., Barnett, T., Dwyer, S., & Chadwick, K. (2004). Cultural diversity in management, firm performance, and the moderating role of entrepreneurial orientation dimensions. *Academy of Management Journal, 47*(2), 255.

Richard, O. C., Murthi, B. P. S., & Ismail, K. (2007). The impact of racial diversity on intermediate and long-term performance: The moderating role of environmental context. *Strategic Management Journal, 28*, 1213–1233.

Rice, T. (2014, July 3). Globalization and the San Antonio Spurs: Success through Diversity. Sports Fitness Network. Retrieved from http://sportsfitnessnetwork.com/2014/07/globalization-and-the-san-antonio-spurs-success-through-diversity/

Riordan, C. M. (2000). Relational demography within groups: Past developments, contradictions, and new directions. *Research in Personnel and Human Resource Management, 19*, 131–173.

Salzbrenner, S. (2014, August 5). Three lessons in cultural diversity management from NBA Champion San Antonio Spurs. Fit Across Cultures. Retrieved from https://www.linkedin.com/pulse/20140805112808-23381296-three-lessons-in-cultural-diversity-management-from-nba-champion-san-antonio-spurs

Sanders, W. G., & Carpenter, M. (1998). Internationalization and firm governance: The roles of CEO compensation. *Academy of Management Journal, 41*, 158–178.

Schuetze, C. F. (2014, August 14). Amsterdam to Refashion 'Black Pete' Character. *New York Times*. Retrieved from https://www.nytimes.com/2014/08/15/world/europe/amsterdam-black-pete-zwarte-piet-verdict.html?_r=0

Schulz-Hardt, S., Jochims, M., & Frey, D. (2002). Productive conflict in group decision making: Genuine and contrived dissent as strategies to counteract biased information seeking. *Organizational Behavior and Human Decision Processes, 88*(2), 563–586.

Schweiger, D. M., Sandberg, W. R., & Ragan, J. W. (1996). Group approaches for improving strategic decision making: A comparative analysis of dialectical inquiry, devil's advocacy, and consensus. *Academy of Management Journal, 29*, 51–72.

Shrader, C. B., Blackburn, V. B., & Iles, P. (1997). Women in management and firm financial performance: An exploratory study. *Journal of Managerial Issues, 9*(3), 355–373.

Sterling, T. (2013, October 17). Opponents of Dutch "Black Pete" speak out. Retrieved January 21, 2015, from http://www.usatoday.com/story/news/world/2013/10/17/dutch-black-pete-netherlands/3000531/

Tajfel, H. (1978). *Differentiation between social groups*. London: Academic Press.

Tajfel, H., & Turner, J. (1986). The social identity of intergroup behavior. In S. Worchel & W. Austin (Eds.), *Psychology of intergroup relations* (pp. 7–24). Chicago: Nelson-Hall.

Taras, V., Steel, P., & Kirkman, B. L. (2012). Improving national cultural indices using a longitudinal meta-analysis of Hofstede's dimensions. *Journal of World Business, 47*, 329–341.

Tihanyi, L., & Thomas, W. B. (2005). Information-processing demands and the multinational enterprise: A comparison of foreign and domestic earnings estimates. *Journal of Business Research, 58*, 285–292.

Todd, A. R., Hanko, K., Galinsky, A. D., & Mussweiler, T. (2010). When focusing on differences leads to similar perspectives. *Psychological Science, 22*, 134–141.

Torchia, M., Calabrò, A., & Huse, M. (2011). Women directors on corporate boards: From tokenism to critical mass. *Journal of Business Ethics, 102*, 299–317.

Triandis, H. C., Hall, E. R., & Ewen, R. B. (1965). Member heterogeneity and dyadic creativity. *Human Relations, 18*(1), 33–55.

Tsui, A., Egan, T. D., & O'Reilly, C. A. (1992). Being different: Relational demography and organizational attachment. *Administrative Science Quarterly, 37*, 549–579.

Tsui, A., & O'Reilly, C. A., III. (1989). Beyond simple demographic effects: The importance of relational demography in superior-subordinate dyads. *Academy of Management Journal, 32*, 402–423.

Tuggle, C. S., Schnatterly, K., & Johnson, R. A. (2010). Attention patterns in the boardroom: How board composition and processes affect discussion of entrepreneurial issues. *Academy of Management Journal, 53*(3), 550–571.

Turner, J. (1985). *Social categorization and the self concept: A social cognitive theory of group behavior* (Vol. 2). Greenwich, CT: JAI Press.

Turner, J. (1987). *Rediscovering the social group: A self-categorization theory*. New York: Basil Blackwell.

USA Today. (2014, July 3). Dutch court: Black Pete is a negative stereotype. Retrieved January 21, 2015, from http://www.usatoday.com/story/news/world/2014/07/03/dutch-court-black-pete-is-a-negative-stereotype/12132299/

van Dick, R., van Knippenberg, D., Hägele, S., Guillaume, Y. R. F., & Brodbeck, F. C. (2008). Group diversity and group identification: The moderating role of diversity beliefs. *Human Relations, 61*, 1463–1492.

van Knippenberg, D., De Dreu, C. K. W., & Homan, A. C. (2004). Work group diversity and group performance: An integrative model and research agenda. *Journal of Applied Psychology, 89*, 1008–1022.

van Knippenberg, D., & Schippers, M. C. (2007). Work group diversity. *Annual Review of Psychology, 58*, 515–541.

Vorauer, J. D., Gagnon, A., & Sasaki, S. J. (2009). Salient intergroup ideology and intergroup interaction. *Psychological Science, 20*(7), 838–845.

Webber, S. S., & Donahue, L. M. (2001). Impact of highly and less job-related diversity on work group cohesion and performance: A meta-analysis. *Journal of Management, 27*, 141–162.

Williams, K. Y., & O'Reilly, C. A. (1998). Demography and diversity in organizations: A review of 40 years of research. *Research in Organizational Behavior, 20*(20), 77–140.

two
Diversity Theories

Opening Case
A Letter to Mr. Spock

The following letter, written by a biracial teenage girl, appeared in the 1968 edition of *FaVE!* magazine (Nimoy, 1968 as reproduced in Epstein, 2013).

"Dear Mr. Spock, I am not very good at writing letters so I will make this short. I know that you are half Vulcan and half human and you have suffered because of this." She went on to explain that her mother was Black and her father was White and she felt like she did not fit in with either group because of this. She explained that Black peers "don't like me because I don't look like them. The White kids don't like me because I don't exactly look like them either. I guess I'll never have any friends." F.C., Los Angeles

The girl writing this letter was addressing her question to Mr. Spock, a famous character in the *Star Trek* science fiction television shows and movies. Mr. Spock was played by Leonard Nimoy. In response to this letter, the magazine printed a two-page reply from Leonard Nimoy giving the girl some wise advice from Mr. Spock. Because Spock was half Vulcan (on his father's side) and half human (on his mother's side), he too had faced the challenges of being biracial.

Leonard Nimoy (speaking on behalf of his character, Mr. Spock) explained that the Vulcans formed groups and often demanded that others be just like them in order to be accepted, which is similar to humans who can be prejudiced. He explained that the most important question in his mind was whether he wanted to be popular among the others or whether he wanted to be true to himself. He explained that it takes courage to go out on your own, but often there is a little voice inside each of us that tells us we need to be true to ourselves. Nimoy further stated that there is usually no good reason for picking on or bullying anyone and that just because someone is different does not mean they are worth any less than anyone else. He continued by stating that Mr. Spock could have let the prejudice he faced get him down, but instead he ultimately realized his worth and the fact that he was equal to everyone else. He advised the girl that she could do the same by overcoming the need to be popular and focusing instead on the people who accept her for who she is. Nimoy closed the letter by providing an example of Mr. Spock, who replaced the idea of being liked with the idea of being accomplished and devoted himself to developing his career and capabilities so that people of all races would recognize his potential as a colleague (Epstein, 2013; Nimoy, 1968).

Today, we have a few prominent examples of individuals who are biracial. The most prominent is probably President Barack Obama, whose mother was White and whose father was Kenyan. In 1968, the year this letter was published, there were not such prominent examples of biracial individuals, and it was more difficult to navigate this environment. Even today, people form many groupings (or categories) on the basis of demographic characteristics including race, sex, age, religion, and other demographics. These characteristics can lead to both inclusion and exclusion, as we will see in the chapter that follows. For individuals who have membership in multiple categories, this can present both challenges and opportunities.

Discussion Questions:

1. Why do you think people who are biracial may encounter prejudice?
2. Do you think there are any advantages to being biracial?
3. In what ways might biracial individuals have a broader knowledge base and mind-set than individuals who are not biracial?
4. Whose responsibility is it (the self, other individuals, employers, society, no one) to help those who are different in some way to be accepted?

Learning Objectives
After reading this chapter, you should be able to:

- Define biases, stereotypes, prejudice, and discrimination
- Understand major theories used in diversity research, including:

  - Self-categorization/social categorization
  - Realistic group conflict

- Social identity
- Similarity attraction
- Relational demography
- Modern sexism and modern racism
- Social dominance
- Critical race
- Status construction

■ Understand two major concepts based on U.S. employment law to identify discrimination in the workplace, including:

- Adverse impact
- Disparate treatment

The purpose of this chapter is to review major diversity theories that are used in diversity and discrimination research. There is an extensive literature examining the reasons why individuals notice differences among people. It is only when one notices that others are different somehow that one might act on those differences. **Biases** are tendencies, inclinations, or feelings, particularly ones that are preconceived and lack reasoning; they are often implicitly, or subconsciously, driven (Greenwald, McGhee, & Schwartz, 1998). **Stereotypes** are defined as generalizations or beliefs about a particular group or its members which are unjustified because they reflect over-generalizations and factual errors as well as misattributions to other groups (Dovidio, Brigham, Johnson, & Gaertner, 1996; Dovidio & Hebl, 2005). **Prejudice** is defined as an unfair negative attitude toward a social group or a person who is a member of that group (Allport, 1954; Dovidio & Hebl, 2005). To treat someone in a way that is less desirable from the way you would normally treat others because of their group membership is **discrimination** (Allport, 1954). In this chapter, we examine a number of major theories that have been put forth to describe how and why people identify and act upon differences.

Social Categorization Theory

One of the most influential people in the study of group differences is **Henri Tajfel**. According to accounts of Tajfel's life, he was a Jew who survived the Nazi Holocaust of World War II. However, his family did not. Tajfel was profoundly impacted by these events, as one could imagine, and he devoted the rest of his life to studying psychology. He became a social psychology professor and dedicated all his efforts to studying why various groups of people grow to dislike and even hate each other. His findings from experiments where groups were formed on almost any trivial basis consistently showed in-group bias favoring one's own group and out-group bias against the other group. Henri Tajfel and his student, John Turner, published what is probably the most influential theory ever written to describe intergroup diversity. It is called **self-categorization** and/or **social categorization theory** and describes the process that people use to categorize themselves and others into social groups and the consequences of such categorization processes.

Social categorization (Tajfel, 1978a, 1978b; Tajfel & Turner, 1986; Turner, 1985, 1987) refers to grouping people into categories based on demographic characteristics including age, sex, and race, among others. These surface-level characteristics are visible and are initially used by people to categorize themselves and others. It is functional for people to perform a quick mental social categorization of others because this process allows people to efficiently categorize the volume of information they are bombarded with daily (Dipboye & Colella, 2005; Heilman, 1995). Therefore, categorizing others is a natural part of human perception. However, this categorization process can also be problematic if it triggers negative stereotypes associated with members of other groups. When people categorize others, they quickly develop a sense for the **in-group** (those who are similar to them) and the **out-group** (those who are different from them). An individual's self-concept includes the fact of membership in various different social groups, and people derive self-esteem from their group membership (Tajfel, 1978). People desire to perceive members of their own category as superior and engage in stereotyping, distancing, and disparaging treatment of people in the out-group. Because of this, categorization can lead to bias, prejudice, and discrimination.

Self-categorization or social categorization is a very robust phenomenon. Empirical evidence for these categorization effects has been found repeatedly in research over the course of many decades. One of the most famous researchers to find categorization effects is **Muzafer Sherif**. His work on **realistic group conflict theory** explains that there are scarce resources such as power, prestige, land, money, and other resources which create intergroup conflict. Realistic group conflict theory has received strong empirical support.

Research shows that scarcity of resources results in conflict and competition between groups. Sherif conducted a famous experiment at a boys' summer camp called Robber's Cave, where he found that hostilities between two different groups of boys happened almost instantly when they were randomly divided and assigned to be in one of two groups, the Eagles or the Rattlers. Indeed, hostilities between the two groups developed so effectively that the researchers decided to stop the friction phase of their experiment and move on to the next phase of their experiment where they attempted to reduce intergroup hostility. Sherif and his research team introduced the notion of **superordinate goals**, or goals that the two different groups have in common, to reduce hostility and promote cooperation. The superordinate goal was successful in reducing intergroup hostilities and restoring good relationships between the two groups of boys (Sherif, 1951).

Other studies have shown similar categorization effects. For example, research shows that intergroup conflict may enhance the intragroup morale, cohesion, and cooperation within each of the competing groups respectively (Fiedler, 1967; Kalin & Marlowe, 1968; Turner, Brown, & Tajfel, 1979). This is one of the reasons why social categorization is robust and can lead to negative consequences. Dislike toward another group can make one group more cohesive and may encourage the members of that group to identify more strongly with their own in-group, thereby associating negative characteristics with the out-group.

Social Identity Theory

Social identity theory (Hogg & Abrams, 1988; Tajfel, 1981; Tajfel & Turner, 1979) describes the cognitive origins of group identification. Social identity is part of an individual's self-concept, and it derives from his/her knowledge of being a member of a social group. People typically attach a value or emotional meaning to the social groups to which they belong because group membership is related to self-concept and self-esteem. Identification with a group means that group membership is important to an individual's self-concept, and the group's interests are of concern to the individual above and beyond his or her own personal self-interest (Brewer, 1991, 1993). People use their social identity with certain groups to bolster their self-image (Tajfel & Turner, 1986). Because people want to have a positive self-image, they are likely to associate positive traits with their in-group members (those who are part of their own group) and negative characteristics with out-group members (those who are not part of their own group). Furthermore, because demographic characteristics like age, sex, and race are readily observable, they are often used to categorize others quickly within a social setting (Clement & Schiereck, 1973; Nelson & Klutas, 2000).

Hogg and Terry (2000) review social identity theory and describe how social categorization processes lead to social identity phenomena. According to these authors, the major motivations for social identity processes are to reduce uncertainty and self-enhancement of one's own self-concept. People are motivated by a need to minimize uncertainty about their own self-concept and how they fit within the social world around them. Self-categorization reduces uncertainty by giving people a set of characteristics that prescribe appropriate social behavior for both them and others. The characteristics of the social groups to which one belongs then form the basis of social identity.

Global View: Iran

In Iran, a British-Iranian woman and other protesters were jailed because they tried to attend a men's volleyball match between Iran and Italy, "in defiance of a push by Iranian hard-liners to enact full gender segregation." The woman was accused and found guilty of acting against the ruling system (*Hindu*, 2014). According to a reporter who interviewed the woman's mother, her daughter was released on almost $30,000 bail. She will remain free until an appeals court rules on her case.

Similarity Attraction and Relational Demography

Similarity-attraction theory predicts that at the individual level people are more attracted to others who are similar to themselves (Byrne, 1971). People who are similar in attitudes or personal traits will be attracted to one another. The theory of **relational demography** is based on the concept of similarity attraction and describes the process by which individuals compare their own demographic characteristics to those of others in their group to decide whether they are similar or dissimilar to the composition of the group (Riordan & Shore, 1997). Relational demography proposes that the more similar an individual employee's demographic characteristics are to the work group, the more positive his or her attitudes and behaviors toward that group will be (Riordan, 2000).

The original work on relational demography was done by Pfeffer (1983), who defined demography as the composition of a group in terms of attributes including age, sex, educational level, tenure, race, and other characteristics. Pfeffer argued that the demographic composition of groups is an important determinant of both processes and performance for individuals and groups in organizations. He examined the distribution of the organization's workforce by organizational tenure and explained that cohorts entering the organization at the same time experience better communication, integration, and cohesion.

Riordan and Weatherly (1999) tested this and found demographic similarity to be strongly related to liking the other person. The theory of relational demography predicts that minority team members who lack **inclusion** may suffer from adverse consequences as a result of negative experiences (Riordan & Shore, 1997; Tsui, Egan, & O'Reilly, 1992). Further, studies examining relational demography have found that when individuals are different from their teams on demographic characteristics, such differences can have negative consequences for both individual and team outcomes due to categorization effects (Riordan & Shore, 1997; Tsui et al., 1992). In diverse teams in which particular individuals are different relative to the team as a whole, minority team members can feel isolated and ignored (Riordan & Shore, 1997; Tsui et al., 1992). They may also receive less help from teammates (Triana, Porter, DeGrassi, & Bergman, 2013).

Katz (1982) describes that when teams are together for a long period of time they tend to increase in behavioral stability, meaning that the group becomes more homogenous and can have selective exposure to different information. This may be one negative consequence of relational demography and similarity-attraction effects in organizations. If people only socialize with others who are most like them, this could limit the flow of information and diverse perspectives between people, which may limit an organization's ability to be innovative.

Modern Racism and Modern Sexism

A number of different authors have proposed that over time discrimination has become much more subtle. There are two major explanations for why discrimination has become subtle over time. One explanation is that old-fashioned blatant racism has become socially unacceptable because we now have laws that prohibit discrimination in employment or society at large against various groups. A second explanation is that people's attitudes have changed and they have really become less prejudiced over time as they have become exposed to ideas of promoting inclusion in society over the years. There is evidence for both of these suggestions. At any rate, discrimination today is typically more subtle than it has been in the past, which is why it is called "modern" discrimination. Modern forms of discrimination are more subtle than blatant, old-fashioned racism and sexism (Dipboye & Colella, 2005).

There are several diversity and discrimination theories whose premise is that modern-day prejudice is subtle. For example, modern sexism (Benokraitis & Feagin, 1995; Glick & Fiske, 1996), modern racism (McConahay, 1983, 1986), aversive racism (Dovidio & Gaertner, 1986), and symbolic racism (Sears & Henry, 2003; Sears, Henry, & Kosterman, 2000) all suggest that modern-day prejudice manifests in subtle ways. **Modern racism theory** and **modern sexism theory** argue that people have deep-seated prejudice but nevertheless behave in socially desirable ways because they are aware that old-fashioned prejudice is socially unacceptable. Therefore, they exhibit biased behavior in subtle ways that are not blatant (although overt prejudice is still exhibited sometimes, too). **Aversive racism theory** also explains that people have deep-seated prejudice but feel it is wrong to have and express such feelings about other groups. **Symbolic racism theory** maintains that prejudice against minority groups including African-Americans is driven by anti-Black emotions and political views. These theories "share the broad assumptions that Whites have become racially egalitarian in principle, and that new forms of prejudice, embodying both negative feelings toward Blacks as a group and some conservative nonracial values, have become politically dominant" (Sears & Henry, 2003, p. 259). Others have also noted that modern-day discrimination is subtle (Benokraitis & Feagin, 1995; Dipboye & Colella, 2005; McConahay, 1986) and contains both **situational ambiguity** (St. Jean & Feagin, 1997) and attributional preferences (Crocker, Major, & Steele, 1998), meaning that the target person the act was directed toward has a hard time identifying what happened and why.

Gaertner and Dovidio (2000) found that self-reported prejudice decreased from 1989 to 1999. They reasoned that modern-day discrimination must come from some other, subtle sources (as also noted by Gaertner & Dovidio, 1986; McConahay, 1986). According to Dovidio and Gaertner (2000), self-reported discrimination among the public has declined substantially over the years. However, discrimination still affects the lives of many people in society. The authors explained that racial prejudice has become less conscious, and more subconscious, over the years. These authors examined aversive racism and found that it accounts for the persistence of racial disparities in society which exist at the same time that people are self-reporting to be less prejudiced. Aversive racism is a racial attitude among Whites who endorse egalitarian values and regard themselves as non-prejudicial individuals, but nonetheless, they discriminate in subtle ways they can rationalize (Gaertner & Dovidio, 1986). According to these authors, this is why racial prejudice is often expressed in indirect or unconscious ways that are not obvious. Furthermore, according to Dovidio et al. (1996), the magnitude of the correlation between conscious biases, prejudices, and acts of discrimination is small to moderate, which provides more evidence that many acts are driven by subconscious biases.

Social Dominance Theory

Social dominance theory was developed by Sidanius and Pratto (1999) to understand how social hierarchies are formed. The theory suggests that societies generate and sustain a trimorphic system and that these systems are typically observed universally across the world. First, the gender system represents status such that men typically have an unequal amount of political and collective power compared to women. Second, the age system explains status such that older people have more social power as compared to children. Third, an arbitrary system of social values based on things like race, class, and religion is typically present and represents levels of social status (Pratto, Sidanius, & Levin, 2006).

Individuals who ascribe to beliefs in line with social dominance theory are said to have high social dominance orientation (SDO). **Social dominance orientation** is defined as "the degree to which individuals desire and support a group-based hierarchy and the domination of 'inferior' groups by 'superior' groups" (Sidanius & Pratto, 1999, p. 48). Individuals who are high in SDO work to maintain traditional social status hierarchies, such as men being more powerful than women and racial majority groups being more powerful than racial minority groups (Sidanius & Pratto, 1999). People with high SDO beliefs tend to favor hierarchy-enhancing types of policies which maintain the current social status and order. People with low SDO beliefs tend to favor hierarchy-attenuating types of beliefs which advocate egalitarianism and moving away from status hierarchies based on social characteristics rather than merit.

Several research studies have found that SDO beliefs are an important predictor of discriminatory behavior. For example, an underlying tenet of social dominance theory is that policies and programs (e.g., affirmative action) which provide opportunities to underrepresented minority groups (e.g., females) are damaging to high status group members (Sidanius, Pratto, & Bobo, 1996). In fact, Aquino, Stewart, and Reed (2005) reported that SDO and affirmative action jointly influence participants' performance expectations of African-American employees. Specifically, social dominance orientation was negatively correlated with the ratings given to an African-American employee on both competence and warmth. There was a negative relationship between SDO and performance expectations from African-American employees, and this relationship was significantly stronger in situations where participants were told that the employees benefited from affirmative action compared to when there was no such statement about affirmative action.

In society, the high status group members typically seek to maintain their wealth, power, and privilege because they enjoy an elevated status within society. Such individuals, especially those high in SDO, are typically opposed to social policies which help minority groups, especially if they utilize a hierarchy-attenuating program like affirmative action (Aquino et al., 2005; Sidanius et al., 1996).

In order to examine the discriminatory tendencies of individuals high in SDO and to test one possible mechanism to attenuate such discriminatory tendencies, one group of researchers conducted two studies and found one mechanism to attenuate the effects of SDO on discrimination toward lower status groups (Umphress, Simmons, Boswell, & Triana, 2008). In this research, the authors pretested candidate descriptions without demographics and established that one of the candidates was particularly well qualified for the position in question given his or her credentials. As part of the experiment, the race of the candidate was varied in one study and the gender of the candidate was varied in another study. Across the two studies, the researchers report that people high in SDO were less likely to select the female candidate and the minority candidate for the position, even when those candidates had the strongest credentials. However, the researchers experimentally manipulated whether an authority figure gave the study participants a directive to strictly focus on job-related qualifications or no directive. In the conditions that did not have the strict directive to focus on job-related qualifications, those high in SDO followed their tendency to discriminate and were less likely to select the most qualified candidate when that person was a woman or a racial minority. However, this tendency of those high in SDO was attenuated when the research team gave participants explicit instructions to focus on job-related qualifications. Therefore, there is some evidence that with the correct set of instructions from an authority figure who is respected in that context, it is possible to mitigate the discriminatory tendencies of people high in SDO.

Global View: Mexico

In an effort to preserve the Wixárika language, the language spoken by Wixaritari people, the University of Guadalajara will begin transmitting news, music, and other pertinent content in the language of the Wixaritari to this ancient and marginalized indigenous group of Mexico. Radio Wixárita's programming, produced and delivered by members of this ancestral community, will reach an area where 72% of the population is Wixaritari but only one in four has an elementary education. A spokesperson for the university explained that in Mexico indigenous people have been forced to learn Spanish while at the same time have been denied the opportunity to preserve their language and culture. University officials hope that the radio station will give a voice to the Wixaritari, thus guaranteeing the protection and preservation of this ancient culture. Moreover, university leaders hope that this community radio station will act as a link between Wixaritari and the university in the hopes of achieving the two-fold goal of promoting continuing education and reducing school drop-out rates. Currently the university supports students of indigenous descent with a monthly stipend of 1,200 pesos through an Economic Stimulus Program for Indigenous Students (Luna, 2016; Universidad de Guadalajara, 2016).

Critical Race Theory

Critical race theory has its origins in law research, and it grew out of dissatisfaction with the results of the civil rights movement in the United States. The originators of the theory are Derrick Bell and Richard Delgado. The mission of this theory is to analyze the relationships among race, racism, and power (Bell, 1995; Delgado & Stefancic, 1993, 1994, 2001). Critical race theory has been used to explain various social issues in a variety of academic disciplines, including education (Ladson-Billings & Tate, 1995; Solorzano, Ceja, & Yosso, 2000), women's studies (Wing, 1997), sociology (Aguirre, 2000), and social work (Abrams & Moio, 2009).

This theory has several different tenets. One is that racism in the United States is endemic and an ordinary occurrence of people of color because it is embedded in the fabric of American society. Another tenet is that race is a category that is socially constructed based on a contrived system of categorizing people according to observable characteristics. The theory also maintains that dominant groups within society can racialize people of other groups in different ways at different times. For example, the way Asian-Americans have been viewed throughout history has changed several times (Abrams & Moio, 2009). Asian-Americans have been exploited with low wages to build America's railroads; they were also viewed with great suspicion and some were forced into internment camps during World War II. More recently, Asian-Americans have been seen as a skilled source of labor and even considered a model minority (Chou & Feagin, 2010). The theory further describes that progressive change around race will only occur when the interests of the powerful White majority happen to converge with those of the racially oppressed (Bell, 1995). Furthermore, the theory explains that the dominant group's accounting of history will routinely exclude racial and other minority perspectives in order to tell its view and legitimize its power (Delgado, 1989). Finally, the theory asserts that an intersection of various oppressions can happen and that a primary focus on race may eclipse other forms of discrimination people may simultaneously experience.

Status Construction Theory

This theory was developed by Cecilia Ridgeway (1991). The theory asks the following question: "How do characteristics of individuals such as sex or race acquire status value in society?" Ridgeway explains that status beliefs which characterize people into a social category, that is, seen as more esteemed and competent compared to people in another category, play an important role in the development of inequality in organizations and society. **Status construction theory** argues that the terms in which people interact across social groups can cause shared status beliefs to form and spread throughout a population.

Status construction theory relies heavily on the foundation of **expectation-states theory** (Berger, Conner, & Fisek, 1974), which maintains that status hierarchy is formed among members of a group or organization and that the status hierarchy is driven by the interactants' expectations about the likely usefulness of each other person's contributions to their shared goals. The issue here is that expectations of another person's abilities are associated with salient characteristics that are attached to social status, including race or sex. Once expectations are formed, or shared, these implicit assumptions about the value added of various individuals in the group can become a self-fulfilling prophecy. Some individuals from higher status groups are assumed to be more competent and capable; hence their actions may be perceived through a filter assuming they know what they are doing, and evaluations of these people are generally positive. The opposite may be true for lower status group members.

Ridgeway's **status construction theory** proposes that inequalities develop in the distribution of resources among the population. The level of resources possessed becomes a meaningful distinction in the population such that people interact more with others who have a similar level of resources. Further, the population is divided into categories of characteristics such as sex, race, or age, and there is a correlation between these characteristics and the resources such that the higher status groups tend to have a higher probability of being resource rich than the lower status groups. Because of these associations of resources and characteristics in society, people tend to develop subconscious associations about the level of resources, and potentially even the level of capabilities, of certain groups which are primed very quickly into the human mind when one sees members of various social status groups. This explanation has been used by Cecilia Ridgeway in her research on status construction theory to explain how gender acquires status value and reproduces inequality. Her work links micro-processes (such as interactions between people in organizations) and macro-structures and processes (such as stereotypes and the distribution of wealth and power in society) to explain how gender hierarchies are preserved over time.

Recent work adopting status construction theory has reported that employed men who are married to women who do not work view the presence of women in the workforce unfavorably, think that organizations with a high number of female employees do not function smoothly, perceive that organizations with female leaders are unattractive places to work, and deny qualified women in the workplace opportunities for advancement more so than their male counterparts who have wives who work outside the home (Desai, Chugh, & Brief, 2014).

Global View: Myanmar

For the 9th East Asia Summit, dignitaries from Southeast Asian nations gathered in Myanmar, Burma. The purpose of the conference was to discuss cooperation on matters pertaining to politics, security, the economy, and other social issues including health, energy, finance, and the environment (Government of India, 2014).

Myanmar is predominantly Buddhist, but approximately 40% of its population is comprised of about 130 ethnic minority groups. The dignitaries attending the conference were greeted by a line of women representing the country's ethnic minority groups. Dressed in traditional clothing representing Myanmar's many ethnic groups, the women welcoming the dignitaries were, in fact, university students, all Burmese (the ethnic majority group), who had been bused in for the event. One young woman in the welcoming line who was wearing a long brass neck coil representing one particular ethnic group's tradition was suddenly seen without her neck adornment. When asked where it was, she purportedly looked offended and replied: "Oh, that's fake! Did you think I was really Kayan Padaung?" (Htusan, 2014).

Adverse Impact and Disparate Treatment

The final two concepts in this chapter have their basis in the United States employment law. The Uniform Guidelines on Employee Selection Procedures (Equal Employment Opportunity Commission, 1978) define a problem called **adverse impact** which occurs when an organization uses a selection mechanism which inadvertently discriminates against members of minority groups, including women and racial minorities. In order to determine whether an organization has an adverse impact problem, an initial check of its employment selection statistics is performed to see whether members of minority groups are selected for positions at a rate of 80% of the rate at which majority groups are selected for that position. For example, if 80% of Caucasian applicants were selected for a particular position, one would expect at least 64% of African-American applicants to be selected as well. Otherwise, there may be something about the selection process that disproportionately disqualifies African-American applicants.

An example of adverse impact would be if an organization sets a selection criteria that has the unintended consequence of eliminating many minorities and women from its final candidate pool. For example, imagine that an organization conducts business in an office setting where the clerks occasionally have to lift parcels that weigh up to 25 pounds. In writing the job description for this position, one might be tempted to request that the candidates be able to lift 50 pounds routinely. After all, being able to lift 50 pounds is better and may mean someone can do a job more efficiently than someone who can lift 25 pounds. However, an unintended consequence of requiring someone to lift 50 pounds rather than 25 pounds could be that the number of women who qualify for this position is severely reduced. Such a job posting might discourage women who are otherwise well qualified from applying. This is called adverse impact.

Disparate treatment is a situation of blatant discrimination which shows an intent to keep certain groups of people from joining or advancing within an organization. While adverse impact is not intentional, disparate treatment is. These concepts will be discussed more in Chapter 3 on employment legislation.

Closing Case
Charlie Hebdo

In January of 2015, two Islamist gunmen attacked the office of a French satirical magazine called *Charlie Hebdo*. The attackers were outraged because the magazine had published cartoons making fun of the Prophet Muhammad, including caricatures of the Prophet Muhammad (*BBC News*, 2015). Twelve people died as a result of this attack. Although there are no explicit prohibitions in the Qur'an about depictions of the Prophet Muhammad, there are cultural taboos on depictions of the Prophet Muhammad and many Muslims find such depictions to be disrespectful (NPR, 2015).

Shortly after the attack at *Charlie Hebdo*, during a trip to Asia which was aimed at improving religious harmony and inclusion, Pope Francis spoke out in relation to this incident and the killing of journalists because of the magazine cover featuring the Prophet Muhammad (Dias, 2015). He said: "Religious freedom and freedom of expression are fundamental human rights," the Pope said, speaking in Italian, but he continued by saying they are also not total liberties: "there is a limit." He concluded, "Every religion has its dignity. I cannot mock a religion that respects human life and the human person" (Dias, 2015). Pope Francis also denounced the Paris violence. He added: "One cannot offend, make war, kill in the name of one's religion, this is, in the name of God," and he added, "To kill in the name of God is an aberration" (Dias, 2015).

Discussion Questions:

1. According to Pope Francis, religious freedom and freedom of expression are fundamental human rights. Can you explain how far one may go in either direction (religious freedom or freedom of expression) without crossing the line?

2. The *Charlie Hebdo* magazine is known for its controversial cartoons on different issues, including its satirical caricatures of the Prophet Muhammad. What was your reaction to the killings which took place?
3. Do you agree with Pope Francis that interreligious harmony and inclusion will create better relations among nations?

References

Abrams, L. S., & Moio, J. A. (2009). Critical race theory and the cultural competence dilemma in social work education. *Journal of Social Work Education, 45*(2), 245–261.

Aguirre, A. (2000). Academic storytelling: A critical race theory story of affirmative action. *Sociological Perspectives, 43*, 319–339.

Allport, G. W. (1954). *The nature of prejudice*. Reading: Addison-Wesley.

Aquino, K., Stewart, M. M., & Reed, A. (2005). How social dominance orientation and job status influence perceptions of African-American affirmative action beneficiaries. *Personnel Psychology, 58*, 703–744.

BBC News. (2015, January 7). Charlie Hebdo gun attack on French magazine kills 12. Retrieved from http://www.bbc.com/news/world-europe-30710883

Bell, D. (1995). *Brown v. Board of Education* and the interest-convergence dilemma. In K. Crenshaw, N. Gotanda, G. Peller, & K. Thomas (Eds.), *Critical race theory: The key writings that formed the movement* (pp. 20–29). New York: New Press.

Benokraitis, N. V., & Feagin, J. R. (1995). *Modern sexism: Blatant, subtle, and covert discrimination* (2nd ed.). Englewood Cliffs, NJ: Prentice-Hall.

Berger, J., Conner, T. L., & Fisek, M. H. (1974). *Expectation states theory: A theoretical research program.* (Reproduced by University Press of America, Lanham, Maryland, 1982.)

Brewer, M. B. (1991). The social self: On being the same and different at the same time. *Personality and Social Psychology Bulletin, 17*, 475–482.

Brewer, M. B. (1993). The role of distinctiveness in social identity and group behaviour. In M. Hogg & D. Abrams (Eds.), *Group motivation: Social psychological perspectives* (pp. 1–16). London: Harvester Wheatsheaf.

Byrne, D. (1971). *The attraction paradigm*. New York: Academic Press.

Chou, R. S., & Feagin, J. R. (2010). *The myth of the model minority: Asian Americans facing racism*. Boulder, CO: Paradigm.

Clement, D. E., & Schiereck, J. J. (1973). Sex composition and group performance in a visual signal detection task. *Memory & Cognition, 1*(3), 251–255.

Crocker, J., Major, B., & Steele, C. (1998). Social stigma. In D. T. Gilbert, S. T. Fiske, & G. Lindzey (Eds.), *The handbook of social psychology* (Vol. 2, pp. 504–553). New York: McGraw-Hill.

Delgado, R. (1989). Storytelling for oppositionists and others: A plea for narrative. *Michigan Law Review, 87*, 2411–2441.

Delgado, R., & Stefancic, J. (1993). Critical race theory: An annotated bibliography. *Virginia Law Review, 79*, 461–516.

Delgado, R., & Stefancic, J. (1994). Critical race theory: An annotated bibliography 1993, a year of transition. *University of Colorado Law Review, 66*, 159–193.

Delgado, R., & Stefancic, J. (2001). *Critical race theory: An introduction.* New York: New York University Press.

Desai, S. D., Chugh, D., & Brief, A. P. (2014). The implications of marriage structure for men's workplace attitudes, beliefs, and behaviors toward women. *Administrative Science Quarterly, 59*(2), 330–365.

Dias, E. (2015, January 15). Pope Francis speaks out on Charlie Hebdo: "One cannot make fun of faith." *Time.* Retrieved from http://time.com/3668875/pope-francis-charlie-hebdo/

Dipboye, R. L., & Colella, A. (2005). *Discrimination at work: The psychological and organizational bases.* Mahwah, NJ: Lawrence Erlbaum Associates.

Dovidio, J. F., Brigham, J. C., Johnson, B. T., & Gaertner, S. L. (1996). Stereotyping, prejudice, and discrimination: Another look. *Stereotypes and Stereotyping, 276,* 319.

Dovidio, J. F., & Gaertner, S. L. (1986). *Prejudice, discrimination, and racism: Historical trends and contemporary approaches.* Orlando, FL: Academic Press.

Dovidio, J. F., & Gaertner, S. L. (2000). Aversive racism and selection decisions: 1989 and 1999. *Psychological Science, 11,* 315–319.

Dovidio, J. F., & Hebl, M. R. (2005). Discrimination at the level of the individual: Cognitive and affective factors. In R. L. Dipboye & A. Colella (Eds.), *Discrimination at work: The psychological and organizational bases* (pp. 11–35). Mahwah, NJ: Lawrence Erlbaum Associates.

Epstein, L. (2013, March 11). Spock's advice to a teenage girl will make you cry. *BuzzFeed.* Retrieved from https://www.buzzfeed.com/leonoraepstein/spocks-advice-to-a-teenage-girl-will-make-you-cry?utm_term=.yrl8aPEvb#.yplMy7zgZ

Equal Employment Opportunity Commission. (1978). Uniform guidelines on employee selection procedures. *Federal Register, 43*(166), 38295–38309.

Fiedler, F. E. (1967). *A theory of leadership effectiveness.* New York: McGraw-Hill.

Gaertner, S. L., & Dovidio, J. F. (1986). The aversive form of racism. In J. F. Dovidio & S. L. Gaertner (Eds.), *Prejudice, discrimination, and racism* (pp. 61–89). San Diego, CA: Academic Press.

Glick, P., & Fiske, S. T. (1996). The ambivalent sexism inventory: Differentiating hostile and benevolent sexism. *Journal of Personality and Social Psychology, 70,* 491–512.

Government of India. (2014, November 13). Chairman's Statement of 9th East Asia Summit (EAS) in Nay Pyi Taw, Myanmar (13 November 2014). Ministry of External Affairs. Retrieved from http://www.mea.gov.in/bilateral-documents.htm?dtl/24252/Chairmans_Statement_of_9th_East_Asia_Summit_EAS_in_Nay_Pyi_Taw_Myanmar_13_November_2014

Greenwald, A. G., McGhee, D. E., & Schwartz, J. L. K. (1998). Measuring individual differences in implicit cognition: The implicit association test. *Journal of Personality and Social Psychology, 74,* 1464–1480.

Heilman, M. E. (1995). Sex stereotypes and their effects in the workplace: What we know and what we don't know. *Journal of Social Behavior and Personality, 10,* 3–26.

Hindu. (2014, November 24). British-Iranian woman jailed for watching men's volleyball released. Retrieved from http://www.thehindu.com/news/international/world/britishi-ranian-woman-jailed-for-watching-mens-volleyball-released/article6629314.ece

Hogg, M. A., & Abrams, D. (1988). *Social identifications: A social psychology of intergroup relations and group processes.* London: Routledge.

Hogg, M. A., & Terry, D. J. (2000). Social identity and self-categorization processes in organizational contexts. *Academy of Management Review, 25,* 121–140.

Htusan, E. (2014, December 27). Myanmar shows illusion of diversity at Asia summit. *Yahoo! News.* Retrieved from http://news.yahoo.com/myanmar-shows-illusion-diversity-asia-summit-132820173.html

Kalin, R., & Marlowe, D. (1968). The effects of intergroup competition, personal drinking habits and frustration in intra-group cooperation. In *Proceedings of 76th Annual Convention APA* (Vol. 3, pp. 405–406). American Psychological Association.

Katz, R. (1982). The effects of group longevity on project communication and performance. *Administrative Science Quarterly, 27*, 81–104.

Ladson-Billings, G., & Tate, W. (1995). Toward a critical race theory of education. *Teachers College Record, 97*, 47–68.

Luna, A. (2016, April 9). Radio Wixárika, difunden la voz indígena de Jalisco. *Exelsior.* Retrieved from http://www.excelsior.com.mx/nacional/2016/04/09/1085490

McConahay, J. B. (1983). Modern racism and modern discrimination: The effects of race, racial attitudes, and context on simulated hiring decisions. *Personality and Social Psychology Bulletin, 9*, 551–558.

McConahay, J. B. (1986). Modern racism, ambivalence, and the Modern Racism Scale. Prejudice, discrimination, and racism. In J. F. Dovidio & S. L. Gaertner (Eds.), *Prejudice, discrimination, and racism* (pp. 91–125). San Diego, CA: Academic Press.

Nelson, L. J., & Klutas, K. (2000). The distinctiveness effect in social interaction: Creation of a self-fulfilling prophecy. *Personality and Social Psychology Bulletin, 26*(1), 126–135.

Nimoy, L. (1968). Spock: Teenage outcast. Fave, pages 37 and 55. Reproduced in Epstein, L. (2013, March 11). Spock's advice to a teenage girl will make you cry. *BuzzFeed.* Retrieved from http://www.buzzfeed.com/leonoraepstein/spocks-advice-to-a-teenage-girl-will-make-you-cry?bftw&utm_term=4ldqpfp#.qglKLMr7x

NPR. (2015, January 10). Depictions Of Muhammad Aren't Explicitly Forbidden, Says Scholar. Retrieved from http://www.npr.org/2015/01/10/376381089/depictions-of-muhammad-arent-explicity-forbidden-says-scholar

Pfeffer, J. (1983). Organizational demography. In B. M. Staw & L. L. Cummings (Eds.), *Research in organizational behavior* (Vol. 5, pp. 299–357). Greenwich, CT: JAI Press.

Pratto, F., Sidanius, J., & Levin. S. (2006). Social dominance theory and the dynamics of intergroup relations: Taking stock and looking forward. *European Review of Social Psychology, 17*, 271–320.

Ridgeway, C. (1991). The social construction of status value: Gender and other nominal characteristics. *Social Forces, 70*(2), 367–386.

Riordan, C. M. (2000). Relational demography within groups: Past developments, contradictions, and new directions. *Research in Personnel and Human Resource Management, 19*, 131–173.

Riordan, C. M., & Shore, L. (1997). Demographic diversity and employee attitudes: An empirical examination of relational demography within work units. *Journal of Applied Psychology, 82*, 342–358.

Riordan, C. M., & Weatherly, E. W. (1999). Defining and measuring employees' identification with their work groups. *Educational and Psychological Measurement, 59*(2), 310–324.

Sears, D. O., & Henry, P. J. (2003). The origins of symbolic racism. *Journal of Personality and Social Psychology, 85*, 259–275.

Sears, D. O., Henry, P. J., & Kosterman, R. (2000). Egalitarian values and contemporary racial politics. In D. O. Sears, J. Sidanius, & L. Bobo (Eds.), *Racialized politics: The debate about racism in America* (pp. 75–117). Chicago, IL: University of Chicago Press.

Sherif, M. (1951). A preliminary study of inter-group relations. In J. H. Rohrer & M. Sherif (Eds.), *Social psychology at the crossroads. The University of Oklahoma lectures in social psychology* (pp. 388–424). Oxford: Harper, viii.

Sidanius, J., & Pratto, F. (1999). *Social dominance: An intergroup theory of social hierarchy and oppression*. Cambridge: Cambridge University Press.

Sidanius, J., Pratto, F., & Bobo, L. (1996). Racism, conservatism, affirmative action, and intellectual sophistication: A matter of principled conservatism or group dominance? *Journal of Personality and Social Psychology, 70,* 476–490.

Solorzano, D., Ceja, M., & Yosso, T. (2000). Critical race theory, racial microaggressions, and campus racial climate: The experiences of African American college students. *Journal of Negro Education, 69,* 60–73.

St. Jean, Y., & Feagin, J. R. (1997). Racial masques: Black women and subtle gendered racism. In N. V. Benokraitis (Ed.), *Subtle sexism: Current practices and prospects for change* (pp. 179–200). Thousand Oaks, CA: Sage.

Tajfel, H. (1978a). *Differentiation between social groups.* London: Academic Press.

Tajfel, H. (1978b). Social categorization, social identity and social comparison. In H. Tajfel (Ed.), *Differentiation between social groups* (pp. 61–76). London: Academic Press.

Tajfel, H. (1981). *Human groups and social categories: Studies in social psychology.* Cambridge: Cambridge University Press.

Tajfel, H., & Turner, J. C. (1979). An integrative theory of intergroup conflict. In W. Austin & S. Worchel (Eds.), *The social psychology of intergroup relations* (pp. 33–48). Pacific Grove, CA: Brooks/Cole.

Tajfel, H., & Turner, J. C. (1986). The social identity of intergroup behavior. In S. Worchel & W. Austin (Eds.), *Psychology of intergroup relations* (pp. 7–24). Chicago: Nelson-Hall.

Triana, M. C., Porter, C. O. L. H., Degrassi, S. W., & Bergman, M. (2013). We're all in this together. . . except for you: The effects of workload, performance feedback, and racial distance on helping behavior in teams. *Journal of Organizational Behavior, 34*(8), 1124–1144.

Tsui, A. S., Egan, T. D., & O'Reilly, C. A., III. (1992). Being different: Relational demography and organizational attachment. *Administrative Science Quarterly, 37,* 549–579.

Turner, J. (1985). *Social categorization and the self concept: A social cognitive theory of group behavior* (Vol. 2). Greenwich, CT: JAI Press.

Turner, J. (1987). *Rediscovering the social group: A self-categorization theory.* New York: Basil Blackwell.

Turner, J. C., Brown, R. J., & Tajfel, H. (1979). Social comparison and group interest in ingroup favouritism. *European Journal of Social Psychology, 9*(2), 187–204.

Umphress, E., Simmons, A., Boswell, W., & Triana, M. (2008). Managing discrimination in selection: The impact of directives from an authority and social dominance orientation. *Journal of Applied Psychology, 93,* 982–993.

Universidad de Guadalajara, Universidad Incluyente. (2016). Radio wixárika, difunden la voz indígena de Jalisco. Retrieved from http://www.excelsior.com.mx/nacional/2016/04/09/1085490

Wing, A. (Ed.). (1997). *Critical race feminism: A reader.* New York: New York University Press.

three
Employment Legislation

Opening Case
A Letter from Tim Cook, the CEO of Apple

Apple has long been a champion of diversity and inclusion. On its web site, Apple states: "The most innovative company must also be the most diverse. At Apple, we take a holistic view of diversity that looks beyond the usual measurements. A view that includes the varied perspectives of our employees as well as app developers, suppliers, and anyone who aspires to a future in tech. Because we know new ideas come from diverse ways of seeing things" (Apple, 2017).

However, the tension between some forms of diversity and religious beliefs has become apparent in the last few years as more religious freedom laws are passed in the United States. According to Sanchez (2016), LGBT rights and freedom of religion have collided, as evidenced by the religious freedom laws passed in Indiana, Mississippi, North Carolina, and Georgia, to name a few. These laws typically protect businesses and groups if they deny services to members of the LGBT (lesbian, gay, bisexual, transgender) community if they do so because of their religious beliefs (Sanchez, 2016).

Tim Cook recently wrote a letter explaining why some religious freedom laws in the United States are dangerous. According to Cook, these bills rationalize the violation of rights and falsely claim to defend something most of us appreciate dearly: freedom. Cook states that these laws are against the principles upon which our country was founded and that they have the power to undo years of advancement toward greater equality between groups in the United States (Cook, 2015).

The business community in America has known for many years that discrimination is not good for business. Cook says Apple's reason for being in business is to empower and improve its customers' lives. Apple puts deliberate effort into conducting business in a manner that is just and fair. Cook adds that he hopes more people will join the movement against such discriminatory laws. Cook states that these new bills will hurt jobs as well as growth in many parts of the United States (Cook, 2015).

Cook pledges: "Apple is open. Open to everyone, regardless of where they come from, what they look like, how they worship or who they love. Regardless of what the law might allow in Indiana or Arkansas, we will never tolerate discrimination" (Cook, 2015).

Cook closes by stating that men as well as women have died fighting to defend the founding laws of the United States, which are based on freedom and equality. He urges the reader to protect those ideals because the times of segregation and discrimination are gone and America must continue to be the land of opportunity for all (Cook, 2015).

Cook is not alone in his opinion. In response to a North Carolina law which prevents transgender people from using the bathroom that corresponds to their gender identity, PayPal announced that it would halt plans to open a new center in Charlotte, North Carolina, costing the city 400 jobs (Sanchez, 2016).

Discussion Questions:

1. According to the article, America must be a land of opportunity for everyone. Do you agree or disagree with this statement? Please give your opinion.
2. "Discrimination is not something that is easy to oppose," Cook says. Do you agree or disagree? Why?

Learning Objectives

After reading this chapter, you should:

- Be aware of the major employment discrimination laws in the United States including Title VII of the Civil Rights Act, the Age Discrimination in Employment Act, the Americans with Disabilities Act, the Equal Pay Act, and the Vietnam Era Veterans' Readjustment Assistance Act
- Be familiar with the International Labor Organization and its mission
- Be aware of average hours worked per week in various countries throughout the world

- Understand International Labor Organization guidelines to foster productive working environments for many groups around the world with respect to:

  - Age discrimination
  - Child labor
  - Forced labor
  - Disability
  - LGBT
  - Migrant workers
  - Seafarers and dock workers
  - Veterans

- Understand maternity and paternity benefits
- Be aware of the wage gap between men and women
- Know what affirmative action is

The purpose of this chapter is to examine major employment legislation. The chapter has a U.S. focus primarily, but it also prominently features guidelines from the United Nations' International Labor Organization, which presents legislation that has been deemed acceptable for employment practices by many countries throughout the world. As organizations become global and conduct business across national boundaries, their human resources and employment practices must follow. Therefore, it is important to be aware of acceptable labor practices as well as agreed-upon standards around the world.

It is important to have legal protections against discrimination and exploitation in organizational settings because discrimination creates discrepancies in outcomes people tend to value at work (Goldman, Gutek, Stein, & Lewis, 2006; Tomaskovic-Devey, Thomas, & Johnson, 2005). Employment consequences of workplace discrimination include preferential hiring and favoritism toward one's in-group members (Pager & Quillian, 2005; Pager, Western, & Bonikowski, 2009) and lower salaries (Cohen & Huffman, 2003; Neckerman & Torche, 2007) and stifled promotions (Kalev, Dobbin, & Kelly, 2006; Stainback & Tomaskovic-Devey, 2009) for individuals who are members of the out-group.

Studies have shown the negative consequences of discrimination in employment decisions. For example, a study found that discrimination at work resulted in minority applicants with no criminal backgrounds being no better off than White applicants with a criminal record (Pager et al., 2009), as well as Blacks being guided into a position lower than that for which they applied (Pager et al., 2009). In another study, men were more likely to receive a call back from a job inquiry than equally qualified women (Correll, Benard, & Paik, 2007).

Laws change over time. Typically, laws are put in place as a result of pressure for societal change. Groups that are somehow discriminated against or disenfranchised will form coalitions and call attention to the problems they face. Prominent examples in the United States include the women's rights movement in the early 1900s, which resulted in women's right to vote, and the civil rights movement of the 1960s, which fostered the **Civil Rights Act of 1964** and the beginning of the end of (legal) racial segregation in the United States. Two other excellent examples are **Title VII of the Civil Rights Act of 1964** and the **Age Discrimination in Employment Act of 1967.** Title VII of the Civil Rights Act of 1964, a major employment law of the land, forbids employment discrimination on the basis of race, sex, religion, color, and national origin (U.S. National Archives, 2015a). It does not cover age. The Age Discrimination in Employment Act forbids employment discrimination against employees 40 years of age or older (U.S. National Archives, 2015b).

Currently, the United States is experiencing another civil rights movement, and that is the struggle for gay rights. The same type of struggle is going on in various parts of the world. As described in Chapter 2, social dominance theory explains that in every society certain groups tend to emerge as the dominant ones, and they hold a disproportionate amount of wealth and power. Inevitably, the minority groups who lack such power, wealth, or equality become frustrated with the status quo and form movements to call attention to the problems. If enough pressure is applied and enough of the population sympathizes with the minority group's cause, the social pressure for change grows and new laws are enacted to reflect such change. However, change is not easy for those who are comfortable with the old ways or those who have the most to lose from the change. Therefore, many resist changes.

This chapter begins with an overview of employment laws and guidelines worldwide. The hours in a workweek are discussed first as well as standards of annual leave worldwide. Then we move on to a discussion of the protections for various types of employment problems that affect various groups of people. This includes problems like discrimination and forced labor which can disproportionately affect various minority groups, the poor, and the uneducated. Throughout this chapter, we draw from several reports from global agencies, including the International Labor Organization.

Global View: The United States

The Obama administration has intervened on behalf of transgender people in North Carolina and 23 other states where state laws threaten the civil rights of these individuals. The U.S. Department of Justice is involved in a lawsuit seeking to overturn H.B. 2, the North Carolina law that went into effect in March of 2016 which "requires people to use public bathrooms that correspond with the sex on their birth certificates even if it conflicts with the gender they identify with. The Justice Department says that it violates federal civil rights laws prohibiting gender discrimination in employment and education" (Wiessner, Garamfalvi, & Gregorio, 2016).

As of the end of 2016, North Carolina legislators stood by this law and did not vote to overturn it. The law has cost the state an estimated tens of millions of dollars because of boycotts from companies, musicians who have refused to perform concerts in the state, and major sporting events that have been moved out of the state (Schuppe & McCausland, 2016).

Overview of Major Laws and Guidelines—A Review From the International Labor Organization and Other Sources

The **International Labor Organization (ILO)** was established in 1919 as part of the Treaty of Versailles. It became a specialized agency of the United Nations in 1946. The ILO has 187 member countries as of the year 2016. The ILO brings together governments, employers, and worker representatives to set labor standards and create policies and programs to promote decent working conditions for men and women. The broad policies of the ILO are set by its member countries, which meet annually at the International Labor Conference. Member countries agree to the standards in principle, as guidelines to follow, but in practice oversight and enforcement of the standards are limited. Nevertheless, the ILO plays a valuable role by creating standards to strive for which inform national labor laws and provide a basis for public pressure when working conditions are poor. The ILO has its headquarters in Geneva, Switzerland, and maintains offices in more than 40 countries worldwide. In 1969, the ILO was awarded a Nobel Peace Prize for its work on bettering working conditions for humanity. In this chapter, we examine information from various ILO reports on the condition of employees throughout the world and summarize this information to provide a snapshot of employee organizational life in various parts of the globe.

Standards for Working Hours and Annual Leave Worldwide

One way in which organizations can provide for the physical and mental health of their employees and facilitate work-life balance is by providing for some annual leave and maintaining reasonable working hours. The ILO has placed a great deal of emphasis on working conditions around the world since its inception. In 2013, the ILO published a report (Ghosheh, 2013) about working conditions in various parts of the world.

With respect to limits on working hours, the ILO (Ghosheh, 2013) reports that during the early 20th century it was not uncommon for people to work 14- to 16-hour days. In the post–World War II time frame, progress was made toward reducing this to 8 hours per day, or 48 hours per week. **ILO conventions No. 1 and No. 30** were held with the goal of reducing the negative impact of excessive work hours on worker lives. Another convention, called the **ILO Forty Hour Week Convention No. 47**, was held in 1935 to establish the possibility of a 40-hour week.

Forty-hour weeks are considered normal in many countries, including the United States. According to the ILO (Ghosheh, 2013), 52% of countries worldwide have legislation which sets the standard hours in a workweek above 40 hours, with the largest cluster of these setting it at 48 hours per week. Thirty-six percent of countries worldwide set the standard working week at 40 hours per week. Only 3% of countries set their limit at fewer than 40 hours per week, and only 1% of countries set their limit at more than 49 hours per week (Ghosheh, 2013). The breakdown of countries is as follows.

In Africa, 35% of countries have set a standard 40-hour week, 27% of countries have set a limit between 42 and 45 hours per week, and 29% of countries have set the limit at 48 hours per week. Only Kenya and Seychelles exceed 49 hours per week. Further, Nigeria and Zimbabwe do not have limits. In Asia and the Pacific regions, 32% of countries endorse a 48-hour workweek. In Asia and the Pacific regions, 46% of countries have set a limit of 40 to 45 hours per week. In Europe, 69% of countries have established the 40-hour workweek, and 16% of countries have laws that exceed the 40-hour workweek, although none of them exceed 48 hours in a workweek. The ILO report also points out that although Germany has no limit to the number of hours in a workweek, national-level collective bargaining for various sectors and industries establishes the standards for work hour limits (Ghosheh, 2013). In addition, the European Union's Charter of Fundamental Rights further protects workers. The Charter states that all workers have the right to "limitation of maximum working hours, to daily and weekly rest periods and to an annual period of paid leave" (Kuddo, 2009).

In the Americas and the Caribbean, 38% of countries follow a 48-hour workweek. A larger proportion of these countries (56%) follow a 40- to 45-hour workweek, and none of the countries had a limit that was over 48 hours. In the Middle East, 90% of countries set a 48-hour workweek limit. Only Syria adhered to a 40-hour workweek (Ghosheh, 2013).

Data compiled by the Organisation for Economic Co-Operation and Development (OECD) through the year 2015 show a consistent trend, with Mexico working the most hours (averaging just over 43 hours per week), followed by Korea, Greece, Chile, Russia, Poland, Iceland, Portugal, Israel, and Estonia in the top 10

ILO 2013 Report on Working Hours Worldwide

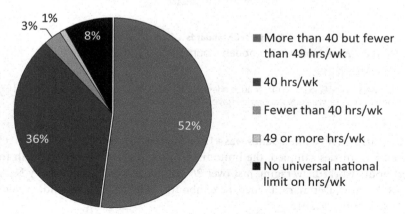

FIGURE 3.1. Percentage of Countries Across the World with Standard Workweek Hours

Source: Ghosheh (2013).

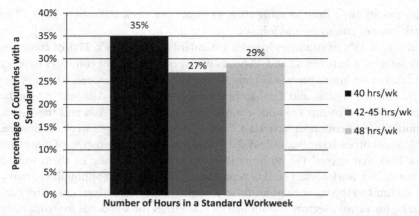

FIGURE 3.2. Work Hours in African Countries

Source: Ghosheh (2013).

Note: Numbers do not add to 100 because Kenya and Seychelles exceed 49 hrs/wk. Nigeria and Zimbabwe do not have a universal national limit on working hours per week.

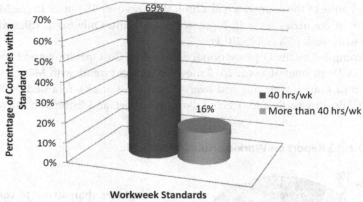

Workweek Standards

FIGURE 3.3. Work Hours in European Countries

Source: Ghosheh (2013).

Note: Numbers do not add to 100 because a few countries do not have a universal national limit on working hours per week. No countries have a limit of more than 48 hrs/wk.

(EOCD, 2016). The United States was #12 averaging just over 34 hours per week. Of the 35 countries sampled, the bottom 10 countries were Germany (with the fewest hours worked, averaging just over 26 hours per week), followed by Netherlands, Norway, Denmark, France, Luxembourg, Belgium, Switzerland, Sweden, and Austria (OECD, 2016).

In examining hours worked, overtime limits must be analyzed because unless there are reasonable limits on overtime, weekly limits may have little effect. The ILO report (Ghosheh, 2013) found that the majority of countries for which data

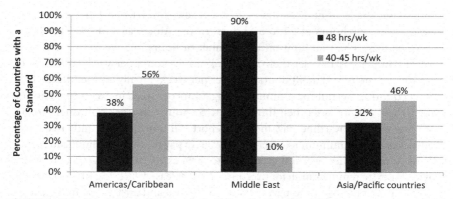

FIGURE 3.4. Workweek Standards in Other Parts of the World

Source: Ghosheh (2013).

Note: For Americas/Caribbean, no country has a limit above 48 hrs/wk. For Asia/Pacific countries, no countries have weekly hour limits above 48 hrs/wk, but some countries have no universal national limit on hours worked per week.

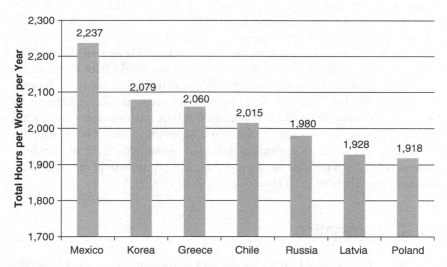

FIGURE 3.5. Countries with the Longest Hours Worked in 2013

Source: World Economic Forum.

were available (75%) establish some sort of limit on overtime hours per week. In
Africa, 55% of countries set total working hours per week at 59 or below, while
20% of African countries set a limit at 60 hours or above, and 8% had no limit.
In Asia and the Pacific, the report observed the highest percentage of countries
(32%) which had no limit on the overtime hours in a workweek. A few countries
in this region (4%) set the limit of hours in a workweek at 48 or fewer, while
29% of countries set the limit at 60 hours per week or more. In Europe, 70%
of countries set the limit of workweek hours at 48 hours or fewer, while 21% of

countries set the limit at 47 hours or fewer. A few countries in Europe (9%) set maximum weekly hours at 49 to 59 hours. In the Americas and the Caribbean, 34% of countries had no limit on the number of hours in a workweek, almost a third of countries (31%) set their limit at 49 to 59 hours per week, and 12% of countries set their limit at 48 hours or fewer per week. Finally, in the Middle East 80% of countries permit maximum working hours per week in excess of 60 hours, while 10% of countries set their limit at 49 to 59 hours per week (Ghosheh, 2013).

With respect to overtime pay, the ILO report (Ghosheh, 2013) finds that most countries do have minimum requirements for extra pay for overtime hours. In Africa, 92% of countries offer overtime pay of up to 50% extra. In Asia, 72% of countries provide for extra remuneration for overtime pay of at least 25% extra. In Europe, 64% of countries require overtime payments between 25% and 50% extra. In fact, since 1999, the European Social Charter, also known as "the Charter," extended additional protection to workers by suggesting that hours worked above the weekly standard "should be considered as overtime." The Charter "suggests recognizing the right of workers to an increase rate of remuneration for overtime work" (Kuddo, 2009). In America and the Caribbean, 100% of countries examined required overtime payments, and the rates ranged between 1% to 75% extra. In the Middle East, all countries offered payment for overtime ranging between 25% to 50% extra (Ghosheh, 2013).

Another way in which organizations contribute to the physical and mental health of their employees and improve their quality of life as a result is by providing effective minimum wages. Researchers for the World Bank conducted a study in 18 countries across the world which revealed that it is not the number of employed adults, but "growth in labor income per adult," that contributes to the reduction of poverty (Azevedo & Inchauste, 2013). A separate quantitative study conducted across 112 countries by the World Economic Forum (WEF) supports this finding. The WEF, an institution dedicated to the betterment of humanity, discovered that "it is possible to be pro-equity and pro-growth at the same time" (Samans, Blanke, Corrigan, & Drzeniek, 2015).

Age Discrimination

According to the ILO (2011), there has been an increase in the number of discrimination claims reported worldwide in the past several years. In the United Kingdom, the claims from the Employment Tribunal Service show an increase in age discrimination claims over the years, with 972 claims in the year 2006–2007 and 3,801 claims in the year 2008–2009 (ILO, 2011). In France, the HALDE received 78 claims in 2005 but 599 claims in 2009 (ILO, 2011). In the United States, there were 16,585 claims filed under the Age Discrimination in Employment Act in 2005, but there were 20,857 claims filed in 2016 (EEOC, 2017).

According to the ILO, 29 countries have employment laws explicitly prohibiting discrimination on the basis of age (ILO, 2011). Several countries including the Netherlands, Norway, Australia, the United Kingdom, and Finland have conducted large government campaigns aimed at encouraging employers to both hire and retain older employees. For example, in the United Kingdom the Age Positive campaign helps promote awareness of the benefits of an age-diverse organization (ILO, 2011). In the Republic of Korea, affirmative action legislation requires that employers employ at least 3% of their workforce from the 55 and older age group. Also in Korea, the Aged Employment Promotion Law specifies certain occupations for which older workers are to be given priority (ILO, 2011; United Nations, 2007).

However, it is important to note that sometimes younger workers may struggle as much as some of the older workers. According to the European Commission (2009), younger employees between the ages of 15 and 24 experienced a 7.3% decline in employment between 2008 and 2009. In both industrialized and developing countries, younger employees tend to find themselves working in situations of informal employment, intermittent employment, and insecure working arrangements with low wages (ILO, 2011). The European Union has started a program called "new start" where young people who have been unemployed for six months or longer are given training, retraining, and job search assistance. An initiative in the United Kingdom called the New Futures Fund (NFF) helps unemployed people between the ages of 16 and 34 (ILO, 2011).

Forced Labor

According to a report by the ILO in 2014, an estimated 20.9 million people around the world are subject to forced labor. Of these, 90% are exploited in private industry by companies or individuals for profit, while 10% are in state-imposed forms of labor. Of those performing forced labor for individuals or companies in the private sector, 22% are victims of forced sexual exploitation, while 68% are in forced labor.

According to the report (ILO, 2014a), vestiges of slavery are still visible in parts of Africa, while forced labor through deceptive or coercive recruiting practices is apparent in Latin America. In numerous countries, there are reports of domestic workers being kept inside of homes through threats. In South Asia, bonded labor persists, and millions of men, women, and children are working to pay off debt. In Europe and North America, there are also reports of trafficking of women and children for the purposes of labor and sexual exploitation (ILO, 2014a). Finally, several countries in the world have also been found to impose forced labor as a means of economic development and retribution for people whose political views clash with the political authorities in the country (ILO, 2014a).

These problems have led a number of countries to act against forced labor. In Brazil, action plans against slave labor were adopted in 2003 and 2008 in coordination with the National Commission to Eradicate Slave Labor. In Peru, the country adopted a second National Commission to Combat Forced Labor in 2013. In Nepal, a National Plan of Action Against Bonded Labor was adopted in 2009 to heighten awareness around the problem of bonded labor (ILO, 2014a).

Child Labor

According to the ILO (2014a) child labor is strongly and positively related to poverty. An estimated 168 million children, or 11% of the children in the world, are considered to be child laborers (ILO, 2014a). There are 77.7 million child laborers between the ages of 5 and 17 in Asia and the Pacific. There are 59 million child laborers in sub-Saharan Africa. There are 12.5 million child laborers in Latin America and the Caribbean. There are 9.2 million child laborers in the Middle East and Northern Africa (ILO, 2014a).

The **Minimum Age Convention of 1973 (No. 138)** set a minimum employment age at 15 years (13 years for light work) and a minimum age of 18 years for hazardous work conditions (16 years under strict conditions). It also put forth a provision for having a minimum working age of 14 years (and 12 years for light work) in countries where the economy and educational infrastructure are not sufficiently developed (ILO, 2014a). In an effort to further protect the young, the European Union's Charter of Fundamental Rights reads that hiring children is forbidden. Any person younger than 15 years of age or who is still subject to the national school age compulsory law is considered a child (Kuddo, 2009).

The **Worst Forms of Child Labor Convention of 1999 (No. 182)** defined a child as a person under the age of 18 and laid out rules which require the ratifying states to abolish the worst forms of child labor, including slavery, the sale or trafficking of children, debt bondage, forced labor, the use of children in armed conflicts, child prostitution or pornography, the use of children for trafficking drugs, and other activities that may be harmful to the health, safety, or morals of the child (ILO, 2014a).

So far, 165 countries have ratified at least one of these two conventions pertaining to child labor. There is evidence that ratifying these rules results in progress. Brazil ratified the convention documents in 2001, and its child labor rate dropped from 18% in 1992 to less than 7% in 2009. School attendance in Brazil rose from 85% to 97% (ILO, 2014a; Understanding Children's Work [UCW] Project, 2011).

Global View: Paraguay

In Paraguay, approximately 47,000 children and adolescents live in what is known as the "criadazgo," or the exploitation of domestic child labor (Latinamerica Press, 2016). The criadazgo is a cultural practice in which poor families give their children to a third party for whom the latter will work in exchange for room and board. Carlos Zárate, minister of childhood and adolescence in Paraguay, explains that the criadazgo system "is detrimental to the rights of boys, girls, and adolescents" and that children in criadazgo run a greater risk of "mistreatment and sexual abuse" (Latinamerica Press, 2016). He adds that the country is working on legislation that will penalize this form of modern slavery.

Disability

According to the ILO report on Achieving Equal Employment Opportunities for People with Disabilities through Legislation, over 1 billion people worldwide have some sort of disability, which accounts for 15% of the world's population (ILO, 2014b). According to the report, "throughout the world there is an undeniable link between disability, poverty, and exclusion" (ILO, 2014b, p. 1).

The report also explains that, for a long time, disability was seen as a social welfare issue and people assumed the disabled should be taken care of through social security systems. The human rights charters adopted from the 1940s through the 1960s do not mention disability (ILO, 2014b). It was only in the 1970s that disability became a human rights issue. In the 1980s and 1990s, councils began adopting (usually nonbinding) instruments, including in the United Nations and in the Council of Europe (ILO, 2014b), to protect individuals with disabilities. The most significant piece of legislation to protect the disabled, the **United Nations Convention on the Rights of Persons with Disabilities (CRPD)**, adopted in 2006, "promotes the full integration of persons with disabilities in societies" (World Bank, 2015). The CRPD requires states to treat the disabled as equal to others without a disability. According to the World Bank, 182 countries have signed the CRPD and 153 have ratified it. Additionally, the World Bank reports that the UN is strengthening its commitment to individuals with disabilities, as evident in the Post-2015 Development Agenda, which states that "disability cannot be a reason or criteria for lack of access to development programming and the realization of human rights" (World Bank, 2015).

Also, according to the ILO report, constitutional law is the highest law of the land. Countries whose constitutions mention disability or address the needs of the disabled are demonstrating the importance they place on this matter (ILO, 2014b). The list of countries that explicitly mention disability in their constitutional law includes: Brazil, Cambodia, Canada, China, Ethiopia, Fiji, Germany, Kenya, Mongolia, New Zealand, Seychelles, Slovenia, South Africa, South Sudan, Tanzania, Thailand, and Uganda.

There is no universal definition of disability. Instead, laws generally take one of two approaches. The first approach is aimed at a narrow beneficiary group and provides a list of conditions or impairments that are covered. If the aim of the law is to provide targeted financial support to those who are most in need (ILO, 2014b), then this approach should be used. The second approach provides broad and inclusive wording to protect people from discrimination on the grounds of a disability. Because many people, including those with temporary disabilities or those perceived as having a disability, can be the targets of discriminatory actions (ILO, 2014b), this approach should be used where the purpose is to broadly protect a social group.

Disability can sometimes affect an individual's capacity to carry out a job in the usual way. This is why the concept of "reasonable accommodation" is typically found in the wording of discrimination law. For example, the U.S. **Americans with Disabilities Act of 1990 (ADA)** prohibits employment discrimination against individuals with a life limiting disability. The law describes disabilities as conditions that limit a major life function such as walking, sitting, breathing, speaking, and thinking, among others. Disabilities may be physical and visible, such as mobility impairment. Disabilities may also be invisible, such as mental disorders including bipolar disorder or schizophrenia. The law maintains that employers must not discriminate against applicants with a disability as long as the applicants are able to meet the essential functions of the job. Essential functions of the job are the skills that are critical to performing the job and must be performed by the employee with or without any accommodation (Americans with Disabilities Act, 2015). For tasks that are helpful but not among the essential functions of the job, employers are encouraged to provide reasonable accommodation for employees with a disability.

Accommodations may come in many forms. If the employee has a physical disability, a reasonable accommodation might be that a coworker who does not have mobility impairment could take over a portion of the job duties which require more physical ability. An individual who is blind should be provided a keyboard with a Braille reader. If the employee has a mental disability, such as bipolar disorder, a reasonable accommodation might be a flexible working schedule which allows the employee to take medication in the morning and come to work later in the day once the medications are effective. Providing a sign language interpreter for a deaf job applicant is another example. According to Lynette A. Barnes, regional attorney for the Equal Employment Opportunity Commission (EEOC)'s Charlotte District, "some employers still judge employees based on a disability rather than on their proven ability to do a job." Her comments follow a lawsuit brought by the EEOC against Correct Care Solutions for disability discrimination against a nurse whom the company fired despite the fact that the nurse's "medical restrictions did not affect her ability to perform her job duties" (EEOC, 2015).

In Ireland, the **Employment Equality Act of 1998** requires reasonable accommodations for the needs of disabled persons by providing for special treatment or facilities. The act explicitly states that "a person who has a disability shall not be regarded as other than fully competent to undertake, and fully capable of undertaking, any duties if, with the assistance of special treatment or facilities, such person would be fully competent to undertake, and be fully capable of undertaking, those duties" (Irish Statute Book [ISB], 2016). This excludes what employees would normally be expected to provide for themselves, including personal care items. In South Africa, reasonable accommodation is required by the **Employment Equity Act of 1998**. This act requires modifications to the job or the working environment to enable the person from the designated group to participate and advance in employment (ILO, 2014b).

A disabled worker who is claiming an accommodation should demonstrate that he or she is otherwise qualified for the job, that the employer is aware of his or her needs, and that with the accommodation, he or she could perform the essential functions of the job (ILO, 2014b). Employers are only exempted from providing reasonable accommodation when they were not aware of the disability, they were not aware of the need for accommodation, an effective accommodation is not available, or the requested accommodation places a disproportionate burden on the employer. In practice, the question of what constitutes a disproportionate burden on the employer depends on cost, the effects on the overall work processes, the size of the organization, the number of disabled persons employed in that organization already, public funding available, and the length of the prospective employment contract (ILO, 2014b).

While implementing reasonable accommodations comes at a cost to employers and society as a whole, "the economic costs of inaction" (Abrahams, 2014) surpass those of action, as revealed by an independent comprehensive report carried out in Australia in 2011 prior to that country's disability system reform. Tony Abrahams of the World Economic Forum informs that the NDIS (the National Disability Insurance Scheme) is now law in Australia, approved by a 79% voter support. The law provides "no-fault, needs-based, individualized funding packages and support for people with a disability, paid for with an increase in 0.5% in personal income tax rates." Abrams also cites a similar UK program for the disabled which "effectively removed financial disincentives for companies to employ disabled workers." The British government has published a return on that investment of 48% (Abrahams, 2014).

LGBT[1] (Lesbian, Gay, Bisexual, and Transgender)

The ILO also maintains some data on the progress that is being made toward the rights of lesbian, gay, bisexual, and transgender employees. The ILO director general often makes a statement about the state of LGBT rights around the world on International Day against Homophobia and Transphobia. According to the data, more than 60 member states of the ILO have prohibited employment discrimination on the basis of sexual orientation in accordance with the **Discrimination (Employment and Occupation) Convention, 1958 (No. 111)**. However, while there has been some progress toward LGBT rights, not all the news is good for LGBT groups. LGBT workers still experience harassment and discrimination both in the workplace and in society at large (ILO, 2013). For example, between 2011 and 2012 the number of countries criminalizing people on the basis of their sexual orientation increased from 76 to 78 countries (ILO, 2013). Furthermore, in 2012 Brazil registered 44% of worldwide homicides committed against LGBT persons (Kaipper Ceratti, 2014). In addition, in 2013 the Pew Research Center surveyed 40,117 respondents in 40 countries about various topics including the morality of homosexuality. The poll revealed that half or more of the survey respondents in the majority of the 40 nations surveyed reported that homosexuality is unacceptable (Pew Research Center, 2014).

As of 2014, the ILO reports that in "78 countries LGBT persons still risk going to prison, or worse, because of laws that criminalize homosexuality." According to the report, most LGBT employees decide to conceal their sexual identity for fear of discrimination in the workplace. Employees who fear that others at work will find out their sexual preference and conceal this part of their identity may develop anxiety in the workplace (ILO, 2014c). Further, prejudice against LGBT groups can adversely affect these individuals not only on the job but also in their personal lives. One study from the United Kingdom based on the Labour Force Survey found that gay men were paid 5% lower wages than their non-gay counterparts (Drydakis, 2009; ILO, 2011). A review of wage differences in the United States Netherlands, UK, Sweden, Greece, France, and Australia revealed that, on average, gay and bisexual men earn 11% less than heterosexual men with the same qualifications (Badgett, 2014; Klawitter, 2015). Moreover, LGBT employees and their partners often do not enjoy the same benefits as non-gay married couples because gay marriage is not recognized in many parts of the world. According to statistics from the World Economic Forum, only 23 nations around the world allow gay marriage either nationally or by jurisdictions (Myers, 2015).

The economic disadvantages that affect the LGBT community affect the world economy at large. The World Bank reported that "social inclusion matters because exclusion is too costly" (World Bank, 2013). Additionally, "Many multinational businesses now recognize the links between inclusion of LGBT employees and business outcomes and have taken voluntary steps to end discrimination against LGBT workers in order to maintain a competitive workforce" (Badgett, 2014).

Maternity Leave and Paternity Leave Worldwide

One challenge that many adults face during their careers is the juggling of simultaneous competing demands such as raising a family, working full-time, and trying to establish their careers. The ILO compiled a report, published in 2014 (Addati, Cassirer, & Gilchrist, 2014), which describes maternity and paternity leave policies throughout the world.

The role of the ILO has been to ensure that employment does not cause potential harm to women or their children and that having a child does not jeopardize a woman's job due to discrimination. To this end, the ILO, which will be 100 years old in 2019, has drafted several key documents for the protection of women and their children. These documents have been adopted by participating countries during the annual ILO conventions. The **ILO Maternity Protection Convention of 2000 (No. 183)** is the most recent convention where a major document was adopted for the benefit of working mothers and their children.

The most recent ILO report (Addati et al., 2014) covers policies in 185 different countries. It finds that 34% of the countries fully meet the requirements of Convention no. 183 by providing at least 14 weeks of paid leave which is paid at a rate of at least two-thirds of the previous salary and is paid by social insurance or public funds such that the employer is not solely liable for the cost. According to the report, the regions of the world with the best maternity benefits are Europe, Central Asia, and the developed economies. Benefits were the lowest in Asia and in the Middle East, while 20% or fewer of the countries in Africa, Latin America, and the Caribbean met the minimum standards of Convention no. 183 (Addati et al., 2014).

The report highlights progress over the years, mentioning that in 1994 only 38% of countries for which information was available at the time provided the minimum of 14 weeks of paid maternity leave. By 2013, 51% of that same group of countries that provided data in 1994 had begun providing the minimum 14 weeks of paid maternity leave. Therefore, good progress has been made. However, the report also highlights several concerns as it states that only 28.4% of all employed women in the world would receive maternity leave benefits. A majority of female workers, representing approximately 830 million women worldwide, would not have adequate maternity leave coverage. About 80% of these women live in Asia and Africa (Addati et al., 2014).

One way to help working women, and working families with children generally, is by providing some paternity leave. According to the ILO report, recognition of men's rights to parenthood, as well as their obligations to share in the household work, will result in more equality between men and women both in employment and at home. In 1994, paternity leave existed in 40 out of the 141 countries for which data were available. By 2013, paternity leave was available in 78 countries out of the 167 countries for which data were available (Addati et al., 2014). Paternity leave is paid in 70% of these countries, although the employing company is the primary source of funding. According to the report, the lowest rates of paternity leave were found in the Middle East, where 80% of companies provided no leave, while 20% of companies provided paternity leave of 1 to 6 days. The most generous paternity leave policies were found in the developed countries, where 33% of companies provided no paternity leave, 17% provided leave between 1 and 6 days, 8% provided leave of 7 to 10 days, 28% provided leave of 10 to 15 days, and 14% provided leave of 16 days or more (Addati et al., 2014).

According to Stéphanie Thomson, an editor at the World Economic Forum, cultural changes must accompany legislative ones if families are to benefit to the full extent that the law allows (Thomson, 2015). As child-rearing is still seen as primarily a woman's job in Korea, only 2% of Korean fathers take advantage of the generous paternity leave offered by this country (Thomson, 2015). In 2011, the Organization for Economic Co-Operation and Development released a "comprehensive assessment of the use of leave" by eligible parents. Their findings show that fathers are less likely to take parental leave than mothers. In Japan, while 72% of mothers took parental leave, only 0.5% of men did. Similarly, in Belgium, Austria, and Canada, men took parental leave at significantly lower rates than women at 27%, 30%, and 55% respectively (OECD, 2014).

Migrant Workers

Unemployment and poverty in underdeveloped countries have led many workers to go to more developed countries that demand labor. There are approximately 232 million migrant workers in the world, which represents 3.1% of the world's population (ILO, 2014a). Women make up almost half of migrant workers, and one in eight migrants are between the ages of 15 and 24 (ILO, 2014a). Migrant workers contribute to the economies of their host country and typically send money home to their families, which also contributes to the economies of their home country. Migrant workers, however, "often enjoy little social protection, face inequalities in the labour market and are vulnerable to exploitation and human trafficking" (ILO, 2014a, p. 82).

The **ILO Global Wage Report for 2014/2015** reported on the status of migrant workers, including "unexplained" differences in pay and the wage gaps between migrant workers and domestic workers. The ILO statisticians decompose wage gaps in two parts, explained portions and unexplained portions. The explained part takes into account experience, education, occupation, economic activity, location, and hours worked. The unexplained portion, or the wage penalty, is what remains after accounting for the explained portion (ILO, 2015).

There are many explanations for the unexplained wage difference, including: the characteristics of the migrant workers including their skill level, prejudice or distrust toward these groups, differences in education, suspicions about the education credentials they bring with them from abroad, perceptions of lower income need (particularly for single migrant workers), and a lack of representation and collective bargaining (ILO, 2015). In every country represented in the ILO report, there is a wage gap for migrant workers that is at least partially unexplained.

The **Migration for Employment Convention (Revised), 1949 (No. 97)** requires members of ratifying states to facilitate international migration processes, provide free assistance and information for migrant workers, and prevent misleading propaganda related to immigration. This includes provisions on medical services available to migrant workers as well as states being required to apply a treatment that is no less favorable than their own nationals with respect to conditions of employment, freedom of association, and social security (ILO, 2014a).

The **Migrant Workers (Supplementary Provisions) Convention of 1975 (No. 143)** puts forth measures to combat illegal immigration as well as provisions for obligations to respect the human rights of migrant workers. It also extends the 1949 convention to ensure equal treatment between national workers and migrant workers with respect to employment and occupations, Social Security, trade unions, cultural rights, and collective freedoms (ILO, 2014a).

Seafarers, Fishers, and Dock Workers

An estimated 90% of world trade is carried on ships which require seafarers to help operate those ships (International Chamber of Shipping, 2015). Very often, seafarers from different parts of the world come together and sail on a ship that is registered or "flagged" in a different country and may be owned by ship owners in yet a different country. According to international law, the country in which the ship is flagged is responsible for the working conditions of the people on board the ship. If the ship flies the flag of a country that does not exercise sufficient control or jurisdiction over the ship, the working conditions on that ship might be poor. In fact, various countries have reported captains who have abused, enslaved, and abandoned employees (ILO, 2014a).

The ILO has established approximately 70 provisions over the years to provide decent work for seafarers. This includes provisions outlining wages, leaves, repatriation, occupational safety and health, medical care, welfare, and social security. Even so, some examples of terrible working conditions for fishermen have been documented worldwide, as shown in the following example.

Global View

Recent articles illustrate the problems experienced by migrant workers on fishing boats. The articles have used the terms "Seafood from Slaves" (Mason, Mendoza, & Htusan, 2015) and "Sea Slaves" (Urbina, 2015) to describe the conditions of migrant workers from Indonesia, Cambodia, and other parts of Asia who were treated as slaves on fishing ships in waters near Thailand. A reporter explains how she found eight men locked in a cage because their captain considered them to be a flight risk, meaning they had a high likelihood of running away while the boat was docked. One of the men said, "All I did was tell my captain that I couldn't take it anymore, that I wanted to go home." The next time the boat docked, he was locked up (Mason et al., 2015).

These men who come from Burma, Cambodia, and other parts of Asia, lived in poverty and were lured onto fishing boats, sometimes under the impression that they would be going somewhere to work in construction and other jobs (Mason et al., 2015; Urbina, 2015). They were brought to Indonesia through Thailand and then forced to fish. The author states that according to some of the men, "the captains on their fishing boats forced them to drink unclean water and work 20- to 22-hour shifts with no days off. Almost all said they were kicked, whipped with toxic stingray tails or otherwise beaten if they complained or tried to rest. They were paid little or nothing . . ." (Mason et al., 2015).

> On the dock in Benjina, former slaves unload boats for food and pocket money. Many are men who were abandoned by their captains—sometimes five, 10 or even 20 years ago—and remain stranded.
>
> (Mason et al., 2015)

A few days after that article broke, approximately 320 of the fishermen on the Indonesian island were rescued and returned home to Burma. The article describes that there could be as many as 4,000 men in the islands surrounding Benjina who were there as a result of being trafficked or enslaved (Associated Press, 2015).

> "I will go see my parents. They haven't heard from me, and I haven't heard from them since I left," said Win Win Ko, 42, beaming, his smile

showing missing teeth. The captain on his fishing boat had kicked out four teeth with his military boots, he said, because Win was not moving fish fast enough from the deck to the hold below.

(Associated Press, 2015)

Examples of abuse such as this bring to light the importance of human rights and employment legislation worldwide. Many of the fish caught by these slave laborers then become part of the food supply of developed countries, providing seafood for restaurants, major grocery chains, and pet food (Mason et al., 2015; Urbina, 2015). According to some of the major merchants the authors interviewed, it is difficult to track supplies of fish throughout the world, and merchants do not always know exactly where their fish came from. Another matter is how much incentive the merchants have to search for these types of problems when everyone is trying to sell a competitive product, which includes being competitive on price.

With respect to the related occupation of dock workers, the ILO has also set guidelines about the occupational safety and health of such workers. The guidelines, known as **Occupational Safety and Health (Dock Workers) Convention, 1979 (No. 152)**, make provisions that stipulate safe access to the workplace, injury-prevention training to employees, providing workers with protective equipment, maintaining adequate first aid equipment, and ensuring proper procedures are followed in case of an emergency (ILO, 2014a).

Wage Gaps Between Men and Women

According to the ILO (2015), women continue to experience a significant wage gap in the amount of pay they obtain for similar jobs compared to their male peers. As explained in the prior section on migrant workers, the ILO statisticians decompose wage gaps into two parts, explained portions and unexplained portions. The explained part takes into account experience, education, occupation, economic activity, location, and hours worked. The unexplained portion, or the wage penalty, is what remains after accounting for the explained portion.

The ILO has developed a detailed breakdown by country comparing how much of the wage gap in that country is explained versus unexplained. According to the ILO (2015), there are unexplained portions of wage gaps (whether small or large) in every country reported in their sample. The report explains that there are several possible explanations for this, including undervaluing women's work, characteristics of the workplace, sex segregation channeling women into lower paid occupations, the wage structure in the country, the perception of women as being economically dependent, and the possibility that women are in occupations that are largely unorganized and do not have representation by unions or other groups

(ILO, 2015). The report stresses that national legislation providing for equal pay between men and women is essential.

However, even in countries where such legislation exists, wage gaps still persist. The United States, for example, has the **Equal Pay Act** which requires equal pay for men and women performing similar jobs. Nevertheless, the wage gap persists in the United States. According to the ILO report, a portion of the wage gap between men and women in the United States is unexplained, meaning that inequities persist (ILO, 2015).

Further, the World Economic Forum (2015) also released its **Global Gender Gap Report for 2015** which shows inequities between men and women in almost every country, including the United States. The World Economic Forum report takes into account four factors, including the economic participation and opportunity for women, educational attainment, health and survival, and political empowerment. They then create an overall ranking. The ranking of the top 15 most egalitarian countries is as follows: Iceland, Norway, Finland, Sweden, Ireland, Rwanda, Philippines, Switzerland, Slovenia, New Zealand, Germany, Nicaragua, Netherlands, Denmark, and France. The United States was ranked 28th overall and 6th in the economic participation and opportunity of women. However, it ranks 40th in educational attainment, 72nd in political empowerment, and 64th in health and survival of women.

Veterans (Ex-Combatants)

As we know, wars and other armed conflicts are fairly common in this world. Men and women who have been involved in armed conflict often face physical or psychological challenges which can take time to heal and may require some assistance to complete the healing process. To assist veterans, the United Nations developed the **Integrated Disarmament, Demobilization and Reintegration Standards (ILO, 2010). Disarmament** is defined as collecting, controlling, and/or disposing of light and heavy weapons. It also includes developing an arms management program. **Demobilization** is defined as discharging active combatants from the armed forces. This is followed by another stage, reinsertion, which provides a support package for the demobilized. **Reinsertion** is defined as the assistance offered to ex-combatants during the process of demobilization. Traditional reinsertion assistance covers the basic costs of food, clothes, medical services, and short-term training to help cover the basic needs of ex-combatants and their families. This reinsertion stage may last up to one year. Finally, the **reintegration** stage is the process where ex-combatants acquire civilian status and return to employment. According to the United Nations, this is a national responsibility of a country and often requires long-term assistance (ILO, 2010).

The United Nations explains that the peace building and economic recovery process includes several steps. The first step is a peace negotiation. This is the stage where stabilizing income and emergency employment is important. The second step is stabilization, which includes providing security, relief, and early recovery.

The third stage is reintegration, which includes reconciliation, peace, equity, and recovery. At this time, local economic recovery should be taking place. The fourth step is transition, which include sustainable growth and social justice. By this point, emergency employment initiatives should be ending and should be replaced with stable employment creation and decent work (ILO, 2010; United Nations, 2008).

There are a number of examples of how different countries have handled reintegration of ex-combatants. The armed conflict between the Sri Lankan government and the separatist group the Tamil Tigers, or the Liberation Tigers of Tamil Eelam (LTTE), illustrates an approach to ex-combatant reintegration. The Sri Lankan Ministry of Disaster Management and Human Rights developed a proposal for the reintegration of the Tamil Tigers into society. Prior to the end of the war, the ILO facilitated sensitization workshops to highlight the disarmament, demobilization, and reintegration challenges that Sri Lanka would face. Government officials, policymakers, and members of the Armed Forces worked together with local advisors to write a National Framework Proposal for Sri Lanka. This framework was validated in a national workshop in July 2009 (ILO, 2010; National Framework Proposal on the Reintegration of Ex-combatants into Civilian Life in Sri Lanka, 2009). This is an example of a readjustment and reintegration procedure within a country where two different groups were at war.

In the United States, efforts to compensate and reintegrate veterans back to civilian life have a long history, and it is one that is dotted with both struggles and successes. Before Congress passed the GI Bill, the legislation that would propel over 7.8 million World War II veterans to participate in an education or training program (U.S. Department of Veterans Affairs, 2013), there was the struggle and the humiliation that World War I veterans and their families had to endure at the hands of the United States government, which was refusing to honor a promise. The conflict began in 1932 with a veteran-led peaceful demonstration at the steps of the U.S. Capitol. These World War I veterans and their families were called the "Bonus Army," and they marched to Washington DC from all over the United States to demand that the government pay the bonuses promised to them in 1918 for their service and sacrifice during World War I. The government, however, claimed that the bonuses could not be paid until 1945. In 1932, with the country in the grip of the Great Depression, the former soldiers were "desperate for relief . . . [and in May of that year] a group of veterans in Portland, Oregon, led by a man named Walter Waters, decided to go to Washington to lobby for early payment of their promised bonus" (Richman & Freemark, 2011). Pulitzer Prize–winning journalist Edward Humes states that this was not the first time America was slow to compensate veterans. He asserts that "most of the Revolutionary War veterans were dead before their pensions, promised 40 years earlier, were finally dispersed" (Callaghan, 2008).

The two month–long peaceful protest led by the determined Bonus Army did not yield immediate results. On July 28 of 1923, the Bonus Army was forced out of their improvised encampment, set afire by the U.S. Army under the leadership of General Douglas McArthur (Richman & Freemark, 2011). Four years later, World War I veterans received their bonuses, and in 1944, "Congress passed the GI Bill to help military veterans transition to civilian life, and to acknowledge the debt owed to those who risk their lives for their country" (Richman & Freemark, 2011). The GI Bill offered veterans benefits such as education and training; loan guaranty for homes, farms, or businesses; and unemployment pay (U.S. Department of Veterans Affairs, 2013).

Thirty years later, the **Vietnam Era Veterans' Readjustment Assistance Act of 1974** was created to help veterans who served in a foreign war readjust to employment when they returned home. This act, still in effect, protects the employment rights of veterans hired by contractors or subcontractors who are awarded contracts by the federal government worth $100,000 or more (National Veterans Foundation, 2015). The law prohibits discrimination against veterans and requires employers to provide affirmative action, which will be described in the section below, "to recruit, hire, promote, and retain" disabled veterans as well as other categories of veterans (Society for Human Resource Management, 2016; U.S. Department of Labor, 2015).

More recently, the U.S. government issued or updated additional bills to assist veterans. The list includes the Active Duty Montgomery GI Bill, the Reserve and Guard Montgomery GI Bill, the Reserve Educational Assistance Program (REAP), the Vocational Rehabilitation and Education Program, and the Post-9/11 GI Bill (Military.com, 2016a). Furthermore, the Transition Assistance Program (Headlee, 2014), a mandatory legal requirement of all military personnel, serves to inform servicemen and women about their benefits before they re-enter civilian life (Military.com, 2016b).

At the international level, the ILO report on guidelines and recommendations toward ex-combatants points out that it is important to promote the entrepreneurship of women after armed conflicts end. Wars make widows, and many times widows and female heads of households lack access to economic wealth (ILO, 2010). The ILO recommends that states ensure women's participation in small business by encouraging business networks and cooperatives and by providing business skills training for women (ILO, 2010).

Affirmative Action

Affirmative action is a concept that is known throughout the world. It is sometimes referred to as positive action (ILO, 2014a). Affirmative action programs are typically aimed at historically disadvantaged groups that have been the target of discrimination. The aim of such programs is to rectify injustices and to restore balance (ILO, 2014a). Affirmative action programs are to be evaluated regularly to ensure they are still needed and should be discontinued when it is deemed that the disadvantaged group has been sufficiently compensated, or caught up, from the disadvantaged position (ILO, 2014a).

Many countries have tried to implement affirmative action programs which attempt to improve employment opportunities for minorities and women. The logic behind affirmative action is that in order to remedy injustices/discrimination perpetrated on groups in the past or in the present, one must provide some favorable treatment to the protected groups harmed by the discrimination to level the playing field in the present. For instance, the practice of slavery in the United States, which persisted for almost 250 years, created a structure whereby the victims of slavery had less education, less money, and no property or resources compared to other groups that were not subject to slavery. This means that after being freed, the people who endured slavery and their descendants were likely to still have little schooling, money, and power for some time because money and education are necessary in order to afford a university degree and obtain access to high-paying professional jobs. Therefore, it would take a great deal of work and many generations in order to overcome the severe lack of resources that social groups are left with when they have been subjected to systematic discrimination.

There are many examples of discrimination throughout the world. Three vivid examples of countries with a history of discrimination as well as affirmative action policies include the United States, India, and South Africa. The United States has its history of slavery, racial segregation, and discrimination against various racial and ethnic minority groups. South Africa has a history of apartheid, or White rule of Blacks by force. Meanwhile, India has a caste system where racially similar people are divided into dissimilar social groups. According to Zacharias and Vakulabharanam (2011), the caste system in India is related to wealth inequality. They examined data from nationally representative household surveys and found that the groups that are traditionally disadvantaged (called the Scheduled Castes or the Scheduled Tribes) have substantially lower wealth than the "forward" caste groups while the "Other Backward Classes and non-Hindus occupy positions in the middle" (Zacharias & Vakulabharanam, 2011, p. 1820).

Several groups of scholars have studied the implementation of affirmative action policies as well as some of the challenges to affirmative action policies. For example, Boston and Nair-Reichert (2003) describe that the United States, Brazil, and India have faced Supreme Court challenges to their affirmative action policies in the past. The paper concludes that if affirmative action policies are to be effective, they must (a) be supported by the state's Constitution that recognizes the policy as restitution for past racial discrimination or caste injustice and (b) have a political party that is supportive of the affirmative action policy (Boston & Nair-Reichert, 2003).

Tummala (1999) assessed affirmative action policies in the United States, India, and South Africa. The article examines lessons learned and provides a list of recommendations for affirmative action policies. This list includes: developing a national consensus that affirmative action is an important public policy, setting a time limit to prevent preference from becoming an entitlement, restoring civility between different groups of people, perhaps downplaying the compensatory justice nature of the preference in favor of other arguments that would justify the preference, and attempting to dislodge the policy from ugly politics (Tummala, 1999). The author acknowledges that these suggestions will be difficult to implement because of the strong feelings that many hold both for and against affirmative action policies.

The United Nations Universal Declaration of Human Rights

Regardless of what particular group we are discussing, the basic principle that applies is that of equality and human dignity. According to the Universal Declaration of Human Rights (United Nations, 1948): "All human beings are born free and equal in dignity and rights. . . ."

Closing Case
The U.S. Supreme Court and Gay Marriage

As you have probably noticed throughout this chapter, laws and regulations surrounding people's rights are influenced by politics. When social support and political pressure grow around a certain topic, laws are put into place to make changes which provide rights that did not exist in the past. A current-day example of this type of law and policy in the making is that of the United States and gay marriage. After many years of sidestepping the issue, or taking on smaller pieces of the issue, the Supreme Court agreed to hear cases and deliberate on the constitutionality of gay marriage in 2015 (The Editorial Board, 2015).

In 2015, the court deliberated over four cases from different states (Tennessee, Ohio, Kentucky, and Michigan) in which same-sex union bans were supported in the Court of Appeals. In doing so, they took on the wide question of the constitutionality of same-sex marriage (The Editorial Board, 2015).

On June 26, 2015, the Supreme Court ruled that state gay marriage bans in the United States were illegal. They upheld gay marriage, thereby making it legal across the United States. In a 5–4 ruling, Justice Kennedy delivered the majority opinion and stated that "their hope is not to be condemned to live in loneliness, excluded from one of civilization's oldest institutions. They ask for equal dignity in the eyes of the law. The Constitution grants them that right" (de Vogue & Diamond, 2015). For gay couples, this is a civil right they have long awaited.

Justice Kennedy wrote "No longer may this liberty be denied... No union is more profound than marriage, for it embodies the highest ideals of love, fidelity, devotion, sacrifice and family" (Liptak, 2015). Chief Justice Roberts wrote the dissenting opinion and stated "The court invalidates the marriage laws of more than half the states and orders the transformation of a social institution that has formed the basis of human society for millennia, for the

Kalahari Bushmen and the Han Chinese, the Carthaginians and the Aztecs . . . Just who do we think we are?" (Liptak, 2015).

Discussion Questions:

1. Do you believe same-sex marriage will be socially accepted now that the Supreme Court has upheld it?
2. Does the Supreme Court decision upholding gay marriage mean discrimination against gays is over? Why or why not?
3. Why do you think it took so long for the Supreme Court to make a decision on the constitutionality of gay marriage and gay marriage bans?

Note

1. Note that LGBT is used as an umbrella term for a community of people. More recently, the term LGBTQIA has been used to be inclusive of more groups in the community. This will be explained in more detail in Chapter 6 on sexual orientation and gender identity.

References

Abrahams, T. (2014, January 16). From charity to insurance: Australia's disability system transformed. World Economic Forum. Retrieved from https://www.weforum.org/agenda/2014/01/charity-insurance-australias-disability-system-transformed/con

Addati, L., Cassirer, N., & Gilchrist, K. (2014). Maternity and paternity at work: Law and practice across the world. Rep. no. 978-92-2-128630-1[ISBN] (print). Geneva: International Labour Office.

Americans with Disabilities Act. (2015). Retrieved from http://www.ada.gov/pubs/adastatute08.pdf

Apple. (2017). Inclusion & Diversity. Retrieved from http://www.apple.com/diversity/

Associated Press. (2015, April 4). "They can all come": More than 300 slave fishermen rescued from Indonesian island. Retrieved from http://www.nydailynews.com/news/world/300-slave-fishermen-rescued-indonesian-island-article-1.2173220

Azevedo, J., & Inchauste, G. (2013). Is labor income responsible for poverty reduction? A decomposition approach. Working paper no. 6414. Washington, DC: World Bank, 2013. Print.

Badgett, M. V. L. (2014). The economic costs of stigma and the exclusion of LBGT people: A case study of India. Retrieved from http://documents.worldbank.org/curated/en/2014/10/23952131/economic-cost-stigma-exclusion-lgbt-people-case-study-india

Boston, T., & Nair-Reichert, U. (2003). Affirmative action: Perspectives from the United States, India, and Brazil. *Western Journal of Black Studies*, 27(1), 3–14.

Callaghan, P. (2008). The road to a better GI Bill. Retrieved from http://www.legion.org/education/911gibill

Cohen, P. N., & Huffman, M. L. (2003). Individuals, jobs, and labor markets: The devaluation of women's work. *American Sociological Review, 68*, 443–463.

Cook, T. (2015, March 29). Tim Cook: Pro-discrimination "religious freedom" laws are dangerous. *Washington Post.* Retrieved from http://www.washingtonpost.com/opinions/pro-discrimination-religious-freedom-laws-are-dangerous-to-america/2015/03/29/bdb4ce9e-d66d-11e4-ba28-f2a685dc7f89_story.html?utm_source=loopinsight.com&utm_medium=referral&utm_campaign=Feed%3A+loopinsight%2FKqJb+(The+Loop)&utm_content=FeedBurner

Correll, S. J., Benard, S., & Paik, I. (2007). Getting a job: Is there a motherhood penalty? *American Journal of Sociology, 112*, 1297–1338.

de Vogue, A., & Diamond, J. (2015, June 26). Supreme Court rules in favor of same-sex marriage nationwide. *CNN.* Retrieved from http://www.cnn.com/2015/06/26/politics/supreme-court-same-sex-marriage-ruling/index.html

Drydakis, N. (2009). Sexual orientation discrimination in the labour market. *Labour Economics, 16*, 364–372.

The Editorial Board. (2015, January 16). The Supreme Court and gay marriage. *New York Times.* Retrieved from http://www.nytimes.com/2015/01/17/opinion/the-supreme-court-and-gay-marriage.html?&_r=0

Equal Employment Opportunity Commission. (2015, November). EEOC sues correct care solutions for disability discrimination health care provider fired employee with seizure disorder despite doctor's clearance, federal agency charges. Washington, DC: U.S. Equal Employment Opportunity Commission.

Equal Employment Opportunity Commission. (2017). Charge Statistics FY 1997 Through FY 2016. Retrieved from https://www.eeoc.gov/eeoc/statistics/enforcement/charges.cfm

European Commission. (2009). *Employment in Europe 2009.* Luxembourg: Office for Official Publications of the European Communities. ISBN 978-92-79-13372-5. Retrieved from http://www.aedh.eu/plugins/fckeditor/userfiles/file/DESC/2009%20Employment%20in%20Europe%20ENG.pdf

Ghosheh, N. (2013). *Working conditions laws report 2012: A global review.* Geneva: International Labour Office. Web. 25 Nov. 2014. ISBN 978-92-2-127515-2 (print version).

Goldman, B. M., Gutek, B., Stein, J. H., & Lewis, K. (2006). Employment discrimination in organizations: Antecedents and consequences. *Journal of Management, 32*, 786–830.

Headlee, C. (2014). You've served your country, now get to class. Retrieved from http://www.npr.org/templates/transcript/transcript.php?storyId=304141184

ILO. (2010). *Socio-economic reintegration of ex-combatants.* Geneva: International Labour Organization. ISBN 9789221231837 (print version). Retrieved from http://www.ilo.org/wcmsp5/groups/public/---ed_emp/documents/instructionalmaterial/wcms_141276.pdf

ILO. (2011). *Equality at work: The continuing challenge.* International Labour Conference, 100th Session 2011, Report I(B). Geneva: International Labour Organization. ISBN 978-92-2-123091-5 (print version). Retrieved April 21, 2015, from http://www.ilo.org/wcmsp5/groups/public/---ed_norm/---relconf/documents/meetingdocument/wcms_154779.pdf

ILO. (2013, May 17). *ILO director-general's statement on international day against homophobia and transphobia.* Geneva: International Labour Organization. Retrieved from http://www.scoop.co.nz/stories/WO1305/S00430/international-day-against-homophobia-and-transphobia.htm

ILO. (2014a). *Rules of the game: A brief introduction to international labour standards* (3rd rev. ed.). Geneva: International Labour Office. ISBN 978-92-2-129063-6 (print version). Retrieved from http://www.ilo.org/global/standards/information-resources-and-publications/publications/WCMS_318141/lang-en/index.htm

ILO. (2014b). *Achieving equal employment opportunity for people with disabilities through legislation: Guidelines.* Geneva: International Labour Organization. ISBN 978-92-2-129121-3 (print version). Retrieved from http://www.oit.org/global/topics/skills-knowl edge-and-employability/disability-and-work/WCMS_322685/lang-en/index.htm

ILO. (2014c, May 17). *Message by Guy Ryder for international day against homophobia and transphobia.* Geneva: International Labour Organization. Retrieved from http://www.ilo.org/global/about-the-ilo/who-we-are/ilo-director-general/statements-and-speeches/WCMS_243297/lang-en/index.htm

ILO. (2015). *Global wage report 2014/2015: Wages and income inequality.* Geneva: International Labour Organization. ISBN 978-92-2-128664-6 (print version). Retrieved from http://www.ilo.org/wcmsp5/groups/public/---dgreports/---dcomm/---publ/doc uments/publication/wcms_324678.pdf

International Chamber of Shipping. (2015). Shipping and world trade. Retrieved from http://www.ics-shipping.org/shipping-facts/shipping-and-world-trade

Irish Statute Book (ISB). (2016). Employment Equality Act, 1998. Government of Ireland. Retrieved from http://www.irishstatutebook.ie/eli/1998/act/21/enacted/en/print#sec2

Kaipper Ceratti, M. (2014, March 4). El Alto Precio De Ser Gay En Latinoamérica. *El Pais Internacional.* Retrieved from http://internacional.elpais.com/internacio-nal/2014/03/07/actualidad/1394211626_115208.html

Kalev, A., Dobbin, F., & Kelly, E. (2006). Best practices or best guesses? Assessing the efficacy of corporate affirmative action and diversity policies. *American Sociological Review, 71,* 589–617.

Klawitter, M. (2015). Meta-analysis of the effects of sexual orientation on earnings. *Industrial Relations: A Journal of Economy & Society, 54*(1), 4–32.

Kuddo, A. (2009). *Labor laws in Eastern European and Central Asian countries: Minimum norms and practices.* SP Discussion paper 0920. Washington, DC: World Bank. Print.

Latinamerica Press. (2016, June 22). "Criadazgo" is a form of modern slavery. Retrieved from http://www.lapress.org/articles.asp?art=7321

Liptak, A. (2015, June 26). Supreme Court Ruling Makes Same-Sex Marriage a Right Nationwide. *New York Times.* Retrieved from https://www.nytimes.com/2015/06/27/us/supreme-court-same-sex-marriage.html

Mason, M., Mendoza, M., & Htusan, E. (2015, March 25). Seafood from slaves: Forced-labor fish harvest enters U.S. supply chain. *Associated Press.* Retrieved from http://www.mlive.com/news/index.ssf/2015/03/fish_from_slavery_trawling_ent.html

Military.com. (2016a). An overview of the GI Bill. Retrieved from http://www.military.com/education/gi-bill/learn-to-use-your-gi-bill.html

Military.com. (2016b). Transition assistance program overview. Retrieved from http://www.military.com/military-transition/transition-assistance-program-overview.html

Myers, J. (2015, November 13). Where is gay marriage legal? World Economic Forum. Retrieved from https://www.weforum.org/agenda/2015/11/where-is-gay-marriage-legal/

National Framework Proposal on the Reintegration of Ex-combatants into Civilian life in Sri Lanka. (2009, July 2). Ministry of Disaster Management and Human Rights. Retrieved from http://www.ilo.org/wcmsp5/groups/public/@ed_emp/@emp_ent/@ifp_crisis/documents/publication/wcms_116478.pdf

Neckerman, K. M., & Torche, F. (2007). Inequality: Causes and consequences. *Annual Review of Sociology, 33,* 335–357.

Organization for Economic Co-Operation and Development (OECD). (2014). PF2.2: Use of childbirth-related leave by mothers and fathers. OECD Family Database. OECD Social Policy Division—Directorate of Employment, Labour and Social Affairs.

Retrieved from http://www.oecd.org/els/soc/PF2_2_Use_of_leave_benefits_by_moth ers_and_fathers_Aug2014.pdf

Organisation for Economic Co-Operation and Development (OECD). (2016). Average annual hours actually worked. Retrieved from http://www.oecd-ilibrary.org/employment/data/ hours-worked/average-annual-hours-actually-worked_data-00303-en

Pager, D., & Quillian, L. (2005). Walking the talk? What employers say and what they do. *American Sociological Review, 70*, 355–380.

Pager, D., Western, B., & Bonikowski, B. (2009). Discrimination in a low-wage labor market: A field experiment. *American Sociological Review, 74*, 777–799.

Pew Research Center. (2014, April 15). Global attitudes and trends. Global views on morality. Pew Research Center. Washington, DC. Retrieved from http://www.pewglobal. org/2014/04/15/global-morality/

Richman, J., & Freemark, S. (2011, November). The bonus army: How a protest led to the GI Bill. Retrieved from http://www.npr.org/2011/11/11/142224795/ the-bonus-army-how-a-protest-led-to-the-gi-bill

Samans, R., Blanke, J., Corrigan, G., & Drzeniek, M. (2015). *The inclusive growth and development report 2015*. Geneva: World Economic Forum.

Sanchez, R. (2016, April 8). Why the onslaught of religious freedom laws? Retrieved from http://edition.cnn.com/2016/04/06/us/religious-freedom-laws-why-now/index.html

Schuppe, J., & McCausland, P. (2016, December 21). HB2 Stays: North Carolina Lawmakers Decline to Repeal Controversial Anti-LGBTQ 'Bathroom' Bill. NBC News. Retrieved from http://www.nbcnews.com/news/us-news/hb2-stays-north-carolina-lawmakers-decline- repeal-controversial-anti-lgbtq-n698696

Society for Human Resource Management. (2016). Vietnam-Era Veterans Readjustment Assistance Act of 1974. Retrieved from https://www.shrm.org/ResourcesAndTools/ legal-and-compliance/employment-law/Pages/Vietnam-EraVeteransReadjustmentAc tof1974.aspx

Thomson, S. (2015, August 7). *Which countries offer the most paternity leave?* Geneva: World Economic Forum.

Tomaskovic-Devey, D., Thomas, M., & Johnson, K. (2005). Race and the accumulation of human capital across the career: A theoretical model and fixed-effects application. *American Journal of Sociology, 111*, 58–89.

Tummala, K. K. (1999). Policy of preference: Lessons from India, the United States and South Africa. *Public Administration Review, 59*(6), 495–508.

Understanding Children's Work (UCW) Project. (2011). *Understanding the Brazilian success in reducing child labour: Empirical evidence and policy lessons*. Rome: ILO office for Italy and San Marino. Retrieved from http://www.ucw-project.org/attachment/Brazil_suc cess_reducing_child_labour20120924_155519.pdf

United Nations. (1948). Universal declaration of human rights. Retrieved from http://www. un.org/en/universal-declaration-human-rights/index.html

United Nations. (2007). *World economic and social survey 2007: Development in an ageing world* (p. 62). New York: Department of Economic and Social Affairs. Retrieved from http://www.un-ngls.org/spip.php?page=article_s&id_article=296

United Nations. (2008). *The United Nations system-wide paper on employment creation, income-generation, and reintegration in post-conflict situations*. New York. Retrieved from http://www.ilo.org/wcmsp5/groups/public/@ed_emp/@emp_ent/@ifp_crisis/docu ments/publication/wcms_117576.pdf

Urbina, I. (2015, July 27). 'Sea Slaves': The human misery that feeds pets and livestock. *The New York Times*. Retrieved from https://www.nytimes.com/2015/07/27/world/ outlaw-ocean-thailand-fishing-sea-slaves-pets.html

U.S. Department of Labor. (2015). Vietnam Era Veterans' Readjustment Assistance Act. Retrieved from http://www.dol.gov/ofccp/regs/compliance/vevraa.htm

U.S. Department of Veterans Affairs. (2013). History and timeline. Retrieved from http://www.benefits.va.gov/gibill/history.asp

U.S. National Archives. (2015a). The Civil Rights Act of 1964 and the Equal Employment Opportunity Commission. Retrieved from http://www.archives.gov/education/lessons/civil-rights-act

U.S. National Archives. (2015b). Equal Employment Opportunity (EEO) laws. Retrieved from http://www.archives.gov/eeo/laws/

Vietnam Era Veteran's Readjustment Assistance Act New Rules. (2015, October 29). National Veterans Foundation. Retrieved from http://nvf.org/vietnam-era-veterans-readjustment-assistance-act-new-rules/

Wiessner, D., Garamfalvi, A., & Gregorio, D. (2016, July 8). Major U.S. companies ask judge to block N.C. transgender bathroom law. *Reuters*. Retrieved from http://www.nytimes.com/reuters/2016/07/08/us/08reuters-usa-companies-transgender.html?_r=1

World Bank. (2013). *Inclusion matters: The foundation for shared prosperity*. Washington, DC: World Bank.

World Bank. (2015). Overview. Retrieved from http://www.worldbank.org/en/topic/disability/overview

World Economic Forum. (2015). The global gender gap report: 2015. Retrieved from http://reports.weforum.org/global-gender-gap-report-2015/

Zacharias, A., & Vakulabharanam, V. (2011). Caste stratification and wealth inequality in India. *World Development, 39*, 1820–1833.

four
Race and Ethnic Origin

Opening Case

How Much Do Different Races of People Differ Genetically? The History of Genetics

In their 1994 manuscript related to population and genetics, Cavalli-Sforza and colleagues described ancestral analysis and genetics. They assessed the genetic structure of the present population and traced ancestral roots for various groups. For example, the genetic group in the United States includes lineage tracing to Hispanic, European, American Indian, and African roots (Cavalli-Sforza, Menozzi, & Piazza, 1994). More recently, in a study conducted by Celera Genomics in the year 2000, it was discovered that human DNA is not highly different across populations. The Celera Genomics study concluded, "We all evolved in the last 100,000 years from the same small number of tribes that migrated out of Africa and colonized the world" (Angier, 2000). Other scientists have stated that people from any part of the globe have about the same percentage of genetic variability (90%) which humanity offers. Also, genes accounting for people's looks account for only 0.01% of human DNA (Angier, 2000).

Beginning in the 1960s scientists started thinking about race as a social construct instead of a biological concept. According to Cavalli-Sforza, "From a scientific point of view, the concept of race has failed to obtain any consensus; none is likely, given the gradual variation in existence. It may be objected that the racial stereotypes have a consistency that allows even the layman to classify individuals. However, the major stereotypes, all based on skin color, hair color and form as well as facial traits, reflect superficial differences that are not confirmed by deeper analysis with more reliable genetic traits and whose origin dates from recent evolution mostly under the effect of climate and perhaps sexual selection" (Cavalli-Sforza et al., 1994).

Discussion Questions:

1. What do you think about the statement that human DNA is not highly different across people/races?
2. If people of all races are almost genetically identical and race is really a socially constructed concept rather than a genetic one, why do you suppose humans find it so important to create barriers between different groups of people and different geographic boundaries, etc.?
3. Scientists are consistently explaining that the planet Earth is one tiny speck in the vast expanse of the Cosmos. If extraterrestrial beings (i.e., aliens) from another planet were to visit us next week, how do you think the ways in which we categorize all sentient beings (racial groups and nationalities from the planet Earth and aliens from outer space) would change? Who would be in the in-group, and who would be in the out-group?

Learning Objectives
After reading this chapter, you should be able to:

- Define race and ethnicity
- Understand some of the history of various racial/ethnic groups in the United States including African-Americans, Hispanics/Latinos, American Indians, Asian-Americans, and White Americans
- Understand discrimination in the United States and how it affects various groups today
- Know about the outcomes of racial discrimination
- Be aware of research on coping with discrimination
- Be aware of recommendations to prevent racial discrimination and enhance racial inclusion in the workplace

In the opening case of this chapter we see that human beings are nearly genetically identical irrespective of their race. The differences in human DNA that make up our variation in skin tone and bodily features are a fraction of a percent of the human DNA. How does such a small difference have such a large social implication for racial group relations in our society? In this chapter, we explore racial/ethnic group differences including discrimination against various groups and the outcomes of discrimination. The chapter begins by investigating groups in the United States and also presents examples of racial and ethnic differences in various parts of the world.

What Are Race and Ethnicity?

Throughout this chapter, the term **race** is used to encompass the social category (as opposed to genetic or biological categories) of racial/ethnic background (Gilroy, 1998; U.S. Census Bureau, 2015a). This is consistent with race as defined by the U.S. government, which refers to social categories that encompass consideration of national origin and sociocultural groups (https://www.census.gov/glossary/#term_Race). The U.S. Census Bureau (2015a) collects racial data in accordance with guidelines from the U.S. Office of Management and Budget (OMB), and these data are based on self-identification. The OMB requires that race be collected for the following groups: White, Black or African-American, American Indian or Alaska Native, Asian, and Native Hawaiian or Other Pacific Islander. White is defined as persons with origins in Europe, the Middle East, or North Africa. Black or African-American is defined as persons with origins in any of the Black racial groups from Africa. American Indian or Alaska Native includes the original peoples of North and South America who maintain tribal affiliation. Asian refers to people with origins in the Far East, Southeast Asia, or the Indian subcontinent. Native Hawaiian or Other Pacific Islander refers to persons with origins in the original peoples of Hawaii, Guam, Samoa, or other Pacific islands (https://www.census.gov/topics/population/race/about.html). The racial categories included in the U.S. Census typically reflect a social definition of race recognized in the United States and are not an attempt to define race biologically, anthropologically, or genetically (U.S. Census Bureau, 2015a). This is in agreement with Gilroy (1998), who argues that race is socially constructed.

    Ethnicity refers to a social group that shares characteristics such as language, religion, and culture. According to the U.S. Census Bureau, there are a minimum of two ethnicity categories: Hispanic or Latino, and not Hispanic or Latino. Hispanics and Latinos may be of any race (https://www.census.gov/glossary/#term_Ethnicity). Consistent with the categories used by the U.S. government to measure and report demographic information on the population and employment statistics for the major racial/ethnic groups in the United States, this chapter discusses White, African-American, Hispanic, Asian, and American Indian racial/ethnic groups. Hispanics can be of any racial origin, and the terms "Hispanic" and "Latino" represent an ethnicity according to the U.S. government.

Description/Brief History of Various Racial/Ethnic Groups in the United States

The United States has a history of being a land of opportunity, but it also has a history of discrimination against many different groups. Qualitative research based on the experiences of minorities also provides evidence describing discrimination against several groups including (a) African-Americans who suffered slavery in U.S. history and now sometimes feel there is a "concrete ceiling" in place which prevents them from advancing in organizations (Feagin & Sikes, 1994), (b) Hispanic-Americans who lost their property to the United States through border and land disputes (Gonzalez, 2000), (c) Asian-Americans who faced stereotypes and mockery of their native languages (Chou & Feagin, 2010) and some of whom served as low-wage laborers to build the U.S. railroads (Boswell, 1986) or were held in internment camps during World War II (Spicer, 1969), (d) American Indians, many of whom died during the colonization of the United States or were moved onto reservation lands (Jahoda, 1975), and also (e) White European immigrants.

Between 2002 and 2012, the U.S. Equal Employment Opportunity Commission (EEOC) data report some increases in the number of minorities in managerial positions. In 2002, 30% of the U.S. workforce belonged to a demographic minority group, and 15% of minorities were in managerial roles. As of 2012, 35% of U.S. employees were from a minority group, and 21% of them were in managerial roles (EEOC, 2014). The EEOC data also show that in 2012, almost 12% of senior-level and executive managerial jobs were held by minorities. While minorities are still underrepresented in managerial jobs given their proportion in the workforce, they are gradually entering more managerial positions over time.

Nevertheless, racial discrimination claims are the most common type of claims to the U.S. Equal Employment Opportunity Commission every year. In 2016, the

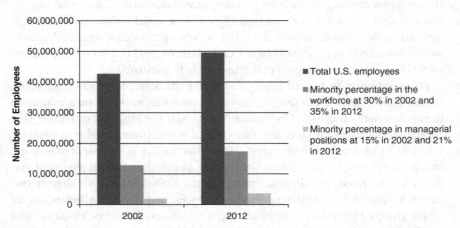

FIGURE 4.1. Number of Minority Employees and Minority Managers Relative to Total U.S. Workforce

Source: Equal Employment Opportunity Commission (2014).

U.S. Equal Employment Opportunity Commission received 91,503 charges of employment discrimination. Of these, race discrimination complaints were the most common (35.3%), followed by sex discrimination complaints (29.4%; EEOC, 2017). This is telling because there are many more women in the United States irrespective of race than there are racial minorities irrespective of sex.

Research has shown that race is one of the strongest, or perhaps the strongest, demographic factor of workplace performance, mistreatment, and other behavior. A study by Harrison, Price, Gavin, and Florey (2002) found that racial diversity was a stronger predictor of participants' perceived surface-level diversity than was sex diversity. Harrison et al. (2002) further reported that racial diversity had stronger negative effects on a team's social integration and collaboration than did sex diversity. Another study also showed that racial diversity had stronger negative effects on individual and team performance compared to sex diversity (Jehn & Bezrukova, 2004). Overall, the research indicates that race seems to have some of the strongest demographic effects on work groups. Racial background influences the way people interact with one another.

America, the Melting Pot

The history of racial tensions in the United States begins very early in this country's history and lingers still today. The Founding Fathers who established the United States and wrote the U.S. Constitution, the highest law of the land, did many things right. For example, the founders established the notion that all men are created equal and that everyone should have the right to life, liberty, and the pursuit of happiness. These are egalitarian ideals. However, one thing that they did wrong, which still affects us today, is that they oppressed some groups for the benefit of other groups. Although the Founding Fathers left Europe and moved to the United States in search of freedom and less oppression, they then made a different set of rules, norms, and decisions that oppressed or discriminated against different groups of people, including African-Americans, American Indians, Hispanic-Americans, Asian-Americans, and other Whites who immigrated later.

With respect to average household income, U.S. Census data from 2013 show that the average White Non-Hispanic household made a median income of $58,270, the average Black household median income was $34,598, the average Asian household median income was $67,065, and the average Hispanic household income was $40,963 (DeNavas-Walt & Proctor, 2014). In 2013, the median household income of American Indian and Alaska Native households was $36,252 (Profile America Facts for Features, 2014). In 2013, 14.5% of all Americans lived in poverty. Broken down by race, the poverty level was 9.6% for White (non-Hispanic) Americans, 27.2% for Blacks, 10.5% for Asians, and 23.5% for Hispanics (who can be of any race; DeNavas-Walt & Proctor, 2014). For American Indians and Alaska Natives, 29.2% lived in poverty in 2013 (Profile America Facts for Features, 2014). With respect to unemployment rates, the Bureau of Labor Statistics (BLS) reports

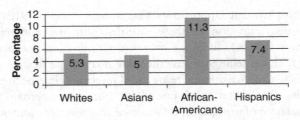

FIGURE 4.2. 2014 Overall Unemployment in the United States by Race

Source: Bureau of Labor Statistics (2015a, 2015b).

that overall unemployment in the United States for 2014 was 6.2%. For Whites, that number was 5.3%; for Asians, it was 5%; and for African-Americans, it was 11.3% (BLS, 2015a). For Hispanics/Latinos, the unemployment rate was 7.4% in 2014 (BLS, 2015b)

Finally, with respect to incarceration, meaning that individuals are being held in state or federal prison, the U.S. Department of Justice figures for 2010 are as follows. On average, data show that minorities are incarcerated (this includes both jail and prison) at a disproportionally high rate relative to their proportion of the population. For males, for every 100,000 people in the United States, 678 White (non-Hispanic), 1,775 Hispanic/Latino, and 4,347 Blacks are incarcerated. For females, for every 100,000 people in the United States, 91 White (non-Hispanic), 133 Hispanic/Latino, and 260 Blacks are incarcerated (Glaze, 2011).

African-Americans/Blacks

African-Americans (i.e., Blacks) currently make up 13% of the U.S. population (U.S. Census Bureau, 2014). As of the 2010 Census, 84.2% of Blacks were high school graduates and 19.8% were college graduates (U.S. Census Bureau, 2012). Africans were first sold as slaves in the United States around the year 1619 (Jordan, 1962). The U.S. Constitution originally stated that enslaved Blacks were worth three-fifths of a White person. This was the law of the land until President Lincoln emancipated slaves with the Emancipation Proclamation of 1863 and the **13th Amendment to the U.S. Constitution** in 1864 (U.S. National Archives, 2015). During the time of slavery, a number of states had laws that prohibited people from teaching slaves reading, writing, and arithmetic, although some people still did so (Pollock, 2001).

In his book *The White Man's Burden: Historical Origins of Racism in the United States*, Winthrop Jordan describes the historical reasons why racial tensions divided the northern and southern United States from the time of colonization to the U.S. Civil War. Because the southern states grew higher concentrations of crops such as tobacco and cotton which required labor to work the land, demand for slave labor was higher in the South than in the North (Jordan, 1974). Leading up to the Civil War, a number of southern slave states seceded from the union and formed the Confederate States of America. By the end of 1865, the North had won the war, thereby reconstituting the United States, and the 13th Amendment was passed to abolish slavery. However, the oppression of Blacks continued. By 1866 the Ku Klux Klan was formed in the South to espouse a message of White supremacy. Jim Crow laws were put in place in the southern United States (as well as many other parts of the country) allowing for legalized segregation in schools, transportation, and public places. Jim Crow laws were supposed to keep the different groups separate but equal. However, there is evidence that the groups were separate and unequal. Examples of segregated facilities include "colored" water fountains and other lower quality facilities for Blacks. It was not until the U.S. Supreme Court decision in **Brown v. the Board of Education of Topeka** that the "separate but equal" educational system was banned and the different groups were to be educated in the same facilities.[1] It is estimated that "between the period from the emancipation to the Great Depression, about 3,000 Blacks were lynched in the American South" (Beck & Tolnay, 1990, p. 526).

Because of the Civil Rights Movement of the 1960s, the Civil Rights Act of 1964, and societal changes, the lives of African-Americans have improved. The examples of this group's hard-fought battles for equal rights are evident in the numerous African-Americans in leadership positions across the United States and across all social levels. Their success is epitomized by Barack Obama, who is half Kenyan and half White and is also the fifth African-American to serve in the U.S. senate and a two-term President of the United States. Another prominent example is Thurgood Marshall, a lawyer who became the first Black U.S. Supreme Court Justice in 1967. However, the long-term effects of systematic discrimination linger today. Blacks are not equal to the majority group (i.e., Whites) with respect to education and income attainment, and they are incarcerated at a higher rate than other racial/ethnic groups.

In a qualitative interview quoted in Feagin and Sikes (1994, pp. 295–296), one man explained why/how discriminatory encounters in society can take a daily toll on African-Americans:

> If you can think of the mind as having one hundred ergs of energy, and the average man uses fifty percent of his energy dealing with the everyday problems of the world . . . then he has fifty percent more to do creative kinds of things that he wants to do. Now that's a White person. Now a Black person also has one hundred ergs; he uses fifty percent the same way a White man does, dealing with what the White man has [to deal with], so he has fifty percent left. But he uses twenty-five percent fighting being Black, [with] all the problems of being Black and what it means.

There are many trailblazers in the African-American community who paved the way for others. An important leader of the Civil Rights Movement in America is Dr. Martin Luther King Jr. He was a powerful orator who delivered passionate speeches and led peaceful protests that swayed public opinion and advanced civil rights. Another prominent activist in the civil rights movement was Rosa Parks. In 1955, Rosa Parks refused to give up her seat to a White man on a bus in Montgomery, Alabama. This precipitated the Montgomery Bus Boycott, where African-Americans refused to ride city buses from December 5, 1955, until December 20, 1956, to protest the segregated seating that required Blacks to sit in the back of the bus (History.com, 2016a). On August 28, 1963, a political rally known as the March on Washington took place. The culmination of this march was Dr. Martin Luther King Jr.'s "I Have a Dream" speech calling for racial equality. The march was a complete success, and over "200,000 Black and White Americans shared a joyous day of speeches, songs, and prayers led by a celebrated array of clergymen, civil rights leaders, politicians, and entertainers" (History.com, 2016b). By July of 1964, President Lyndon B. Johnson signed the Civil Rights Act of 1964 which includes Title VII, one the most important antidiscrimination employment laws to date.

Whites

Whites are the majority group in the United States today both because they are the most populous (63% of the population; U.S. Census Bureau, 2014) and because Whites hold the majority of the most powerful and highest-level positions in organizations (EEOC, 2014). As of the 2010 Census, 87.6% of Whites were high school graduates, and 30.3% were college graduates.

The term **Caucasian** is often used to refer to White people in general. The definition of Caucasian refers to the inhabitants of Caucasus, a region of Southeastern Europe between the Black and Caspian Seas which is divided by the Caucasus Mountains. This includes a region roughly spanning from southern Russia (northern boundary) to Turkey (southern boundary) and the land in between those boundaries bounded by the Caspian Sea on the east and the Black Sea on the west. The term "Caucasian" is also broadly used to refer to people native to Europe, North Africa, and Southwest Asia, particularly people of European descent who have light skin pigment (Merriam-Webster, 2016). Therefore, the term "Caucasian" is often misused in the United States to represent light-skinned people of primarily European descent. This is why the term **White** has been more commonly used in the United States both by researchers and by the U.S. government in its population reports to represent light-skinned people of primarily European descent. It is important to note that this refers to Whites who are non-Hispanic. As mentioned earlier in the chapter, **Hispanic/Latino** refers to an ethnic group whose roots originate from Spanish-speaking countries, particularly those from Latin America. Hispanics/Latinos may be of any race. The U.S. Census reports Hispanic and White (non-Hispanic) categories separately for that reason.

From the 1820s to the 1920s, almost 40 million Europeans from many countries, including Germany, Italy, Greece, Poland, Ireland, England, and others, immigrated to the United States (Wray, 2006). Discrimination has been documented against many White immigrant groups, including Irish, Italians, Jews, and others (Feagin & Feagin, 1993). There was a pecking order among these White groups, with English immigrants who immigrated to the United States first at the top, then Germans,

Irish, Italians, and Poles. English immigrants who arrived first believed themselves to be superior to the later White immigrants and tried to avoid them in both work and domestic contexts (Wray, 2006). Indeed, the waves of immigration to the United States in the late nineteenth century prompted warnings by those groups already established in the United States about the "mongrelization" of the Nordic and Anglo-Saxon races in the United States as immigrants from Southeastern Europe and Central America arrived in the United States (Sacks, 2003). This is a common attitude toward newly arrived immigrants, as many ethnic groups in the United States now enjoy higher status than they once did (Lee & Fiske, 2006). As a result, there were several tensions between these various groups of immigrants related to conflicts about work, and racial segregation within residential areas was common (Wray, 2006).

The U.S. Census also differentiated between different types of Whites until about 1850. Before 1850, the category "free Whites" appeared on the Census to identify Whites who were free as opposed to indentured servants. This category was removed and simply became "Whites" after 1850 because all Whites were free at that time (Rodriguez, 2000). According to Brodkin (1998, 2004), Jewish people were initially identified as a separate race and then changed to be considered White. Irish Catholics, who also faced discrimination and exclusion in the United States initially (Ignatiev, 1995), bonded together for protection and ultimately were instrumental in the formation of labor unions (Kennedy, 1999). Brodkin (2004) explains that in the 1930 Census, there was a distinction between Whites who were more recent immigrants versus those who were earlier immigrants and considered to be native Whites. However, by the 1940 Census this distinction between Whites was no longer made (Brodkin, 2004).

Quantitative studies have shown that Whites have a higher social status in virtually every part of the world than minorities (McConahay, 1983; Sidanius & Pratto, 1999). However, as a result of affirmative action programs that attempt to rectify past and current discrimination against women and minority groups, some White men today feel like they are being penalized for past wrongs they personally did not commit (Feagin & O'Brien, 2003). In a qualitative interview (Feagin & O'Brien, 2003, p. 85), one White man describes why he feels disadvantaged.

> I feel you're at a disadvantage today if you're White and male. There are a couple of different factors working against you. It's like basically if you're White and you're born here, I believe it's a disadvantage—as opposed to coming into the country, not even being White, especially . . .

Title VII of the Civil Rights Act of 1964 is the major employment discrimination law of the land. This law protects people from discrimination on the basis of race and sex. While it is understood that the protected classes are typically minority groups due to their history of experienced discrimination, the wording of the law is such that the protected group is "race" and "sex." This means that people of all races and all sexes are protected and can file grievances under the law. Therefore, if a White male perceives that he has been discriminated against, he could file what is called a reverse discrimination complaint seeking protection under Title VII. According to Schaefer (2002) and a *New York Times* article published in 1995 (Associated Press, 1995), of the more than 3,000 discrimination lawsuit opinions produced in federal courts from 1990 to 1994, fewer than 100 of these dealt with the issue of reverse discrimination. Further, reverse discrimination was only established in six of these cases.

According to Catalyst (2015), in the Standard & Poor's 500 (an index of the largest firms in the United States), there are currently 23 female CEOs. In the Fortune 500 (another index of the largest firms in the United States), there are 5 Black CEOs (Black Profiles, 2015). Therefore, the large majority of top executives appear to be White and also male.

Finally, it is important to note that many Whites have been and still are advocates of minority rights. Feagin and Sikes (1994) refer to numerous examples of Whites helping people of color. During times of slavery and also during the civil rights movement of the 1960s, a number of White people stood alongside Blacks and other people of color to show their support for equal rights of all groups. A number of these White were injured and some were even killed trying to support rights for Blacks and other minority groups during the Civil Rights Movement. The role of these White progressive individuals who serve as champions for civil rights has been and continues to be critical to civil rights for minorities. Indeed, because Whites and men are the majority groups and continue to hold much power and wealth in U.S. society, some of the most convincing advocates for civil rights are White males.

Hispanics/Latinos

Hispanics/Latinos currently make up 17% of the U.S. population (U.S. Census Bureau, 2014). According to the Pew Research Center, as of 2011 the Hispanic population in the United States came from many different countries/territories including: Mexico (64.6%), Puerto Rico (9.5%), El Salvador (3.8%), Cuba (3.6%), Dominican Republic (2.9%), Guatemala (2.3%), Columbia (1.9%), Spain (1.4%), Honduras (1.4%), Ecuador (1.2%), Peru (1.1%), Nicaragua (0.8%), Venezuela (0.5%), and Argentina (0.5%) (Lopez, Gonzales-Barrera, & Cuddington, 2013).

As of the 2010 Census, 62.9% of Hispanics were high school graduates, and 13.9% were college graduates (U.S. Census, 2012). Hispanics are the fastest growing and largest minority group in the United States and are expected to be over 24% of the U.S. population by 2050 (Blancero & Del Campo, 2012; Cisneros, 2009). In 1999, Sidanius and Pratto published the results of a large-scale study which indicates that this is the perceived order of race status in the United States: Whites, Asians, Blacks, and Latinos (p. 78).

People from Mexico represent the most populous group of Latinos in the United States. The ancestors of Mexican-Americans have a long history of residing in the southwestern U.S. as well as in Mexico before the arrival of Europeans from Spain

(Saenz, 1999). Spaniards arrived in the area in 1519 and established colonies along with a colonization process in the areas where indigenous peoples lived. Marriages between Spanish men and indigenous women led to many mestizo children (of heritage from both White Europeans and Indigenous peoples of the Americas) being born (Saenz, 1999). The area in the southern part of the United States where many Mexican-Americans live today eventually won its freedom from Spain in 1821. However, disputes between the United States and Mexico about the boundaries of Texas continued. The Mexican-American War determined that Texas would belong to the United States, and Mexicans residing in Texas at the time had the option of remaining on their land in the United States Many chose to do so, thereby becoming Mexican-American citizens of the United States (Saenz, 1999).

Puerto Ricans are the next most populous group of Latin Americans in the United States. During the Spanish-American War, Puerto Rico was seized by the U.S. military in 1898 (Aranda, 2008). The Jones Act of 1917 established that Puerto Ricans would have U.S. citizenship. Therefore, children born in Puerto Rico have dual citizenship (Aranda, 2008). Although Puerto Rico is a U.S. territory, it is not one of the 50 states in the United States.

One of the most comprehensive accounts of Hispanics in the United States was written by Gonzalez (2000), who is Puerto Rican. He reveals several forces which have led Latin Americans to be "invisible." First, the fact that Latinos mainly speak Spanish as their first language and English as their second language puts them at a disadvantage when they enter the United States, where day-to-day transactions and business are conducted in English. Second, because of their vast diversity, Latin Americans differ in terms of the experiences that unite them and their social capital. Finally, there are also conflicts both between Latin American groups and within Latin American groups which cause tension and make it more difficult for the groups to unite with the common purpose of advancing the status of all Latin Americans in the United States. In the following, I elaborate on each of these three points.

The first and most obvious challenge facing Latin Americans in the United States is the language barrier. Some Spanish-speaking children report getting in trouble in school when they are caught speaking Spanish (Gonzalez, 2000). Particularly along the U.S.-Mexico border, racial tensions still linger. Gonzalez gives detailed examples of how Mexican-American land was appropriated by English-speaking settlers who created new laws and rules in English and utilized rules and contracts written in English (which Mexican people did not understand) to take land away from Mexican-American people (p. 99). The ability to speak fluent English is clearly of crucial importance to Latin Americans, as demonstrated by the fact that speaking English is one of the primary goals of LULAC (League of United Latin American Citizens) (Gonzalez, 2000). However, even when Latin Americans have a good command of the English language, Latinos (particularly first-generation American immigrants) often speak with a Spanish accent. This accent may then have negative repercussions for Latin Americans because of the stigma that is often placed on non-native speakers of English (Lippi-Green, 1997).

For example, although being bilingual is mostly considered to be an asset, Latinos have sometimes faced discrimination for speaking Spanish. Gonzalez presents an example of a Spanish-speaker facing scrutiny when a district judge in Texas ordered a Mexican-American mother to stop speaking Spanish to her five-year-old daughter *at home* because she was "abusing that child and relegating her to the position of a housemaid." The judge added that it was not in the child's "best interest to be ignorant" (Gonzalez, 2000, p. 206). It is important to note here that this issue is not unique to the Latino community. Immigrants of all races (e.g., Asians, Hispanics, Africans, and others including Whites) who speak English with an accent are often portrayed in stereotypical ways. In an analysis of what we teach children about spoken accents, Lippi-Greene reports that in Disney cartoons, the characters who are non-native English speakers and speak with an accent are twice as likely to be evil than are native English speakers (Lippi-Green, 1997).

Second, because of the tremendous diversity among the Latin American groups, these different groups may share the Spanish-language, and often the Catholic religion, but differ in terms of their experiences and other characteristics. Because Latin Americans are such a diverse group and come from many countries such as Mexico, Puerto Rico, Cuba, Honduras, Guatemala, and the Dominican Republic, just to name a few, there are a number of differences among these groups with respect to Spanish dialect, ethnic foods, holidays, and traditions. There are also differences in the way these groups have experienced discriminatory treatment in the United States.

Gonzalez (2000) describes derogatory nicknames ascribed to the various Latin American groups, which are consistent with the stereotypes for that particular group. For example, Gonzalez writes about Puerto Ricans being called derogatory names (Gonzalez, 2000, p. 88). The Cuban stereotype is that of the people who arrived in the United States through the Mariel boat wave in 1980 (Gonzalez, 2000, p. 109) or subsequently on rafts. Along the Mexico/Texas border, people also use derogatory terms for individuals whom they presume have illegally crossed the Rio Grande in order to enter Texas. Most Latin American groups seem to experience stereotypes which, in turn, create a within-group bond that is not shared with other Latino groups.

Third, Gonzalez (2000) demonstrates that there is a certain amount of conflict both between and within the Latin American communities. Gonzalez talks about tensions between Puerto Ricans and Dominicans resulting from illegal Dominican immigration into Puerto Rico (p. 126). Gonzalez also alludes to the fact that some Latin Americans view Cuban-Americans as "special refugees" (p. 108) who had easier entry into the United States from the Florida coast than other immigrants from countries such as Haiti (p. 108). This intergroup tension between Latin Americans may be one of the reasons why Gonzalez describes how Cuban-Americans developed "intensely loyal internal markets among their own" and "hired workers and purchased goods from within their own community" (p. 111).

In addition to some conflict between Latin Americans from different countries, there is also conflict *within* these individual Latin American groups. This tension is often racially driven. Because Latin America was colonized by Spain and was also a region where the slave trade from Africa flourished, there are racial tensions within each of these countries. For example, Gonzalez (2000) mentions that wealthy lighter skinned Puerto Ricans used to have Black slaves and/or servants (p. 82). The same was true in Cuba many decades ago. Gonzalez also discusses a revolt by Black sugar workers on the island of Cuba in 1912 (p. 24) who were seeking fair wages from their employers. Finally, we can see examples of these racial tensions in the press. A few years ago, a Black caricature named Memin Pinguin appeared on Mexican postage stamps. Memin is a little Black boy with exaggerated African features who is naughty and gets into trouble (Krauze, 2005). This example from Mexico indicates that there is racial tension within the Mexican community as well.

A prominent Mexican-American leader in the U.S. civil rights movement of the 1960s is Cesar Chavez. He was born in Yuma, Arizona, and grew up in very poor conditions in California, where he and his family worked as migrant workers. During the 1960s, Cesar Chavez led peaceful demonstrations including worker strikes and hunger strikes. He worked to organize farm workers, register them to vote, and fight for farm worker rights including pay and working conditions. In 1962, Cesar Chavez founded the National Farm Workers Association, and together with Dolores Huerta, a Latina feminist and civil rights activist, this organization became the United Farm Workers. The United Farm Workers is a union which negotiates and advocates for the rights of farm workers (United Farm Workers, 2016).

Global View: Mexico

The Mexican government currently does not include questions about African ethnic origin in its national census. According to some, "the black population has been invisible" (Archibold, 2014). The census has typically asked only whether an indigenous language is spoken at home, and this has been used to identify the native Indian population, which is approximately 6% of the population (Archibold, 2014). African Mexicans are stating that Mexico has ignored its African roots, and they are requesting a census count in order to be recognized by the government.

According to the U.S. Central Intelligence Agency (2015), the majority of the population in Mexico is 62% mestizo (Amerindian-Spanish), with 21% predominantly Amerindian, 7% Amerindian, and 10% other (mostly European). There are several accounts of how discrimination, whether blatant or subtle, is present in Mexican society. For example, Mexico's largest bakery, Bimbo, changed the name of one of its most popular snack cakes, the "Negrito," or little black one, as it began the doing business internationally. They now call the snack cake "Nito" and the cartoon of the little boy on the wrapping of the snack has changed over the years. He still has an Afro hairstyle, but his skin has become lighter over the years and his facial features have become more European (Mexican, 2013).

An advertisement in 2013 for Aeromexico, Mexico's largest airline, sought models for an advertisement and requested "nobody dark skinned." The airline later apologized (Archibold, 2014).

American Indians and Alaska Natives

The native people of the United States are American Indians. This group is also sometimes referred to as Native Americans. However, the term "Native American" came into use to describe groups served by the U.S. government's Bureau of Indian Affairs, and many Indian groups do not like this name. The preferred term is "American Indian." American Indians are currently 1.2% of the U.S. population (U.S. Census Bureau, 2014). According to the 2000 U.S. Census special report on American Indians and Alaska Natives, they comprised 1.53% of the U.S. population as of the 2000 Census with 1.02% American Indian with one tribal grouping (Apache, Cherokee, Chippewa, Choctaw, Creek, Iroquois, Lumbee, Navajo, Pueblo, or Sioux), 0.04% Alaska Native with one tribal grouping (Alaska Athabascan, Aleut, Eskimo, or Tlingit-Haida), and about 0.45% one or more other specified tribal groupings. For American Indians and Alaska Natives educational attainment is as follows: 27.4% have less than a high school diploma, 29% are high school graduates, 31.5% have some college or an associate degree, and 12.1% have a college degree (Ogunwole, 2006). The overall labor force participation for men ages 16 and older was 66.7%, and for women it was 57.6% (Ogunwole, 2006). Average annual income for American Indian males was $28,890, and for females it was $22,762, and the overall poverty rate for American Indians was 25.8% whereas the overall poverty rate for the U.S. population was 12.4% (Ogunwole, 2006). Finally, the majority of American Indians (64.1%) live outside of Indian reservations (Ogunwole, 2006).

American Indians were already present in the United States when Christopher Columbus arrived in America in 1492. This group lost many of its people during the colonization of the United States. Disputes over land ensued as European settlers immigrated to the United States and began moving westward across the country. A law called the **Indian Removal Act of 1830** and political support from President Andrew Jackson resulted in an enforced relocation process known as the Trail of Tears. During this process, several American Indian tribes including the Cherokee, Muskogee, Seminole, Chickasaw, and Choctaw tribes were relocated by force from their homelands in the southeastern United States to an area west of the Mississippi River designated Indian Territory (Public Broadcasting Service [PBS], 2015).

The Cherokee, who lived in the southeastern United States, had lands confiscated and were moved by force. In the winter of 1838, the Cherokee began a 1,000-mile march on foot from Tennessee to Illinois. Many of them died of exposure to the cold, disease, or were murdered. According to a Georgia soldier who participated in the removal, "I fought through the War Between the States and have seen many men shot, but the Cherokee Removal was the cruelest work I ever knew" (Remini, 2000, p. 170).

American Indians were not counted in the U.S. Census until 1860, and at the time, they were only counted if they were living in the general population (not on an Indian reservation). However, by the 1890 Census, American Indians were counted whether they were living on or off a reservation (U.S. Census Bureau, 2015b). We are not certain how many American Indians were present in the United States before the colonization and the Trail of Tears. Estimates of the number of American Indians in the United States range from 1 to 8 million (Thornton, 2004). By the 1890 census, the first official recorded count of American Indians was 248,253 (U.S. Census Bureau, 1894).

According to a quote in the *Denver Times* in 1879 referring to the Ute Indian tribe which once had a nomadic life style spanning an area larger than the state of Colorado, "Either they (the Utes) or we must go, and we are not going . . . The Western Empire is an inexorable fact. He who gets in the way of it will be crushed" (Colorado Historical Society, 2015). As the European colonization process continued westward throughout the United States, American Indian children were often forced to attend American schools but were forbidden from speaking their native languages (Wildenthal, 2003). Ironically, 63 years later, the language of the American Indian Navajos proved life-saving to American troops fighting the Japanese in the Pacific during World War II.

It is interesting that the Navajo helped the U.S. government win World War II using the very language they were forbidden to speak in school. In essence, the United States could not conceal its war plans and operations from the Japanese because the enemy had become highly adept at breaking the U.S. security codes. Apparently, many Japanese cryptographers had been educated in the United States and understood English perfectly. Therefore, once the Americans' code was broken, battle plans were well-known to the enemy almost immediately, which resulted in a large loss of American lives (Wilsont, 1997).

In February of 1942, a man named Philip Johnston, a civil engineer who lived in Los Angeles and had grown up on a Navajo reservation, had an idea. He recalled that the Navajo language was very unique and required a series of sounds and intonations virtually incomprehensible to anyone else. He told the military about his recollection, which resulted in the recruitment of a number of bilingual Navajos to assist in the war effort. The Navajos created a new language based on their native tongue which the Marines used in the Pacific to communicate, and this allowed them to have a secret code the Japanese were unable to break. According to Teddy Draper Sr., a Navajo code talker, "When I was going to boarding school [before the war], the U.S. government told us not to speak Navajo, but during the war, they wanted us to speak it!" (Wilsont, 1997).

In December of 1971, President Richard Nixon presented Navajo code talkers a certificate of appreciation for their courage and patriotism. "Those brave veterans had given the Marine Corps its only unbreakable means of battlefield communication, saving thousands of American lives in the process" (Wilsont, 1997).

Asians

According to the U.S. Census Bureau, Asian-Americans make up approximately 5% of the population (U.S. Census Bureau, 2014). As of the 2010 Census, 88.9% of Asians and Pacific Islanders had graduated from high school, and 52.4% had a college degree (U.S. Census, 2012). This is a diverse group of people who come from many countries including Korea, Vietnam, Japan, India, Thailand, China, the Philippines, Singapore, and Sri Lanka, among other countries in that region of the world. As of the 2010 Census in the United States, Asian-Americans were primarily Chinese (22.8%), Asian Indian (19.4%), Filipino (17.4%), Vietnamese (10.6%), Korean (9.7%), and Japanese (5.2%), among others (Jones, 2012). This is also a diverse group in terms of its religious beliefs, with 42% Christian, 26% unaffiliated, 14% Buddhist, 10% Hindu, 4% Muslim, 1% Sikh, and 2% other, including Jain (Pew Research Center, 2012).

As of 2012, Asians had the highest educational attainment level and income of any demographic group in the U.S. (Taylor et al., 2012). Asians have sometimes been referred to as the "model minority" (Lee, 1996), probably because they are highly educated and successful as a group overall.

However, Asian-Americans have also faced discrimination in the U.S. Chinese immigrants began arriving in the United States in the 1850s, and many worked in domestic service and laundry, fishing, agriculture, as miners during the California gold rush, and also on the transcontinental railway (Lin, 1999). Some researchers have discussed whether Chinese laborers may have served as replacements for African slaves after the slave trade became illegal in the 1840s (Lin, 1999). Reports state that Chinese railroad workers were paid less than their White European-American counterparts (Lin, 1999; Takaki, 2008; Zia, 2000). Once the transcontinental railroad was finished, that made it easier for East Coast workers to move westward, and the labor force competition resulted in anti-Chinese sentiment including rioting and lynching in the 1870s and 1880s (Lin, 1999; Takaki, 2008; Zia, 2000). Further, the Chinese Exclusion Act, a law signed by President Chester Arthur in 1882, prohibited all immigration of Chinese laborers. This restricted Chinese immigration to the United States for several decades.

Perhaps the most egregious example is the discrimination that Japanese-Americans faced when anti-Asian sentiment reached a climax during World War II. Japanese immigrants first arrived in the United States in 1843, and a large proportion of the ancestors of current Japanese-Americans arrived between about 1884 and 1924 (Fujiwara & Takagi, 1999). In 1942, President Roosevelt signed an executive order which required that all Americans of Japanese descent be moved into internment camps that were often located in remote, desert-like places of the U.S., including Arizona. This executive order encompassed everyone who had at least one-eighth Japanese ancestry (Schaefer, 2002) and accounted for over 90% of Japanese-Americans at the time (Fujiwara & Takagi, 1999). Over 127,000 American citizens were imprisoned in the early 1940s during World War II for being of Japanese ancestry. Many Japanese-American families sold their homes and their businesses hastily, and for a low price, because they had no assurances that they would be allowed to return or whether their homes and businesses would still be there to return to. Almost two-thirds of those in the internment camps were Nisei, meaning that they were born in the United States and had never been to Japan. Even some people who were Japanese-American veterans of World War I were required to leave their homes and go to the internment camps (U.S. History, 2016). Other reports describe that one battalion included Japanese-American soldiers who were drafted from the internment camps to serve in the war (Fujiwara & Takagi, 1999).

Toyosaburo "Fred" Korematsu challenge the legality of **Executive Order 9066**, but the U.S. Supreme Court ruled that it was a necessity during the wartime. According to the Supreme Court records, the dissenting Justice Jackson expressed the following:

> Korematsu was born on our soil, of parents born in Japan. The Constitution makes him a citizen of the United States by nativity and a citizen of California by [323 U.S. 214, 243] residence. No claim is made that he is not loyal to this country. There is no suggestion that apart from the matter involved here he is not law-abiding and well disposed. Korematsu, however, has been convicted of an act not commonly a crime. It consists merely of being present in the state whereof he is a citizen, near the place where he was born, and where all his life he has lived.
>
> (U.S. Supreme Court, 1944)

After the war, when the order was repealed, many of these Japanese-Americans attempted to return to their home communities but could not because anti-Japanese sentiment remained high. Therefore, they scattered across the country. In 1988, the U.S. government attempted to apologize for these internment camps by awarding every surviving intern $20,000 (U.S. History, 2016).

Inevitably, where there are differences and where there is diversity, discrimination will often be present. In a book published on discrimination in organizations, Dipboye and Colella (2005) state in their final chapter that whether we like it or not, to be human is to discriminate in one form or another. Therefore, the final section of this chapter turns to a discussion of racial discrimination, the outcomes of racial discrimination, and some research findings on coping as a response to racial discrimination.

Global View: Indonesia

Although racial differences usually result in discrimination for the minority group, occasionally the minority group members excel in spite of the challenges they face. A recent headline from Indonesia explains that a man who is of Chinese origin was elected governor of Jakarta, Indonesia. According to the article, Chinese were restricted from running for political office in Indonesia prior to 1999 (Cochrane, 2014). In spite of such past discrimination against his racial group, Basuki Tjahaja Purnama has been elected governor.

According to the U.S. Central Intelligence Agency (CIA), the racial/ethnic makeup of Indonesia is as follows: Javanese 40.1%, Sundanese 15.5%, Malay 3.7%, Batak 3.6%, Madurese 3%, Betawi 2.9%, Minangkabau 2.7%, Buginese 2.7%, Bantenese 2%, Banjarese 1.7%, Balinese 1.7%, Acehnese 1.4%, Dayak 1.4%, Sasak 1.3%, Chinese 1.2%, other 15% (CIA, 2015).

Purnama is also a Christian in a country that is predominantly Muslim. "I asked them why they wanted me to run, because I am of Chinese descent and a Christian," he recalled asking the local residents who approached him. "They said, 'We don't care—we know who you are. We know your character'" (Cochrane, 2014). Purnama has also had challenges. He is the first non-Muslim governor of Jakarta and is in an environment where Chinese make up 1% of the population. Islamic groups have protested against him as he runs for re-election and accused him of insulting the Qur'an while campaigning (*BBC News*, 2016).

Global View: Czech Republic

According to some civil rights groups, the Czech Republic is defying a European court ruling by placing Roma children who do not have special needs into special education classes. In November 2007, the European Court of Human Rights ruled that the Czech Republic must stop putting Roma students who do not need special education into special needs classes (Associated Press, 2014). Amnesty International and six other human rights groups state that at least one-third of students in schools for pupils with mental disabilities are Roma. They explained that the Roma students are experiencing segregation in education (Associated Press, 2014). According to Amnesty International (2017), there is a history of discrimination and segregation of Romani children in Czech schools. Between 1.4% and 2.8% of the Czech population is Roma, but 32% of the students in programs for students with mild mental disabilities come from Roma backgrounds. Further, 30% of Roma between the ages of 20 and 24 have a general or vocational secondary education while 82% of those from non-Roma backgrounds have such an education (Amnesty International, 2017).

Outcomes of Racial Discrimination

Individuals who perceive discrimination are more likely to experience negative feelings including distress (Leary, Koch, & Hechenbleikner, 2001). Stress is a main mechanism by which discrimination perceptions affect mental and physical health, work-related outcomes/behaviors, and employee work-related attitudes (e.g., Pascoe & Richman, 2009). Physical health effects can include increased stress, loss of appetite, headaches, loss of sleep, lack of energy, high blood pressure, ulcers, and chest pain (Pascoe & Richman, 2009). Psychological/mental health effects can include lack of self-confidence, mental distress, low self-esteem, anxiety, depression, lack of cooperation, insecurity, and a feeling of helplessness (Jones, Peddie, Gilrane, King, & Gray, 2016; Lee & Ahn, 2011, 2012; Schmitt, Branscombe, Postmes, & Garcia, 2014). Work-related attitudes that may be affected include job satisfaction, organizational commitment, and intent to quit. Work-related outcomes/behaviors can include reduced productivity (Jones et al., 2016). In a sample that was almost half African-American, Bauermeister et al. (2014) found that work discrimination was negatively associated with self-rated health and was associated with a greater number of days when physical and mental health was not good.

Several large-scale studies known as meta-analyses, which aggregate the findings of many other studies, have reached similar conclusions: discrimination is bad for the victim (e.g., Jones et al., 2016; Lee & Ahn, 2011, 2012; Pascoe & Richman, 2009). The findings show that perceived discrimination is negatively related to work outcomes and helpful work behaviors, as well as mental and physical health. Lee and Ahn studied individual-level discrimination outcomes of Latin Americans and Asians. They examined the mental health outcomes of general discrimination for Asians (Lee & Ahn, 2011) as well as the effects of general discrimination on mental health, physical health, employment, and educational outcomes for Latinos (2012). For the meta-analysis on Asian samples, which aggregated effects from several studies, they found that discrimination was positively related to depression, anxiety, and psychological distress (Lee & Ahn, 2011). Similarly, the study examining Latinos found positive associations between perceived racial discrimination and anxiety, depression, psychological distress, and job dissatisfaction (Lee & Ahn, 2012).

In a meta-analysis about perceived racial discrimination in the workplace, Triana, Jayasinghe, and Pieper (2015) found that perceived racial discrimination was negatively related to job attitudes, physical health, psychological health, organizational citizenship behavior, and perceived diversity climate, but positively related to coping behavior. Results provide some evidence that the effects of discrimination were stronger the more women and minorities were in the samples, indicating that these groups are more likely to perceive discrimination and/or respond more strongly to perceived discrimination. Results also showed that the negative relationship between perceived racial discrimination and employee job attitudes was stronger after the passage of the **Civil Rights Act of 1991** than before. The Civil Rights Act of 1991 strengthened the civil rights antidiscrimination legislation and provided the possibility of punitive damages (i.e., financial compensation paid as a penalty) for employees whose employers were found guilty of discriminating against them. Therefore, the authors reasoned that the threshold for feeling deprived of good treatment was lowered after the strengthening of the law in 1990 and, subsequently, employees felt discrimination was a greater wrong.

In a different meta-analysis which examined several types of discrimination, Jones et al. (2016) compared the relationship between subtle and blatant discrimination with psychological health, physical health, and work-related outcomes. They found that subtle and overt forms of discrimination correlate in similar ways to relevant outcomes. This suggests that subtle acts of discrimination such as incivility, undermining, and microaggressions can be just as damaging as blatant discrimination. This is important, especially in today's environment, because research shows that discrimination tends to unfold in subtle ways since most people know that blatant, old-fashioned racism is socially unacceptable (Dipboye & Colella, 2005; Dovidio & Gaertner, 1986). The new and subtle form of racial discrimination is called "modern racism" (McConahay, 1983). It is subtle in nature and is difficult to detect because of situational ambiguity (St. Jean & Feagin, 1997). For example, avoiding contact with someone, not sharing information with someone, not volunteering to mentor or help someone, not inviting someone to social outings, monitoring someone, or showing subtle signs of disrespect like undermining someone's authority or interrupting them while they speak are all examples of subtle ways in which racism can manifest today. If such acts are disproportionately targeted at some individuals who are of one racial or ethnic group compared to individuals of a different racial or ethnic group, that would be modern discrimination because it meets the definition of treating someone differently (and in a way that is worse than one would treat members of another group) on the basis of their demographic characteristics (Allport, 1954).

Research Findings on Coping with Racial Discrimination

Workplace discrimination has costs associated with it including a decrease in employee attitudes and increased turnover intentions (King, Hebl, George, & Matusik, 2010; Madera, King, & Hebl, 2012). Therefore, researchers have examined the process by which discrimination has its deleterious effects. Several studies have tested ways to remedy employment discrimination by exploring contextual factors that can buffer the harmful effects of perceived discrimination on employee outcomes. Pascoe and Richman (2009) reported that **social support** and **social coping** are effective at reducing the effects of discrimination. Social support refers to the network of people around individuals who can help them cope with life's challenges. Social coping is the act of reaching out to one's social support network for advice in order to resolve some matter that is causing one stress. However, not all forms of coping behavior were equally successful. **Active or problem-focused coping** with an emphasis on ways of resolving the problem was the most effective. **Emotion-focused coping** which involves eating or using alcohol or drugs may remove the immediate negative mood effects of stressors but may lead to longer-term problems including addiction or obesity (Pascoe & Richman, 2009).

Researchers have found that coping can be **adaptive** and buffer the harmful effects of discrimination, but it could also be **maladaptive** and cause other negative outcomes. For example, one common maladaptive coping strategy is smoking (Purnell et al., 2012; Shih, Young, & Bucher, 2013). One study found that some populations (e.g., migrant female workers in China) could be more vulnerable to coping with stressors in maladaptive ways such as smoking (Shih et al., 2013). Purnell et al. (2012) studied perceptions of racial discrimination in the workplace and in health care settings and found that the relationship between perceived racial discrimination and smoking was more relevant in the workplace setting than in the health care settings (Purnell et al., 2012). Perhaps racial encounters in the workplace have a stronger impact on individuals as compared to racial encounters in a health care setting because the workplace is very important for one's livelihood needs and employees are in the workplace much more regularly than in a health care setting. Therefore, the workplace context is important and should be examined further.

Other studies have found that people sometimes cope with discrimination through **identity management strategies** (e.g., identity switching and identity redefinition). Identities are the group memberships that we define ourselves as being members of, and we derive our sense of self and our esteem through our identity groups (Hogg & Abrams, 1988; Hogg & Terry, 2000). Redefining one's identity is one way to protect one's self-esteem from the harmful effects of discrimination. Shih et al. (2013) note that strategies for coping with discrimination are short-term tools. Thus, it is important to examine the long-term consequences of discrimination. A study by Madera et al. (2012) found that group identity management (meaning the participants either manifested a group identity or suppressed a group identity) was associated with perceived discrimination, which in turn was associated with lower job satisfaction and higher intentions to quit.

Finally, the type of coping strategy and how closely tied it is to the type of perceived discrimination also matters. Stainback and Irvin (2012) examined an organization's demographic composition and found that Whites, Blacks, and Latinos were less likely to experience discrimination when the majority of their coworkers were of their same race. However, perceived racial discrimination reduced loyalty to the employer and increased job search intentions regardless of which racial group the employees belonged to. This implies that the consequences of discrimination may differ based on whether the organization's demographic composition matches the employee's demographic characteristic. This would be consistent with at least three major theories of diversity and discrimination in organizations. The first is Kanter's (1977) theory on **tokenism** which states that individuals whose demographic group comprises 15% or less of an organization's demographic will be highly visible and will have the potential to feel isolated or excluded. The second is Byrne's (1971) **similarity-attraction hypothesis** which states that people like others who are similar to themselves and gravitate toward those people. As a result, they generally have a better experience when they are with similar others. The third is **relational demography theory** which has shown that people working in groups who are similar to themselves in demographic characteristics are more likely to enjoy being part of that group, have a tighter knit group, and be more productive in the group (O'Reilly, Caldwell, & Barnett, 1989; Pfeffer, 1983; Riordan, 2000; Tsui, Egan, & O'Reilly, 1992; Tsui & O'Reilly, 1989).

Recommendations for Organizations

It is important for organizations and individuals to recognize that all of us have biases and are capable of discriminatory behavior. As you will see in Chapter 14

(Subconscious/Implicit Bias), biases are deeply seated, and subconscious bias is very common. Some organizations have begun conducting subconscious bias training to alert employees to the fact that most people hold biases, which makes them capable of having prejudiced opinions about some groups of people and discriminating against them. This is problematic for organizations both because discrimination is illegal (as we saw in Chapter 3, Employment Legislation), and because biases can hinder decision-making and prevent organizations from making the best decisions in hiring, promotion, evaluation, and other employment decisions. Therefore, employees, particularly those with managerial and selection responsibilities, should be aware of biases (ideally aware of their own biases) and should be instructed to make decisions on the basis of job-related qualifications. In fact, a research study conducted by Umphress, Simmons, Boswell, and Triana (2008) demonstrated that people who have a tendency to discriminate against highly qualified women and racial minority group members do so less often when they are instructed by a leader to make decisions on the basis of job-related qualifications and ignore irrelevant factors.

It is also important for organizations to encourage employees' ethical behavior with respect to diversity and inclusion. Many times, people see discriminatory behavior and say nothing, becoming bystanders, because they do not want to confront their colleagues or might be afraid of backlash. If the organizational leaders sent a norm of ethical and inclusive behavior, whereby it is acceptable to remind others of biases and to discourage biased language and behavior, this empowers members of organizations to be agents of change rather than bystanders.

Obviously, it is also important for organizations to be clear that they have a zero-tolerance policy for discrimination. This follows the requirements of Title VII of the Civil Rights Act of 1964, a major employment law in the United States. It also sends a signal that the organization strives for equal employment opportunity for all groups and to be inclusive in its practices.

Another important practice that organizations can utilize to avoid discrimination and to reap the benefits of a diverse organization is to recruit from diverse talent pools that contain qualified minority applicants. Universities in various regions of the country and various professional organizations are well poised to provide diverse applicant pools of qualified minorities. For example, Historically Black Colleges and Universities (HBCUs) and universities that are designated as Hispanic-Serving Institutions are good sources of diverse applicant pools with a high proportion of qualified minority candidates. Universities in New Mexico and Arizona including the University of Arizona, the University of New Mexico, and New Mexico State University have fairly strong representation of American Indian students and are also good sources to recruit diverse applicant pools. Organizations could recruit at some of these institutions in addition to other institutions from which they may recruit that have primarily White student bodies. Professional organizations are another good source from which to recruit a diverse applicant pool. For example, recruiters in the market for MBA students regularly attend the National Black MBA Association and Prospanica (the National Society for Hispanic MBAs).

Both of these organizations host a large national conference that draws many recruiters as well as applicants from various demographic backgrounds.

Finally, organizations should also be aware of discrimination against Asians. Because of the "model minority" stereotype and the fact that Asians as a whole tend to be highly educated and have a high level of income, sometimes people assume that all Asians do not need help. In reality, not all Asians are wealthy and well educated. The overgeneralization of the model minority hinders some Asians from modest backgrounds from receiving assistance they could use. For a thorough review, see the book written by Chou and Feagin (2010) called *The Myth of the Model Minority*. Stereotypes about Asian groups are common, and this may also prevent them from advancing to managerial positions in organizations.

Concluding Remarks

This chapter has covered the major racial groups in the United States, the discrimination they have faced, and the outcomes of discrimination and some coping mechanisms. Perhaps the best way to think about racial discrimination is to determine how to prevent it in the first place. One way is through social rules and legislation including employment legislation prohibiting discrimination (covered in Chapter 3). Another way is through strong diversity management practices within organizations, which will be discussed in Chapter 15.

Closing Case

Nurse Sues Michigan Hospital for Following Parents' Request: No African-American Nurse to Take Care of Baby

A Michigan hospital has been charged with racial discrimination by an African-American nurse. Tonya Battle, a certified nurse who has worked for the same hospital for many years and has worked in the Intensive Care Unit for newborn babies, "was barred from treating an infant patient" (Gates, 2013). Her skin color was the reason for her removal from her assignment.

Nurse Battle was reassigned after the baby's father requested that no African Americans take care of his child. As he made the request, he pulled up his shirt sleeve and displayed a tattoo which appeared to be "a swastika of some kind" (NBC News, 2013). The hospital complied and reassigned the baby to another nurse.

In addition, the court proceeding states that a note was attached to the infant's file saying, "No African American nurse to take care of baby" (Gates, 2013). Even though attorneys for the hospital presented a different argument, it seems that "the hospital honored the patient's request for more than a month" (Gates, 2013; NBC News, 2013).

Nurse Battle, who filed a discrimination claim, is asking for compensation for damages to her reputation and stress-related problems in her lawsuit.

Discussion Questions:

1. How would you have reacted to this situation?
2. How would you feel about this issue emotionally?
3. Do you think the hospital acted in an appropriate manner? Please explain.

Note

1. For a timeline of events leading up to the Brown v. Board of Education decision, see the following link: http://www.archives.gov/education/lessons/brown-v-board/time-line.html.

References

Allport, G. W. (1954). *The nature of prejudice*. Reading, MA: Addison-Wesley.

Amnesty International. (2017). Czech Republic: Roma Progress Report. Retrieved from https://www.amnesty.org/en/latest/campaigns/2016/08/czech-republic-roma-progress-report/

Angier, N. (2000, August 22). Do races differ? Not really, DNA shows. *New York Times*. Retrieved from http://partners.nytimes.com/library/national/science/082200sci-genetics-race.html

Aranda, E. M. (2008). Class backgrounds, modes of incorporation, and Puerto Ricans' pathways into the transnational professional workforce. *American Behavioral Scientist, 52*, 426–456.

Archibold, R. C. (2014, October 25). Negro? Prieto? Moreno? A question of identity for Black Mexicans. *New York Times*. Web. 27 Nov. 2014. Retrieved from http://www.nytimes.com/2014/10/26/world/americas/negro-prieto-moreno-a-question-of-identity-for-black-mexicans.html#slideshow/100000003197258/100000003197259

Associated Press. (1995, March 31). Reverse discrimination complaints rare, labor study reports. *New York Times*, p. A23. Retrieved from ProQuest Historical Newspapers: The New York Times (1851–2009).

Associated Press. (2014, November 13). Rights groups: Czechs still segregating Gypsy kids. Web. 26 Nov. 2014. Retrieved from http://news.yahoo.com/rights-groups-czechs-still-segregating-gypsy-kids-124921558.html

Bauermeister, J. A., Meanley, S., Hickok, A., Pingel, E., Vanhemert, W., & Loveluck, J. (2014). Sexuality-related work discrimination and its association with the health of sexual minority emerging and young adult men in the Detroit Metro area. *Sexuality Research & Social Policy: Journal of NSRC: SR & SP, 11*(1), 1–10.

BBC News. (2016, November 16). 'Ahok': Police name Jakarta governor as blasphemy suspect. Retrieved from http://www.bbc.com/news/world-asia-37996350

Beck, E. M., & Tolnay, S. (1990). The killing fields of the deep South: The market for cotton and the lynching of Blacks, 1882–1930. *American Sociological Review, 55,* 526–539.

Black Profiles. (2015). African American Chairman & CEO's of Fortune 500 companies. Retrieved from http://www.blackentrepreneurprofile.com/fortune-500-ceos/

Blancero, D. M., & Del Campo, R. G. (2012). *Hispanics at work: A collection of research, theory and application.* New York: Nova Science Publishers.

Boswell, T. E. (1986). A split labor market analysis of discrimination against Chinese immigrants, 1850–1882. *American Sociological Review, 51,* 352–371.

Brodkin, K. (1998). *How Jews became White folks & what that says about race in America.* New Brunswick, NJ: Rutgers University Press.

Brodkin, K. (2004). How Jews became White. In J. F. Healey & E. O'Brien (Eds.), *Race, ethnicity, and gender* (pp. 283–294). Thousand Oaks, CA: Pine Forge Press.

Bureau of Labor Statistics. (2015a). Household data annual averages. Table 5. Employment status of the civilian noninstitutional population by sex, age, and race. Retrieved from http://www.bls.gov/cps/cpsaat05.pdf

Bureau of Labor Statistics. (2015b). Household data annual averages. Table 6. Employment status of the Hispanic or Latino population by sex, age, and detailed ethnic group. Retrieved from http://www.bls.gov/cps/cpsaat06.pdf

Byrne, D. (1971). *The attraction paradigm.* New York: Academic Press.

Catalyst. (2015). Women CEOs of the S&P 500. Retrieved from http://www.catalyst.org/knowledge/women-ceos-sp-500

Cavalli-Sforza, L. L., Menozzi, P., & Piazza, A. (1994). *The history and geography of human genes.* Princeton, NJ: Princeton University Press.

Central Intelligence Agency. (2015). World factbook: Country comparison to the world. Retrieved from https://www.cia.gov/library/publications/the-world-factbook/fields/2075.html

Chou, R. S., & Feagin, J. R. (2010). *The myth of the model minority: Asian Americans facing racism.* Boulder, CO: Paradigm.

Cisneros, H. G. (2009). *Latinos and the nation's future.* Houston, TX: Arte Publico Press.

Cochrane, J. (2014, November 22). An Ethnic Chinese Christian, breaking barriers in Indonesia. *New York Times.* Retrieved from http://www.nytimes.com/2014/11/23/world/asia/an-ethnic-chinese-christian-breaking-barriers-in-indonesia.html?src=me&_r=2

Colorado Historical Society. (2015). Vanishing homeland. Historical marker about the Ute American Indian tribe of Colorado and Utah displayed in the city of Durango, Colorado, in Santa Rita Park. Photographed by author on May 30, 2015.

DeNavas-Walt, C., & Proctor, B. D. (2014, September). Income and poverty in the United States: 2013. United States Census Bureau. Retrieved from http://www.census.gov/content/dam/Census/library/publications/2014/demo/p60-249.pdf

Dipboye, R. L., & Colella, A. (2005). *Discrimination at work: The psychological and organizational bases.* Mahwah, NJ: Lawrence Erlbaum Associates.

Dovidio, J. F., & Gaertner, S. L. (1986). *Prejudice, discrimination, and racism: Historical trends and contemporary approaches.* Orlando, FL: Academic Press.

Equal Employment Opportunity Commission (EEOC). (2014). Job patterns for minorities and women in private industry (EEO-1). Retrieved from http://www.eeoc.gov/eeoc/statistics/employment/jobpat-eeo1/

Equal Employment Opportunity Commission (EEOC). (2017). Charge statistics FY 1997 through FY 2016. Retrieved from https://www.eeoc.gov/eeoc/statistics/enforcement/charges.cfm

Feagin, J. R., & Feagin, C. B. (1993). *Racial and ethnic relations* (4th ed.). Englewood Cliffs, NJ: Prentice Hall.

Feagin, J. R., & O'Brien, E. (2003). *White men on race: Power, privilege, and the shaping of cultural consciousness.* Boston, MA: Beacon Press.

Feagin, J. R., & Sikes, M. P. (1994). *Living with racism: The black middle-class experience.* Boston, MA: Beacon Press.

Fujiwara, J. H., & Takagi, D. Y. (1999). Japanese Americans: Stories about race in America. In A. G. Dworkin & R. J. Dworkin (Eds.), *The minority report* (3rd ed., pp. 297–320). Fort Worth, TX: Harcourt Brace Publishers.

Gates, S. (2013, February 16). Tonya Battle, African American nurse, sues Michigan hospital for race discrimination. *Huffington Post.* Retrieved from http://www.huffingtonpost.com/2013/02/16/tonya-battle-hurley-medical-center-race-discrimination_n_2702373.html

Gilroy, P. (1998). Race ends here. *Ethnic and Racial Studies, 21,* 839–847.

Glaze, L. (2011). *Correctional populations in the United States, 2010.* Report NCJ 236319. U.S. Department of Justice. Retrieved from http://bjs.ojp.usdoj.gov/content/pub/pdf/cpus10.pdf

Gonzalez, J. (2000). *Harvest of empire: A history of Latinos in America.* New York: Penguin Books.

Harrison, D. A., Price, K. H., Gavin, J. H., & Florey, A. T. (2002). Time, teams, and task performance: Changing effects of surface- and deep-level diversity on group functioning. *Academy of Management Journal, 45,* 1029–1045.

History.com. (2016a). Rosa Parks. Retrieved from http://www.history.com/topics/black-history/rosa-parks

History.com. (2016b). March on Washington. Retrieved from http://www.history.com/topics/black-history/march-on-washington

Hogg, M., & Abrams, D. (1988). *Social identification.* London: Routledge.

Hogg, M., & Terry, D. J. (2000). Social identity and self-categorization processes in organizational contexts. *Academy of Management Review, 25,* 121–140.

Ignatiev, N. (1995). *How the Irish became White.* New York: Routledge.

Jahoda, G. (1975). *The trail of tears: The story of the American Indian removals 1813–1855.* New York: Wings Books.

Jehn, K., & Bezrukova, K. (2004). A field study of group diversity, workgroup context, and performance. *Journal of Organizational Behavior, 25,* 703–729.

Jones, K. P., Peddie, C. I., Gilrane, V. L., King, E. B., & Gray, A. L. (2016). Not so subtle: A meta-analytic investigation of the correlates of subtle and overt discrimination. *Journal of Management, 42,* 1588–1613. doi:10.1177/0149206313506466.

Jones, N. A. (2012, May 2). The Asian population in the United States: Results from the 2010 census. Presentation for the 2010 Asian Profile America Event, United States Census Bureau, Washington, DC, May 2, 2012. Retrieved from http://www.census.gov/newsroom/releases/pdf/2012-05-02_nickjones_asianslides_2.pdf

Jordan, W. D. (1962). Modern tensions and the origins of American slavery. *Journal of Southern History, 28,* 18–30.

Jordan, W. D. (1974). *The White man's burden: Historical origins of racism in the United States.* London: Oxford University Press.

Kanter, R. M. (1977). *Men and women of the corporation.* New York: Basic Books.

Kennedy, R. E., Jr. (1999). Irish Catholic Americans: A successful case of pluralism. In A. G. Dworkin & R. J. Dworkin (Eds.), *The minority report* (3rd ed., pp. 395–414). Fort Worth, TX: Harcourt Brace Publishers.

King, E. B., Hebl, M. R., George, J. M., & Matusik, S. F. (2010). Understanding tokenism: Negative consequences of perceived gender discrimination in male-dominated organizations. *Journal of Management, 36,* 482–510.

Krauze, E. (2005, July 17). Two sides of reality on race in Mexico. *Houston Chronicle.* Retrieved from http://www.chron.com/opinion/outlook/article/Two-sides-of-reality-on-race-in-Mexico-1950008.php

Leary, M. R., Koch, E. J., & Hechenbleikner, N. R. (2001). Emotional responses to interpersonal rejection. In M. Leary (Ed.), *Interpersonal rejection* (pp. 145–166). New York: Oxford University Press.

Lee, D. L., & Ahn, S. (2011). Racial discrimination and Asian mental health: A meta-analysis. *The Counseling Psychologist, 39*(3), 463–489. doi:10.1177/0011000010381791.

Lee, D. L., & Ahn, S. (2012). Discrimination against Latina/os: A meta-analysis of individual-level resources and outcomes. *The Counseling Psychologist, 40*(1), 28–65.

Lee, S. (1996). *Unraveling the "model minority" stereotype: Listening to Asian American youth.* New York: Teachers College Press.

Lee, T. L., & Fiske, D. W. (2006). Not an outgroup, not yet an ingroup: Immigrants in the stereotype content model. *International Journal of Intercultural Relations, 30,* 751–768.

Lin, J. (1999). Chinese Americans: From exclusion to prosperity? In A. G. Dworkin & R. J. Dworkin (Eds.), *The minority report* (3rd ed., pp. 321–342). Fort Worth, TX: Harcourt Brace Publishers.

Lippi-Green, R. (1997). *English with an accent: Language, ideology, and discrimination in the United States.* New York: Psychology Press.

Lopez, M. H., Gonzales-Barrera, A., & Cuddington, D. (2013, June 19). Diverse origins: The nation's 14 largest Hispanic-origin groups. Pew Research Center. Hispanic Trends. Retrieved from http://www.pewhispanic.org/2013/06/19/diverse-origins-the-nations-14-largest-hispanic-origin-groups/

Madera, J. M., King, E. B., & Hebl, M. R. (2012). Bringing social identity to work: The influence of manifestation and suppression on perceived discrimination, job satisfaction, and turnover intentions. *Cultural Diversity & Ethnic Minority Psychology, 18*(2), 165–170. doi:10.1037/a0027724.

McConahay, J. B. (1983). Modern racism and modern discrimination: The effects of race, racial attitudes, and context on simulated hiring decisions. *Personality and Social Psychology Bulletin, 9,* 551–558.

Merriam-Webster. (2016). Dictionary. Definition of Caucasian. Retrieved from http://www.merriam-webster.com/dictionary/Caucasian

Mexican, M. (2013, November 22). Bimbo says adios to 'Negrito'—snack cake is now 'Nito'. Retrieved from http://www.pocho.com/bimbo-says-adios-to-negrito-snack-cake-is-now-nito/

NBC News. (2013, February 19). Hospital granted dad's request: No black nurses, lawsuit says. Retrieved from http://vitals.nbcnews.com/_news/2013/02/19/17021357-hospital-granted-dads-request-no-black-nurses-lawsuit-says?lite

Ogunwole, S. (2006). We the people: American Indians and Alaska Natives in the United States. Census 2000 special reports. CENSR-28. United States Census Bureau. Issued February, 2006. Retrieved from http://www.census.gov/prod/2006pubs/censr-28.pdf

O'Reilly, C. A., III, Caldwell, D., & Barnett, W. P. (1989). Work group demography, social integration, and turnover. *Administrative Science Quarterly, 34,* 21–37.

Pascoe, E. A., & Richman, L. S. (2009). Perceived discrimination and health: A meta-analytic review. *Psychological Bulletin, 135*(4), 531–554.

Pew Research Center. (2012, July 19). Asian Americans: A mosaic of faiths. The Pew Forum on Religion & Public Life. Retrieved from http://www.pewforum.org/2012/07/19/asian-americans-a-mosaic-of-faiths-overview/

Pfeffer, J. (1983). Organizational demography. In B. M. Staw & L. L. Cummings (Eds.), *Research in organizational behavior* (Vol. 5, pp. 299–357). Greenwich, CT: JAI Press.

Pollock, B. H. (2001). An act prohibiting the teaching of slaves to read. In B. H. Pollock (Ed.), *Zamani to Sasa: Readings on the Black quest for freedom, identity, and power in America* (pp. 107–108). Dubuque, IA: Kendall/Hunt Publishing Company.

Profile America Facts for Features. (2014, November 12). American Indian and Alaska native heritage month: November 2014. U.S. Census Bureau. U.S. Department of Commerce. Retrieved from http://www.census.gov/content/dam/Census/newsroom/facts-for-features/2014/cb14ff-26_aian_heritage_month.pdf

Public Broadcasting Service (PBS). (2015). Indian removal. Retrieved from http://www.pbs.org/wgbh/aia/part4/4p2959.html

Purnell, J. Q., Peppone, L. J., Alcaraz, K., McQueen, A., Guido, J. J., Carroll, J. K., & Morrow, G. R. (2012). Perceived discrimination, psychological distress, and current smoking status: Results from the behavioral risk factor surveillance system reactions to race module, 2004–2008. *American Journal of Public Health, 102*(5), 844–851. doi:10.2105/AJPH.2012.300694.

Remini, R. (2000). *Invasion. The Earth shall weep: A history of native America.* New York: Grove Press.

Riordan, C. M. (2000). Relational demography within groups: Past developments, contradictions, and new directions. *Research in Personnel and Human Resource Management, 19*, 131–173.

Rodriguez, C. (2000). *Changing race: Latinos, the census, and the history of ethnicity in the United States.* New York: New York University Press.

Sacks, K. B. (2003). How Jews became White. In R. E. Ore (Ed.), *The social construction of difference & inequality.* Boston, MA: McGraw-Hill.

Saenz, R. (1999). Mexican Americans. In A. G. Dworkin & R. J. Dworkin (Eds.), *The minority report* (3rd ed., pp. 209–229). Fort Worth, TX: Harcourt Brace Publishers.

Schaefer, R. T. (2002). *Racial and ethnic groups, census 2000 update* (8th ed.). Upper Saddle River, NJ: Pearson Education.

Schmitt, M. T., Branscombe, N. R., Postmes, T., & Garcia, A. (2014). The consequences of perceived discrimination for psychological well-being: A meta-analytic review. *Psychological Bulletin, 140*, 921–948. doi:10.1037/a0035754.

Shih, M., Young, M. J., & Bucher, A. (2013). Working to reduce the effects of discrimination: Identity management strategies in organizations. *American Psychologist, 68*(3), 145–157. doi:10.1037/a0032250.

Sidanius, J., & Pratto, F. (1999). *Social dominance: An intergroup theory of social hierarchy and oppression.* Cambridge: Cambridge University Press.

Spicer, E. H. (1969). *Impounded people: Japanese-Americans in the relocation centers.* Tucson, AZ: University of Arizona Press.

St. Jean, Y., & Feagin, J. R. (1997). Racial masques: Black women and subtle gendered racism. In N. Benokraitis (Ed.), *Subtle sexism: Current practices and prospects for change* (pp. 179–201). Thousand Oaks, CA: Sage Publications.

Stainback, K., & Irvin, M. (2012). Workplace racial composition, perceived discrimination, and organizational attachment. *Social Science Research, 41*(3), 657–670.

Takaki, R. (2008). *A different mirror.* Boston, MA: Back Bay Books.

Taylor, P., Cohn, D., Wang, W., Passel, J. S., Kochhar, R., Fry, R., Parker, K., Funk, C., Livingston, G. M., Patten, E., Motel, S., & Gonzalez-Barrera, A. (2012, July 12). The rise of Asian Americans (PDF). Pew Research Social & Demographic Trends. Retrieved from http://www.pewsocialtrends.org/files/2013/01/SDT_Rise_of_Asian_Americans.pdf

Thornton, R. (2004). Trends among American Indians in the United States. In J. F. Healey & E. O'Brien (Eds.), *Race, ethnicity, and gender* (pp. 195–210). Thousand Oaks, CA: Pine Forge Press.

Triana, M., Jayasinghe, M., & Pieper, J. (2015). Perceived workplace racial discrimination and its correlates: A meta-analysis. *Journal of Organizational Behavior, 36*(4), 491–513.

Tsui, A., Egan, T. D., & O'Reilly, C. A. (1992). Being different: Relational demography and organizational attachment. *Administrative Science Quarterly, 37*, 549–579.

Tsui, A., & O'Reilly, C. A., III. (1989). Beyond simple demographic effects: The importance of relational demography in superior-subordinate dyads. *Academy of Management Journal, 32*, 402–423.

Umphress, E. E., Simmons, A. L., Boswell, W. R., & Triana, M. C. (2008). Managing discrimination in selection: The influence of directives from an authority and social dominance orientation. *Journal of Applied Psychology, 93*, 982.

United Farm Workers. (2016). Retrieved from http://ufw.org/_page.php?menu=about&inc=about_vision.html

U.S. History. (2016). America in the Second World War. 51e. Japanese-American Internment. Retrieved from http://www.ushistory.org/us/51e.asp

United States Census Bureau. (1894). Report on Indians taxed and Indians not taxed in the United States (except Alaska). Department of the Interior, Census Office. Eleventh Census: 1890. Retrieved from http://www2.census.gov/prod2/decennial/documents/1890a_v10-01.pdf

United States Census Bureau. (2012). Table 229. Educational attainment by race and Hispanic origin: 1970 to 2010. Retrieved from http://www.census.gov/compendia/statab/2012/tables/12s0229.pdf

United States Census Bureau. (2014). Population estimates. Current estimates data. PEPSR6H-sex-both sexes, year-April 1, 2010 census, Hispanic origin-total. Annual estimates of the resident population by sex, race, and Hispanic origin for the United States, states, and counties: April 1, 2010 to July 1, 2013. Retrieved from http://www.census.gov/popest/data/index.html

United States Census Bureau. (2015a). Race. Retrieved from http://www.census.gov/topics/population/race.html

United States Census Bureau. (2015b). Censuses of the American Indians. Retrieved from http://www.census.gov/history/www/genealogy/decennial_census_records/censuses_of_american_indians.htmlUnited States Supreme Court. Toyosaburo Korematsu v. United States, 323, U.S. 214 (1944). Retrieved from http://caselaw.lp.findlaw.com/scripts/getcase.pl?navby=CASE&court=US&vol=323&page=214

U.S. National Archives. (2015). United States Constitution. Retrieved from http://www.archives.gov/historical-docs/document.html?doc=3&title.raw=Constitution%20of%20the%20United%20States

Wildenthal, B. H. (2003). *Native American sovereignty on trial.* Santa Barbara, CA: ABC-CLIO.

Wilsont, W. R. (1997, February). World War II: Navajo Code Talkers. *American History Magazine.* Retrieved from http://www.historynet.com/world-war-ii-navajo-code-talkers.htm

Wray, M. (2006). *Not quite White.* Durham, NC, and London: Duke University Press.

Zia, H. (2000). *Asian American dreams: The emergence of an American people.* New York: Farrar, Straus, and Giroux.

five
Sex/Gender

Opening Case
Harvard's Secret "Computers"

In 1881, the astronomer Edward Pickering, who worked at the Harvard College Observatory, had the ambitious idea of mapping the skies. After firing a male staffer who was not doing a sufficiently good job cataloging stars, Mr. Pickering decided to hire women to work in the observatory basement to help him reach his goal (American Museum of Natural History, 2015; Pandika, 2014). Because cataloging stars in the night sky was considered a tedious and secretarial task, Mr. Pickering employed several women to complete the task, among whom was his maid, Williamina Fleming (American Museum of Natural History, 2015; Geiling, 2013; Pandika, 2014).

This group of at least 80 women astronomers took images of the night sky and printed them onto glass plates. The women then made written copies from the glass plates into their notebooks. Some of the women classified stars, while others cataloged pictures, writing the date and location on the plates. Their salary was 25–50 cents per hour. Men's salaries were twice that amount (American Museum of Natural History, 2015; Geiling, 2013; Pandika, 2014).

"The women were not allowed to use the observatory telescopes, but that did not prevent them from making important discoveries" (Pandika, 2014). Antonia Maury, one of the workers, made a significant discovery. "She identified the second binary star shortly after Pickering discovered the first. She was also the first to calculate the path of these stars' orbits and the time needed to complete them" (Pandika, 2014). However, Maury was never recognized for her contribution. Similarly, Annie Jump Cannon's and Henrietta Leavitt's hard work, dedication, and findings were not acknowledged. Cannon cataloged 350,000 stars and simplified Maury's system. In fact, Cannon "classified hundreds of thousands of stars" and developed a star classification system which is still used today (American Museum of Natural History, 2015). She was the first woman to serve as an officer in the American Astronomical Society as well as to earn an honorary degree from Oxford (American Museum of Natural History, 2015). However, this system was not named after Cannon. Instead, it is called the Harvard system of spectral classification (Geiling, 2013; Pandika, 2014).

Two years before Ms. Cannon retired in 1940, Harvard acknowledged her work by naming her the William C. Bond Astronomer. Mr. Pickering had a 42-year career at Harvard Observatory, during which he received many awards "including the Bruce Medal, the Astronomical Society of the Pacific's highest honor. Craters on the moon and on Mars are named after him" (Geiling, 2013).

To place this case in its historical context, Harvard University was established in 1636 and was dedicated to educating an all-male student body. Radcliffe was established as a "Harvard Annex" for women and opened its doors in 1879 with an all-male faculty to educate the all-female student body. Harvard and Radcliffe merged their admissions in 1975, and it was in 1977 that Harvard's ratio of accepting four men for every one woman accepted ended and was replaced by sex-blind admissions. In 1999, Radcliffe officially merged with Harvard (Walsh, 2012).

Discussion Questions:

1. Do you think that the discoveries these women made compare in importance or significance to the work of their male counterparts? Please explain.
2. Women worked as hard as men in the basement of the Harvard College Observatory. They had to classify stars, catalog pictures, and transcribe information into tables. Why were their salaries so meager? Why have we never heard of these women?

Learning Objectives

After reading this chapter, you should be able to:

- Understand the gender gap
- Be familiar with some of the countries that are the best and the worst in the world with respect to the gender gap according to the Global Gender Gap Index ranking

- Define sex discrimination
- Be aware of gender role differences between men and women and how this may contribute to the gender gap
- Understand how gender differences contribute to the glass ceiling, glass cliff, sticky floor, and glass escalator
- Be aware of differing expectations in extra-role behavior for male and female employees and how this may contribute to the gender gap
- Understand how country culture and cultural values can contribute to the gender gap
- Be familiar with several steps companies can take to remove barriers to women's advancement in organizations
- Know several recommendations for organizations to diminish the gender gap

Perhaps one of the most popular topics in the study of diversity is that of gender. The population in the world is roughly 50% men and 50% women, which makes this a topic that is relevant for most everyone. An example of the popularity of gender diversity and male/female differences is Sheryl Sandberg's book titled *Lean In: Women, Work and the Will to Lead*. Sandberg is the chief operating officer of Facebook and one of the most successful businesswomen in the United States and the world. Her book was published on March 11, 2013, and has since become a best-selling book, selling approximately 1.6 million copies by early 2015. This book brings attention to the fact that there is still a lack of women advancing to the most senior-level positions in organizations.

Please note that the words "sex" and "gender" are used interchangeably throughout this chapter, as they are often used interchangeably in society. However, there is a distinction between the two words. Sex refers to one's biological sex (i.e., male or female). Gender has more connotations about how one is expected to behave as a result of one's biological sex. For example, stereotypical gender roles for women are different than gender roles for men.

This chapter begins by examining the status of women both in the United States and throughout the world. We then review information from several sources that conclude there is a gender gap whereby men have higher status and power in the world than women. There is also a wage gap in both the United States and various countries of the world. This wage gap is discussed, and then we review the extensive research on gender roles and stereotypes which helps us understand why gender gaps between men and women persist. We then discuss the outcomes of these gender roles and stereotypes including the glass ceiling, the glass cliff, the sticky floor, and the glass escalator (all defined later in the chapter). This is followed by a discussion explaining why it may sometimes be difficult for women to reject these stereotypes and behave in counter-stereotypical ways. Finally, the chapter concludes with some recommendations that address these existing gender gaps between men and women in organizations.

The Status of Women and Men: The Gender Gap

The World Economic Forum (2014) *Global Gender Gap Report* for 2014 ranks the status of women in countries worldwide and considers four factors: economic participation and opportunity for women, educational attainment, health and survival, and political empowerment. The United States ranks 4th in the economic participation and opportunity of women, 39th in educational attainment, 54th in political empowerment, and 62nd in health and survival of women. The United States ranks 20th in the world overall for the quality of life for women. The most highly ranked countries (in the overall ranking across categories) for women worldwide are Iceland, Finland, Norway, Sweden, and Denmark, in that order. For a complete list of all countries ranked in the gender gap report by the World Economic Forum, see Table 5.1.

According to the *Global Gender Gap Report* for 2014 (World Economic Forum, 2014), women have achieved the most equality compared to men in Iceland. This report measures the gap between women and men on a scale ranging from 0 to 1, where 0 equals complete inequality and 1 equals complete equality. The index for equality of women compared to men in Iceland is 0.859 for the overall measure of equality. Therefore, in the best country in the world for women, they are roughly 86% equal to men. This overall measure is comprised of the four individual measures mentioned in the previous paragraph. The educational attainment score in Iceland was a 1.0, meaning that in this category, women have achieved full equality compared to men. The health and survival score in Iceland was 0.965. The economic participation score was 0.817. Finally, the political empowerment score was 0.655. With these scores, Iceland has been ranked the #1 country with the smallest gender gap between men and women for six consecutive years, from 2009 to 2014 (World Economic Forum, 2014).

One characteristic that may help the economic attainment of women in Iceland is the country's generous maternity and paternity leave policy. Maternity leave benefits extend up to 90 calendar days, paid at a rate of 80% of the women's regular wages, and 100% of this benefit is provided by the government. Men receive this same benefit in the form of paternity leave for the birth of a child. Taken together, this means that a married couple is guaranteed a total of six months maternity and paternity leave with 80% of their regular wages paid for by the government. This benefit most certainly helps many women stay in the labor force after the birth of a child (World Economic Forum, 2014).

Sex Discrimination Statistics and the Wage Gap

Despite employment laws against discrimination and increased corporate investments in diversity management practices (Richard, Roh, & Pieper, 2013),

TABLE 5.1. Global Gender Gap Index Ranking by Country

1	Iceland	37	Kenya	73	Honduras	109	Suriname
2	Finland	38	Lesotho	74	Montenegro	110	Burkina Faso
3	Norway	39	Portugal	75	Russian Federation	111	Liberia
4	Sweden	40	Namibia	76	Vietnam	112	Nepal
5	Denmark	41	Madagascar	77	Senegal	113	Kuwait
6	Nicaragua	42	Mongolia	78	Dominican Republic	114	India
7	Rwanda	43	Kazakhstan	79	Sri Lanka	115	United Arab Emirates
8	Ireland	44	Lithuania	80	Mexico	116	Qatar
9	Philippines	45	Peru	81	Paraguay	117	Korea, Rep.
10	Belgium	46	Panama	82	Uruguay	118	Nigeria
11	Switzerland	47	Tanzania	83	Albania	119	Zambia
12	Germany	48	Costa Rica	84	El Salvador	120	Bhutan
13	New Zealand	49	Trinidad and Tobago	85	Georgia	121	Angola
14	Netherlands	50	Cape Verde	86	Venezuela	122	Fiji
15	Latvia	51	Botswana	87	China	123	Tunisia
16	France	52	Jamaica	88	Uganda	124	Bahrain
17	Burundi	53	Colombia	89	Guatemala	125	Turkey
18	South Africa	54	Serbia	90	Slovak Republic	126	Algeria
19	Canada	55	Croatia	91	Greece	127	Ethiopia
20	United States	56	Ukraine	92	Swaziland	128	Oman
21	Ecuador	57	Poland	93	Hungary	129	Egypt
22	Bulgaria	58	Bolivia	94	Azerbaijan	130	Saudi Arabia
23	Slovenia	59	Singapore	95	Cyprus	131	Mauritania
24	Australia	60	Lao PDR	96	Czech Republic	132	Guinea
25	Moldova	61	Thailand	97	Indonesia	133	Morocco
26	United Kingdom	62	Estonia	98	Brunei Darussalam	134	Jordan
27	Mozambique	63	Zimbabwe	99	Malta	135	Lebanon
28	Luxembourg	64	Guyana	100	Belize	136	Côte d'Ivoire
29	Spain	65	Israel	101	Ghana	137	Iran, Islamic Rep.
30	Cuba	66	Chile	102	Tajikistan	138	Mali
31	Argentina	67	Kyrgyz Republic	103	Armenia	139	Syria
32	Belarus	68	Bangladesh	104	Japan	140	Chad
33	Barbados	69	Italy	105	Maldives	141	Pakistan
34	Malawi	70	Macedonia, FYR	106	Mauritius	142	Yemen
35	Bahamas	71	Brazil	107	Malaysia		
36	Austria	72	Romania	108	Cambodia		

Source: Data are from Global Gender Gap Report published by the World Economic Forum (2014), Table 5.3: Global rankings.

employees still experience workplace discrimination (Dipboye & Colella, 2005; Equal Employment Opportunity Commission [EEOC], 2015b; Goldman, Gutek, Stein, & Lewis, 2006; Tomaskovic-Devey, Thomas, & Johnson, 2005). **Discrimination** is defined as denying equality of treatment to individuals on the basis of their group membership (Allport, 1954). Title VII of the U.S. Civil Rights Act forbids employment discrimination on the basis of sex, race, color, religion, and national origin (EEOC, 2015a). In 2014, the U.S. Equal Employment Opportunity Commission (EEOC), the government agency that enforces Title VII, received 88,778 discrimination charges. Of these, sex discrimination claims were prevalent, with 29.30%, or 26,027 claims, made during the year (EEOC, 2015b). Monetary awards to sex discrimination victims totaled $106.5 million in 2014 (EEOC, 2015c). In addition to the financial costs of workplace discrimination, there is a human cost to sex discrimination including many employee problems such as stress, job dissatisfaction, and physical symptoms (Dipboye & Colella, 2005; Raver & Nishii, 2010; Shrier et al., 2007). Research also shows that perceived sex discrimination is negatively related to perceptions of fairness (Blau, Tatum, Ward-Cook, Dobria, & McCoy, 2005; Foley, Hang-Yue, & Wong, 2005; Foley, Kidder, & Powell, 2002) and career satisfaction (Shrier et al., 2007) and positively related to conflict with the supervisor (Jeanquart, 1991), job pressure, and job threat (Rospenda, Richman, & Shannon, 2009).

In the United States, women experience a wage gap and make, on average, 81% of the median earnings of their male counterparts (Bureau of Labor Statistics, 2013). Across the world, just over 50% of women eligible for labor force participation are active in the global economy (International Labor Organization, 2009, as cited in the Economist Intelligence Unit, 2012, p. 4). According to Catalyst (2014), women held 24% of senior management roles globally in the year 2013. By region, women held 32% of senior management roles in Southeast Asian countries, 25% in Europe (except for the Nordic countries), 24% in the Nordic countries, 23% in Latin America, and 21% in North America.

Gender Role Differences and Their Origins

Differences in gender roles in the United States have been documented as far back as the 1830s when Alexis de Tocqueville wrote *Democracy in America*. He explained that in Europe there are people who "confounding together the different characteristics of the sexes, would make men and women into beings not only equal but alike" (p. 696). By contrast, he writes that in America they had carefully divided

> the duties of man from those of women in order that the great work of society may be the better carried on. America is the one country where the most consistent care has been taken to trace clearly distinct spheres of action for the two sexes and where both are required to walk at an equal pace but along paths that are never the same.
>
> (de Tocqueville, 2003 reprint, p. 697)

Anecdotal evidence tells us that there are differences between men and women which can sometimes lead to friction. The phrase "battle of the sexes" is so common that a search on google.com produced 13.2 million results (i.e., "hits"). Elvis Presley sang a tune describing conflict between men and women as "the cause of trouble ever since the world began." The song, *Hard Headed Woman*, was so famous that it became the first rock-and-roll song to be awarded the "gold record" designation by the Recording Industry Association of America. The book *Men Are from Mars, Women Are from Venus*, which discusses differences between the sexes that can cause communication problems, was a #1 *New York Times* bestseller. Clearly, people understand that there are differences between men and women which can be problematic.

Researchers have also noted differences between men and women, including the status they are afforded in society. Sidanius and Pratto (1999) state that in every society males are the dominant sex. In a survey of over 11,000 people from all over the world, these researchers found that people always ranked males above females in terms of their social status. Put simply, males dominate (Sidanius & Pratto, 1999). How does this happen?

Research on Gender Diversity in Groups and Organizations

Research investigating diversity in teams is typically grounded in theories that explain how people mentally categorize themselves and others, with what groups people identify, and to whom they tend to be attracted.

Stereotypes

People form stereotypes about groups of people in much the same way that they generalize about any aspect of their environment (Heilman, 1995). Categorizing people into groups is functional because it helps us make sense of the world. However, in the case of stereotypes about sex, social categorization may trigger male and female behavior that is not conducive to equal participation or opportunity in organizations. Stereotypes about male and female behavior generally involve males playing a very active role, while females play a more subdued and supportive role. For example, adjectives used to describe women are generally along the lines of nurturing, tender, understanding, concerned for others, kind, helpful, and sympathetic. The adjectives used to describe men are generally along the lines of independent, decisive, ambitious, forceful, and aggressive (Heilman, 1995, 2001).

There is substantial evidence that differences between males and females, likely exacerbated by social categorization and sex stereotypes, affect the way that men and women interact in teams. Empirical studies have shown that mixed-sex teams report more conflict, more interpersonal tension, and less friendly behavior compared to all-male teams (Alagna, Reddy, & Collins, 1982; see Devine et al., 1999, for additional findings). Other studies investigating sex diversity in teams have also reported process losses, or inefficiencies that make the team less productive (Clement & Schiereck, 1973; Pelled, 1996). For example, Pelled (1996) found that sex dissimilarity among team members increased perceptions of emotional conflict and led to reduced perceptions of team performance.

Proportions Matter

In the process of investigating sex diversity and its effect in organizations, one finding that is fairly consistent is that the proportion of men and women in the group seems to be important (Williams & O'Reilly, 1998). These findings are consistent with the classic work of Kanter (1977), which predicted that when women make up less than 15% of the group, they will often be seen as **tokens** and will be stereotyped and marginalized. **Tokenism** is defined as the idea that one person (i.e., a token) serves to represent an entire group of people. The term often has negative connotations, denoting that the token person may be devalued relative to others if his or her presence is seen as satisfying a need or checking a box so the company can say they have one woman, minority, man (or whatever the case may be) in the group. Particularly when women are "solo," or the only one of their kind in the group, they become especially salient. It is not until the minority group comprises 35% or more of the total group that the minority group will have influence in the larger group's decision-making. Some support for Kanter's theory came from Sackett, DuBois, and Noe (1991), who found that when the proportion of women in a group was small, they received lower performance ratings after the effects of ability, education, and experience were accounted for.

Although Kanter's theory has received mixed support overall (Mannix & Neale, 2005), there is evidence that females do tend to feel more included in the team as their numbers increase. This is consistent with research showing that as a particular minority group becomes increasingly small in proportion to the total group, those who are part of that minority group will become increasingly aware of their identity (Ethier & Deaux, 1994; Mullen, 1983). This is also consistent with findings showing that women in predominately male organizations have been treated with hostility by male coworkers (O'Farrell & Harlan, 1982), that women in majority-male teams are not well integrated (Brass, 1985; Ibarra, 1992; Kanter, 1977), and that sexist stereotyping is more common in majority-male groups than in majority-female groups (Konrad, Winter, & Gutek, 1992). However, men in predominantly female groups seem to be better integrated socially and treated in a more egalitarian manner (Fairhurst & Snavely, 1983). In addition, while solo women in male-dominated groups speak the least of all the team members, solo men in female-dominated groups speak the most (Myaskovsky, Unikel, & Dew, 2005).

Evidence That Men and Women Are Socialized to Behave Differently

Overall, the findings described previously are consistent with sociological research which suggests that from the time of socialization as children, females are taught to interact in a way that is inclusive of others while males are taught to interact in a way that is more competitive (Wood, 1994). For example, some researchers have observed that men and women exhibit different speech patterns (Tannen, 1990). Women's speech tends to be characterized by equality between people (Aries, 1987), supporting others, sustaining conversations by prompting others to speak, and responsiveness via showing concern for others and making them feel included and valued. Women's speech also tends to be more tentative than that of men, including words like "kind of," "probably," or ending in a question such as "don't you think?" which then invites others to be included in the conversation (Kemper, 1984; Lakoff, 1975; Wood, 1994, p. 143). Men's speech, on the other hand, tends to focus more on exhibiting knowledge or ability, accomplishing instrumental objectives, controlling the conversation by challenging other speakers or taking the stage away from them, and expressing themselves in ways that are more absolute, direct, and confident (Wood, 1994). These learned patterns of speech and behavior could then potentially create a challenge for women within university and organizational settings as they try to compete with men for top grades, advanced degrees, and promotions in predominantly male settings.

There is also research on interaction in groups that indicates some employee ideas may be overlooked in organizational settings (Benokraitis & Feagin, 1995; Cleveland, Stockdale, & Murphy, 2000; Dubrovsky, Kiesler, & Sethna, 1991; Kimmel, 2000), resulting in underutilization of an organization's human capital. Research has demonstrated that a number of demographic characteristics, including sex, tend to be related to lower participation rates in team discussions. For example, studies have shown that in mixed-sex teams, men get more attention and have more speaking turns (i.e., opportunities to speak) than women. This finding holds true across many settings, including business organizations (Benokraitis & Feagin, 1995; Bernard, 1972), educational classrooms (Kimmel, 2000; Wood, 1994), and laboratory settings (Hilpert, Kramer, & Clark, 1975; Ritter & Yoder, 2004; Swacker, 1975). For example, in a study of male-female dyads, compared to women, men spoke more than 59% of the time (Bhappu, Griffith, & Northcraft, 1997; Hilpert et al., 1975).

Ritter and Yoder (2004) extended these results by showing that even women who scored high on dominance (as measured by the California Psychological Inventory dominance scale) spoke less when they were paired with men who scored low on dominance. In fact, the only time the high dominance women out-talked the low dominance men was when they were asked to discuss a highly feminine task (i.e., planning a wedding). In a laboratory study on mixed-sex teams, women averaged

3 minutes of speaking whereas men averaged approximately 13 minutes (Swacker, 1975). In organizational settings, studies have shown that men out-talk women and that women often have difficulty getting an opportunity to speak; when they do get to speak they are interrupted more often than men (Bernard, 1972).

Empirical studies (primarily conducted in North America) have demonstrated that men, due to their higher status and privilege in society (Sidanius & Pratto, 1999), dominate group discussions because they display more assertive nonverbal behavior, speak more often, interrupt others more often, give more commands, and generally have more opportunity to influence others (Hearn & Collinson, 2006; Merrill-Sands, Holvino, & Cumming, 2000). This evidence suggests that women have less opportunity to speak their minds and share ideas in group settings.

If certain team members struggle to voice their thoughts and opinions, this may result in feelings of injustice and potentially demoralize these individuals, making them less likely to participate in group processes. Qualitative data from interviews with women working in organizations have echoed these frustrations. For example, one female editor at the *New York Times* described her frustration with the "old boys' network" and said that managerial meetings on the news floor were stressful for her:

> We are drowned out, not listened to, we are dismissed, passed over. It makes me crazy. The men running the *Times* now truly do not believe themselves capable of sexist feelings. They have serious wives. They help with the dishes. But they are still looking for, and are only comfortable with, people in their own image—in other words, other white men. They have a joking camaraderie together that walls us out.
>
> (Benokraitis & Feagin, 1995, p. 114)

Why Don't Women Reject These Stereotypes and Assert Their Rights?

Research on sex discrimination in the workplace shows that women can be penalized for acting outside of their prescribed gender stereotypes (Dipboye, 1985; Heilman, 1983, 1995; Heilman & Eagly, 2008; Heilman & Okimoto, 2007; Heilman, Wallen, Fuchs, & Tamkins, 2004). A common explanation for harsh reactions toward women who do not conform to their traditional gender role stereotypes is the **lack of fit model** (Heilman, 1983, 2001), which predicts that people sense a mismatch between the target person's group stereotype and the person's actual behavior (Dipboye, 1985; Heilman, 1983, 2001). According to Heilman's lack of fit model (1983), when people see others acting in a way that is incongruent with their stereotypical gender roles, they sense something is not right and does not fit with how things ought to be. People form stereotypes about other people through the social categorization process. Once categorized, we see and interpret the behavior of others on the basis of the knowledge and the expectations we hold about that group/category (Heilman, 1995). People commonly categorize others based on sex because sex is a readily observable, surface-level characteristic (Harrison, Price, & Bell, 1998). This categorization process allows us to quickly recall the behavior that should be associated with a man or a woman. As stated earlier, adjectives used to describe "feminine" behavior generally include nurturing, tender, understanding, concerned for others, kind, helpful, and sympathetic. Adjectives used to describe "masculine" behavior typically include independent, decisive, ambitious, forceful, and aggressive (Heilman, 1995, 2001). There is much evidence that these gender role stereotypes influence how men and women are perceived and treated in society (Cleveland, Stockdale, & Murphy, 2000; Dipboye & Colella, 2005; Heilman, 1995, 2001).

"Ice Queens" and "Iron Maidens"

If women are being excluded from predominantly male teams because their more subdued speech patterns and behavior do not allow them to break into male conversations, then one obvious solution would be for women to be more assertive and to force their way into the discussion. However, research shows that women are often penalized for acting outside of their prescribed sex stereotypes. Because stereotypes about female behavior maintain that females should be kind, gentle, considerate, and not aggressive, people usually expect females to behave in a more submissive and passive manner than males (Cleveland et al., 2000; Heilman, 1995). These stereotypes then put pressure on women to behave in accordance with their prescribed sex roles. For example, research has demonstrated that women who act outside of their prescribed sex roles by exhibiting masculine traits such as confidence in their abilities and assertiveness are often thought to be cold individuals, or "ice queens," and are interpersonally derogated (Heilman, 1995; Heilman, Wallen, Fuchs, & Tamkins, 2004). In a review of the gender discrimination literature, which was largely based on U.S. studies, Heilman (2001, p. 668) describes that women who are agentic (i.e., confident, take charge) and successful tend to be derogated and have been described using the following terms: "bitch," "quarrelsome," and "selfish." This is consistent with Kanter's (1977) theory which stated that assertive women in the corporate environment would be categorized as "iron maidens." This also holds true in the popular press. For example, during the Enron trial, it became known that Sharon Watkins, the high-ranking female who blew the whistle on Enron's corrupt and illegal business practices, was commonly referred to as "the buzz saw" (a power-operated circular saw named after the noise it makes) by her male peers (Flood, 2006).

Inclusion and participation for women in male-dominated teams, then, is not easy. On the one hand, women are socialized to be supportive and somewhat passive members of society, which makes it difficult for them to take very active roles within male-dominated teams. On the other hand, if they do act assertively in their interactions, their behavior is often seen as inappropriate, and they may be ridiculed, nicknamed, or treated as tokens. In many cases, it is simply easier for women to recede from group discussions than it is to assert themselves and face social or professional rejection (Benokraitis & Feagin, 1995).

The Outcomes of These Gender Differences

The **glass ceiling** is the invisible but strong barrier which keeps women from ascending to the top layers of organizational management (Morrison, White, & Van Velsor, 1992). In the United States, while women make up roughly 50% of lower-level employees and first-level managers, their numbers dwindle in the higher ranks of organizations. They make up 19.2% of directors at U.S. stock index companies (Catalyst, 2015a), and they are 4.6% of CEOs of Standard & Poor's 500 companies (Catalyst, 2015b).

The **glass cliff** theory predicts that women and minorities are more likely to be promoted to leadership positions in organizations that are having a crisis or are struggling and at risk of failure (Ryan, Haslam, Hersby, & Bongiorno, 2007). Cook and Glass (2014) found that minorities were more likely than White men to be promoted to be the CEOs of poorly performing firms. When the firm performance declined during their tenure as CEO, these minority CEOs were then likely to be replaced by White men, a phenomenon the authors described as the "savior effect."

The **sticky floor** is a situation where women tend to get stuck at the bottom of the distribution in pay. It is a situation where equally qualified men and women may be appointed to the same pay scale or job rank, but the women are appointed at the bottom of the pay scale while men are appointed higher on the pay scale (Booth, Francesconi, & Frank, 2003). The "sticky floor" means that women tend to linger in the low-paying, low-mobility jobs at the bottom of the employment pool (Berheide, 1992). Booth et al. (2003) used data from the British Household Panel Survey and found that full-time working women were just as likely as men to get promoted but were more likely to receive smaller wage increases upon promotion. They explained this model by calling it a sticky floor of pay and promotion. In the model, women are just as likely as men to be promoted, only to find themselves at the bottom of the pay scale for their new grade.

The **glass escalator** effect is a phenomenon whereby men in traditionally female (pink-collar) occupations tend to get promoted more quickly than their equally qualified female peers. Williams (1992) found this phenomenon in pink-collar jobs, primarily in the nursing and elementary school teaching occupations. Hultin (2003) also found support for the glass escalator effect in a nursing setting in Europe. Nevertheless, people can also react negatively to men who work in stereotypically female roles. Qualitative interviews with men in nursing and elementary school teaching suggest they may be disrespected and pressured to look for more masculine, better paying, and more prestigious work (Hultin, 2003; Williams, 1992).

But Haven't Gender Roles Changed Over Time as Women Enter the Workforce?

Somewhat. Estimates reveal "the presence of a growing number of married couples in which traditional gender roles vis-à-vis labor market activity may be reversed" whereby the wife is the primary wage earner and the husband is the secondary wage earner (Winkler, 1998, p. 42; Winkler, McBride, & Andrews, 2005). Among dual-earner couples in the United States, 24% of wives earn more than their husbands (Winkler, 1998; Winkler et al., 2005). Despite evidence that wage earner roles are changing, most couples still exhibit the traditional model with the male being the primary wage earner in the family (Winkler, 1998; Winkler et al., 2005). Consequently, the situation where the wife earns more than her husband has been termed the "innovative" pattern (Kulik & Rayyan, 2003). Thus, female primary wage earners and male secondary wage earners are still a minority.

Recent Changes in Gender Roles—But Males Still Predominantly Primary Wage Earners

According to the lack of fit model (Heilman, 1983), people should be surprised to see others who are exhibiting gender role incongruent behavior. As more women enter the workforce and the roles of men and women change, people should express less surprise to see gender role incongruent behavior in the form of female primary wage earners and male secondary wage earners. However, population survey data still show that males are overwhelmingly the primary wage earners in their families (Winkler et al., 2005).

Over the last 50 years in the United States, the percentage of married women who work outside the home rose from 25% to 60%, and the proportion of dual-earner couples increased from 39% to 61% of all married couples (Winkler, 1998; Winkler et al., 2005). In addition, the proportion of married couples in which only the wife works rose to 7% by 2003 (Winkler et al., 2005). In other words, gender roles in the family are shifting as more women become the main wage earners and more men become the secondary wage earners for the household. Nevertheless, men are still the primary breadwinners in 76% of American families (Winkler et al., 2005), although that is changing slowly.

As more females become the family's main source of income and more males take up the secondary wage earner status, it remains to be seen how others in the workplace will react to this innovative pattern. In an initial experimental study to examine how research participants reacted to female primary wage earners and male secondary wage earners, Triana (2011) found that people were more surprised to see women in primary wage earner roles compared to the traditional secondary wage earner roles and to see men in secondary wage earner roles compared to primary wage earner status. Female primary wage earners were also given slightly lower reward recommendations than their equally qualified male peers who were also primary wage earners in their families.

The Second Shift

Housework and childcare also factor into the explanation of the wage gap. Important research on the **second shift** (Hochschild, 1989) shows that women do more childcare and household work than men, even when they also hold full-time jobs. The second shift refers to all the extra work moms do after they finish a full day of work for their employer. Hochschild (1989) found that while men do their fair share of the housework when both spouses work and make roughly equal amounts of money, women once again take on a disproportionate amount of the housework when their income exceeds their husband's (Bittman, England, Sayer, Folbre, & Matheson, 2003). According to Bittman et al. (2003, p. 186), in households where the woman makes more than half of the family income, the housework again shifts mostly to the woman as if to compensate for this gender role incongruence and ensure their spouses do not feel emasculated. Hochschild and Machung (2012) updated Hochschild's classic work from 1989 and reported similar findings. The authors still describe that women do more housework, have more childcare responsibilities, and make trade-offs in their careers to accommodate family obligations, which make them more likely to have non-traditional careers.

Global View: Scotland

Nicola Sturgeon, Scotland's first female to hold the position of first minister, has said that resolving inequality is at the heart of everything she does and that she would like to smash the glass ceiling in Scotland to "smithereens" (*BBC News*, 2014). Her cabinet is the first to have an equal number of men and women (Dickie, 2014). She has vowed to increase free childcare if she is still in power after the 2016 elections, and she has challenged businesses to ensure that their boards of directors have an equal representation of men and women (*BBC News*, 2014).

Higher Service Expectations for Women, More Benefit of the Doubt for Men

Gender research (especially the work of Heilman and colleagues) suggests that having ambiguous credentials will penalize women more than men. Heilman and coauthors (Heilman, Block, & Lucas, 1992; Heilman, Block, & Stathatos, 1997) showed that women who were seen as having benefited from affirmative action were judged to be less competent by their coworkers (called the stigma of incompetence). Heilman et al. (1997) found that the stigma of incompetence was alleviated when the organization presented unambiguous information about the women's credentials. Therefore, having unambiguously strong credentials helps women avoid getting stereotyped to some degree.

There is also some evidence that gender stereotypes might make it more difficult for women in leadership positions. While a meta-analysis of gender and perceptions of leader effectiveness found that men and women leaders do not differ with respect to perceived leader effectiveness (Paustain-Underdahl, Walker, & Woehr, 2014), another meta-analysis showed evidence that the "think manager think male" paradigm still exists (Koenig, Eagly, Mitchell, & Ristikari, 2011). People tend to associate leadership with males and masculine characteristics (Koenig et al., 2011). One possible disadvantage that women have in leadership positions, and in most any job within an organization, is a somewhat higher expectation of doing service. Due to social stereotypes about women being caring and helpful (Heilman, 2001), women are expected to be relationship oriented. This behavior overlaps with the characteristics of transformational leadership, which includes having consideration for subordinates, and such leadership behaviors may not be as attention grabbing when performed by a female leader (compared to a male leader).

Research shows that females receive less recognition than males for performing organizational citizenship behavior (discretionary behavior which is not part of one's formal job requirements but helps the functioning of the organization; Organ, 1988), which would be consistent with stereotypes about women being kind and helpful (e.g., Allen & Rush, 2001). In a study examining altruistic helping behavior performed by men and women, Heilman and Chen (2005) reported that when men and women both performed helpful behaviors, men were given more credit for it than women in the form of significantly higher performance evaluations and reward recommendations. When the men and women did not perform the altruistic helping behavior, the men were still rated significantly higher on both performance and reward recommendations than the women. It is as if women's actions of performing helpful behavior are simply taken for granted whereas helpful behavior for men may be seen as an extra-role behavior that goes beyond society's expectations of men. Unfortunately, this is another factor that may keep qualified women from deserved rewards, raises, and promotions. Research shows, for example, that women leaders place value on fostering relationships with their subordinates. However, these efforts have not been considered "real" work, being relegated to things one would expect from women (Fletcher, Jordan, & Miller, 2000). In one study, female supervisors were rated as less competent than male supervisors when providing criticism to their subordinates (Sinclair & Kunda, 2000). Stereotypes about women still persist, and this makes it difficult for women to exhibit agentic behavior without incurring penalties.

With respect to male leaders, research suggests that men tend to get more credit from subordinates than women leaders because the former are the dominant sex in society and people may assume they are more capable than their female counterparts (Benokraitis & Feagin, 1995; Glick & Fiske, 1996; Sidanius & Pratto, 1999). Foschi (2000) proposed that minority group members (who have lower social status) will have their successful performance scrutinized more than majority group members (who have higher social status). When high status group members fail, they will be scrutinized less than lower status group members would be. "The higher the status, the more convincing the demonstration of *incompetence* will have to be"

(Foschi, 2000, p. 25) for the high status group member to be penalized. This would explain why male leaders are evaluated better than female leaders, as research on leadership shows (Eagly, Makhijani, & Klonsky, 1992; Eagly & Johannesen-Schmidt, 2001; Eagly & Karau, 2002; Heilman, 2001). If men get the benefit of the doubt, they can display more incompetence before incurring penalties equal to their female counterparts.

Global View: The Church of England

In 2014, the Church of England allowed women to become bishops for the first time (Castle, 2014). The church had voted on this matter several times before, and it had defeated the petition to recognize female bishops as recently as 2012. However, earlier in 2014, Archbishop Welby, senior bishop in the Church of England, warned his fellow church leaders that if they continued to exclude women from this role, the public would find it "almost incomprehensible" (Bennhold, 2014). The vote involved making one change to Canon 33 to read: "A man or a woman may be consecrated to the office of bishop" (Bennhold, 2014). Prime Minister David Cameron supported this change, and so did Deputy Prime Minister Nick Clegg, who stated that "allowing women to become bishops is another long overdue step towards gender equality in senior positions" (Castle, 2014).

While many welcomed the vote as exciting news and agreed to allow the church members to move forward with the legislation, others disagreed. There was opposition from a conservative group called Reform, which expressed that "the divine order of male headship" makes it "inappropriate" for women to lead dioceses. Reform claimed that at least 25% of the church found this change incompatible with their beliefs (Bennhold, 2014).

Cultural Values as a Potential Contributing Factor to Women's Status in Organizations

Gender egalitarianism is a society's beliefs about whether a person's gender should determine the roles the person plays in the home, in business, and in the community (House, Hanges, Javidan, Dorfman, & Gupta, 2004). The less a society believes that gender should drive a person's roles, the more egalitarian the society. Global Leadership and Organizational Behavior Effectiveness, or GLOBE, is the name of a landmark study which sampled 62 different countries and ranked them into bands A, B, and C for egalitarian practices, with A being the most egalitarian. Measured on a scale from 1 to 7, where 7 is more egalitarian, the United States scored a mean of 5.06 for egalitarian values, placing it into band A. However, the United States scored a mean of 3.34 on society's practices, which placed it in band B. Overall, based on the GLOBE data, there is evidence the United States values egalitarianism in theory but not as much in practice. This may explain why gender gaps persist in the United States compared to other countries in the world which value gender egalitarianism more in both theory and practice. With legal protections including Title VII of the Civil Rights Act which prohibits sex discrimination in employment and the Equal Pay Act which requires equal pay for equal work, other more subtle (yet persistent) forces like bias and cultural values are likely at work. In countries that have high gender egalitarianism practices, the societal norm is to reject differences that make distinctions between the genders and to avoid elevating one gender to a higher status than another (House et al., 2004).

Masculinity/femininity (Hofstede, 2001) refers to dominant gender role patterns such that men show more masculine behavior and women show more feminine behavior. In societies that value masculinity, men should be tough, assertive, and focused on material success, while women should be tender, modest, and concerned for quality of life (Hofstede, 2001). In countries where femininity is valued, both men and women are supposed to be tender, modest, and concerned with the quality of life (Hofstede, 2001). Out of 53 countries and regions sampled by Hofstede (2001), the United States ranked as the 15th highest in masculinity. By contrast, the countries with the lowest masculinity values in the sample were Sweden, Norway, the Netherlands, Denmark, Costa Rica, Yugoslavia, and Finland. Several of these countries include those with the most equality between men and women according to the *Global Gender Gap Report* (World Economic Forum, 2014) data presented earlier in this chapter. High masculinity scores may help explain why gender gaps persist between men and women in the United States and other advanced countries in spite of legal protections against sex discrimination.

Global View: Turkey

Recep Tayyip Erdogan, the president of Turkey, stated in 2014 that women should not be seen as equal to men because pregnancy represents an obstacle for them in the workplace. "You cannot put women and men on an equal footing," Mr. Erdogan said "it is against her nature—because her nature is different, her bodily constitution is different" (Arsu, 2014).

The president's comments drew applause from the Women and Democracy Association, a conservative organization that sponsored the conference where he was speaking. However, it drew criticism from the women's rights movement in Turkey. One activist was quoted as saying, "There is an apparent effort in changes made to the labor law to lock women indoors, and we should be aware of Erdogan's constant threat against us" (Arsu, 2014).

Turkey was ranked as country number 125 out of the 142 countries rated in the *Global Gender Gap Report* (World Economic Forum, 2014).

Things That Can Be Done to Improve Gender Equality

Diversity Training

One possibility is to make people aware of the biases (both blatant and subtle) women face in the workplace. As more women enter leadership roles, it is in our best interest to help women succeed in those positions. In a study about subtle (i.e., subconscious) bias against women leaders, Dasgupta and Asgari (2004) found that when female participants were exposed to information about famous female leaders, they were less likely to show stereotyping of women in a subsequent experimental activity. In a college sample, Dasgupta and Asgari (2004) found that stereotyping of women leaders was more likely to happen in the coed college (where men and women go to school together) compared to the women's college. It appears that both the environment and exposure to counter-stereotypical examples seem to matter. It seems that when men and women coincide in the same setting, gender stereotypes can be triggered, and it is all the more important to use counter-stereotypical examples of successful female leaders to counteract such stereotypes.

Another consideration with diversity training involves who to train and the topic of the training. For example, while men (as the stereotypically dominant sex) would seem like the natural targets for sex diversity training, there is evidence to suggest that females perpetrate just as much bad behavior toward each other. Researchers have shown that women often see each other as competitors and become envious of one another (Eichenbaum & Orbach, 1987) and that women in positions of power sometimes abuse their female employees (Rollins, 1985). Particularly if women ascribe to sexist beliefs themselves (Glick & Fiske, 1996) or are high in **social dominance orientation** (the belief that some groups in society are better than others and that the social hierarchy of majority groups (Whites, males) in a position of power over minority groups (racial minorities, females) is appropriate (Sidanius & Pratto, 1999)), women may treat other women badly.

Researchers have coined names to describe the bad behavior that women sometimes inflict on other women. One is the **queen bee syndrome**, which refers to women who have achieved success within the social structure and then endorse traditional sex roles and deny that there is discrimination against women (Abramson, 1975, p. 55; Staines, Travis, & Jayerante, 1973). Consequently, these female leaders show no sympathy or support toward other working women, especially their subordinates. Women do not like to work for these female leaders (Gini, 2001). Therefore, although there is evidence that women feel more optimistic and better supported in organizations where there is a large proportion of female leaders (Ely, 1994), this situation is very different when the female leaders are tokens. When female leaders are isolated within a male-dominated team, they are more likely to behave in ways which help them fit in with their males peers while simultaneously isolating themselves from their female subordinates (Nieva & Gutek, 1981).

Overall, although diversity training is good in theory, it may be difficult to implement well in practice. Organizations have had mixed results using diversity training because it can create a backlash among males who may feel they are being targeted, and it can sometimes reinforce negative stereotypes. Therefore, trainers must be careful to avoid these issues. In addition, there is evidence to suggest that targeting training at men may be inappropriate because women need sex diversity training just as much as men do.

Empowering Mind-Sets That May Help Women

The concept of **womanism** stems from work studying feminism. Womanism is defined as a commitment to fuse multiple identities and to combat multiple oppressions (Garth, 1994). **Feminism** is a term which means individuals identify with being pro-women's rights and may also be engaged in women's rights activism (Downing & Roush, 1985; Duncan, 1999). This frame of mind could help women buffer against the negative effects of sexism to reduce psychological distress (DeBlaere & Bertsch, 2013). Drawing from critical race theory (Solorzano, 1998), womanism allows sexual minority women of color to identify and analyze the aspects of society that maintain oppressive systems (e.g., racism, sexism). A study by Holland and Cortina (2013) examined feminism related to women's experiences of sexual harassment as both a cost (increasing exposure to harassment) and a benefit (decreasing harassment-related outcomes). They predicted that both feminist-identified and feminist-active women would experience negative outcomes of harassment to a lesser extent. Only women who were active in feminist movements experienced a lesser degree of some negative occupational outcomes.

Another study also found that women who are committed to womanism are more likely to experience less negative effects of perceived lifetime sexist events on psychological distress (DeBlaere & Bertsch, 2013). Specifically, sexual minority women of color with a framework of womanism were better able to put their sexist experiences in context, which allowed them to externalize and minimize the negative effects of those experiences (Landrine & Klonoff, 1997).

Organizational and National Employment Policies

In a comprehensive report about *Barriers to Work Place Advancement Experienced by Women in Low-Paying Occupations*, Harlan and Berheide (1994) provided an extensive analysis about various factors that contribute to women experiencing both the glass ceiling and the sticky floor. They also provided several policy recommendations which individual employers and governments can use to mitigate these problems for women.

According to Harlan and Berheide (1994), barriers to advancement for women include the following:

- Educational systems that use gender, race, or class because they restrict opportunities for women, minorities, immigrants, and low-income people to obtain high-quality education

- **Occupational segregation**, which means that there is an overrepresentation of women and minorities in the lowest paying jobs; segregation occurs when members of one sex comprise 70% or more of an occupation (Anker, 1998); almost 70% of the full-time female labor force is employed in low-wage occupations
- Wage differentials by gender and race which channel women and minorities into low-paying jobs
- Social class, meaning that class-based economic power is associated with division of labor along sex and race lines
- The growing contingent workforce—women and African-Americans are over-represented in these temporary and part-time jobs

Harlan and Berheide (1994) also point out barriers to advancement that are driven by organizational culture, including:

- Gender and race are often synonymous with one's place in the organizational hierarchy. The people in the highest positions have a vested interest in maintaining traditional rules that work to their advantage.
- Social relationships at work between women and men and between racial minority and majority members can limit upward mobility. These barriers include things like sexual harassment, exclusion from informal support systems, and resistance to equal employment opportunity policies.
- Low-paying jobs are often not connected to any pipeline of advancement or job ladder in the organization. Women tend to occupy many of these low-paying jobs.
- Hiring practices used by employers sometimes result in placing women into jobs that have a short job ladder and limited room for growth.
- Job incumbents who work in predominantly female jobs have lower rates of promotion than those whose jobs are predominantly male or mixed-gender jobs.
- Women who might move into predominantly male or mixed-gender jobs with more opportunities may be blocked by eligibility requirements, seniority rules, or a lack of training and career development.
- Rigid work schedules require high time commitments and lack flexibility to accommodate family responsibilities.
- Job evaluation systems encourage compensation policies which devalue the content of women's work.

The Equal Employment Opportunity Commission (EEOC) Women's Work Group, established in 2010 to study existing obstacles in the U.S. federal government which hinder the hiring and advancement of women, found similar challenges to those presented above. This group found six fundamental obstacles to women attaining equal success as men in the federal workplace:

1. "Inflexible workplace policies create challenges for women in the federal workforce with caregiver obligations."

2. "Higher level and management positions remain harder to obtain for women."
3. "Women are underrepresented in science, technology, engineering, and mathematics (STEM) fields in the federal workforce."
4. "Women and men do not earn the same average salary in the federal government."
5. "Unconscious gender biases and stereotypical perceptions about women still play a significant role in employment decisions in the federal sector."
6. "There is a perception that Agencies lack commitment to achieving equal opportunities for women in the federal workplace."

The group also made recommendations to remedy employment discrimination and promote equal opportunities for women (EEOC Women's Work Group Report, 2013). Some of the recommendations directly addressed workplace policies such as implementing more flexible work schedules, additional training, and more parental leave. Other recommendations called for formal and informal opportunities for women to network and seek mentoring. Due to some of the historic systemic issues resulting in biases and stereotypes that start in elementary school socialization, some of the recommendations also involved partnering with primary and secondary schools, offering scholarships at the collegiate and graduate level, and providing more internships for female college students interested in STEM careers (EEOC Women's Work Group Report, 2013).

Harlan and Berheide (1994) also provide several recommendations for organizations and for national policymakers in order to advance women out of the lowest paying jobs, including:

- Raising the wages of low-paying jobs
- Examining the talent pipeline to determine whether career ladders can be built to advance people out of low-paying jobs
- Investing in education and training for low-level employees
- Providing flexible work arrangements to accommodate family responsibilities
- Expanding union coverage, as unions have been shown to close the wage gap between men and women
- Increasing access to higher education
- Expanding equal pay legislation to prohibit wage discrimination on the basis of sex, race, or national origin
- Expanding the coverage of national labor laws to include small firms and to allow part-time and temporary workers to be represented by collective bargaining agreements
- Strengthening employment legislation to protect women against all forms of sexual harassment; in the United States this suggests amending the Civil Rights Act of 1991 to apply to employers with fewer than 15 employees and to remove the limits on financial awards to people who are victims of sexual harassment (note that men must also be protected against sexual

harassment since about 16% of claims are filed by men, most of whom are harassed by other men (EEOC, 2002))

- Increasing federal agency monitoring and enforcement of employment discrimination laws
- Having labor unions participate in government and employer equal opportunity negotiations that influence the labor unions
- Adopting a national skill-based industry certification standard to allow for a common understanding of the qualifications that workers need to be upwardly mobile (irrespective of race, sex, or other characteristics)
- Providing better paid leave for employees with family responsibilities
- Providing childcare programs, especially for low-income women
- Opposing arbitrary limits to the length of time low-income women can stay on federal assistance programs
- Expanding federal resources for education and training programs that benefit women, minorities, and low-income workers to help them obtain the education and training that provide advancement opportunities

Recommendations for Organizations

Organizations must have a zero-tolerance policy for sex discrimination, and they must be especially mindful of sexual harassment. Hostile work environment and quid pro quo acts of sexual harassment make it untenable for women to perform at their full potential. Moreover, if the organization is seen as one that tolerates harassment or creates a toxic work environment, many women will leave the employment situation, which decreases their organizational tenure and work experience. Providing a professional work environment free from sex discrimination and harassment is essential for women to achieve parity with men at work. According to the EEOC, 74.4% of gender discrimination cases filed in 2014 were filed by women, and the most frequent charges were for discharge, harassment, and sexual harassment (EEOC, 2016).

Organizations should also consider qualified women for all positions, including senior management and executive positions when they become available. Managers should be aware of the "think manager think male" bias that still exists (Koenig, Eagly, Mitchell, & Ristikari, 2011) as well as subconscious biases that lead people to associate men with careers and leadership more so than women. To remedy such biases, companies should consciously ask themselves whether there are qualified women who have been overlooked in the selection process for a desirable job or promotion every time they fill a position.

Companies can also facilitate success for women through mentoring programs that provide senior-level mentors who can give women valuable career advice and potentially advocate for them when there is an opportunity for a promotion. Companies and individuals can also encourage women to follow their passions and enter careers they are interested in as opposed to careers that are predominantly female and considered good/safe careers for women. Predominantly female occupations (i.e., pink-collar) tend to be associated with lower wages, and when women self-select into these careers or are encouraged into these careers by others, that contributes to lower average pay among women. If women truly have a passion to be in pink-collar jobs, that is obviously their prerogative, but all careers should be open for women who want to experience them. Both organizations and individuals should be supportive of such career choices even if women are entering traditionally male fields. A good example of an organization helping young women make inroads into computer programming (a predominantly male STEM—Science, Technology, Engineering, and Math—field) is called Girls Who Code (https://girlswhocode.com/about-us). This program invites young women to visit high-tech organizations such as Twitter and other companies to learn about computer programming and gain hands-on experience at an early age. These types of experiences could prove to be invaluable for girls to make inroads into careers where they are underrepresented.

Finally, in order to support women's careers it is also helpful for organizations to provide reasonable maternity and paternity benefits. Paternity benefits allow women to stay more engaged in their work and return to work more promptly after the birth of a child. These benefits also allow men to become more engaged with their children and develop a bond with their children early on. In the United States, the Equal Employment Opportunity Commission (EEOC, 2015d) provided guidance that under the Pregnancy Discrimination Act of 1978 companies are obligated to treat men and women the same with regard to parental leave policies. Companies are beginning to offer more generous leave policies for both men and women, which helps parents remain employed while striving for work-life balance. In 2016, Twitter announced that it would provide 20 weeks of fully paid time off to any employee who became a parent. This includes maternity leave and paternity leave. Further, more organizations including Facebook and others are adopting similar policies (Lev-Ram, 2016).

Closing Case

High-Profile Sex Discrimination Case in Silicon Valley

Ellen Pao, a Princeton graduate with business and law degrees from Harvard, formally charged the Silicon Valley venture capital firm Kleiner Perkins on the grounds of gender discrimination. Pao, who claims she was sexually harassed after she ended a relationship with a coworker, argued that the firm created conditions where females were forced not to complain (Dillion, 2015; Streitfeld, 2015). According to Pao, after the breakup, she was not invited to important reunions, email groups, and company dinners since women "kill the buzz" on those festive occasions (Dillion, 2015).

Pao also asserted that the corporation did not promote her due to her gender. In addition, Pao's performance reviews criticized her for having "sharp elbows." Comments related to Pao's male coworkers were also negative, but those male colleagues were promoted nonetheless. Pao's attorney contended that the firm was discriminating against women, punishing them for being ambitious instead of rightfully promoting them (Lowrey, 2015).

Pao, who was fired in 2012, says that she was terminated due to her discrimination complaints. However, the firm claims that it was due to her poor performance. The firm hired Pao in 2005 as chief of staff for a senior partner (Dillion, 2015). In her lawsuit, Pao asked for unspecified damages. However, a lawyer from the firm stated that Pao requested $16 million for back pay and future wages lost (Dillion, 2015).

Felicia Medina, a managing partner for Sanford Heisler Kimpel who is knowledgeable regarding gender discrimination lawsuits, stated: "I don't think they got away with anything . . . Ellen Pao had her day—many days— in court, and the whole world knows now what goes on in that place. They are going to have to do a lot to mend that reputation. This topic is not going to go away. It's now at the forefront of public discourse" (Cole, 2015).

The jury made its decision in favor of Kleiner Perkins, arguing that there was no gender discrimination against Pao. However, one member of the jury, Marshalette Ramsey, said she believes Pao experienced discrimination at Kleiner Perkins. She explained that male junior partners at the firm "had those same character flaws that Ellen was cited with" but those men were promoted nevertheless (Streitfeld, 2015).

Discussion Questions:

1. Do you feel this case deals with sex discrimination? How likely do you think it is that Pao was a poor performer on the job?
2. What should be done in order to improve conditions for women in the workplace? Please explain.

References

Abramson, J. (1975). *The invincible woman: Discrimination in the academic profession.* London: Jossey-Bass.

Alagna, S., Reddy, D., & Collins, D. (1982). Perceptions of functioning in mixed-sex and male medical training groups. *Journal of Medical Education, 57,* 801–803.

Allen, T. D., & Rush, M. C. (2001). The influence of ratee gender on ratings of organizational citizenship behavior. *Journal of Applied Social Psychology, 31*, 2561–2587.

Allport, G. (1954). *The nature of prejudice*. Boston, MA: Beacon Press.

American Museum of Natural History. (2015). The Harvard Computers. Retrieved from http://www.amnh.org/explore/news-blogs/news-posts/the-harvard-computer

Anker, R. (1998). *Gender and jobs: Sex segregation of occupations in the world*. Geneva: International Labour Organization.

Aries, E. (1987). Gender and communication. In P. Shaver & C. Hendricks (Eds.), *Sex and gender* (pp. 149–176). Newbury Park, CA: Sage.

Arsu, S. (2014, November 24). Turkish president says women shouldn't be considered equals. *New York Times*. Retrieved from http://www.nytimes.com/2014/11/25/world/europe/turkish-president-says-women-shouldnt-be-considered-equals.html?src=me

BBC News. (2014, November 28). Sturgeon out to smash glass ceiling. Retrieved from http://www.bbc.com/news/uk-scotland-scotland-politics-30252007

Bennhold, K. (2014, November 17). Church of England approves plan allowing female bishops. *New York Times*. Retrieved from http://www.nytimes.com/2014/11/18/world/europe/church-of-england-approves-plan-allowing-female-bishops.html?action=click&contentCollection=Europe&region=Footer&module=MoreInSection&pg-type=article

Benokraitis, N. V., & Feagin, J. R. (1995). *Modern sexism: Blatant, subtle, and covert discrimination* (2nd ed.). Englewood Cliffs, NJ: Prentice-Hall.

Berheide, C. W. (1992, Fall). Women still "stuck" in low-level jobs. *Women in Public Service: A Bulletin of the Center for Women in Government, 3*, 1–4.

Bernard, J. (1972). *The sex game*. New York: Atheneum.

Bhappu, A. D., Griffith, T. L., & Northcraft, G. B. (1997). Media effects and communication bias in diverse groups. *Organizational Behavior and Human Decision Processes, 70*, 199–205.

Bittman, M., England, P., Sayer, L., Folbre, N., & Matheson, G. (2003). When does gender trump money? Bargaining and time in household work. *American Journal of Sociology, 109*, 186–214.

Blau, G., Tatum, D. S., Ward-Cook, K., Dobria, L., & McCoy, K. (2005). Testing for time-based correlates of perceived gender discrimination. *Journal of Allied Health, 34*(3), 130–137.

Booth, A. L., Francesconi, M., & Frank, J. (2003). A sticky floors model of promotion, pay, and gender. *European Economic Review, 47*(2), 295–322.

Brass, D. J. (1985). Men's and women's networks: A study of interaction patterns and influence in an organization. *Academy of Management Journal, 28*, 327–343.

Bureau of Labor Statistics. (2013, October). *Highlight of women's earnings in 2012*. Report 1045. Washington, DC: U.S. Bureau of Labor Statistics.

Castle, S. (2014, July 14). Church of England Votes to Accept Women as Bishops. *New York Times*. Retrieved from https://www.nytimes.com/2014/07/15/world/europe/church-of-england-votes-to-allow-women-as-bishops.html

Catalyst. (2014, April 28). *Women in management, global comparison*. New York. Retrieved from http://www.catalyst.org/knowledge/women-management-global-comparison

Catalyst. (2015a). *2014 Catalyst census: Women board directors*. New York. Retrieved from http://catalyst.org/system/files/2014_catalyst_census_women_board_directors_0.pdf

Catalyst. (2015b). *Women CEOs of the S&P 500*. New York. Retrieved from http://catalyst.org/knowledge/women-ceos-sp-500

Clement, D., & Schiereck, J. (1973). Sex composition and group performance in a signal detection task. *Memory and Cognition, 1*, 251–255.

Cleveland, J. N., Stockdale, M., & Murphy, K. R. (2000). *Women and men in organizations: Sex and gender issues at work.* Mahwah, NJ: Lawrence Erlbaum Associates.

Cole, S. (2015, March 27). Jury determines Kleiner Perkins did not discriminate against Ellen Pao. Retrieved from http://m.fastcompany.com/3044395/strong-female-lead/jury-determines-kleiner-perkins-did-not-discriminate-against-ellen-pao?partner=rss&google_e

Cook, A., & Glass, C. (2014). Above the glass ceiling: When are women and racial/ethnic minorities promoted to CEO? *Strategic Management Journal, 35*(7), 1080–1089.

Dasgupta, N., & Asgari, S. (2004). Seeing is believing: Exposure to counterstereotypic women leaders and its effect on the malleability of automatic gender stereotyping. *Journal of Experimental Social Psychology, 40*(5), 642–658.

De Tocqueville, A. (2003). *Democracy in America.* London: Penguin Books.

DeBlaere, C., & Bertsch, K. N. (2013). Perceived sexist events and psychological distress of sexual minority women of color: The moderating role of womanism. *Psychology of Women Quarterly, 37*(2), 167–178. doi:10.1177/0361684312470436.

Devine, D. J., Clayton, L. D., Philips, J. L., Dunford, B. B., & Melner, S. B. (1999). Teams in organizations: Prevalence, characteristics, and effectiveness. *Small Group Research, 30,* 678–711.

Dickie, M. (2014, November 21). Nicola Sturgeon balances genders in Scottish cabinet reshuffle. *Financial Times.* Retrieved from https://www.ft.com/content/aba8f5d4-717f-11e4-818e-00144feabdc0

Dillion, M. (2015, February 23). Trial nears in high-profile Silicon Valley sex bias case. Retrieved from http://www.capitalbay.com/news/728819-trial-nears-in-high-profile-silicon-valley-sex-bias-case.html

Dipboye, R. L. (1985). Some neglected variables in research on unfair discrimination in appraisals. *Academy of Management Review, 10,* 116–127.

Dipboye, R. L., & Colella, A. (2005). *Discrimination at work: The psychological and organizational bases.* Mahwah, NJ: Lawrence Erlbaum Associates.

Downing, N. E., & Roush, K. L. (1985). From passive acceptance to active commitment: A model of feminist identity development for women. *The Counseling Psychologist, 13,* 695–709. doi:10.1177/0011000085134013.

Dubrovsky, V. J., Kiesler, S., & Sethna, B. N. (1991). The equalization phenomenon: Status effects in computer-mediated and face-to-face decision-making groups. *Human-Computer Interaction, 6,* 119–146.

Duncan, L. E. (1999). Motivation for collective action: Group consciousness as a mediator of personality, life experiences, and women's rights activism. *Political Psychology, 20,* 611–635. doi:10.1111/0162-895X.00159

Eagly, A. H., & Johannesen-Schmidt, M. C. (2001). The leadership styles of women and men. *Journal of Social Issues, 57,* 781–797.

Eagly, A. H., & Karau, S. J. (2002). Role congruity theory of prejudice toward female leaders. *Psychological Review, 109*(3), 573.

Eagly, A. H., Makhijani, M. G., & Klonsky, B. G. (1992). Gender and the evaluation of leaders: A meta-analysis. *Psychological Bulletin, 111,* 3–22.

Economic Intelligence Unit. (2012). Democracy index 2012: Democracy is at a standstill. Retrieved from http://www.eiu.com/public/topical_report.aspx?campaignid=DemocracyIndex12

Eichenbaum, L., & Orbach, S. (1987). *Between women: Love, envy and competition in women's friendships.* New York: Viking Penguin.

Ely, R. J. (1994). The effects of organizational demographics and social identity on relationships among professional women. *Administrative Science Quarterly, 39*, 203–238.

Equal Employment Opportunity Commission. (2002, October 25). EEOC sues Kraft foods North America for same-sex harassment of men. Retrieved from http://www.eeoc.gov/eeoc/newsroom/release/archive/10-25-02.html

Equal Employment Opportunity Commission. (2013). EEOC Women's Work Group Report. US Equal Employment Opportunity Commission. Retrieved from https://www.eeoc.gov/federal/reports/women_workgroup_report.cfm

Equal Employment Opportunity Commission. (2015a). Charge statistics FY 1997 through FY 2014. Retrieved from http://www1.eeoc.gov/eeoc/statistics/enforcement/charges.cfm

Equal Employment Opportunity Commission. (2015b). Sex-based charges FY 1997 through FY 2014. Retrieved from http://eeoc.gov/eeoc/statistics/enforcement/sex.cfm

Equal Employment Opportunity Commission. (2015c). Title VII of the Civil Rights Act of 1964. Retrieved from http://www.eeoc.gov/laws/statutes/titlevii.cfm

Equal Employment Opportunity Commission. (2015d, June 25). EEOC issues updated pregnancy discrimination guidance. Retrieved from https://www.eeoc.gov/eeoc/newsroom/release/6-25-15.cfm

Equal Employment Opportunity Commission. (2016). Women in the American workforce. Retrieved from https://www.eeoc.gov/eeoc/statistics/reports/american_experiences/women.cfm

Ethier, K. A., & Deaux, K. (1994). Negotiating social identity when contexts change. *Journal of Personality and Social Psychology, 67*, 243–251.

Fairhurst, G. T., & Snavely, B. K. (1983). A test of the social isolation of male tokens. *Academy of Management Journal, 26*, 353–361.

Fletcher, J. K., Jordan, J. V., & Miller, J. B. (2000). Women and the workplace: Applications of a psychodynamic theory. *American Journal of Psychoanalysis, 60*, 243–261.

Flood, M. (2006, March 16). Whistle-blower tells jury of "blatant" lies. *Houston Chronicle,* p. A1.

Foley, S., Hang-Yue, N., & Wong, A. (2005). Perceptions of discrimination and justice: Are there gender differences in outcomes? *Group & Organization Management, 30*(4), 421–450.

Foley, S., Kidder, D. L., & Powell, G. N. (2002). The perceived glass ceiling and justice perceptions: An investigation of Hispanic law associates. *Journal of Management, 28*, 471–496.

Foschi, M. (2000). Double standards for competence: Theory and research. *Annual Review of Sociology, 26*, 21–42.

Garth, P. H. (1994). A new knowledge: Feminism from an Afrocentric perspective. *Thresholds in Education, 20*, 8–13.

Geiling, N. (2013, September 18). The Women Who Mapped the Universe And Still Couldn't Get Any Respect. *Smithsonian.* Retrieved from http://www.smithsonianmag.com/history/the-women-who-mapped-the-universe-and-still-couldnt-get-any-respect-9287444/

Gini, A. (2001). *My job myself: Work and the creation of the modern individual.* London: Routledge.

Glick, P., & Fiske, S. T. (1996). The ambivalent sexism inventory: Differentiating hostile and benevolent sexism. *Journal of Personality and Social Psychology, 70*, 491–512.

Goldman, B., Gutek, B., Stein, J. H., & Lewis, K. (2006). Employment discrimination in organizations: Antecedents and consequences. *Journal of Management, 32*, 786–830.

Harlan, S. L., & Berheide, C. W. (1994). *Barriers to work place advancement experienced by women in low-paying occupations.* Washington, DC: U.S. Glass Ceiling Commission.

Harrison, D. A., Price, K. H., & Bell, M. P. (1998). Beyond relational demography: Time and the effects of surface- and deep-level diversity on group cohesion. *Academy of Management Journal, 41*, 96–107.

Hearn, J., & Collinson, D. (2006). Men, masculinities and workplace diversity/diversion: Power, intersections and contradictions. In A. M. Konrad, P. Prasad, & J. K. Pringle (Eds.), *Handbook of workplace diversity* (pp. 299–322). Thousand Oaks, CA: Sage.

Heilman, M. E. (1983). Sex bias in work settings: The lack of fit model. *Research in Organizational Behavior, 5*, 269–298.

Heilman, M. E. (1995). Sex stereotypes and their effects in the workplace: What we know and what we don't know. *Journal of Social Behavior and Personality, 10*, 3–26.

Heilman, M. E. (2001). Description and prescription: How gender stereotypes prevent women's ascent up the organizational ladder. *Journal of Social Issues, 57*, 657–674.

Heilman, M. E., Block, C. J., & Lucas, J. A. (1992). Presumed incompetent? Stigmatization and affirmative action efforts. *Journal of Applied Psychology, 77*(4), 536.

Heilman, M. E., Block, C. J., & Stathatos, P. (1997). The affirmative action stigma of incompetence: Effects of performance information ambiguity. *Academy of Management Journal, 40*(3), 603–625.

Heilman, M. E., & Chen, J. J. (2005). Same behavior, different consequences: Reactions to men's and women's altruistic citizenship behavior. *Journal of Applied Psychology, 90*(3), 431.

Heilman, M. E., & Eagly, A. H. (2008). Gender stereotypes are alive, well, and busy producing workplace discrimination. *Industrial and Organizational Psychology, 1*, 393–398.

Heilman, M. E., & Okimoto, T. G. (2007). Why are women penalized for success at male tasks? The implied communality deficit. *Journal of Applied Psychology, 92*, 81–92.

Heilman, M. E., Wallen, A. S., Fuchs, D., & Tamkins, M. M. (2004). Penalties for success: Reactions to women who succeed at male gender-typed tasks. *Journal of Applied Psychology, 89*, 416–427.

Hilpert, F., Kramer, C., & Clark, R. (1975). Participants' perceptions of self and partner in mixed sex dyads. *Central States Speech Journal, 26*, 52–56.

Hochschild, A. (1989). *The second shift: Working parents and the revolution at home.* New York: Viking Penguin.

Hochschild, A., & Machung, A. (2012). *The second shift: Working families and the revolution at home.* New York: Penguin Books.

Hofstede, G. (2001). *Culture's consequences: Comparing values, behaviors, institutions, and organizations across nations* (2nd ed.). Thousand Oaks, CA: Sage.

Holland, K. J., & Cortina, L. M. (2013). When sexism and feminism collide: The sexual harassment of feminist working women. *Psychology of Women Quarterly, 37*(2), 192–208. doi:10.1177/0361684313482873.

House, R. J., Hanges, P. J., Javidan, M., Dorfman, P. W., & Gupta, V. (2004). *Culture, leadership, and organizations: The GLOBE study of 62 societies.* Thousand Oaks, CA: Sage.

Hultin, M. (2003). Some take the glass escalator, some hit the glass ceiling? Career consequences of occupational sex segregation. *Work and Occupations, 30*, 30–61.

Ibarra, H. (1992). Homophily and differential returns: Sex differences in network structure and access in an advertising firm. *Administrative Science Quarterly, 37*, 422–447.

Jeanquart, S. (1991). *Felt conflict of subordinates in vertical dyadic relationships when supervisors and subordinates vary in gender or race* (Doctoral dissertation). Retrieved from Proquest Dissertations and Theses database. (UMI No. 9219744).

Kanter, R. M. (1977). *Men and women of the corporation.* New York: Basic Books.

Kemper, S. (1984). When to speak like a lady. *Sex Roles, 10*, 435–443.

Kimmel, M. S. (2000). *The gendered society.* New York: Oxford University Press.

Koenig, A. M., Eagly, A. H., Mitchell, A. A., & Ristikari, T. (2011). Are leader stereotypes masculine? A meta-analysis of three research paradigms. *Psychological Bulletin, 137,* 616–642.

Konrad, A. M., Winter, S., & Gutek, B. A. (1992). Diversity in work group sex composition: Implications for majority and minority members. In P. Tolbert & S. B. Bacharach (Eds.), *Research in the sociology of organizations* (Vol. 10, pp. 115–140). Greenwich, CT: JAI Press.

Kulik, L., & Rayyan, F. (2003). Wage-earning patterns, perceived division of domestic labor, and social support: A comparative analysis of educated Jewish and Arab-Muslim Israelis. *Sex Roles, 48,* 53–66.

Lakoff, R. (1975). *Language and woman's place.* New York: Harper and Row.

Landrine, H., & Klonoff, E. A. A. (1997). *Discrimination against women: Prevalence, consequences, remedies.* Thousand Oaks, CA: Sage.

Lev-Ram, M. (2016, April 5). Exclusive: Twitter to give all new parents 20 weeks of paid leave. *Fortune.* Retrieved from http://fortune.com/2016/04/05/twitter-20-weeks-parental-leave/

Lowrey, A. (2015, March 30). Ellen Pao and the sexism you can't quite prove. Retrieved from http://nymag.com/daily/intelligencer/2015/03/ellen-pao-and-the-sexism-you-cant-quite-prove.html

Mannix, E., & Neale, M. A. (2005). What differences make a difference? *Psychological Science in the Public Interest, 6*(2), 31–55.

Merrill-Sands, D., Holvino, E., & Cumming, J. (2000). *Working with diversity: A focus on global organizations.* Boston, MA: Center for Gender in Organizations.

Morrison, A. M., White, R. P., & Van Velsor, E. (1992). *Breaking the glass ceiling: Can women reach the top of America's largest corporations?* Reading, MA: Addison-Wesley Publishing Co.

Mullen, B. (1983). Operationalizing the effect of the group on the individual: A self-attention perspective. *Journal of Experimental Social Psychology, 19,* 295–322.

Myaskovsky, L., Unikel, E., & Dew, M. A. (2005). Effects of gender diversity on performance and interpersonal behavior in small work groups. *Sex Roles, 52,* 645–657.

Nieva, V. F., & Gutek, B. (1981). *Women and work: A psychological perspective.* New York: Praeger.

O'Farrell, B., & Harlan, S. L. (1982). Craft workers and clerks: The effect of male co-worker hostility on women's satisfaction with non-traditional jobs. *Social Problems, 29,* 252–265.

Organ, D. W. (1988). *Organizational citizenship behavior: The good soldier syndrome.* Lexington, MA: Lexington Books.

Pandika, M. (2014, January 3). Harvard's secret "computers." Retrieved from http://www.ozy.com/flashback/harvards-secret-computers/4140.article

Paustain-Underdahl, S. C., Walker, L. S., & Woehr, D. J. (2014). Gender and perceptions of leadership effectiveness: A meta-analysis of contextual moderators. *Journal of Applied Psychology, 99,* 1129–1145.

Pelled, L. H. (1996). Relational demography and perceptions of group conflict and performance: A field investigation. *International Journal of Conflict Resolution, 22,* 54–67.

Raver, J. L., & Nishii, L. H. (2010). Once, twice, or three times as harmful? Ethnic harassment, gender harassment, and generalized workplace harassment. *Journal of Applied Psychology, 95,* 236–254.

Richard, O. C., Roh, H., & Pieper, J. P. (2013). The link between diversity and equality management practice bundles and racial diversity in the managerial ranks: Does firm size matter? *Human Resource Management, 52*(2), 215–242.

Ritter, B. A., & Yoder, J. D. (2004). Gender differences in leader emergence persist even for dominant women: An updated confirmation of role congruity theory. *Psychology of Women Quarterly, 28,* 187–193.

Rollins, J. (1985). *Between women.* Philadelphia, PA: Temple University Press.

Rospenda, K. M., Richman, J. A., & Shannon, C. A. (2009). Prevalence and mental health correlates of harassment and discrimination in the workplace: Results from a national study. *Journal of Interpersonal Violence, 24,* 819–843.

Ryan, M. K., Haslam, S. A., Hersby, M., & Bongiorno, R. (2007). Think crisis-think female: Glass cliffs and contextual variation in the think-manager-think male stereotype. *Journal of Applied Psychology, 96*(3), 470–484.

Sackett, P. R., DuBois, C. L., & Noe, A. W. (1991). Tokenism in performance evaluation: The effects of work group representation on male-female and white-black differences in performance ratings. *Journal of Applied Psychology, 76,* 263–267.

Shrier, D. K., Zucker, A. N., Mercurio, A. E., Landry, L. J., Rich, M., & Shrier, L. A. (2007). Generation to generation: Discrimination and harassment experiences of physician mothers and their physician daughters. *Journal of Women's Health, 16*(6), 883–894.

Sidanius, J., & Pratto, F. (1999). *Social dominance: An intergroup theory of social hierarchy and oppression.* New York: Cambridge University Press.

Sinclair, L., & Kunda, Z. (2000). Motivated stereotyping of women: She's fine if she praised me but incompetent if she criticized me. *Personality and Social Psychology Bulletin, 26,* 1329–1342.

Solorzano, D. G. (1998). Critical race theory, race and gender microaggressions, and the experience of Chicana and Chicano scholars. *International Journal of Qualitative Studies in Education, 11*(1), 121–136.

Staines, G., Travis, C., & Jayerante, T. E. (1973). The queen bee syndrome. *Psychology Today, 7,* 55–60.

Streitfeld, D. (2015, March 27). Ellen Pao Loses Silicon Valley Bias Case Against Kleiner Perkins. *New York Times.* Retrieved from https://www.nytimes.com/2015/03/28/technology/ellen-pao-kleiner-perkins-case-decision.html

Swacker, M. (1975). The sex of the speaker as a sociolinguistic variable. In B. Thorne & N. Henley (Eds.), *Language and sex: Difference and dominance* (pp. 76–83). Rowley, MA: Newbury House.

Tannen, D. (1990). *You just don't understand: Women and men in conversation.* New York: William Morrow.

Tomaskovic-Devey, D., Thomas, M., & Johnson, K. (2005). Race and the accumulation of human capital across the career: A theoretical model and fixed-effects application. *American Journal of Sociology, 111,* 58–89.

Triana, M. (2011). A woman's place and a man's duty: How gender role incongruence in one's family life can result in home-related spillover discrimination at work. *Journal of Business and Psychology, 26,* 71–86.

Walsh, C. (2012, April 26). Hard-earned gains for women at Harvard: Horowitz reveals obstacles, milestones in Radcliffe lecture. *Harvard Gazette.* Retrieved from http://news.harvard.edu/gazette/story/2012/04/hard-earned-gains-for-women-at-harvard/

Williams, C. L. (1992). The glass escalator: Hidden advantages for men in the "female" professions. *Social Problems, 39,* 253–267.

Williams, K. Y., & O'Reilly, C. A., III. (1998). Demography and diversity in organizations: A review of 40 years of research. *Research in Organizational Behavior, 20,* 77–140.

Winkler, A. E. (1998). Earnings of husbands and wives in dual-earner families. *Monthly Labor Review, 121,* 42–48.

Winkler, A. E., McBride, T. D., & Andrews, C. (2005). Wives who outearn their husbands: A transitory or persistent phenomenon for couples? *Demography, 42*, 523–536.

Wood, J. T. (1994). *Gendered lives: Communication, gender and culture*. Belmont, CA: Wadsworth Publishing Company.

World Economic Forum. (2014). *The global gender gap report: 2014*. Retrieved from http://reports.weforum.org/global-gender-gap-report-2014/

six
Sexual Orientation

Opening Case

Employee Lawsuit Over Sexual Orientation Harassment

An Oak Park, Illinois, city worker filed a civil claim against the suburban town saying that he was badgered and dismissed from work due to his sexual orientation (Jaworski, 2010). Michael Aguayo, who began working for the county in 2001 and revealed his sexual orientation to his coworkers in 2007, filed a lawsuit against the town and a few of its employees (Jaworski, 2010).

According to the lawsuit, Aguayo received unfair censure and write-ups. In addition, he was harassed and discharged after coworkers learned of his sexual orientation (Cora, 2010). The suit states that Aguayo was also subjected to insults which created an adverse work environment, causing him to seek medical treatment for psychological and physical illness resulting from the harassment (Jaworski, 2010). For example, some of his coworkers would refer to things that did not work properly in the office as "being gay," and he was told that certain statements he made about his sexual orientation could get him fired. According to the lawsuit, when Aguayo brought these issues to the attention of the village officials, they did not investigate the remarks, and Aguayo was reprimanded and demoted for raising these issues (Huffington Post, 2011).

Tom Barwin, the village manager, does not accept Aguayo's complaint of being fired from work, saying: "It's just false, I am the ultimate authority in termination cases, and I have not signed a termination sheet" (Jaworski, 2010).

Adam Rosen, the communications director of the Service Employees International Union Local 73, said his organization represented Aguayo, who took time off from work after his partner's mother passed away (Jaworski, 2010). According to Rosen, "Aguayo was terminated Feb. 10 and reinstated after union representatives met with the village" (Jaworski, 2010). Aguayo's attorney said that "Aguayo was dismissed over a Family Medical Leave Act dispute and then reinstated" (Jaworski, 2010).

Aguayo is asking for compensation due to damages with a sum exceeding $600,000. In addition, he is asking for medical and court fees remuneration.

Discussion Questions:

1. Do you think that sexual orientation has anything to do with work performance?
2. What action could the supervisors have taken in order to stop the write-ups and verbal abuse which created a hostile environment?
3. Why might there be a discrepancy in the story told by the employee, Aguayo, versus that of the village manager, Barwin?

Learning Objectives

After reading this chapter, you should be able to:

- Define what the acronym LGBTQIA stands for
- Define gender identity and sexual orientation
- Have a rough idea of how much of the U.S. population may be LGBT
- Understand the history of discrimination against the LGBT community
- Be aware of relevant employment legislation and recent lawsuits protecting LGBTQ workers
- Understand the life experiences of LGBT people compared to heterosexual people
- Understand the tensions between some religious beliefs and LGBT rights
- Know about research findings pertaining to LGBT families
- Be aware of recommendations for organizations to be inclusive of the LGBT community

This chapter begins by defining terminology including LGBT and LGBTQIA. We define gender identity and sexual orientation and present figures on what proportion of the U.S. population may be LGBT. The chapter examines the history of discrimination against the LGBT community as well as the relevant legislation protecting LGBT workers. Then, we turn our attention to the life experiences of LGBT people compared to heterosexual people. The chapter also presents findings regarding LGBT families. Finally, the chapter concludes with recommendations for organizations to follow in order to be inclusive of the LGBT community.

What Does the Acronym LGBT Stand For?

LGBT means lesbian, gay, bisexual, and transgender. To be **lesbian** means that you are a woman who is sexually attracted to other women. Likewise, **gay** men are attracted to other men. **Bisexual** people are attracted to individuals of both male and female sexes. **Transgender** people believe they were assigned the incorrect gender at birth. In other words, they were assigned to one gender at birth but identify as being of the other gender. Many transgender people take hormones and undergo sex reassignment surgery to alter their gender, becoming trans men (female-to-male) and trans women (male-to-female) (Marshall & Hernandez, 2013). (See the documentary *Growing Up Trans* by PBS, 2015, for a thorough review.) Other comprehensive and helpful guides and introductions to the transgender community can be found at the National Center for Transgender Equality (NCTE) at http://www.transequality.org/issues/resources/under standing-transgender-people-the-basics.

The terms "male" and "female" are used to describe physical/biological sex (or sex assigned at birth); "man" and "woman" are terms used to describe gender identity (one's true sense of internal self); "masculine" and "feminine" are terms used to describe a person's gender expression (how a person expresses/communicates aspects of gender to the outside world). **Cisgender** refers to people whose gender identity aligns with the gender assigned to them at birth. In other words, "cisgender" is the general term for someone who does not identify as transgender, in the same way that the word "heterosexual" describes someone who is not LGB. For example, a person born male, who also feels as if he is a man, would likely identify as cisgender.

Heterosexuality refers to people whose primary attraction is to individuals of the opposite sex (Mayo, 2007). In other words, they have a heterosexual sexual orientation. The terms "heterosexual" and "homosexual" were introduced in the United States in medical journals in the year 1914 (Eaklor, 2008). The term "homosexual" dates from around the late 1860s when a Hungarian named Karl Maria Kertbeny coined the term in defense of same-sex male love (Eaklor, 2008). The term refers to people who are primarily attracted to those of their same sex. However, it is no longer a preferred term according to the American Psychological Association (APA) because it may perpetuate negative stereotypes due to (a) "its historical associations with pathology," (b) its ambiguous nature, which is often "assumed to refer exclusively to men and thus renders lesbians invisible," and (c) its unclear nature (APA, 2016). Therefore, the preferred terminology is lesbian, gay, bisexual, or transgender when referring to members of the LGBT community. GLAAD, an LGBT media resource, has good tips on terminology use for describing LGBT communities at http://www.glaad.org/reference/lgb.

It is important to note that gender identity and sexual orientation are two separate constructs. **Gender identity** refers to whether a person identifies as being of male or female gender. **Sexual orientation** refers to whom individuals are sexually/romantically attracted, and this could mean they are attracted to males, females, both, or neither. Further, the fact that one may be transgender is indepen-dent from one's sexual orientation. Transgender people may be attracted to males, females, both, or neither, just as cisgender heterosexual people might be.

The acronym LGBT is sometimes written with other letters at the end. It some-times has an *I* at the end to be inclusive of intersex people. According to the Accord Alliance (2015), **intersex** is defined as a condition where a person is born with a sexual anatomy that does not fit the traditional definition of male or female. The ILGA formally defines its name as the International Lesbian, Gay, Bisexual, Trans, and Intersex Association to be inclusive of intersex people. Sometimes there is also a Q in the acronym: LGBTQ. The Q stands for **queer**, which Lugg (2003) explains is meant to encompass people who are gay, lesbian, bisexual, transgen-der, and intersex. Other times there is also an A at the end of the LGBT acronym, which means **asexual**, or people with a sexual orientation characterized by a lack of sexual attraction or desire for a sexual partner (UC Davis, 2015). Therefore, the term LGBTQIA is the most inclusive term and encompasses all groups, whereas the terms LGBT or LGBTQ are often used as umbrella terms used to refer to the community as a whole (UC Davis, 2015). See the LGBTQIA resource center glos-sary at UC Davis for an excellent summary. Other excellent glossaries and sources include the following:

- Human Rights Campaign (HRC) web site (http://www.hrc.org/resources/glossary-of-terms)
- Ally's Guide to Terminology from GLAAD and the Movement Advance-ment Project (http://www.glaad.org/sites/default/files/allys-guide-to-terminology_1.pdf)
- National Gay and Lesbian Journalists Association Stylebook (http://www.nlgja.org/stylebook)
- Fenway Health LGBT Health Education Center (http://www.lgbthealtheducation.org/lgbt-education/lgbt-health-resources)

Global View: Malaysia

In Malaysia, three transgender women have won a court case appealing a law which prohibits Muslim men from wearing women's clothing. Under those laws, people violating the rule could serve three years in jail. The appellants are all Muslims who were assigned a male gender at birth based on their sexual organs but identify as being female. They were arrested four years ago and put in jail because of their appearance. "Appeals court Judge Mohamad Yunus said the 'degrading, oppressive and inhumane' law discriminated against people with gender issues" (*BBC News*, 2014a). Activists in Malaysia called this a major win for the LGBTQ community.

What Percentage of the Population Is LGBT?

We do not have an exact number. In 1948, Kinsey, Pomeroy, and Martin wrote a book called *Sexual Behavior in the Human Male* and estimated that 10% of all men were homosexual. More recently, the Family Research Report estimated that 2% to 3% of men and 2% of women are gay, lesbian, or bisexual (Robison, 2002). On the upper end of the estimates, the Gallup Poll conducted a survey of Americans in 2002 asking them to estimate what percentage of the population they thought was gay. The average estimates were that 21% of men could be gay and 22% of women could be lesbian (Robison, 2002). These estimates of the LGBT community may underestimate the percentage of the population because they focus on sexual identity, and the *T* from LGBT (i.e., transgender) is likely omitted from these estimates. The Williams Institute, a division of the UCLA School of Law which conducts research on LGBT demographics, released updated information in 2016 estimating that there are 1,400,000 transgender adults in the United States, or 0.6% of the adult population (Flores, Herman, Gates, & Brown, 2016).

According to a study by the National Bureau of Economic Research in 2013, approximately 20% of the population in the United States reports being attracted to their own gender. The study was conducted in a way that either assured participants of anonymity or provided a veiled method of collecting responses which concealed individual responses further. The veiled method allowed for more truthful responses, according to the authors of the research. Findings showed that in the veiled condition, self-reports of non-heterosexual identity increased by 65% and reports of same-sex sexual activity increased by 59%. The veiled condition also increased the instances of anti-gay sentiment. Participants were 67% more likely to express disapproval of gay managers at work and 71% more likely to say that it was fine to discriminate against LGBT individuals.

In sum, the LGBT community could encompass from 4% to 20% of the total U.S. population. To put this in perspective, see Figure 6.1. African-Americans currently make up about 13% of the U.S. population, while Hispanics make up about 17% and Asians make up about 5% of the population. This means that there are about as many people in the LGBT community as there are Asians on the low end and almost as many as Hispanics and Asians combined on the high end of the estimates (U.S. Census Bureau, 2015). Members of the LGBT community are part of every racial group, so they may belong to multiple minority groups. It is important to clarify that it does not matter how large a group is if they are oppressed. If a group experiences oppression, society should take note and aim to rectify the situation whether the group is large or small. The purpose of these comparative statistics is to point out that the LGBT community also happens to be a sizable minority group in the United States.

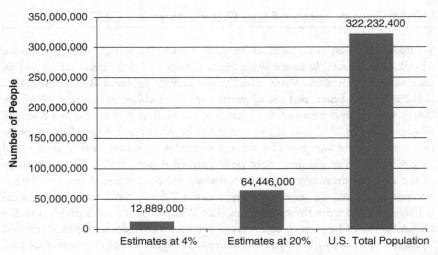

U.S. Percentage of LGBT Individuals Compared to Total U.S. Population

FIGURE 6.1. United States LGBT Population Estimates

Source: U.S. Census Bureau (2015).

LGBT Community Historical Background

There have always been people in the LGBT community. The fact that we are not
sure how many of them there are is telling because the topic of sexual identity
is personal and discussions about being non-heterosexual have been somewhat
taboo in the past (and also in the present in many parts of the world). In addition,
some people in the LGBT community conceal their sexual identity, or remain **in
the closet**, as it is sometimes referred to, in order to avoid the stigma and discrimination that can come with identifying themselves as members of the LGBT
community. Kenneth Roth, executive director of the Human Rights Watch, writes
that almost "2.8 billion people are living in countries where identifying as gay
could lead to imprisonment, corporal punishment or even death" (Roth, 2015).
As a result, many individuals **pass**, meaning they conceal their identity and let
others think they belong to a group when they in fact do not. Passing can apply
to different groups of people. For example, gay or lesbian people may let others
believe they are heterosexual, or fair-skinned African-Americans or Latinos(as)
may let others believe they are White. The choice of whether to reveal their sexual
identity or to pass is a daily one for members of the LGBT community. For example, a gay man may simply not have the time or energy to correct others whenever
people presume he is heterosexual (e.g., ask him about his wife). LGBT individuals
may also decide to avoid challenges that may arise from revealing one's sexual
identity in certain company where it may not be safe to do so if that information
may be used against them. For a source addressing common microaggressions that
LGBTQ people experience regularly and suggestions for how to avoid committing them, see the following article by Nadal (2014) titled "Stop Saying 'That's So

Gay!': 6 Types of Microaggressions That Harm LGBTQ People": https://psychologybenefits.org/2014/02/07/anti-lgbt-microaggressions.

The concept of passing is also related to **privilege**, which refers to certain advantages the majority group experiences in daily life because society makes assumptions that their situation is the norm. For instance, a White heterosexual male would have privilege compared to a White gay male because he can go about his day without correcting inaccurate assumptions others make about him, noticing that others are staring when he is in public with his partner, or mentally debating whether or not it is safe to explain his sexual orientation when others ask him what he did over the weekend or how his family is doing. That mental overhead that minority groups, including members of the LGBT community and other minority groups, experience on a regular basis denotes a lack of privilege.

Attitudes Toward the LGBT Community Past and Present

Discrimination Toward LGBT Groups

An important reason why members of the LGBT community conceal their identity is because of the discrimination they have faced both in the past and in the present. This is true both in the United States and around the world. During the time of American colonization, and prior to the formation of the current United States, sodomy, defined in part as copulating with a member of the same sex, was a crime in most states (although enforcement would wax and wane). The Carolinas were the last states to drop the death penalty for sodomy, in the years after the Civil War (Eaklor, 2008).

During the time of the American Revolution, Thomas Jefferson, the primary author of the Declaration of Independence and someone who would become one of the most famous presidents of the United States, briefly turned his attention to Virginia's sodomy law (Eaklor, 2008). At the time that Jefferson wrote the following statement, the state of Virginia had a law which imposed the death penalty for acts of sodomy. Thomas Jefferson attempted to introduce Bill 64 which would provide a more lenient penalty. His proposed punishment was as follows.

> Whosoever shall be guilty of Rape, Polygamy, or Sodomy with man or woman shall be punished, if a man, by castration, if a woman, by cutting thro' the cartilage of her nose a hole of one half diameter at the least.
> (Eaklor, 2008, p. 31; The Papers of Thomas Jefferson, 1950)

There is also documented evidence of persecution against gays and lesbians by the Nazis during World War II. Male prisoners were sent to Nazi concentration camps because of their homosexuality. They were identified by a pink downward-pointing triangle which they wore to symbolize that they were homosexuals. The Nazis also required sexual offenders, including rapists and pedophiles (Plant, 2011), to wear the same pink triangle. It is estimated that about 100,000 gay men were arrested;

about 50,000 were found guilty of being homosexual and sent to Nazi concentration camps, where between 5,000 and 15,000 of them were killed (Eaklor, 2008; Ziv, 2015).

LGBT Rights Over the Years and Pioneers of the LGBT Rights Movement

Globally, the International Lesbian, Gay, Bisexual, Trans, and Intersex Association (ILGA; http://ilga.org/) reports that same-sex relationships are understood and either tolerated or accepted in many parts of the world. Acceptance appears highest in Europe, Canada, the United States, and Australia, while there is tolerance (meaning same-sex relationships are not widely accepted but are mostly tolerated) in most parts of Central and South America, China, and parts of northern Asia. In Russia, same-sex relationships are somewhat tolerated, but the ILGA classifies that country as having anti-LGBT propaganda and restricting freedom of expression and association (World Economic Forum, 2015). However, same-sex relationships are not well understood, accepted, or tolerated in many parts of the Middle East, Africa, and some parts of South Asia. In parts of the world where the LGBT community is not understood or accepted, gay, lesbian, bisexual, and transgender individuals can face discrimination and hate crimes. According to the World Economic Forum (2015), 2.8 billion people in the world live in a country where being gay is a crime. Being gay is punishable by imprisonment in 78 countries and by the death penalty in five countries located in the Middle East and Africa as well as in parts of Nigeria and Somalia (World Economic Forum, 2015). For a map of the world color-coded to show the level of LGBT rights around the globe, see the report "LGBT: Moving Towards Equality" published by the World Economic Forum in 2015 and found at this link: http://reports.weforum.org/outlook-glob al-agenda-2015/wp-content/blogs.dir/59/mp/files/pages/files/lgbt.pdf

Because of the discrepancy in treatment and acceptance between LGBT people and heterosexual people throughout the world, there has been a push for equal rights for the LGBT community both in the past and in the present. Eaklor (2008) wrote an extensive book called *Queer America* which documents the history of the LGBT community and their fight for equal rights. According to Eaklor (2008), in the late 1800s and early 1900s, a group of physicians who have been referred to as "the sexologists" were busy studying homosexuality and trying to understand whether this condition was something a person was born with or whether it was a choice. It is generally understood today that this is a predisposition people are born with, although there was much debate about this in the past, and some dissent and debate remain today.

The German sexologist Magnus Hirschfeld was an openly homosexual physician and a pioneer of gay rights in the early 1900s (Rudacille, 2005). During 1871, Germany adopted the Prussian legal code (paragraph 175), which stated that homosexual acts between males were "unnatural fornication" and made them criminal offenses (Eaklor, 2008, p. 34). Hirschfeld rejected theories about "mental illness and degeneracy" as the cause of homosexuality and instead proposed the idea of a "Uranian," which means an intermediate condition, or a "third sex," that exists (Eaklor, 2008, p. 34). Hirschfeld founded the Scientific Humanitarian Committee in 1897 and then founded the Institute for Sexual Science in 1919 (Rudacille, 2005). He continued to oppose paragraph 175 of the German law, and while it was successfully revoked in 1929, the repeal apparently never took effect, and paragraph 175 remained in the legal code until 1994 (Eaklor, 2008). Hirschfeld lived until 1935. He witnessed the Nazis rise to power and destroy his work by burning his library (Rudacille, 2005).

Meanwhile, in England, sodomy was considered a capital offense from the 16th century until 1861 and was punishable by life imprisonment. In 1886, a "purity crusade" in England and the United States took place, and sexual acts between men were defined as indecent and criminal activity, irrespective of age or consent (Eaklor, 2008). One of England's most prominent writers, Oscar Wilde, was put on trial for being gay in 1895, found guilty, and sentenced to the maximum penalty, which was two years of hard labor, which he served (Braithwaite, 2016). This trial made popular the phrase "the love that dare not speak its name," which is from a poem written by Wilde's companion, Lord Alfred Douglas (Braithwaite, 2016).

With time, sexologists realized that homosexuality was an inborn condition that was not changing with counseling. Sigmund Freud, one of the most famous psychologists to write about sex and psychology, had doubts about changing homosexuality and whether there was a need to do so. In a letter written by Freud to a mother who sought advice from him because her son was gay, Freud told her there was "nothing to be ashamed of" and that homosexuality could not be classified as an illness (Sleczkowski, 2015). Helene Deutsch, one of Freud's students, tells that she had been treating a lesbian patient and concluded that after successful treatment the woman could deal with many problems in her life, but she was still a lesbian. Deutsch worried about what Freud would say regarding the outcome of her patient's treatment. When the two spoke on the subject, the exchange unfolded as follows. Freud said, "Congratulations on your great success with Miss X." Helene Deutsch replied, "But she's still a Lesbian," to which Freud responded, "What does it matter as long as she's happy?" (Eaklor, 2008, p. 35).

One of the most important moments in LGBT history occurred when Henry Gerber founded the Society for Human Rights in December 1924. This organization is significant because it was the first LGBT rights organization in the United States. Gerber, a German immigrant who had come to the United States in 1913 and served in WWI at a post in Germany, was influenced by the world's first movement on homosexual rights in Germany. The Society for Human Rights was short-lived, lasting only until mid-1925 when it was brought to an end, in part because of a scandal involving its vice president (Eaklor, 2008; Janega, 2013). After the scandal, Gerber moved to New York City and continued to write articles and books advocating for gay and lesbian rights until his death in 1972. The Gerber/Hart Library in Chicago, founded in 1981, is named after him (Eaklor, 2008; Katz, 1992).

As you can see from this history, a lot of stigma regarding LGBTQ people is based in deep histories of discrimination by various institutions against LGBTQ people. For example, the American Psychiatric Association categorized homosexuality as a mental illness until 1973. It was in 1973 that they removed the diagnosis of "homosexuality" from their *Diagnostic and Statistical Manual*'s second edition (Drescher, 2015). The Stonewall Uprising (also referred to as the Stonewall Riots) marked the birth of the modern LGBTQ civil rights movement. On June 28, 1969, police officers raided a popular gay bar in the Greenwich Village section of New York City called the Stonewall Inn. Police raids on gay bars were common during that time, but that night "the street erupted into violent protests and demonstrations that lasted for the next six days" (Corporation for Public Broadcasting, 2016).

Global View: The United Nations

As recently as 2010, the United Nations General Assembly voted to remove the words "sexual orientation" from a resolution calling on its member countries to investigate killings motivated by prejudice and carried out outside the judicial system or on an arbitrary basis. This resolution was passed only after the objectionable words were removed at the request of several countries including: China, Iraq, Iran, Nigeria, South Africa, and Cuba. The United Kingdom and Ireland voted to include the words "sexual orientation" in the resolution, but they were outvoted 79 to 70 by the member countries (Crawley, 2010; OutRight Action International, 2010). The International Gay and Lesbian Human Rights Commission provided the following response to this decision.

"This decision in the General Assembly flies in the face of the overwhelming evidence that people are routinely killed around the world because of their actual or perceived sexual orientation, and renders these killings invisible or unimportant. The Special Rapporteur on Extrajudicial, Summary or Arbitrary Executions has highlighted documented cases of extrajudicial killings on the grounds of sexual orientation including individuals facing the death penalty for consensual same-sex conduct; individuals tortured to death by State actors because of their actual or perceived sexual orientation; paramilitary groups killing individuals because of their actual or perceived sexual orientation as part of 'social cleansing' campaigns; individuals murdered by police officers with impunity because of their actual or perceived sexual orientation; and States failing to investigate hate crimes and killings of persons because of their actual or perceived sexual orientation" (Crawley, 2010).

Discrimination Toward the LGBT Community in Employment

Employment discrimination against members of the LGBT community may derive from the beliefs of the business leaders themselves. However, it may also stem from pressures in the community or from customers who do not approve of the LGBT community. In a qualitative study, a participant living in rural America described the following situation.

I still live in my hometown community and the acceptance level of LBGT has remained the same, in my opinion. Recently, the town is buzzing about the two lesbians that live in the yellow house on the corner. One of the women was hired at the local grocery store, which surprised me, because I didn't think that the local owner would be very accepting, but what I think has happened is he was unaware and now the town is letting him "in" on the situation.

(Marshall & Hernandez, 2013, p. 470)

A research study conducted by Badgett (1995) on earnings differences between gays and lesbians compared to heterosexuals found that gay men earned 11% to 27% less than heterosexual men. However, the study did not find a significant difference between the earnings of lesbian and heterosexual women. The research took into account education, work experience, occupation, geographic area, and marital status of the participants (Badgett, 1995). A different study conducted by Ragins and Cornwell (2001) found that gay and lesbian employees who worked with other gay and lesbian employees had lower earnings than gay and lesbian employees who worked with mostly heterosexual employees or a balance of employees of differing sexual orientations. The authors suggest that either gays and lesbians may be channeled into certain occupations that are deemed appropriate for them or that perhaps they opt to work with similar others in the hopes of finding a supportive work environment (Ragins & Cornwell, 2001).

Relevant Legislation

There is currently no federal law in the United States that explicitly prohibits employment discrimination against LGBT groups. For many years, members of Congress have introduced the Employment Nondiscrimination Act (ENDA), which would prohibit private employers with more than 15 employees from discriminating on the basis of sexual orientation or gender identity, with exemptions provided for religious organizations and some nonprofit groups. However, this legislation has never been passed by the U.S. Congress. Nevertheless, a number of states and cities have passed their own laws over the years prohibiting discrimination on the basis of sexual orientation. According to the American Civil Liberties Union (2015), there are currently 19 out of 50 states in the United States that protect against employment discrimination on the basis of sexual orientation and gender identity. There are also three additional states that cover employment discrimination on the basis of sexual orientation but do not cover gender identity.

Executive Order 11478 (Equal Employment Opportunity in the Federal Government) also prohibits discrimination in federal civilian workplaces on the basis of sexual orientation, but this order does not extend to other employers across the country. This executive order was enacted in 1998, and it was updated by President Barack Obama in 2014. President Obama enacted an executive order to amend Executive Order 11478 as well as **Executive Order 11246 (Equal Employment Opportunity)**, enacted in 1965, which prohibits discrimination among federal contractors with contracts of more than $10,000. The new executive order amends Executive Order 11478 to include both sexual orientation and gender identity instead of only sexual orientation. It also updated Executive Order 11246, which had previously covered sex and national origin, to include sexual orientation and gender identity in addition to the other categories previously covered (race, color, religion, sex, and national origin) (Office of Federal Contract Compliance Programs, 2016; White House, 2014).

An organization called the **Human Rights Campaign (HRC)** works for LGBT rights, maintains extensive information on the current situation for members of the LGBT community, and documents information about various injustices in employment or in society at large faced by members of the LGBT community. Among the data collected by the HRC with respect to LGBT employees, the latest statistics show that among the Fortune 500, the largest companies in the United States, 89% prohibit discrimination on the basis of sexual orientation, 66% prohibit discrimination on the basis of gender identity (compared to only three companies that did so in the year 2000), and 66% provide domestic partner health insurance benefits for their employees (Human Rights Campaign, 2016). The HRC's work with the Corporate Equality Index (http://www.hrc.org/campaigns/corporate-equality-index) is significant because the Index has helped define the categories that measure the LGBT inclusion of a particular company.

Many large corporations and entities also establish LGBT Employee Resource Groups to support LGBT people in their organizations. For example, the American Federation of Labor and Congress of Industrial Organizations (AFL-CIO) has an LGBTQ organization called Pride at Work (http://www.prideatwork.org). There is also an organization for LGBT people in the financial sector called Out on the Street (http://outleadership.com/out-on-the-street), and it is the first global LGBT leadership organization in the financial industry. These are just two examples among many others.

In December of 2012, the Equal Employment Opportunity Commission (EEOC) adopted its current Strategic Enforcement Plan (SEP) to include "... lesbian, gay, bisexual and transgender individuals under Title VII's sex discrimination provisions ..." (EEOC, 2016). The SEP was promptly implemented in September 2013, when the Fifth Circuit Court of Appeals upheld that Chuck Wolfe, supervisor of an all-male construction crew, had harassed one of his subordinates, Kerry Woods, creating a hostile work environment (EEOC v. Boh Bros. Constr., 2013). In the case summary it is written that "The Court ... ruled that the Commission had offered sufficient evidence to sustain the jury's verdict that Wolfe harassed Woods because of sex (here, because Wolfe viewed Woods as "not manly enough"), and that Wolfe's harassment of Woods was sufficiently severe or pervasive to create a hostile environment" (EEOC, 2013). Since then, the EEOC has successfully defended the rights of several LGBT individuals whose civil rights have been violated.

More recently, in 2016, the EEOC made history again by entering into a settlement on one of the first lawsuits it has ever filed on the basis that discrimination based on sexual orientation violates Title VII of the Civil Rights Act of 1964. The wording of Title VII of the Civil Rights Act of 1964 prohibits discrimination on the basis of race, sex, religion, color, and national origin. It does not explicitly include sexual orientation or gender identity, which is why this action by the EEOC is significant and represents a willingness of this major federal agency to consider sexual orientation as part of the groups covered under Title VII. Furthermore, the EEOC was demonstrating consistency in following their 2012 Strategic Enforcement Plan, which, as stated earlier, includes "... lesbian, gay, bisexual and transgender individuals under Title VII's sex discrimination provisions ..." (EEOC, 2016). The 2016 lawsuit involved a lesbian woman, Yolanda Boone, who was working as a forklift operator and faced harassment from her manager at her employer, IFCO Systems. Boone complained about the harassment to her supervisor, but nothing was done. When she complained to the general manager and human resources, she was discharged soon thereafter (Smith, 2016a). The EEOC claimed sex discrimination in early 2016 on the grounds of Boone's sexual orientation. The end result was that the company must pay $182,200 to Boone and $20,000 to the Human Rights Campaign. The company also agreed to hire an expert on sexual orientation, gender identity, and transgender training to develop a module on sexual orientation and gender identity issues in the workplace. The EEOC will then use this module in future settlements (Smith, 2016a).

Global View: Russia

After current Apple CEO Tim Cook announced publicly that he was gay, the Russian government removed a giant iPhone statue displayed in honor of the company's former CEO, Steve Jobs.

"Russian legislation prohibits propaganda of homosexuality and other sexual perversions among minors," ZEFS wrote in a statement published on the web site of Russian radio station Ekho Moskvy. "After Apple CEO Tim Cook publicly called for sodomy, the monument was dismantled pursuant to Russian federal law on the protection of children from information that promotes the denial of traditional family values" (Demirjian, 2014).

Research Findings on the Experiences of LGBT People Compared to Those of Heterosexual People

Research in this area shows differences in experiences between members of the LGBT community and those of the heterosexual community from an early age. A study on victimization over the lifespan comparing lesbian, gay, bisexual, and heterosexual siblings found that sexual orientation was a significant predictor of victimization. Gay, lesbian, and bisexual participants reported more physical and psychological abuse by their caretakers as children, more childhood sexual abuse, more psychological and physical victimization from a partner in adulthood, and more sexual assault experiences in adulthood than did their heterosexual counterparts (Balsam, Rothblum, & Beauchaine, 2005).

In a qualitative study interviewing gay and lesbian participants, researchers concluded that although the LGBT community is becoming more accepted socially, bullying of gays and lesbians is pervasive. The participants in the qualitative interviews described the bullying as something that comes from many different sources including peers, adults, teachers, religious leaders, social support staff, public transit staff, and the police (Mishna, Newman, Daley, & Solomon, 2009). Participants also described harassment from family members who feared and disapproved of the gay people in their lives and would make comments such as, "Oh my god, did you see that gay person? They're going to hell!" (Mishna et al., 2009).

Bullying and violence against LGBT adolescents has produced higher levels of suicide attempts and suicides among this group. In one study, almost 20% of lesbian and gay youths and 22% of bisexual youths revealed attempting suicide at least one time in the previous year, compared with 4% of their heterosexual counterparts (Hatzenbuehler, 2011; Marshall & Hernandez, 2013). Attempted suicide rates are even higher for transgender people. According to a recent study by the American Foundation for Suicide Prevention and the Williams Institute, 41% of transgender people attempt suicide at some point during their lives compared to 4.6% of the general population. The data that these organizations analyzed comes from the National Transgender Discrimination Survey (Ungar, 2015). These suicide attempt rates are largely fueled by bullying, harassment, discrimination, and a general lack of understanding and empathy toward transgender individuals (Ungar, 2015).

The Process of Coming Out of the Closet

Research provides some insight as to the trajectory of LGBT people as they consider coming out, or disclosing their LGBT identity, to others. Some "stages," or hallmarks, of the coming out process include: identity confusion, comparison, identity acceptance, immersion, and identity synthesis (Corrigan & Matthews, 2003). This process primarily addresses the *L*, *G*, and *B* in LGBT because it focuses on revealing one's sexual identity. It does not address the process for the *T* in LGBT because for transgender people the process would involve revealing their true gender identity. During the identity confusion stage, people may begin to question who they are. During the comparison stage they may feel alienated from the rest of the population that is different from them, but they may also learn to tolerate this identity and seek out similar others. During the identity acceptance stage, they would reveal the identity to other trusted persons. During the immersion stage, concern about one's identity may subside and be replaced by a sense of connection and pride to the new identity. This immersion stage may involve joining other groups that are associated with the new identity and becoming active in them. Finally, during the identity synthesis stage the activism that may have been exhibited during the immersion stage subsides and people gradually accept the new identity as only one aspect of their overall identity and self (Corrigan & Matthews, 2003).

According to Corrigan and Matthews (2003), there are both advantages and disadvantages to coming out of the closet. Advantages include psychological well-being, an increase in self-esteem, a decrease in distress, diminished risky behavior, facilitation of interpersonal relationships, and enhanced relatedness with key institutions including their place of employment. Disadvantages include physical harm due to crimes, social avoidance by others, and social disapproval (Corrigan & Matthews, 2003).

The Human Rights Campaign has published a resource called "A Resource Guide to Coming Out" (Human Rights Campaign, 2014). The guide includes information about telling others, as well as a list of resources and a glossary of terms.

Homophobia

Homophobia is defined as "fear, hatred, or intolerance of lesbians and gay men or any behavior that falls outside of traditional gender roles" (Blumenfeld, 1992; Griffin & Harro, 1997, p. 146). This may be related to **heterosexism**, which is defined as attitudes or actions that stigmatize or belittle people who are not heterosexual. **Transphobia** is the fear, hatred, or intolerance of transgender people. On the other end of the continuum, an **ally** is a heterosexual or cisgender person who supports the rights of the LGBT community (Gay, Lesbian, & Straight Education Network, 2011).

In a study conducted about homophobia among a group of people who were preparing to be high school principals in America, the researchers, Marshall and Hernandez (2013), found that the participants in the high school principal preparation program had varied experiences with members of the LGBT community and that the participants' own perceptions about sexual orientation were complicated by their Christian beliefs. Chapter 3 referenced the survey conducted by the Pew Research Center in 2013 on the morality of various issues including homosexuality. In the United States, 37% of those polled indicated that homosexuality is unacceptable while 23% stated that it is acceptable and 35% responded that it is not a moral issue at all (Pew Research Center, 2014). A similar survey requested by the European Commission's Directorate General for Justice and Consumers Office revealed that Europeans' attitudes have become more tolerant of LGBT persons. Of the respondents, 71% agreed that gay, lesbian, and bisexual people should have the same rights as heterosexual people while 61% agreed that same-sex marriages should be allowed throughout Europe (European Commission, 2015)

Global View: The European Union

According to the *BBC News* (2014b), a court in the European Union has blocked a gay asylum test. The court ruled that refugees who seek asylum on the grounds that they are gay should not have to prove it. Homosexual acts are illegal in many African countries, including Uganda. The court case centered around three men, including a Ugandan and another man from a Muslim country, who were denied asylum because a Dutch Court said they had not proved their sexuality. In the past, tests of sexuality have included a "phallometric" test which involves demonstrating an erection (FRA, 2010). The United Nations criticized the Czechoslovakian authorities in 2011 for using such a test, which dates back to communist times (*BBC News*, 2014b).

In the ruling, the European Union court said that the decisions of courts have to be consistent with European Union law and respect people's rights to privacy in their family life (FRA, 2010). The court said that "evidence of homosexual acts submitted from tests or on film infringed human dignity, even if it was proposed by the asylum applicant" (*BBC News*, 2014b).

Religion and Attitudes Toward the LGBT Community

From qualitative interviews with research participants, it is clear that religious beliefs shape attitudes toward the LGBT community. Perhaps the following quotations from the participants say it best.

In one situation, a participant describes the outcome of a Christian background that taught that homosexuality is a sin. "I come from a devout Christian family and I believe being in a homosexual relationship is a sin. But . . . I would not consider myself a 'homophobe'" (Marshall & Hernandez, 2013, p. 469).

However, Christianity also teaches that hate is a sin. Another participant describes being in a church service where the pastor was condemning homosexuality. The participant stood up and left the church "because I felt the sermon was hateful" (Marshall & Hernandez, 2013, p. 469).

Another interviewee described feeling so much tension between religious beliefs and personal beliefs on the matter of LGBT rights that the individual eventually changed churches. "Throughout college as an RA [resident assistant] I became more and more exposed to diversity. Even so, I struggled with sexual orientation because I was leaning on my religious beliefs and prejudice. Since then, I have changed my religious affiliation and political viewpoints regarding same-sex marriage. I have joined an inclusive church" (Marshall & Hernandez, 2013, p. 470). Some churches have embraced the LGBT community and have LGBT leaders. For example, the Anglican Church consecrated its first openly gay bishop, Reverend Canon Gene Robinson, in 2003 (*BBC News*, 2003), and the Episcopal Church consecrated its first openly lesbian bishop, Reverend Mary Glasspool, in 2010 (CNN, 2010). Some of the denominations that are among the more inclusive of the LGBT community include: the United Church of Christ, Episcopalian, Anglican, Lutheran (Evangelical Lutheran Church of America), and Unitarian denominations.

By contrast, in November 2015, the Mormon Church decided that "the children of same-sex parents will be banned from blessings and baptism until they turn 18 and disavow gay marriage under a new Mormon Church policy that deems homosexual parents to be apostates, or people who have renounced their faith" (Muskal, 2015). The new policies are included in "Handbook 1," which is a guide for lay leaders of the Mormon Church, formally known as the Church of Jesus Christ of Latter-day Saints. The information was first posted on Facebook by John Delin, a former member of the Mormon Church, who was excommunicated earlier in 2015 because he was an advocate for same-sex marriage as well as a supporter of women's rights to become priests in the all-male Mormon priesthood (Muskal, 2015).

Elsewhere, there is evidence of confusion and differences of opinion within religious organizations about how to handle LGBT issues within the church. Within the Catholic Church, Pope Francis recently responded to a question about gay priests by saying: "If someone is gay and he searches for the Lord and has good will, who am I to judge?" This is a change from his predecessor, Pope Benedict, who was of the opinion that no one with homosexual tendencies should become a priest, even if he was celibate (Donadio, 2013). "Francis certainly was not advocating homosexual acts among priests or anybody else. It's unlikely that priests will be able to marry or that women will become priests. But experts note the tone does matter in rejuvenating the church . . ." (Donadio, 2013, quoting a video with the *New York Times*' Ian Fisher).

Research About LGBT Families

A research paper published by Biblarz and Savci (2010) provides a comprehensive review of the research findings about LGBT families. Overall, the majority of evidence focuses on families led by lesbian couples, followed by gay couples. There is very little research on bisexual and transgender couples and families.

Findings show that lesbian families have children either because one or both of the partners gave birth to them in a prior heterosexual relationship, through donor insemination, or through adoption. According to the research, children raised by lesbian mothers are similar to children raised by heterosexual parents with respect to psychological well-being, relationships with peers, and social adjustment (Biblarz & Savci, 2010). The research studies have included teacher and parent ratings of behavior in children ages 5 to 12 (Bos & van Balen, 2008; Bos, Gartrell, van Balen, Peyser, & Sandfort, 2008; Gartrell, Deck, Rodas, Peyser, & Banks, 2005; Golombok et al., 2003; MacCallum & Golombok, 2004) and play narratives of 8-year-old children that measured the quality of parent-child relationships, family interactions, and the children's adjustment (Perry et al., 2004). Research has also examined levels of self-esteem, anxiety, depression, and perceptions of social acceptance among children ages 10 to 12 (Bos, van Balen, Sandfort, & van den Boom, 2006; Vanfraussen, Ponjaert-Kristoffersen, & Brewaeys, 2002). The study conducted by MacCallum and Golombok (2004) included assessment of the children's socioemotional development by a child psychiatrist who was unaware which children had lesbian co-mothers versus heterosexual parents. This study found no differences among children across the two types of households.

In a study of gender behavior of children raised by lesbian couples compared to heterosexual couples, there were no significantly different results. Among 4- to 6-year-old children, their preferences for traditionally masculine and feminine activities did not vary depending upon having lesbian or heterosexual parents (Fulcher, Sutfin, & Patterson, 2008). Among 5- to 10-year-old children, perceived acceptance by peers and the quality of the relationships with peers did not vary significantly whether they had lesbian mothers or heterosexual parents (Golombok et al., 2003; MacCallum & Golombok, 2004). No differences were reported in adolescent self-esteem, depression, school grade-point average, delinquent behavior, or drug and alcohol use (Wainright & Patterson, 2006; Wainright, Russell, & Patterson, 2004). Also, no differences were found in the odds of adolescents having sex, the age when they had sex, or the number of sexual partners (Biblarz & Savci, 2010; Davis & Freil, 2001; Wainright et al., 2004).

With respect to gay men being fathers, the research shows that they become parents through surrogacy, adoption, or coparenting arrangements they negotiated with women, mainly lesbians, who wanted male sperm donors and were willing to be a part of the children's lives (Biblarz & Savci, 2010; Stacey, 2006).

Some research points to one aspect that could be more challenging for LGBT couples: raising sons as opposed to daughters. For lesbian couples, it may more difficult to raise a son than a daughter because of the societal expectations around gender roles (Biblarz & Savci, 2010). In a book called "My Two Moms", Zach Wahls describes his experience growing up in a household with lesbian mothers. He describes how many challenges originate from society and gives the example of the most common question he gets asked by other people: Are you gay? He explains that he is not gay, but this is a common misperception among people he encounters because of stereotypes about his family. Wahls concludes that the sexual orientation of his parents has had no effect on his character and that what matters most is growing up in a family where one is loved (Wahls & Littlefield, 2012).

Teaching boys masculine behavior seems to be something all parents are aware of. For example, one might imagine that other types of households (other than traditional heterosexual married couple households) such as single mothers raising male sons might have similar questions about how to teach males sons what constitutes appropriate masculine behavior. Kane (2006) conducted a study on all parents' (LGBT and heterosexual) attitudes about their children's gender nonconformity. They found that while many parents welcomed gender nonconformity in their daughters, they had more complex reactions to gender nonconformity in their sons. All parents, including heterosexual mothers, gay fathers, and lesbian mothers, said their concerns about their sons' feminine behavior stemmed from fears about whether their sons would be socially accepted. For heterosexual male fathers, they linked their concerns to their own sense of personal responsibility and their masculine competence (Biblarz & Savci, 2010).

Very little research has studied the children of gay fathers. In one study by Barrett and Tasker (2001), gay fathers were asked about the attitudes of their children regarding their sexual orientation. The results showed that daughters were more sympathetic and supportive than sons (Barrett & Tasker, 2001). In a study about gay and lesbian adoptive parents, Ryan and Brown (2012) point out that in the United States there are about 115,000 children who are available for adoption through the child welfare system (Child Welfare League of America, 2008). These authors collected survey data from gay and lesbian parents who adopted children. Their overall conclusion is that children "growing up in gay and lesbian households are doing well" (p. 199) and that it would be helpful for adoption practitioners to be aware of the issues facing gay and lesbian parents "such as stigma and secrecy" (p. 198) so they may provide referrals to support groups and resources that can help these parents (Ryan & Brown, 2012).

Recommendations for Organizations

Employment legislation regarding the LGBT community is regularly being shaped and updated as a result of lawsuits and social change. The trend over the years is moving in the direction of employers being required to offer more equality to LGBT employees, as evidenced by the executive order updates by President Obama in 2014, by the EEOC 2012 Strategic Enforcement Plan which protects lesbian, gay, bisexual, and transgender individuals' civil rights under Title VII, and by the results of lawsuits since then ruling in favor of plaintiffs on the grounds of sexual orientation as a form of sex discrimination. Some important ways in which employers can support LGBT employees and avoid lawsuits are by 1) making sexual orientation and gender identity a part of their zero tolerance for discrimination policy, 2) providing access to quality health care including partner/spousal benefits and medication, and 3) providing appropriate health care coverage for transgender employees.

Another issue that organizations should be aware of regards HIV/AIDS medication. **HIV** stands for human immunodeficiency virus. When this virus enters the body, it resides primarily in the white blood cells, which normally protect us from disease. HIV is the virus that causes **AIDS**, which stands for acquired immunodeficiency syndrome. As the HIV virus grows, it damages the immunity cells and weakens the body, leaving the person susceptible to illnesses ranging from pneumonia to cancer. When someone with HIV begins to exhibit these conditions, they are diagnosed with AIDS (amfAR, 2016a). According to amfAR, the Foundation for AIDS Research, there were 36.7 million people worldwide living with AIDS in 2015, and 150,000 of these were children under the age of 15 (amfAR, 2016b). In the United States, over 1.2 million people live with HIV, although the number of new HIV diagnoses has declined by 19% over the past decade. Gay and bisexual men are the most heavily affected by HIV and account for 83% of diagnoses among men and 67% of diagnoses overall (AIDS.gov, 2016). Employers should be aware of some current issues in this area including the cost of HIV medication as well as health care benefits for transgender employees. With regard to HIV medication, the issue involves the price of such medication. Organizations will need to determine how much to subsidize the cost of these medications to make them affordable for anyone living with HIV, regardless of their sexual orientation or gender identity. Providing equal access to health care, including affordable medication for people living with HIV/AIDS, can also help reduce the stigma associated with this disease.

With regard to transgender employees, a current concern is obtaining benefits related to gender reassignment surgery. According to the Human Rights

Campaign (2015), individuals in the United States may secure health insurance coverage for gender reassignment surgery through one of three sources: employer group plans, government-subsidized plans including Medicare and Medicaid, and individual plans purchased through State Insurance Exchanges. As a number of employers have started providing more benefits for transgender employees, the former will have to determine how to best meet the health care needs of the latter. For a list of businesses with transgender-inclusive benefits policies from the Human Rights Campaign, see this link: http://www.hrc.org/resources/corporate-equality-index-list-of-businesses-with-transgender-inclusive-heal.

Another matter which has received media attention recently is access to restrooms for transgender people. Some transgender individuals (or individuals who were thought to be transgender) have faced harassment when using public restrooms. For example, in 2016 the state of North Carolina passed a bill requiring people to use the restroom that corresponds to the gender on their birth certificate rather than their gender identity. The state received backlash to this new rule, both from the public and from employers who favor LGBT rights. According to the Society for Human Resource Management, organizations should allow transgender employees to use the restroom that corresponds to their gender identity. Providing an option to use unisex bathrooms whereby no one can question anyone's ability to use those restrooms can be helpful, but it is important to note that organizations must not require transgender people (or anyone else) to use the unisex restrooms. The Occupational Safety and Health Administration (OSHA, 2016) has published a document called *A Guide to Restroom Access for Transgender Workers*, which requires that all employers provide restroom options that are safe, convenient, and respectful of transgender employees (Smith, 2016b). Also, according to the Society for Human Resource Management, the EEOC determined in 2015 that a government employer had discriminated against a transgender employee in the process of transitioning from male to female when that organization required the employee to use a unisex bathroom because the employee's use of the women's restroom made coworkers uncomfortable (Smith, 2016b).

Organizations should strive to treat all employees with dignity and respect. This includes empathy, understanding, and inclusion regardless of their sexual orientation and gender identity. This also includes empathy, understanding, and inclusion for employees whose religious, personal, or political beliefs may not align with LGBTQ equity. These groups must coexist in the workplace and treat each other with respect. The key question for employers should be based on employees' talent and their ability to contribute to the organization. People from all different groups, irrespective of any demographic characteristic, have talents and skills to contribute to organizations. The largest employment law of the land in the United States is Title VII of the Civil Rights Act, and the spirit of this law indicates that employers should focus on providing equal opportunity to people from all groups and should base all employment decisions on the match between employees' knowledge, skills, abilities, and other characteristics and the job requirements for the task at hand. If employees are able to meet the job requirements, their other characteristics which have nothing to do with those job demands or obligations should be irrelevant to making employment decisions. If employers focus on job-related qualifications, hire qualified employees, and then treat all of those employees equally, with dignity, respect, and equal access to opportunity, this should positively contribute to employee morale and organizational productivity (Cox, 1994).

Closing Case
Gay Marriage in France

When a law allowing gay marriage was implemented in France, a state of agitation developed among some citizens as protesters demonstrated in the streets shortly after President Hollande signed a law legalizing gay marriage in May of 2013 (*BBC News*, 2013). Some individuals sought to "awaken consciences" and stir others against "the erosion of European civilization" (Baruch, 2013). For example, Dominique Venner killed himself at Notre Dame Cathedral. Other groups protesting the law cited a large list of what they considered to be proper natural standards described by various famous intellectuals from Thomas Aquinas to Joseph de Maistre (Baruch, 2013).

Protesters opposing gay marriage include the Catholic Church which argues "the bill will undermine an essential building block of society" (*BBC News*, 2013). According to sociologist Hervieu-Leger who wrote in *Le Monde*, "The rhetoric used by the Church (that same-sex couples equals the end of civilization, that they kick out the foundations of human identity, and that they imperil the nuclear family and blur the difference between the sexes) was exactly the rhetoric used in earlier struggles against women's work or the legalization of divorce by mutual consent" (Baruch, 2013).

Expressing another point of view, Dany Robert Dufour, a libertarian teaching at the University in Paris, wrote in *Le Monde*, "Let homosexuals marry if they so desire. Let them create and subvert roles and signs of masculinity and femininity. . . .[But] homosexuals should realize that they will never be able to claim full equality with heterosexual couples because the capacity to have children is not a natural function they are missing, but a basic impossibility" (Baruch, 2013).

These comments demonstrate the tension that continues to surround gay marriage in France. During the annual meeting of the association of mayors, most of whom are conservative, President Hollande said that mayors can always refer to the "conscience clause" if they do not want to marry gay couples. This was a surprise coming from the president, both because he is expected to uphold the law and because in French law a "conscience clause" does not exist (Baruch, 2013). However, some mayors have requested a conscience clause which would allow them to refuse to marry gay couples based on their personal beliefs (Clavel, 2012).

Discussion Questions:

1. After reading this article, what is your reaction to issues around gay marriage?
2. What do you believe drives most of the apprehension conservative groups have toward gay marriage?
3. How effective are the arguments used for or against gay marriage in the article? In your response consider the opinion expressed by the French instructor at the University of Paris who stated that homosexual couples can never obtain equality with heterosexual couples because they cannot have children together biologically. Also, reflect on the fact that some heterosexual couples are not able to have children.
4. Are gay couples less capable of being good parents?

References

Accord Alliance. (2015). Intersex. Retrieved from http://www.accordalliance.org/?s=intersex

AIDS.gov. (2016). U.S. Statistics. U.S. Department of Health and Human Services. Retrieved from https://www.aids.gov/hiv-aids-basics/hiv-aids-101/statistics/

American Civil Liberties Union. (2015). Non-Discrimination Laws: State by state information—map. Retrieved from https://www.aclu.org/map/non-discrimination-laws-state-state-infor mation-map

American Psychological Association. (2016). Avoiding heterosexual bias in language. Reprinted information from an article in *American Psychologist, 46*, 973–974. Retrieved from http://www.apa.org/pi/lgbt/resources/language.aspx

amfAR. (2016a). Basic facts about HIV/AIDS. The Foundation for AIDS Research. Retrieved from http://www.amfar.org/About-HIV-and-AIDS/Basic-Facts-About-HIV/# What_is_HIV?

amfAR. (2016b). Statistics worldwide. The Foundation for AIDS Research. Retrieved from http://www.amfar.org/worldwide-aids-stats/

Badgett, M. L. (1995). The wage effects of sexual orientation discrimination. *Industrial & Labor Relations Review, 48*(4), 726–739.

Balsam, K. F., Rothblum, E. D., & Beauchaine, T. P. (2005). Victimization over the life span: A comparison of lesbian, gay, bisexual, and heterosexual siblings. *Journal of Consulting and Clinical Psychology, 73*(3), 477.

Barrett, H., & Tasker, F. (2001). Growing up with a gay parent: Views of 101 gay fathers on their sons' and daughters' experiences. *Educational and Child Psychology, 18*, 62–77.

Baruch, M. O. (2013, Fall). Gay marriage and the limits of French liberalism. Retrieved from https://www.dissentmagazine.org/article/gay-marriage-and-the-limits-of-french-liberalism

BBC News. (2003, August 3). Anglican Church approves gay bishop. Retrieved from http://news.bbc.co.uk/onthisday/hi/dates/stories/august/3/newsid_3909000/3909559.stm

BBC News. (2013, May 18). France gay marriage: Hollande signs bill into law. Retrieved from http://www.bbc.com/news/world-europe-22579093

BBC News. (2014a, November 7). Malaysian court overturns cross-dressing ban. Retrieved from http://www.bbc.com/news/world-asia-29947393

BBC News. (2014b, December 6). EU court blocks gay asylum tests. Retrieved from http://www.bbc.com/news/30290532

Biblarz, T. J., & Savci, E. (2010). Lesbian, gay, bisexual, and transgender families. *Journal of Marriage and Family, 72*(3), 480–497.

Blumenfeld, W. J. (Ed.). (1992). *Homophobia: How we all pay the price.* Boston, MA: Beacon Press.

Bos, H. M. W., Gartrell, N. K., van Balen, F., Peyser, H., & Sandfort, T. G. (2008). Children in planned lesbian families: A cross-cultural comparison between the United States and the Netherlands. *American Journal of Orthopsychiatry, 78,* 211–219.

Bos, H. M. W., & van Balen, F. (2008). Children in planned lesbian families: Stigmatisation, psychological adjustment and protective factors. *Culture, Health and Sexuality, 10,* 221–236.

Bos, H. M. W., van Balen, F., Sandfort, T. G. M., & van den Boom, D. C. (2006). Children's psychosocial adjustment and gender development in planned lesbian families. Working paper, Social and Behavioral Sciences Department of Education, University of Amsterdam. *CNN.* (2010, May 15). Episcopal Church consecrates first openly lesbian bishop. Retrieved from http://www.cnn.com/2010/US/05/15/episcopal.lesbian.bishop/

Brathwaite, L. F. (2016, May 25). Today in Gay History: Oscar Wilde Convicted of Gross Indecency. *Out Magazine.* Retrieved from http://www.out.com/today-gay-history/2016/5/25/today-gay-history-oscar-wilde-was-convicted-gross-indecency

Child Welfare League of America. (2008). Standards of excellence for adoption services. Washington, D.C.

Clavel, P. G. (2012, October 12). Gay Marriage In France Will Inspire Mayors To Cite 'Conscience Clause,' Refusing To Perform Weddings. *The Huffington Post.* Retrieved from http://www.huffingtonpost.com/2012/10/12/gay-marriage-french-mayors-conscience-clause_n_1962011.html

Cora, C. (2010, November 16). Update: Suit Alleges Oak Park Employee Fired After Gay Harassment. *Oak Park Patch.* Retrieved from http://patch.com/illinois/oakpark/suit-alleges-oak-park-employee-fired-after-gay-harassment

Corporation for Public Broadcasting. (2016). Stonewall uprising. Retrieved from http://www.pbs.org/wgbh/americanexperience/features/introduction/stonewall-intro/

Corrigan, P., & Matthews, A. (2003). Stigma and disclosure: Implications for coming out of the closet. *Journal of Mental Health, 12*(3), 235–248.

Cox, T. H., Jr. (1994). *Cultural diversity in organizations: Theory, research and practice.* San Francisco, CA: Berrett-Koehler.

Crawley, W. (2010). Does the UN now support the execution of gays? Retrieved from http://www.bbc.co.uk/blogs/ni/2010/11/does_the_un_now_support_the_ex.html

Davis, E. C., & Freil, L. V. (2001). Adolescent sexuality: Disentangling the effects of family structure and family contexts. *Journal of Marriage and Family, 63,* 669–681.

Demirjian, K. (2014, November 3). Russian monument to Steve Jobs taken down after Apple CEO Cook says he is gay. Retrieved from https://www.washingtonpost.com/news/worldviews/wp/2014/11/03/russian-monument-to-steve-jobs-taken-down-after-apple-ceo-cook-says-he-is-gay/

Donadio, R. (2013, July 29). On gay priests, Pope Francis asks, "who am I to judge?" *New York Times.* Retrieved from http://www.nytimes.com/2013/07/30/world/europe/pope-francis-gay-priests.html?_r=0. See also an accompanying video by Reem Makhoul, Alyssa Kim, and Ian Fisher.

Drescher, J. (2015). Out of DSM: Depathologizing homosexuality. *Behavioral Sciences, 5,* 565–575. Retrieved from http://www.ncbi.nlm.nih.gov/pmc/articles/PMC4695779/

Eaklor, V. (2008). *Queer America: A people's GLBT history of the United States.* New York: The New Press.

Equal Employment Opportunity Commission (EEOC) (2013, September 30). Fifth circuit court of appeals reinstates same-sex harassment verdict against Boh Bros. Construction Co. Retrieved from https://www.eeoc.gov/eeoc/newsroom/release/9-30-13b.cfm

Equal Employment Opportunity Commission (EEOC). (2016, July 8). Fact sheet: Recent EEOC litigation regarding title VII & LGBT-related discrimination. Retrieved from https://www.eeoc.gov/eeoc/litigation/selected/lgbt_facts.cfm

European Commission. (2015). Discrimination in the EU in 2015. Special Eurobarometer 437. European Union. Retrieved from http://ec.europa.eu/public_opinion/index_en.htm

Flores, A. R., Herman, J. L., Gates, G. J., & Brown, T. N. (2016). How many adults identify as transgender in the United States. The Williams Institute, University of California School of Law. Retrieved from http://williamsinstitute.law.ucla.edu/research/how-many-adults-identify-as-transgender-in-the-united-states/

FRA. (2010, September 12). The practice of 'phallometric testing' for gay asylum seekers. FRA: European Union Agency for Fundamental Rights. Retrieved from http://fra.europa.eu/en/news/2011/practice-phallometric-testing-gay-asylum-seekers

Fulcher, M., Sutfin, E. L., & Patterson, C. J. (2008). Individual differences in gender development: Associations with parental sexual orientation, attitudes, and division of labor. *Sex Roles, 58*, 330–341.

Gartrell, N., Deck, A., Rodas, C., Peyser, H., & Banks, A. (2005). The national lesbian family study: 4. Interviews with the 10-year-old children. *American Journal of Orthopsychiatry, 75*, 518–524.

Gay Lesbian and Straight Education Network (GLSEN). (2011). *Educator's guide to ally week*. New York: GLSEN. Retrieved from https://www.glsen.org/sites/default/files/Safe%20Space%20Kit.pdf

Golombok, S., Perry, B., Burston, A., Murray, C., Mooney-Somers, J., Stevens, M., & Golding, J. (2003). Children with lesbian parents: A community study. *Developmental Psychology, 39*, 20–33.

Griffin, P., & Harro, B. (1997). Heterosexism curriculum design. In M. Adams, L. A. Bell, & P. Griffin (Eds.), *Teaching for diversity and social justice: A sourcebook* (pp. 141–169). New York: Routledge.

Hatzenbuehler, M. L. (2011). The social environment and suicide attempts in lesbian, gay, and bisexual youth. *Pediatrics, 127*(5), 896–903.

Huffington Post. (2011, May 25). Michael Aguayo sues Oak Park over anti-gay harassment. Retrieved from http://www.huffingtonpost.com/2010/11/16/michael-aguayo-sues-oak-p_n_784460.html

Human Rights Campaign. (2014). A Resource Guide to Coming Out. Retrieved from http://hrc-assets.s3-website-us-east-1.amazonaws.com//files/assets/resources/resource_guide_april_2014.pdf

Human Rights Campaign. (2015). Creating equal access to quality healthcare for transgender patients. Retrieved from http://www.hrc.org/resources/finding-insurance-for-transgender-related-healthcare

Human Rights Campaign. (2016). LGBTQ equality at the Fortune 500. Retrieved from http://www.hrc.org/resources/lgbt-equality-at-the-fortune-500

Janega, J. (2013, October 30). First gay rights group in the US (1924). *Chicago Tribune*. Retrieved from http://www.chicagotribune.com/bluesky/series/chicago-innovations/chi-first-gay-rights-group-us-1924-innovations-bsi-series-story.htm

Jaworski, J. (2010, November 16). Employee sues Oak Park, claims he was harassed over sexual orientation. *Chicago Tribune*. Retrieved from http://articles.chicagotribune.com/2010-11-16/news/ct-met-oak-park-suit-1117-20101116_1_sexual-orientation-victim-of-sexual-harassment-employee

Kane, E. W. (2006). "No way my boys are going to be like that!": Parents' responses to children's gender nonconformity. *Gender and Society, 20,* 149–176.

Katz, J. N. (1992). *Gay American history: Lesbians and gay men in the U.S.A.* New York: Penguin Books.

Kinsey, A. C., Pomeroy, W. B., & Martin, C. E. (1948). *Sexual behavior in the human male.* Philadelphia, PA: Saunders.

Lugg, C. A. (2003). Sissies, faggots, lezzies, and dykes: Gender, sexual orientation, and a new politics of education? *Educational Administration Quarterly, 39*(1), 95–134.

MacCallum, F., & Golombok, S. (2004). Children raised in fatherless families from infancy: A follow-up of children of lesbian and single heterosexual mothers at early adolescence. *Journal of Psychology and Psychiatry, 45,* 1407–1419.

Marshall, J. M., & Hernandez, F. (2013). "I would not consider myself a homophobe" learning and teaching about sexual orientation in a principal preparation program. *Educational Administration Quarterly, 49*(3), 451–488.

Mayo, C. (2007). Queering foundations: Queer and lesbian, gay, bisexual, and transgender educational research. *Review of Research in Education, 31*(1), 78–94.

Mishna, F., Newman, P. A., Daley, A., & Solomon, S. (2009). Bullying of lesbian and gay youth: A qualitative investigation. *British Journal of Social Work, 39*(8), 1598–1614.

Muskal, M. (2015, November 6). New Mormon policy bans acceptance of children of same-sex couples. *Los Angeles Times.* Retrieved from http://www.latimes.com/nation/la-na-mormons-same-sex-marriage-20151106-story.html

Nadal, K. L. (2014). Stop Saying "That's So Gay!": 6 Types of Microaggressions That Harm LGBTQ People. American Psychological Association. Retrieved from https://psychologybenefits.org/2014/02/07/anti-lgbt-microaggressions.

National Bureau of Economic Research. (2013, October 24). What percent of the population is gay? More than you think. Retrieved from http://www.smithsonianmag.com/smart-news/what-percent-of-the-population-is-gay-more-than-you-think-5012467/

Occupational Safety and Health Administration (OSHA) (2016). A guide to restroom access for transgender workers. Department of Labor. Retrieved from https://www.osha.gov/Publications/OSHA3795.pdf

Office of Federal Contract Compliance Programs. (2016). Executive order 11246—Equal Employment Opportunity. Retrieved from https://www.dol.gov/ofccp/regs/compliance/ca_11246.htm

OutRight Action International. (2010, November 17). Governments remove sexual orientation from UN resolution condemning extrajudicial, summary or arbitrary executions. Retrieved from https://www.outrightinternational.org/content/governments-remove-sexual-orientation-un-resolution-condemning-extrajudicial-summary-or

The Papers of Thomas Jefferson. (1950). *A bill for proportioning crime and punishments in cases heretofore capital.* Ed. Julian P. Boyd (Vol. 2, p. 497). Princeton, NJ: Princeton University Press.

PBS. (2015, June 30). Growing up trans. *Frontline.* Retrieved from http://www.pbs.org/wgbh/pages/frontline/growing-up-trans/

Perry, B., Burston, A., Stevens, M., Golding, J., Golombok, S., & Steele, H. (2004). Children's play narratives: What they tell us about lesbian mother families. *American Journal of Orthopsychiatry, 74,* 467–479.

Pew Research Center. (2014, April 15). Global attitudes and trends. Global views on morality. Pew Research Center. Washington, DC. Retrieved from http://www.pewglobal.org/2014/04/15/global-morality/table/homosexuality/

Plant, R. (2011). *The pink triangle: The Nazi war against homosexuals.* London: Palgrave Macmillan.

Ragins, B. R., & Cornwell, J. M. (2001). Pink triangles: Antecedents and consequences of perceived workplace discrimination against gay and lesbian employees. *Journal of Applied Psychology*, *86*(6), 1244.

Robison, J. (2002, October 8). What percentage of the population is gay? Retrieved from http://www.gallup.com/poll/6961/what-percentage-population-gay.aspx

Roth, K. (2015, November 26). *LGBT: Moving towards equality*. World Economic Forum. Retrieved from http://reports.weforum.org/outlook-global-agenda-2015/wp-content/blogs.dir/59/mp/files/pages/files/lgbt.pdf

Rudacille, D. (2005). *The riddle of gender*. New York: Anchor Books.

Ryan, S., & Brown, S. (2012). Gay and Lesbian Adoptive Parents. In D. M. Brodzinsky & A. Pertman (Eds.), *Adoption by Lesbians and Gay Men: A New Dimension in Family Diversity* (pp. 184–203). New York: Oxford University Press.

Sleczkowski, C. (2015, February 18). Unearthed Letter From Freud Reveals His Thoughts On Gay People. *The Huffington Post*. Retrieved from http://www.huffingtonpost.com/2015/02/18/sigmund-freud-gay-cure-letter_n_6706006.html

Smith, A. (2016a, July 11). EEOC enters first settlement in sexual orientation case. Society for Human Resource Management. Retrieved from https://www.shrm.org/ResourcesAndTools/legal-and-compliance/employment-law/Pages/sexual-orientation-training.aspx

Smith, A. (2016b, March 28). Anxiety over transgender women in restrooms persists. North Carolina law was a response to such concerns but, but it exists elsewhere, too. Society for Human Resource Management. Retrieved from https://www.shrm.org/ResourcesAndTools/legal-and-compliance/state-and-local-updates/Pages/Anxiety-Over-Transgender-Women-in-Restrooms-Persists.aspx

Stacey, J. (2006). Gay parenthood and the decline of paternity as we knew it. *Sexualities*, *9*, 27–55.

UC Davis. (2015). Lesbian, gay, bisexual, transgender, queer, intersex, asexual resource center. Retrieved from lgbtqia.ucdavis.edu

Ungar, L. (2015, August 16). Transgender people face alarmingly high risk of suicide. *USA Today*. Retrieved from http://www.usatoday.com/story/news/nation/2015/08/16/transgender-individuals-face-high-rates--suicide-attempts/31626633/

U.S. Census Bureau. (2015). State & county QuickFacts. *USA QuickFacts*. Retrieved from http://quickfacts.census.gov/qfd/states/00000.html

Vanfraussen, K., Ponjaert-Kristoffersen, I., & Brewaeys, A. (2002). What does it mean for youngsters to grow up in a lesbian family created by means of donor insemination? *Journal of Reproductive and Infant Psychology*, *20*, 237–252.

Wahls, Z., & Littlefield, Br. (2012). *My Two Moms*. New York: Gotham Books.

Wainright, J. L., & Patterson, C. J. (2006). Delinquency, victimization, and substance use among adolescents with female same-sex parents. *Journal of Family Psychology*, *20*, 526–530.

Wainright, J. L., Russell, S. T., & Patterson, C. J. (2004). Psychosocial adjustment, school outcomes, and romantic relationships of adolescents with same-sex parents. *Child Development*, *75*, 1886–1898.

White House. (2014, July 1). Executive order—further amendments to executive order 11478, Equal Employment Opportunity in the Federal Government, and executive order 11246, Equal Employment Opportunity. Retrieved from https://www.whitehouse.gov/the-press-office/2014/07/21/executive-order-further-amendments-executive-order-11478-equal-employment

Ziv, S. (2015, May 31). Pink triangles and prison sentences: Nazi persecution of homosexuals. *Newsweek*. Retrieved from http://www.newsweek.com/pink-triangles-prison-sentences-nazi-persecution-homosexuals-337840

seven
Religion

Opening Case

Mayor of a Dallas/Fort Worth City Takes Efforts to Prevent Shariah Law Influence

> I will fight this with every fiber of my being.
> —Beth Van Duyne

Beth Van Duyne, the mayor of Irving, Texas, has pushed back on Muslim imams who wanted to establish what has been referred to as a "Sharia light" (Hohmann, 2015) process in Irving. Shariah refers to Islamic law and following the straight path of God. Van Duyne is making an effort to avoid Islamic law taking a foothold in the United States (Izadi & Bever, 2015). There are two ways of looking at Van Duyne—she could be the mayor who took a firm position against the implementation of Shariah law in the United States or she could be an "Islamophobic bigot" trying to make political gains by playing on fears related to Islamic extremists (Hohmann, 2015).

This matter originated in mosques near Dallas, Texas, where some imams would get together to "mediate disputes," acting as judges to settle disputes among Muslims who, of their own free will, surrendered to the panel's authority. Imams are Muslim religious leaders who lead prayers. The imams said this was not a Shariah court. According to them, they were going to discuss nonbinding decisions such as business issues, divorces, and other family problems similar to other groups which have resolved disputes for people of Christian and Jewish faiths for many years in America (Izadi & Bever, 2015).

Van Duyne worked with state lawmakers to create a bill which would make it illegal for a court in the United States to use a foreign legal system as the basis for its rulings. Neither Islam nor any other religion appeared in the bill. The Irving City Council endorsed the bill (Hohmann, 2015).

Van Duyne's local newspaper referred to her as someone who uses "gifted speaking skills" to "get a crowd on her side" (Selk, 2015). "The dispute has made Van Duyne a hero among a fringe movement that believes Muslims—a tiny fraction of the U.S. population—are plotting to take over American culture and courts" (Selk, 2015). The newspaper also quoted a local imam, Zia Sheikh, who says that the mayor's attitude "fuels anti-Islamic hysteria" and is "very Islamophobic." Van Duyne is well liked by some U.S. conservatives since they believe that state and federal leaders regularly yield to the demands of the Council on American-Islamic Relations (CAIR), a nonprofit advocacy group for Muslim Americans (Hohmann, 2015).

According to Dr. Mark Christian, who was raised in a Muslim family in Egypt but later became a Christian as an adult and now resides in the United States, he is opposed to the panels. Dr. Christian, who also previously lived in Great Britain, said, "I have seen these tribunals in operation in Britain. They supplant the laws of the host nation by forcing Muslims to abandon their inherent rights under our law and submit instead to Shariah, many times to their own detriment." He continued, "I applaud the mayor for her strength of conviction. She isn't denying rights to Muslims; she is preserving them for Muslims" (Hohmann, 2015).

Discussion Questions:

1. Do you think immigrants who move from one country to another should have the freedom to abide by laws from the old country while living in the new country?
2. In the United States, citizens have a right to freedom of religion, and, at the same time, there is a legal separation between religious organizations and the judicial/legal system. In what ways is there a tension between following the established legal system to settle disputes versus allowing for religious freedom, which is also protected under law?
3. In what ways would following Shariah law be positive for Muslims living in the United States? In what ways might it be negative for Muslims living in the U.S.?
4. Many Christians in the United States go to members of the clergy (e.g., a pastor) for advice. In what ways is that similar to or different from Muslims going to their imam for advice in the article described here?

5. How would Muslims going to an imam to resolve a conflict be the same as or different from other U.S. citizens going through a mediation/arbitration process that results in them settling their differences?

Learning Objectives

After reading this chapter, the reader should be able to:

- Define religion
- Have a high-level understanding of major religions in the world
- Understand that religion shapes beliefs and relationships which have evolved over many centuries
- Know which religions tend to be prominent in different countries/regions of the world
- Understand the role of women and men in major religious groups
- Be aware of best-known practices in managing religious diversity from the Equal Employment Opportunity Commission and the Society for Human Resource Management
- Comprehend the importance of being respectful of different religious beliefs

The purpose of this chapter is to define religion, present a brief description of some major religions in the world, and provide recommendations for organizations with employees who hold a diversity of religious beliefs. The chapter primarily focuses on recommendations for U.S. organizations, but many global examples are included.

Religion is defined as a set of beliefs about what people hold sacred. It is a way of seeing, behaving, and experiencing the world (Esposito, Fasching, & Lewis, 2012). According to the Pew Research Center, the world population is approximately 31.5% Christian, 23.2% Muslim, 16.3% Unaffiliated, 15% Hindu, 7.1% Buddhist, 5.9% Folk Religions, 0.8% Other Religions, and 0.2% Jewish (Pew Research Center, 2014). The "Unaffiliated" category refers to atheists, agnostics, and those with no other particular religious beliefs. The "Folk Religions" category refers to folk or traditional religions including African traditional religions, Chinese folk religions, Native American religions, and Australian aboriginal religions. The "Other Religions" category includes Baha'i, Jain, Shinto, Sikh, Taoist, Tenrikyo, Wicca, and Zoroastrian religions (Pew Research Center, 2014).

One important distinction is whether beliefs are **theistic** or not – that is, whether they believe in the existence of a god or multiple gods or whether they do not believe in god. **Atheists** do not believe in god. However, it is possible not to believe in god but still have religious beliefs. For example, atheists may have a deeply held set of beliefs and values about what is right and wrong. Buddhists also do not believe in god, but they are religious in that they revere and follow the teachings of Buddha in their path toward enlightenment. Christians, Muslims, Hindus, and Jews believe in one or more gods. Some religions are monotheistic and others

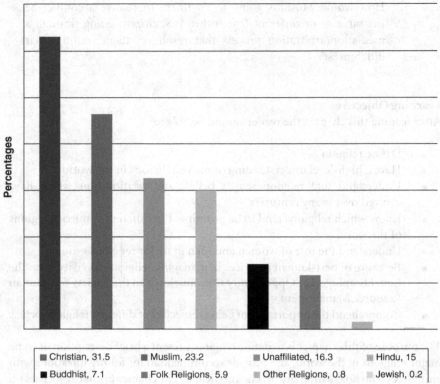

FIGURE 7.1. Religious Beliefs Worldwide

Source: Pew Research Center (2014).

are polytheistic. **Monotheistic** religions are those that believe in a single god, and examples of such religions are the Christian, Muslim, and Jewish faiths. **Polytheistic** religions believe in multiple gods and goddesses. **Henotheistic** refers to religions that believe there is one ultimate god or goddess but that there are also many other deities which can be manifestations of the supreme god (Hinnells, 1995).

In the following pages, I provide a brief overview of some of the major religions referenced earlier. For an exhaustive review of world religions, see Esposito et al. (2012), *World Religions Today*; Earhart (1993), *Religious Traditions of the World*; Fisher (2002), *Living Religions*; Oxtoby (1996), *World Religions*; and Noss (1999), *A History of the World's Religions*.

Christianity

The name "Christianity" refers to walking the path with Christ, the son of God. The vast majority of Christians believe that God exists as three beings, or the **Trinity** (Father, Son, and Holy Spirit), which are manifestations of God's revelation

(Earhart, 1993). The "Son" refers to Jesus Christ, who is the son of God who was born on earth of the Virgin Mary. The Christian holy book is the **Bible**. Christians worship in churches, and their religious leaders are typically referred to as priests and nuns (in the Catholic Church) or pastors (Protestant churches).

The largest denomination within Christianity is the Roman Catholic Church, which is led by the Pope in the Vatican. However, there is much diversity within the Christian faith, including many Protestant denominations. The Protestant denominations of Christianity began in a 16th-century movement to reform Catholicism. Specifically, Martin Luther, a Catholic monk, posted a 95-page thesis on a church door in 1517, marking the beginning of the Protestant Reformation (Esposito et al., 2012). According to the *Christian Post*, the largest Protestant denominations in North America are as follows: the Southern Baptist Convention, the United Methodist Church, the Church of God in Christ, National Baptist Convention, Evangelical Lutheran Church, National Baptist Convention of America, Assemblies of God, Presbyterian Church, African Methodist Episcopal Church, National Missionary Baptist Convention of America, the Lutheran Church-Missouri Synod, the Episcopal Church, Churches of Christ, Pentecostal Assemblies of the World, and the African Methodist Episcopal Zion Church (Rainer, 2013). Other common Christian faiths include Eastern Orthodoxy, Oriental Orthodoxy, Anglicanism, the Church of Jesus Christ of Latter-Day Saints (Mormonism), and Jehovah's Witnesses (Pew Research Center, 2015).

Christians believe that Jesus Christ, the son of God, was born of the Virgin Mary, became man, and spent his brief time on earth preaching, teaching, and healing. During Christ's time on earth, he devoted time to his twelve disciples/apostles preaching and teaching them the will of God. Several of these apostles went on to write parts of the Bible within the New Testament. The Old Testament in the Bible comes from the Hebrew Bible. The New Testament was written after the Old Testament and includes information about the life, works, and teachings of Christ. The Old Testament establishes foundational principles and shows the wrath of God against sin. For example, the story of Noah's Ark appears in Genesis within the Old Testament. God instructs Noah to build an ark and to take his family as well as a male and female of many species of animals so that they may all take shelter within the ark and survive a major flood that God used to wipe wicked people from the earth. The Old Testament (also in Genesis) further describes the destruction of the cities of Sodom and Gomorrah which God had deemed to be excessively sinful. God sent two angels to Sodom to investigate the situation, and these angels were met by a man named Lot. The angels determined that the people of Sodom were wicked and instructed Lot to take his family (who were deemed virtuous enough to be spared) and leave before the city was destroyed. Therefore, the Old Testament has many stories about sin and the wrath of God against sinful people, but it also shows evidence of God's grace and forgiveness toward the righteous. The Old Testament also contains prophecies that a Messiah was yet to come, and Christians believe these prophecies point to the coming of Jesus Christ and were fulfilled through the life and works of Jesus Christ as described in the New Testament. Christ was born of the Virgin Mary and became man to show humanity how to live a spiritual life and fulfill God's will. The teachings of Christ as described in the New Testament are strongly influenced by salvation through faith and God's grace. Christ was compassionate, performed miracles to heal the sick, and showed compassion, teaching/guidance, kindness, and forgiveness toward sinners who repented. Christians believe that the actions and example of Jesus Christ illustrate the path to salvation and eternal life in Heaven.

Christ was crucified in the year 31 CE under the ruler Pontius Pilate. (Christians would refer to the year of Christ's death as 31 AD because they count time using the life of Christ as the reference point, with BC meaning before Christ and AD meaning Anno Domini, or in the year of the Lord.) Christ became a man, suffered, and died for the sins of humanity to help save mankind. He resurrected on the third day after he was buried and ascended into Heaven. The birth and death of Jesus Christ mark the two largest Christian holidays, Christmas, which commemorates the birth of Jesus Christ, and Easter Sunday, which commemorates the resurrection of Jesus Christ three days after he was crucified and died on Good Friday. During Christmas time, Christians decorate a Christmas tree, attend church services, and exchange presents. The giving of gifts at Christmas commemorates the gifts presented to Baby Jesus by the Three Magi (sometimes called the Three Kings or the Three Wise Men). The Bible describes that the Three Magi were guided to Jesus's location by the Star of Bethlehem and that they visited Baby Jesus, his mother Mary, and Mary's husband, Joseph, in a stable where Jesus Christ was born in Bethlehem. The Three Magi paid homage to Jesus and gave him three gifts: gold (something valuable), frankincense (a perfume), and myrrh (an anointing oil). The birth of Christ is observed on December 25, and many Christian denominations also observe the Epiphany on January 6 to commemorate the day the Three Magi visited Jesus in Bethlehem. That is why many churches of these denominations and their members often do not remove their Christmas trees until after January 6.

Furthermore, Christians believe that Jesus Christ will return in the future, on a day known only to the Lord, to judge the living and the dead. Following the teachings of Christ and the Apostles, most Christians believe they are saved by the grace of God through faith, not by their good works alone. Justifying grace is experienced when one is restored to a right relationship with God. This does not happen by one's own effort, but through God's favor revealed in Jesus Christ in his death on the cross. With this understanding of grace, all are predestined to be saved if they repent of their sins and accept by faith the relationship of love that God offers them. Christians also believe that faith must be accompanied by deeds and good works, done in Christ's name, and that they are empowered by Christ. Therefore, Christians strive to follow the teachings of Christ. This includes following the Ten Commandments presented by the Lord to Moses. The Ten Commandments are as follows according to the King James Bible, in the fifth chapter of Deuteronomy from the Old Testament:

- I am the Lord thy God. Thou shalt have no other gods before me.
- Thou shalt not make unto thee any graven image.
- Thou shalt not take the name of the Lord thy God in vain.
- Remember the Sabbath day, to keep it holy.

- Honor thy father and thy mother.
- Thou shalt not kill.
- Thou shalt not commit adultery.
- Thou shalt not steal.
- Thou shalt not bear false witness against thy neighbor.
- Thou shalt not covet thy neighbor's house, thy neighbor's wife, thy neighbor's land or property, or anything belonging to thy neighbor.

Some Christian denominations emphasize the concept of the seven deadly sins, sometimes called capital vices or cardinal sins. The seven deadly sins are pride, greed, lust, envy, gluttony, wrath, and sloth. Although these seven deadly sins are not explicitly listed in the Bible, several of them are mentioned or alluded to in Galatians 5:19–21. Although it is sometimes difficult to do so, Christians strive to avoid these sins and follow the teachings of the Bible and the example of Jesus Christ in order to obtain salvation.

Islam

Muslims follow the Islamic faith. Islam is a way of life which covers physical, intellectual, and spiritual needs. Islam covers divine law, beliefs, and ethics and moral character (The Islamic Supreme Council of America, 2016). Muslims study the holy book called the **Qur'an**. Muslims worship in mosques, and their religious leaders are imams. Mecca is the most holy city in Islam, as it is the birthplace of the Prophet Muhammad. Muslims pray five times a day, and they turn in the direction of Mecca when they do so. The foundations of Islam are a belief in God and in God's messenger, the **Prophet Muhammad**. When Muslims write the name of the Prophet Muhammad they include the statement "peace be upon him" or the letter S, which stands for "peace be upon him," as a sign of respect. Muslims refer to their God as **Allah**, the Arabic word for "The God." While Christians and Jews claim they descend from Abraham and his wife, Sarah, through their son, Isaac, Muslims trace their heritage back to Abraham through Ishmael, his firstborn son with Hagar, Sarah's Egyptian handmaiden (Esposito et al., 2012; Fisher, 2002; Oxtoby, 1996). Muslims follow Shariah law, which means the "path" in Arabic. Shariah law guides all aspects of daily life including daily routines, family and religious obligations, and financial dealings. Shariah law is derived primarily from the Qur'an and the **Sunna**, the sayings, practices, and teachings of the Prophet Muhammad.

There are five pillars of Islam. First, the Declaration of Faith (Shahadah) maintains that a Muslim is a person who bears witness that "there is no God but the God and Muhammad is the messenger of God." The second pillar is prayer (Salat), as Muslims pray throughout the day (dawn, noon, midafternoon, sunset, and evening) to worship God. The third pillar is almsgiving (Zakat), which means that Muslims have a duty to attend to the social welfare of their community. This entails an annual contribution of 2.5% of one's accumulated wealth and assets, not just income. The fourth pillar is the Fast of Ramadan. Muslims fast (Sawm) during the month of Ramadan, which is the ninth month in Islam's lunar calendar. From dawn until dusk, healthy Muslims are expected to abstain from food, drink, and sex. Their focus during this time should be on reflection, discipline, and performing good deeds. The fast ends at the end of each day with a light meal. The fifth pillar of Islam is that of pilgrimage (Hajj) to Mecca. The pilgrimage season comes after Ramadan, and each adult Muslim who is financially and physically able to perform the pilgrimage to Mecca in Saudi Arabia is expected to do so at least once in their lifetime (Earhart, 1993; Esposito et al., 2012; Fisher, 2002).

Jihad is sometimes referred to as a sixth pillar of Islam. Sometimes jihad is mentioned in news from the Middle East where extremist groups have declared a holy war against Islam's enemies with whom they disagree, whether those enemies are Christian or Muslim. However, according to religious scholars, that is not the most proper definition of jihad. The proper definition of **jihad** means an exertion or a struggle as one strives to realize the will of God, lead a life of virtue, and fulfill the mission of Islam (Fisher, 2002; Oxtoby, 1996). "A famous teaching of Muhammad's holds that the 'greater jihad' is the spiritual struggle that each individual has with her or his own faith and need for repentance, whereas jihad as armed conflict is called the 'lesser' exertion" (Earhart, 1993, p. 648). According to Esposito et al. (2012), jihad is popularly used to describe struggles for social or educational reform, such as fighting drugs or working for social justice. While jihad is not supposed to mean warfare, that term has been used as a tactic invoked by extremists such as Osama bin Laden, the terrorist organization Al Qaeda, and other extremist groups to justify their actions.

Muhammad was from central Arabia. He was orphaned at an early age and raised by an uncle. Muhammad had one wife, Khadija, for well over 20 years until her death. He had many other wives after she passed away but only one wife while he was married to her (Esposito et al., 2012; Oxtoby, 1996). Khadija proposed marriage to Muhammad, and they were married when he was about 25; she was several years (about 15 years) older than he was (Earhart, 1993; Fisher, 2002). It is said that Khadija was his closest confidant and strongest supporter. "Muhammad had the greatest affection and respect for Khadija, who did so much to support him during difficult times in his life, especially when he first began receiving his prophetic revelations around 610" CE (Earhart, 1993, p. 624). Muhammad and Khadija had six children, including four daughters as well as two sons who died in their infancy (Esposito et al., 2012; Fisher, 2002; Oxtoby, 1996).

Muhammad was born in and lived in Mecca much of his life, and he preached a message of social justice, condemning economic and social inequalities of the time and denouncing exploitation of poor people, orphans, and widows as well as corrupt business practices including false contracts. He also denounced polytheism. Because Muhammad's message brought problems to light and he disagreed with some powerful people in Mecca about religion, daily life in Mecca became more difficult for him and his followers. After years of rejection and persecution in Mecca, Muhammad and his followers migrated to Yathrib, which they renamed Medina in 622 CE. This emigration from Mecca to Medina is referred to as **hijra**, and it is an important point in Muhammad's life and in the history of Islam. This is why Muslims date their calendar after the hijra, and the year 622 CE became 1 AH (after the hijra) (Esposito et al., 2012).

The time of Muhammad and his first four successors, or caliphs, is seen as "the formative, normative, exemplary period of Muslim faith and history" (Esposito et al., 2012, p. 232). Muhammad died in 632 CE, and ensuing disagreements about succession eventually developed into the Sunni and Shia divide we see today. While some favored succession based on election by prominent members of the Islamic community, others favored succession based on Muhammad's bloodline. The ones favoring election (the Sunni majority) wanted Abu Bakr, who became the first caliph after the Prophet Muhammad, to be the successor. The ones favoring bloodline (the Shia minority) wanted Ali ibn Abi Talib, Muhammad's younger cousin and son-in-law, to be the successor (Council on Foreign Relations, 2016). Ali ibn Abi Talib eventually became the fourth caliph in 656 CE, and a civil war occurred during the time of Caliph Ali. Soon after he came to power, Caliph Ali was challenged by Muhammad's widow, Aisha, the daughter of Caliph Abu Bakr. A group of Caliph Ali's followers known as the Kharajites also broke away from the religion, and some members of this group emerged as revolutionaries who inspired modern radical groups. Another issue was that the governor of Syria, Muawiya, waited until Caliph Ali was assassinated in 661 CE by a member of the Kharajites and then established the Umayyad dynasty from 661–750 CE, which ushered in a rapid spread of Islam that created opposition to what Muslim historians have called impious caliphs and resulted in calls for reform from groups including the Shia and the Kharajites (Earhart, 1993; Esposito et al., 2012; Fisher, 2002; Oxtoby, 1996).

It was around this time that groups claiming to follow the Qur'an, but having a different interpretation of Muhammad's teachings, expressed that they were the instruments of God's justice and used violence, death, guerrilla warfare, and revolution to punish unbelievers. According to some members of the Kharajites, even other Muslims who did not follow the letter of the law as they interpreted it should be fought against and killed for committing treason if they did not repent. These same ideas can be found in the writings and practices of modern-day extremist groups including the Muslim Brotherhood, Al Qaeda, Islamic Jihad (Esposito et al., 2012), and the Islamic State. A second major revolution initiated by opposition to the Umayyad rule was the rebellion of those who followed the fourth caliph, Caliph Ali. In 680 CE Caliph Ali's son, Hussein, led an army against the superior forces of the caliph in Karbala, Iraq. Hussein's forces were defeated, and he was beheaded, and this deepened the divide between Sunnis and Shias because Shias consider Ali to be their first imam and Hussein to be their third imam (Shuster, 2007). These are the origins of the two major branches of Islam we see today, the Sunni majority and the Shia minority. The followers of Caliph Ali became the Shia minority. Sunni Muslims represent 85% of the Islamic community while Shia Muslims represent 15% of the Islamic community (Council on Foreign Relations, 2016; Esposito et al., 2012).

Hinduism

Hinduism is the oldest organized religion in the world (Frost, 1972). It is polytheistic (although it also resembles henotheism) and varies greatly in practices and beliefs (Hinnells, 1995). Most Hindus believe that all of the gods and goddesses are embodiments of the Brahma, the creator god or Ultimate Being. Some Hindus worship many gods and goddesses simultaneously while others recognize all but worship one god or goddess as being higher than the others. Some Hindus believe that god is inherent to the world, a form of monotheism. Finally, another segment of Hinduism (Monism) believes that reality is an un-personified essence of all life. This group argues that gods and goddesses only have a provisional reality and are ultimately unreal.

Hinduism reflects a combination of spiritual traditions originating in South Asia, including India and Nepal. Two Muslim nations, Pakistan and Bangladesh, are also home to Hindu minorities. Indonesia, Sri Lanka, Malaysia, Myanmar, Fiji, and the Caribbean also contain small communities of Hindus. There are Hindu minorities in North America and in Europe as well. Hindus worship in temples, and masters of the Hindu faith are referred to as **gurus**. Hinduism lacks a holy book that is accepted by all followers and has no single institution that exerted control over its development or its fundamental practices. However, the most sacred texts shaping this religion are four Vedas, "Books of Knowledge," some of the oldest texts in human history (3,500 years old). Each Veda is different, and the Vedas were originally transmitted orally among the priestly class. The Rig Veda is the oldest and most important of these and includes a collection of 1,028 hymns of praise and supplication directed at the gods (Earhart, 1993; Esposito et al., 2012; Fisher, 2002; Frost, 1972). Another collection of Hindu texts called the Upanishads followed the Vedas. These contain the most central philosophies and concepts of Hinduism. It is in these texts that concepts central to Hindu philosophy (Brahman, or Ultimate Reality, and Ātman, or Soul) are introduced. The Bhagavad Gita, a 700-verse Hindu scripture which is part of the Hindu epic Mahabharata, is another important holy book in Hinduism (Fisher, 2002; Noss, 1999).

Dominant themes in Hinduism include reincarnation, the law of karma, and the concept of dharma, or duty. **Karma** is the notion of cause and effect, that good deeds eventually yield good consequences while bad deeds yield negative consequences. **Dharma** refers to the idea that one must live in accordance with individual ethics and obligations and one's place in the world and must perform the proper duties of one's particular caste. **Bhakti** means devotion to and love of a divinity. Some traditions of the Hindu faith include yoga, which is meant to train the body for flexibility and mental peace as well as transcendental meditation. **Yoga** refers to various practices through which humans can focus their bodily power to realize their true spiritual essence. **Reincarnation** refers to the concept that a living being can begin a new life in a different body after death.

A group of texts known as the Dharmashastras (Treatises on Dharma) assume that an individual's place in society is defined in terms of karma and that one's birth location is telling of one's karma since karma provides a way of explaining the destiny of a being according to its moral past (Esposito et al., 2012). It is from these texts that the caste system originated. The caste system in India is a social structure whereby there are four or five social groups which have different degrees of social status. Brahmins have the highest social status and are priests (Noss, 1999). Kshatriyas are next, and they are warriors and rulers. Vaishyas are merchants, tradesmen, and farmers, and Shudras are the laboring classes which serve the other classes. There is also another group outside the formal caste system known as Untouchables which is subordinate to all the other groups and fill the least prestigious roles and occupations in society. These Dharmashastras would argue that a high-status birth reflects one's good karma in the past, and this, together with the desire of some groups to maintain a social hierarchy that benefits them, is how the caste system has been justified over time.

Hindus believe in a **Brahman**, which is a universal spirit. Brahma (the creator), Vishnu (the preserver), and Shiva (the destroyer) are part of a Hindu Trinity and are viewed as a form of the Brahman. They also believe in **Ātman**, which is an inner self or soul (Fisher, 2002; Noss, 1999). There are also many deities in Hinduism. Some of the great deities of Hinduism include Vishnu, Shiva, Ganesha, Rama, Krishna, and the Devis. Ganesha (depicted with an elephant head) is the most popular divinity, and many Hindus worship Ganesha to secure his help in removing obstacles from worldly life. Shiva's essence can be found in our energies of the world, and one can find his or her own divine nature by dedicating devotional faith, or bhakti, to Shiva. Hindu legend maintains that Shiva saved the world many times, but Shiva also has a wrathful side which punishes humans. Vishnu devotees maintain that he underlies all reality, as Vishnu is the only one who appears in the Vedas. A theme of Vishnu is that of different incarnations, or avatars, which were sometimes animals and other times local heroes. For example, Rama, one of Vishnu's incarnations, is a hero described in a great Hindu epic called Ramayana, where Rama slays a demon called Ravana and demonstrates the ideals of obedience to one's parents, loyalty to brothers, and the conduct of Hindu kings. Krishna is the most complex of Vishnu's avatars and is revered in many different forms. The Devis refers to several goddesses who are born of the earth and bestow its wealth. For example, rivers are all goddesses according to Hinduism. There are several different goddesses. For instance, Saraswati is the goddess of knowledge, wisdom, and learning. Lakshmi (the wife of Vishnu) is the goddess of wealth, fortune, and prosperity. Parvati (the wife of Shiva) is the goddess of fertility, love, and devotion. The earth goddess is called Amba. Durga is a goddess beyond reach who is pure energy and formless. Kali is associated with empowerment and the destruction of evil forces. (Earhart, 1993; Esposito et al., 2012; Fisher, 2002; Noss, 1999).

Global View: India

Dr. Bhimrao Ramji Ambedkar is a founding father of modern-day India. He is known as the architect of the Indian Constitution and a champion of rights for people in the Untouchable caste. He was born into a family in the Untouchable Dalit caste in India. Ambedkar worked and studied very hard, ultimately receiving a Ph.D. in Economics from Columbia University in the United States. Ambedkar was the first highly educated and politically prominent person from India's Untouchable caste. Ambedkar worked tirelessly to change India's caste system and fight for the rights of the Untouchable Dalit caste. Ambedkar wrote *Annihilation of Caste* in 1936 for a meeting of a community of liberal Hindu caste reformers. The group rescinded their invitation to Ambedkar after seeing a draft of his speech. Thus, he decided to publish the book himself, and it became a classic. He was honored by Columbia University in 1952 with an honorary degree as a social reformer and defender of human rights. For more information about Dr. Ambedkar, please see the following web site at Columbia University: http:// globalcenters.columbia.edu/mumbai/content/bhimrao-ramji-ambedkar

In 1935, Ambedkar, a prominent Indian leader and first law minister at the time, declared that he would not die a Hindu because that religion perpetuates the caste injustices. He was then courted by many religions who wanted him and the Untouchable Dalits to convert to their respective religions. Ambedkar publicly converted to Buddhism in 1956 after writing a series of articles and books explaining that Buddhism was the only way for Untouchables to gain equality (Bellwinkel-Schempp, 2004).

Buddhism

Buddhism is over 2,500 years old and began in India (Frost, 1972), although there are few Buddhists in India today. Buddhists revere the Buddha, which means the enlightened one. They go for refuge in the Buddha, in the teachings, and in the community. Buddhism is the fourth largest world religion, and over 98% of Buddhists live in Asia. The Buddha provided extensive teachings, and although some disagree about which teachings are most important, a prominent collection of Buddha's numerous teachings is called the Tipitaka (Hinnells, 1995). Buddhists today are divided into two groups, those who follow the Mahayana, or Great Vehicle (about 62%), and those who follow the Theravada, or Teachings of the Elders (about 38%). Mahayana Buddhists seek enlightenment through the dodhisattva path, which refers to people who are aspiring to be Buddhas either in the present life or a future life. Theravada Buddhists seek to escape a cycle of suffering and rebirth. Buddhists are the majority of the population in Japan, Thailand, Myanmar, Sri Lanka, Thailand,

Laos, and Cambodia, while they represent a significant minority in Nepal, China, South Korea, Singapore, and a smaller minority in Malaysia, Indonesia, and India (Esposito et al., 2012). Buddhists worship in temples, and their religious leaders are monks and nuns. The famous Dalai Lama is a Tibetan Buddhist monk.

The Buddha lived from 563–483 BCE (Frost, 1972). The foundation of Buddhism is based on **The Three Jewels**, or **The Three Refuges**, which are Buddha (the highest spiritual achievement that exists in humans), Dharma (the teachings of the Buddha which reveal the path to enlightenment), and Sangha (the community of those who have obtained enlightenment; used more broadly it refers to the community of Buddhist monks and nuns). The followers of the practices of the Buddha can be divided into two groups of people, those who are ordained as monks or nuns and lay people, or lay-Buddhists.

Today's Buddhism was influenced by the Sramana movement, an Indian religious movement which developed at a similar time and in parallel with the Vedic movement, when the Vedas were compiled in Sanskrit, the primary sacred language of Hinduism. The Sramana movement refers to people who perform acts of austerity, or are ascetic. Therefore, the **shramanas** of the Sramana movement moved away from Vedic traditions and pursued a path of ascetic acts to achieve liberation and realize the essence of human life and consciousness. Most shramanas believe that life consists of a series of rebirths that are determined by an individual's karma, which accrues from one's deeds, and these rebirths will continue until one reaches a state of moral perfection and burns off one's karma in a state of liberation which is called **nirvana** (Earhart, 1993; Esposito et al., 2012; Fisher, 2002). The Sramana movement gave rise to Buddhism as well as Jainism, another ancient Indian religion that prescribes a path of non-violence toward all living beings.

The Buddha was originally named Siddhartha Gautama and was the son of warrior-caste parents from the Himalayan foothills. Siddhartha means "the one who attains the goal," and he had a life-changing event when he took a trip and saw four passing sights (a sick man, an old man, a dead man, and a shramana) (Fisher, 2002; Noss, 1999). After that, he left his old life and began studying with shramana gurus (Alara Kalama was his first teacher, followed by Uddaka Ramaputta) about meditation and how to achieve a state of meditative consciousness. Gautama discovered what the Buddhists call the Middle Way, which means a path of moderation that moves away from both extreme self-indulgence and extreme asceticism (Noss, 1999). There are stages on the path to enlightenment. For example, Gautama achieved **dhyana**, which refers to a cultivated state of mind that leads to perfect awareness. He also achieved a state referred to as **prajna**, which means wisdom, or insight, that results from moral and mental discipline and leads to nirvana. **Bodhi** means "awakening" and refers to a state of enlightenment where one understands the nature of things. From this point forward, the term "Buddha" was applied to Siddhartha (Earhart, 1993; Esposito et al., 2012). Buddha did not believe in God or the idea of a universal spirit. He only believed in the Three Jewels, or Three Refuges.

Buddhists seek enlightenment by following the teachings of the Buddha. The earliest Buddhist teachings include the Four Noble Truths, which are 1) "All life entails suffering," 2) "The cause of suffering is desire," 3) "Removing desire removes suffering," and 4) "The way for removing desire is to follow the Eightfold Path." The Eightfold Path centers around the practices of reality, meditation, and wisdom and is as follows (Earhart, 1993; Esposito et al., 2012; Fisher, 2002; Noss, 1999).

- First, one must have the Right Views, especially of the Four Noble Truths.
- Second, Right Thought means thoughts are detached from hatred and cruelty.
- Third, Right Speech means avoiding gossip, frivolity, and falsehood.
- Fourth, Right Action means one must not kill, steal, or harm.
- Fifth, Right Livelihood means that one does not live by casting magical spells or performing careers that inflict harm or kill others.
- Sixth, Right Effort means to clear and calm one's mind.
- Seventh, Right Mindfulness means a form of meditation that observes clearly the mind and body and cultivates detachment.
- Eighth, Right Concentration refers to another form of advanced meditation which reaches the mastery of trance states.

Judaism

The Jewish religion is characterized by diversity. Jewish people worship in synagogues, and their religious leaders are called rabbis. A very important holy book in Judaism is the **Torah,** or the Pentateuch. This includes the first five books of the Hebrew Bible: Genesis, Exodus, Leviticus, Numbers, and Deuteronomy. The **Tanakh** is an acronym which refers to the division of the Bible of Judaism into the Torah (teachings), Nevi'im (books of the prophets, for example, Jeremiah, Ezekiel, Amos, Hosea), and Ketuvim (writings, for example, Proverbs, Ecclesiastes, Job) (Earhart, 1993; Esposito et al., 2012; Fisher, 2002; Hinnells, 1995).

There are different groups within the Jewish faith with varying beliefs. Reform Jews believe that the core of Judaism is its ethics and that, while this must not be changed, other beliefs about the supernatural and rituals can be changed as necessary. Conservative Jews want the Jewish rituals to remain unchanged but believe that supernatural beliefs can be changed. Orthodox Jews maintain that neither beliefs nor rituals should be changed, but they allow for some aspects of Jewish life such as work and education to be carried out in the secular world. Ultra-Orthodox Jews want nothing about the Jewish faith to be changed and wish to have a way of life that is separate from the modernizing forms of Judaism as well as the surrounding non-Jewish (gentile) world (Esposito et al., 2012; Fisher, 2002; Noss, 1999).

Jewish history describes migrations. For example, the family of Abraham's great-grandson, Joseph, migrated to Egypt during a famine. Abraham's descendants were enslaved in Egypt, but then God sent Moses to guide them out of slavery. This story, the Exodus, describes how God helped Moses free the tribes of Israel from slavery by sending plagues upon the Egyptians and then parting the

Red Sea to enable the Israelites to leave Egypt and make their way to the Promised Land. Along the way, on Mount Sinai, God gave Moses the Ten Commandments on two stone tablets written by the finger of God (Exodus 31:18).

The tribes of Israel wandered through the desert for 40 years and then reached the Promised Land. King David was the second king of Israel, and it was his army that captured Jebus, a Canaanite city, and renamed it Jerusalem, which means "God's peace." In the year 721 BCE the Assyrians conquered Israel and took its inhabitants into slavery. In the year 586 BCE, the Babylonians conquered the Assyrians and took the inhabitants of the southern kingdom of Judah into exile and slavery. However the Persians then conquered the Babylonians in the year 538 BCE and the Israelites were allowed to return. Alexander the Great conquered this part of the world in the fourth century BCE, and when he died in the year 323 BCE, his empire was split among his generals. Ptolemies ruled Israel between 301 and 198 BCE. Then, Seleucids, who governed this area between 198 and 167 BCE, began requiring the conquered people to adopt Greek beliefs including venerating many gods. Jews who refused to do so were persecuted, and in the middle of the second century BCE, Judas Maccabaeus and his brothers led a revolt which gained the Jewish people some independence, which lasted into the first century CE. In the year 63 BCE, the Jewish people invited the Romans to protect them in an effort to further resist control by the Seleucids (Earhart, 1993; Esposito et al., 2012; Fisher, 2002; Noss, 1999; Oxtoby, 1996).

It was around this time, at the end of the 1st century CE, that the Tanakh came into being. Two active groups within the Jewish faith at that time were the Sadducees and the Pharisees. Rome accepted only the five books of Moses and wanted an adherence to the written Torah. The Sadducees agreed to placate Rome. However, the Pharisees did not agree because they accepted the books of Moses in addition to those of the prophets and other historical writings. Jews who were dispersed, or scattered, across the Roman Empire (parts of Europe and Asia) because of persecution from Rome are referred to as Jews of the Diaspora. Influenced by the Pharisees, the dispersed Jews shaped the development of the modern Tanakh (Earhart, 1993; Esposito et al., 2012; Fisher, 2002; Noss, 1999; Oxtoby, 1996).

The height of **anti-Semitism**, or prejudice, hatred, and discrimination against Jews, came during the Holocaust in World War II. Under Adolf Hitler, Nazi Germany captured, tortured, and killed millions of Jews in a number of concentration camps designed for mass extermination. We do not know the exact number of Jews who were killed, but many estimates say the number is about six million (Fisher, 2002). This is an estimate attributed to a statement by a Gestapo chief, Adolph Eichmann, chief of the Jewish Section of the Gestapo. A colleague of his presented this testimony during the Nuremberg Trials after World War II. Of these, four million Jews were said to have been killed in the many extermination camps such as Auschwitz or Dachau, typically in gas chambers, while two million Jews were killed by execution squads, disease, and other causes (Nizkor Project, 1945).

Emil Fackenheim, a Jew, argues that after Auschwitz, a 614th commandment should be added to the 613 commandments found in the Torah. The commandment should be that Jews are forbidden from giving Adolf Hitler victory. They should survive as Jews so the Jewish people can persist. They should not despair in the God of Israel, otherwise Judaism may perish, thus completing the work of Hitler for him (Fackenheim, 1997).

Religious Diversity Around the World

A report on religious diversity conducted by the Pew Research Center has calculated a Religious Diversity Index (RDI) to assess the diversity of various regions and countries in the world. The RDI is a 10-point scale (with 10 being the most diverse) and is divided into four groupings. Countries with a score of 7.0 or higher (the top 5%) are categorized as having a very high degree of religious diversity. Countries scoring between 5.3 to 6.9 (the next highest 15%) are considered to have a high degree of religious diversity. Countries with scores from 3.1 to 5.2 (the following 20%) are considered to have moderate diversity, while those remaining are considered to have little religious diversity (Pew Research Center, 2014). The breakdown of religious diversity for the various regions in the world is as follows. See Figures 7.2–7.7.

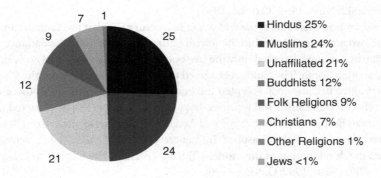

FIGURE 7.2. Religious Diversity in Asia-Pacific

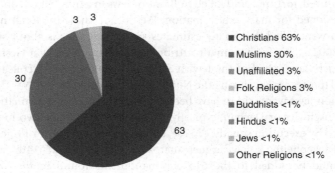

FIGURE 7.3. Religious Diversity in Sub-Saharan Africa

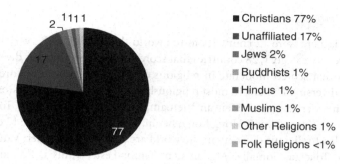

FIGURE 7.4. Religious Diversity in North America

- ■ Christians 77%
- ■ Unaffiliated 17%
- ■ Jews 2%
- ■ Buddhists 1%
- ■ Hindus 1%
- ■ Muslims 1%
- ▦ Other Religions 1%
- ▦ Folk Religions <1%

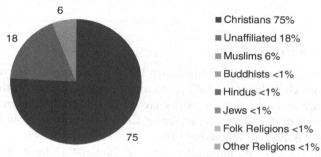

FIGURE 7.5. Religious Diversity in Europe

- ■ Christians 75%
- ■ Unaffiliated 18%
- ▦ Muslims 6%
- ■ Buddhists <1%
- ■ Hindus <1%
- ▦ Jews <1%
- ▦ Folk Religions <1%
- ▦ Other Religions <1%

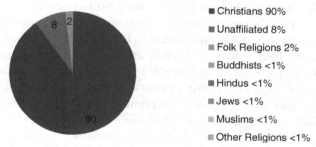

FIGURE 7.6. Religious Diversity in Latin America–Caribbean

- ■ Christians 90%
- ■ Unaffiliated 8%
- ▦ Folk Religions 2%
- ■ Buddhists <1%
- ■ Hindus <1%
- ■ Jews <1%
- ▦ Muslims <1%
- ▦ Other Religions <1%

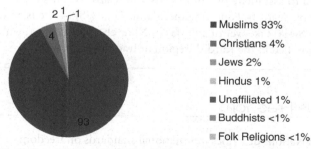

FIGURE 7.7. Religious Diversity in the Middle East–North Africa

- ■ Muslims 93%
- ■ Christians 4%
- ▦ Jews 2%
- ▦ Hindus 1%
- ■ Unaffiliated 1%
- ■ Buddhists <1%
- ▦ Folk Religions <1%

Sources: Pew Research Center (2014). Religious groups are in order from the largest to the smallest by percentage of the population. "Folk Religions" include African traditional religions, Chinese folk religions, Native American religions, and Australian aboriginal religions. The "Other Religions" category includes Baha'is, Jains, Sikhs, Shintoists, Taoists, followers of Tenrikyo, Wiccans, Zoroastrians, and other faiths.

Overall, there were 12 countries in the world that scored in the very high religious diversity category, 28 countries that scored in the high religious diversity category, 58 that scored moderate in religious diversity, and 134 that scored low in religious diversity. The top 12 most religiously diverse countries in the world are as follows, in order: Singapore, Taiwan, Vietnam, Surinam, Guinea-Bissau, Togo, Ivory Coast, South Korea, China, Hong Kong, Benin, and Mozambique. The 12 countries with the least religious diversity in the world are as follows, in order: Vatican City, Morocco, Tokelau, Somalia, Afghanistan, Timor-Leste, Tunisia, Romania, Iran, Western Sahara, Papua New Guinea, and Mauritania (Pew Research Center, 2014).

Global View: Iraq

According to the Pew Research Center, Iraq has a Religious Diversity Index of 0.2, which makes it the 12th least religion-diverse country in the world. There are many religious minority groups in Iraq that represent a small percentage of the population including Christians, Yazidis, Shabak, Sabian Mandaeans, Bahais, Kakais, and Faili Kurds. These groups have lived in Iraq for centuries or even thousands of years (al-Lami, 2014). Most of them live in Nineveh, a province about 250 miles northwest of Baghdad. "Persecuted under the Ottomans, Saddam Hussein's Baathists and nowadays by jihadists, and facing prejudice and intolerance, some of the smaller minority groups, such as the Shabak and Yazidis, have led a life of secrecy" (al-Lami, 2014).

Turkmen, Iraqi citizens of Turkish origin, are the third largest ethnic group in Iraq after Arabs and Kurds, and they are said to number about 3 million of Iraq's 34.7 million citizens according to the Iraqi Ministry of Planning (Bassem, 2016). They are primarily Muslim, with the minority being Catholic. They live mostly along the dividing line between the Arab and Kurdish regions of Iraq in the Nineveh provinces. They often get caught in conflicts between the central government and the Kurdish region and are pressured to assimilate by both Kurds and Arabs. Turkmen have also been attacked by jihadists. Following the Islamic State (ISIS—the Islamic State of Iraq and Syria) takeover of Tal Afar in Nineveh, most of the town's 250,000 population fled to the Kurdish region of Iraq (al-Lami, 2014).

Religious Freedom

The United Nations describes international standards on freedom of religion primarily based on article 18 of the Universal Declaration of Human Rights,[1] article 18 of the International Covenant on Civil and Political Rights, and the Declaration on the Elimination of All Forms of Intolerance and of Discrimination Based on Religion or Belief (United Nations, 2015). Freedom of religion or belief is described as three main rights. First, people should have the freedom to adopt, to change, or to renounce a religion or belief. Second, people should have freedom from coercion, which means that no one should be forced to adopt certain beliefs. Third, a person should have the right to manifest his/her religion or beliefs. This standard advocates for an individual's freedom to worship and the liberty to choose a place of worship, religious symbols, observed holidays, and days of rest. In addition, this third principle of religious freedom, as defined by the United Nations, supports the freedom to appoint clergy, the option to teach and disseminate information through missionary activities, and the rights of parents to morally educate their children. Furthermore, the right to registration (which refers to the right to maintain religious and charitable institutions) and the right to communicate with religious communities at both the national and international levels, establishing religious and charitable institutions which can solicit and receive funding, as well as the right to conscientious objection (which refers to refusing military service that is in conflict with one's religion), are also included in this third standard (United Nations, 2015).

A report published by the Pew Research Center in 2011 revealed that between 2006 and 2009, restrictions on religious beliefs and practices rose in 12% (23 of 198) of the world's countries, decreased in 6% (12) of countries, and stayed the same in 82% (163) of countries. One in eight countries increased religious restrictions or hostility in areas where approximately one-third of the world's population resides. Listed in order, the top countries where government religious restrictions rose are as follows: Egypt, France, Algeria, Uganda, Malaysia, Yemen, Syria, and Somalia. The top countries where government religious restrictions declined are as follows, in order: Greece, Togo, Nicaragua, Republic of Macedonia, Guinea-Bissau, Timor-Leste, Equatorial Guinea, and Nauru (Pew Research Center, 2011).

Women in Religion

The **stained glass ceiling** is a term used to refer to the fact that women are often restricted to junior roles in the clergy compared to their male counterparts (Purvis, 1995; Sullins, 2000). There are a number of examples of religions where women have obtained more opportunities over the years as well as examples where they have not.

For instance, in Christianity men have historically played the greatest roles, as Christianity arose in a patriarchal (male-dominated) environment (as did most other religions). Currently, the Roman Catholic and Orthodox churches do not ordain women, arguing that all of Jesus's apostles were male, which implies a divine intention for an all-male priesthood. Women began to be ordained in some Protestant denominations in the 19th century (Fisher, 2002). Congregationalists were the first to ordain a female in 1853, and they were followed by other religious groups including Universalists as well as Methodists, Presbyterians, Episcopalians, and Lutherans (Esposito et al., 2012). However, some Protestant churches still do not allow women to serve as pastors or to hold office as leaders of the congregation.

Islam also developed in a patriarchal society whereby women and men were expected to perform their roles inside and outside the home respectively. More recently, Muslim women in Egypt, Jordan, Malaysia, and the United States are forming women-led prayer groups. Many Muslim women also wear a headscarf, or hijab. For many, this symbolizes their ability to be both modest and to participate in functions outside of the home, including employment (Esposito et al., 2012; Fisher, 2002).

Similar to Islam and Christianity, Judaism also developed in a patriarchal society where it was long assumed that men were given the primary responsibility for the order of things while women were created to help men. This goes back to the idea that God first created Adam and then he created Eve from one of Adam's ribs as a helper and companion for Adam (Esposito et al., 2012). However, women also have a prominent role in Judaism because matriarchs were important in the Torah. Also, in the Jewish religion, a child is considered Jewish if the mother is Jewish rather than the father. This means that if a Jewish man and a non-Jewish woman marry, the children are not Jewish according to the religion. According to Esposito et al. (2012), the greatest equality for women has been achieved in the secular forms of Judaism, such as Jewish socialism and Zionism, and among the more secular forms of religious Judaism with Reform first, then Conservative, and least among Orthodox Jews. Women began to be ordained as rabbis in the 1970s.

In Hinduism, although men generally have higher social status than women, women's social status and ability to be religious leaders depends on what region they live in and the extent to which goddesses are worshiped in that region. For example, in some parts of India and Asia "lesser good karma is said to be the reason for birth as a female, and the troubles of menstruation and childbirth are accordingly their burden. In the public life, the submission of women to men is clear, a norm underwritten by religious sanction" (Esposito et al., 2012, p. 370; Noss, 1999). However, goddesses are prominent in the Hindu religion, and there are some female Hindu gurus among the male majority. There are matriarchal societies in South India and Northeast India where women are heads of households and inherit wealth.

Hinduism has a strong presence of the divine feminine dating back to ancient times. In fact, the 10th chapter of the Rig Veda refers to the supreme consciousness behind all of the cosmos as being feminine. In a hymn called Devi Sukta the Rig Veda states, "I am the Queen, the gatherer-up of treasures, most thoughtful, first of those who merit worship. Thus Gods have established me in many places with many homes to enter and abide in" (Rig Veda, 10.125.3–10.125.8). Ancient and medieval Hindu texts and epics discuss a woman's position and role in society across a continuum ranging from a self-sufficient, marriage-eschewing powerful goddess, to one who is subordinate and whose identity is defined by men rather than her, and to one who sees herself as a human being and spiritual person while being neither feminine nor masculine. Many (Western) scholars point out that women are accorded a fairly low status in the Hindu texts that deal with law and ethics (the Dharmashastras). However, these texts were not well-known and utilized in many parts of Hindu India. Local custom and practice were more important than the dictates of these legal texts. Therefore, the social status of women and their ability to be leaders in society, including gurus, varies across various groups and parts of India.

Among Buddhists, the Buddha allowed women to join the sangha, the religious order of monks and nuns, but with stricter rules and with nuns being under the authority of monks (Fisher, 2002; Noss, 1999). Buddhists in Indonesia and Tibet are somewhat more restrictive of women than other countries in Asia. In Theravada Buddhism today, full ordination for women has been restored in Sri Lanka. That is not the case in Tibetan Buddhism. Since 2000, over 400 women have moved to Chinese Mahayana monasteries in mainland China and Taiwan to obtain full and official ordination as nuns (Esposito et al., 2012).

Global View: Nigeria

Boko Haram is an Islamist extremist group whose name roughly translates as "Western education is forbidden" (Human Rights Watch, 2014). Boko Haram has carried out an insurgency in Nigeria for over six years. The group has abducted over 2,000 women and girls as well as some men and boys (Amnesty International, 2015; New York Times, 2014). Amnesty International estimates that at least 5,500 civilians were killed between January 2014 and April 2015 (Amnesty International, 2015). During 2014, Human Rights Watch interviewed 30 women and girls who were captured by Boko Haram but escaped. They were all abducted while working on farms, getting water, or attending school. The women and girls said that for refusing to convert to Islam, they saw many in their camp physically and psychologically abused, subjected to forced labor, forced to participate in military operations, and also sexually abused/raped. They were also made to cook, clean, perform other household duties, and carry items stolen by the insurgents from attacked towns and villages. While some of the women and girls seem to have been taken arbitrarily, most of them were kidnapped because they were students, Christians, or both (Human Rights Watch, 2014).

By the end of 2015, the Nigerian military made progress against the Boko Haram insurgents and pushed them out of most regions in the country, rescuing some of the women and girls who were abducted. However, by then many of the young girls had been forced to marry their captors and were several months pregnant or had already become mothers (Stanglin, 2015). When one of the abducted girls, who was 15 years old, complained to a Boko Haram commander that she and the other girls who had been abducted were too young to get married, he pointed at his five-year-old daughter and stated, "If she got married last year, and is just waiting till puberty for its consummation, how can you at your age be too young to marry?" (Human Rights Watch, 2014).

Recommendations for Managing Religious Diversity in Organizations

The purpose of this chapter has been to provide managers and employees with a brief background of some major religions in the world so that organizations may better understand what religious diversity entails. Religious beliefs and practices are deep seated and affect employees' perceptions, interactions with others, and expectations both from other people and from organizations. We now turn to a discussion of what this means for organizations that need to manage diversity. The chapter primarily focuses on recommendations for U.S. organizations and includes examples from the Equal Employment Opportunity Commission and the Society for Human Resource Management, but many of these recommendations are also applicable in other countries, per managerial judgment and adherence to their employment laws.

Work Situations

According to the United States Equal Employment Opportunity Commission (EEOC), religious discrimination entails unfavorable treatment toward someone (an applicant or an employee) because of his or her religious beliefs. Title VII of the Civil Rights Act prohibits discrimination on the basis of religion. This applies to any aspect of employment including selection, pay, promotion, training, benefits, and dismissal, as well as any other employment condition.

Harassment

It is illegal to harass someone on the basis of his or her religious beliefs. This includes making offensive remarks about a person because of his or her religious beliefs or practices. According to the EEOC (2015a), the harasser in question could include the person's supervisor, a coworker, or someone else such as a customer.

Segregation

Further, the law also prohibits discrimination on the basis of segregation. For example, if someone is assigned to a position where they do not have contact with customers because of dress or grooming practices which are associated with their religion, this could be considered segregation (EEOC, 2015a).

Reasonable Accommodation

Employers are expected to provide reasonable accommodations for employees' religious beliefs and practices unless it would cause an undue hardship for the employer. For example, employers should accommodate an employee's request to change his/her schedule or have time off during religious holidays. Typical accommodations include flexible work schedules or being able to change work shifts with other coworkers, as well as modification to some work practices or policies.

Dress and Grooming Policies

Religious accommodations also include dress and grooming practices which employees follow for religious reasons. Examples include wearing a Muslim headscarf, a Jewish yarmulke, or a Sikh turban; hairstyles such as Rastafarian dreadlocks; and facial hair such as Sikh uncut hair and beard. This also includes respecting prohibitions against wearing certain types of clothing. For example, a woman should not be forced to wear pants or a miniskirt if that is against her religious beliefs. When employees need dress or grooming accommodations for religious reasons, they must inform their employer of this. The employer may request additional information if needed, and, if the accommodation does not cause an undue hardship to the employer, they must grant the accommodation (EEOC, 2015a).

> Some courts have concluded that it would pose an undue hardship if an employer was required to accommodate a religious dress or grooming practice that conflicts with the public image the employer wishes to convey to customers. While there may be circumstances in which allowing a particular exception to an employer's dress and grooming policy would pose an undue hardship, an employer's reliance on the broad rubric of "image" to deny a requested religious accommodation may amount to relying on customer religious bias ("customer preference") in violation of Title VII. There may be limited situations in which the need for uniformity of appearance is so important that modifying the dress code would pose an undue hardship. However, even in these situations, a case-by-case determination is advisable" (EEOC, 2011) [and so is seeking legal counsel prior to making the decision].

Reasonable Accommodation and Undue Hardship

Employers do not have to accommodate religious requests if granting them creates an undue hardship for them. Examples of undue hardship include requests that are expensive, jeopardize workplace safety, decrease organizational efficiency, infringe on other employees' rights, or require other employees to do more than their fair share of hazardous or burdensome work (EEOC, 2015a).

Employment Policies/Practices

Furthermore, employees must not be forced to participate (or not participate) in religious activities as a condition of their employment (EEOC, 2015a).

Example of a Religious Discrimination Case in the U.S. Supreme Court

In 2015, the United States Supreme Court heard a case presented against the large retail company Abercrombie & Fitch. The plaintiff, Samantha Elauf, a Muslim teenager, was denied a job with the retailer because she wore a headscarf. At the time, Abercrombie maintained a "Look Policy" which focused on its employees looking sexy, attractive, and preppy. Abercrombie had paid $71,000 in 2013 to settle two similar cases. In April 2015, Abercrombie finally abandoned this dress policy, and company representatives explained that their sales force would focus on selling clothes instead of obsessing about a prescribed look. In its defense against Elauf's case, Abercrombie maintained that they did not have knowledge that she wore her headscarf for religious reasons. A federal appeals court supported Abercrombie, but then Elauf appealed to the Supreme Court (EEOC, 2015b). On June 1, 2015, the Supreme Court ruled in an eight-to-one decision written by Justice Antonin Scalia "that an employer may not refuse to hire an applicant if the employer was motivated by avoiding the need to accommodate a religious practice. Such behavior violates the prohibition on religious discrimination contained in Title VII of the Civil Rights Act of 1964" (EEOC, 2015b).

Recommendations From the Society for Human Resource Management and the Equal Employment Opportunity Commission

Dress Codes

The Society for Human Resource Management interviewed employment law experts to request their opinion about dress code policies. Tamara Devitt, a partner in a Silicon Valley office of Haynes and Boone, a corporate law firm, advises a written policy instructing employees to contact their management or human resources department if they feel the need for a religious accommodation for religious beliefs, observances, or practices (Wilkie, 2015). This puts the responsibility on the employee and prevents the employer from having to ask employees questions which may be considered discriminatory.

David Baron, an attorney with Cozen O'Connor in Houston, explains that it is important to have a clear dress code policy in advance which anticipates the situation and explains what is acceptable with respect to clothing, tattoos, piercings, and head coverings. If an employee is found to be violating a dress code, management should ask the employee to correct the violation of the dress code. If the employee says there is a religious reason for his or her noncompliance of the dress code, the employer must investigate whether reasonable accommodation can be made. According to Baron, "Only at that point should the employer have a detailed discussion about the religious beliefs of the employee and the possibility for an exception to policy. Absent a legitimate need for such a discussion about [apparel], the employer runs the risk of offending the employee and creating evidence of harassment or discrimination" (Wilkie, 2015).

Suggestions for Ramadan

As the number of Muslim employees in America, Europe, and other parts of the world grows, it is important to consider workplace accommodations for Ramadan. The Society for Human Resource Management has provided guidance about workplace accommodations for Muslim employees during the month of Ramadan. According to Imam Johari Abdul-Malik, of the Northern Virginia mosque Dar Al-Hijrah, because Ramadan is one of the five pillars of the Muslim faith, even Muslims who are not particularly observant the rest of the year fast from dawn until sunset and pray five times a day during the month of Ramadan. Ramadan follows the lunar calendar, which is 11 months long. Therefore, it falls on a different month every year according to the standard solar calendar. Abdul-Malik says he checks the web site of the Islamic Society of North America for calculations about when Ramadan begins and how long the fasting day will last between dawn and sunset. The month of Ramadan ends with Eid al-Fitr, which is an important family celebration that is similar in importance to the days of Christmas or Easter in the Christian faith (Lytle, 2015).

Fasting during Ramadan means that some employees will be abstaining from food and water all day long, and this is difficult, particularly for employees in physically demanding jobs. Therefore, the Society for Human Resource Management suggests some ways in which employers can accommodate Muslim employees during the month of Ramadan (Lytle, 2015).

- Adjust work hours. Being allowed to start work before the heat of the day or after sunset will be especially helpful for employees working outdoors or in warm climates.
- Provide a supportive environment whether an employee is fasting or not.
- Offer light-duty jobs or job swaps with another employee for employees who are fasting.
- Allow flexible breaks. For example, an employee who is not eating lunch may wish to work through the lunch hour and leave earlier at the end of the day.
- Offer a place for prayer. Making an empty conference room available will be helpful for those who need to pray five times per day.
- Find a place where those fasting can nap during breaks if the fast makes them tired.
- Be mindful about requiring employees to attend lunch meetings. Watching everyone else eat while one is fasting can make things difficult. Companies should try to schedule meetings during other times or allow employees who are fasting to be excused from the meetings and informed afterwards about the meeting content.

- Let people use their time off during Ramadan and especially during Eid al-Fitr.

Imam Abdul-Malik said, "Accommodations give employees a sense of being valued. That sensitivity breeds productivity" (Lytle, 2015).

These recommendations from the Society for Human Resource Management are grounded in regulations from the Equal Employment Opportunity Commission (EEOC). The EEOC adds the following suggestions in their documentation on Best Practices for Eradicating Religious Discrimination in the Workplace.

Employers should let employees know that they will make reasonable efforts to accommodate their religious needs. Employers should also train managers on how to recognize religious accommodation requests from employees and have a process to handle such requests. Managers should also be trained on how to identify alternative ways of handling the requested accommodation. For example, if one accommodation is deemed to cause an undue hardship on the employer, there may be other effective alternatives which can be provided. If an employer receives an accommodation request which they cannot grant, they should consider granting an alternative accommodation which is effective in the short-term while they investigate other long-term solutions. Further, if the employee's proposed accommodation is denied it would create undue hardship or because the employer chooses to implement another alternative that is effective, the employer must communicate to the employee what is being done and why (EEOC, 2008).

Summary of Recommendations for Organizations

Building on the prior recommendations, it is important for managers in organizations to recognize the vast diversity of religious beliefs their employees hold. Employees who are religious will have widely varying religious beliefs and religious holidays, as described in this chapter. Other employees will not have any religious beliefs. Organizations should strive to create a respectful and welcoming environment so that employees can be productive and effective in the workplace regardless of their religious beliefs.

As suggested previously by the Society for Human Resource Management, organizations should be very careful about appearance requirements which could lead to religious discrimination. If appearance requirements are not clearly related to a business necessity, organizations should avoid dress codes and other appearance requirements which could be interpreted as discriminatory against particular religious groups. Further, with respect to religious holidays, organizations should be flexible and equitable with employees. Employees should be given the flexibility to work on the days they choose and take religious holidays on the days they choose in order to be productive employees but also meet the requirements of their faith.

Finally, please see the following link for the Interfaith Calendar, which lists the dates and important holy days and religious customs for many faiths around the world: http://www.interfaithcalendar.org.

Closing Case

United Nations Told Atheists Face Discrimination Worldwide

Recently the United Nations was told that atheists, humanists, and free-thinkers are facing discrimination in all parts of the world. Their views have been treated as criminal, and in some countries, atheists have faced capital punishment (Evans, 2013).

A document from the Human Rights Council, a worldwide organization connecting people who do not adhere to an organized religion, said that atheism was prohibited by law in several states where people were forced to adopt a faith (Evans, 2013). According to the International Humanist and Ethical Union, atheists have been beaten, lashed, jailed, and killed for not adhering to a religion (IHEU, 2016; O'Casey, 2016).

In Afghanistan, Iran, Pakistan, Saudi Arabia, Sudan, Mauritania, and Maldives, "Atheists can face the death penalty on the grounds of their belief" (Evans, 2013), even though this is a violation of United Nations human rights (United Nations Universal Declaration of Human Rights, 2017).

Discussion Questions:

1. Do religion and morality always go together? In other words, can one be a moral person without religion, and can one be a religious person who lacks morality? Please explain.
2. There have been a number of conflicts related to the religious beliefs of various groups around the world. Do you have any suggestions for finding solutions so the different groups can have better relations? Please explain.
3. How can countries achieve a situation where people of many different religious beliefs respect each other?

Note

1. The Universal Declaration of Human Rights is a standard that countries should aspire to achieve, but it is nonbinding. Many countries do not follow this closely, and some countries do not follow it even loosely.

References

al-Lami, M. (2014, July 21). Iraq: The minorities of Nineveh. *BBC News*. Retrieved from http://www.bbc.com/news/world-middle-east-28351073

Amnesty International. (2015, April 14). Nigeria: Abducted women and girls forced to join Boko Haram attacks. Retrieved from https://www.amnesty.org/en/latest/news/2015/04/nigeria-abducted-women-and-girls-forced-to-join-boko-haram-attacks/

Bassem, W. (2016, October 14). Iraq's Turkmens call for independent province. *Al-Monitor*. Retrieved from http://www.al-monitor.com/pulse/originals/2016/10/turkmens-iraq-mosul-tal-afar.html

Bellwinkel-Schempp, M. (2004). Roots of Ambedkar Buddhism in Kanpur. In S. Jondhale & J. Beltz (Eds.), *Reconstructing the world: B.R. Ambedkar and Buddhism in India* (pp. 221–244). New Delhi: Oxford University Press.

Council on Foreign Relations. (2016). The Sunni-Shia divide. Retrieved from http://www.cfr.org/peace-conflict-and-human-rights/sunni-shia-divide/p33176#!/?cid=otr-marketing_url-sunni_shia_infoguide

Earhart, H. B. (1993). *Religious traditions of the world*. New York: Harper Collins.

Equal Employment Opportunity Commission (EEOC). (2008, July 23). Best Practices for Eradicating Religious Discrimination in the Workplace. Retrieved from https://www.eeoc.gov/policy/docs/best_practices_religion.html

Equal Employment Opportunity Commission (EEOC). (2011). Questions and answers: Religious discrimination in the workplace. Retrieved from https://www.eeoc.gov//policy/docs/qanda_religion.html

Equal Employment Opportunity Commission (EEOC). (2015a). Religious discrimination. Retrieved from http://www.eeoc.gov/laws/types/religion.cfm

Equal Employment Opportunity Commission (EEOC). (2015b, June 1). Supreme Court rules in favor of EEOC in Abercrombie religious discrimination case. Retrieved from https://www.eeoc.gov/eeoc/newsroom/release/6-1-15.cfm

Esposito, J. L., Fasching, D. J., & Lewis, T. (2012). *World religions today* (4th ed.). New York: Oxford University Press.

Evans, R. (2013, February 25). U.N. told Atheists face discrimination around globe. Retrieved from http://articles.chicagotribune.com/2013-02-25/news/sns-rt-us-rights-atheists-religious-discrimination-around-globe

Exodus. *The Holy Bible*. King James version. (1999). New York: American Bible Society.

Fackenheim, E. L. (1997). *God's presence in history*. Northvale, NJ and Jerusalem: Jason Aronson, Inc.

Fisher, M. P. (2002). *Living Religions* (5th ed.). Upper Saddle River, NJ: Prentice Hall.

Frost, S. E., Jr. (1972). *The sacred writings of the world's great religions*. New York: McGraw-Hill.

Hinnells, J. R. (1995). *A New Dictionary of Religions*. Oxford: Penguin Books.

Hohmann, L. (2015, March 24). Mayor takes stand against Muslim Shariah courts. Retrieved from http://www.wnd.com/2015/03/mayor-wont-back-down-from-muslim-brotherhood/

Human Rights Watch. (2014, October 27). Those terrible weeks in their camp: Boko Haram violence against women and girls in Northeastern Nigeria. Retrieved from http://features.hrw.org/features/HRW_2014_report/Those_Terrible_Weeks_in_Their_Camp/index.html

IHEU. (2016, April 4). Atheist student Nazimuddin Samad killed in Bangladesh. International Humanist and Ethical Union. Retrieved from http://iheu.org/atheist-student-nazimuddin-samad-killed-in-bangladesh/

Islamic Supreme Council of America. (2016). Understanding Islamic Law. Retrieved from http://www.islamicsupremecouncil.org/understanding-islam/legal-rulings/52-understanding-islamic-law.html

Izadi, E. & Bever, L. (2015, September 16). The history of anti-Islam controversy in Ahmed Mohamed's Texas city. *The Washington Post*. Retrieved from https://www.washingtonpost.com/news/acts-of-faith/wp/2015/09/16/the-history-of-anti-islam-controversy-in-ahmed-mohameds-texas-city/?utm_term=.7eaf16540152

Lytle, T. (2015, June 1). Prayer breaks, flexible hours help during Ramadan. Society for Human Resource Management. Retrieved from http://www.shrm.org/hrdisciplines/diver sity/articles/pages/ramadan-2015.aspx?utm_source=HR%20Week%20June%208%20 2015%20(1)&utm_medium=email&utm_content=June%2008,%202015&MID= 01197622&LN=Triana&spMailingID=22799495&spUserID=ODM1OTI2MDk3NDUS1& spJobID=580754229&spReportId=NTgwNzU0MjI5S0

New York Times. (2014, November 10). Explaining Boko Haram, Nigeria's Islamist insurgency. Retrieved from http://www.nytimes.com/2014/11/11/world/africa/boko-haram-in-nigeria.html?action=click&contentCollection=Africa&module=RelatedCoverage&region=Marginalia&pgtype=article

Nizkor Project. (1945). The trial of German major war criminals. Sitting at Nuremberg, Germany December 3 to December 14, 1945. Retrieved from http://www.nizkor.org/hweb/imt/tgmwc/tgmwc-02/tgmwc-02-20-05.shtml

Noss, D. S. (1999). *A History of the World's Religions* (10th ed.). Upper Saddle River, NJ: Prentice Hall.

O'Casey, E. (2016, March 15). Jailed and lashed for atheism – At UN, IHEU highlights Saudi and Egypt's treatment of those with no religion. International Humanist and Ethical Union. Retrieved from http://iheu.org/jailed-lashed-for-atheism-at-un-iheu-highlights-saudi-egypts-treatment-of-those-with-no-religion/

Oxtoby, W. G. (1996). *World Religions: Western Traditions.* Ontario: Oxford University Press.

Pew Research Center. (2011, August 9). Rising restrictions on religion: One-third of the world's population experiences an increase. Washington, DC: Pew Research Center. Retrieved from http://www.pewforum.org/2011/08/09/rising-restrictions-on-religion2/

Pew Research Center. (2014, April 4). Global religious diversity: Half of the most religiously diverse countries are in Asia-Pacific region. Washington, DC: Pew Research Center. Retrieved from http://www.pewforum.org/2014/04/04/global-religious-diversity/

Pew Research Center. (2015, May 12). America's changing religious landscape. Washington, DC: Pew Research Center. Retrieved from http://www.pewforum.org/2015/05/12/americas-changing-religious-landscape/

Purvis, S. B. (1995). *The stained glass ceiling: Churches and their women pastors.* Louisville, KY: Westminster John Knox Press.

Rainer, T. (2013, March 27). The 15 largest Protestant denominations in the United States. *Christian Post.* Retrieved from http://www.christianpost.com/news/the-15-largest-pro testant-denominations-in-the-united-states-92731/

Selk, A. (2015, March 24). Dispute over Islam lands Irving Mayor Beth Van Duyne on national stage. *Dallas Morning News.* Retrieved from http://www.dallasnews.com/news/community-news/northwest-dallas-county/headlines/20150324-dispute-over-islam-lands-irving-mayor-beth-van-duyne-on-national-stage.ece

Shuster, M. (2007, February 12). Chronology: A history of the Shiite-Sunni split. Retrieved from http://www.npr.org/2007/02/12/7280905/chronology-a-history-of-the-shia-sunni-split

Stanglin, D. (2015, May 2). Nigerian military: 234 girls, women rescued from Boko Haram. *USA Today.* Retrieved from http://www.usatoday.com/story/news/world/2015/05/01/nigeria-rescue-boko-haram/26755427/

Sullins, P. (2000). The stained glass ceiling: Career attainment for women clergy. *Sociology of Religion, 61*(3), 243–267. United Nations. (2015). International standards on freedom of religion or belief. United Nations Human Rights. Office of the High Commissioner. Retrieved from http://www.ohchr.org/EN/Issues/FreedomReligion/Pages/Standards.aspx

United Nations. (2017). *Universal Declaration of Human Rights.* Retrieved from http://www.ohchr.org/EN/UDHR/Documents/UDHR_Translations/eng.pdf

Wilkie, D. (2015, May 18). Abercrombie case leaves companies in the dark on dress codes. *Society for Human Resource Management.* Retrieved from http://www.shrm.org/hrdisciplines/diversity/articles/pages/abercrombie-dress-code.aspx?utm_source=HR%20Week%20May%2025%202015%20(1)&utm_medium=email&utm_content=May%2027,%202015&MID=01197622&LN=Triana&spMailingID=22722063&spUserID=ODM1OTI2MDk3NDUS1&spJobID=562658686&spReportId=NTYyNjU4Njg2S0

eight
Age

Opening Case

It Takes People of All Ages: The Need for Older Workers in the Computer Industry

Computer programming is an example of a job where workers of all ages are required. One of the current challenges faced by the computer industry is the need to fill programming positions that maintain legacy languages such as COBOL and FORTRAN. COBOL is a language that was written in 1959. A poll conducted in 2013 showed that 73% of college instructors teaching information technology classes today do not teach COBOL (Shead, 2013). Young graduates do not want to learn old languages. They prefer to learn newer programming languages such as Java. However, there is a need for people who can program in COBOL because an estimated 220 billion lines of this code are running many business applications to this day (Hacker-Rank, 2015). "It would be a herculean feat to replace every single business program with a brand new language without introducing detrimental bugs" (HackerRank, 2015). Therefore, the cost of replacing the COBOL code has not outweighed the benefits of using this older language. As a result, the average age of COBOL programmers is estimated to be in the fifties, and these programmers can make a good living filling an important need.

Meanwhile, the National Air and Space Administration (NASA) also has a need for computer programmers who know FORTRAN. The Voyager 1 and 2 spacecraft, which are still active and will be for many years to come, contain computers that were programmed in these legacy languages. The last Voyager engineer from the original project team that launched the satellites is now retiring, and the person who replaces him on the job will need to have a specific skill set, including maintaining legacy computer programs, in order to service the Voyager crafts (Wenz, 2015).

Discussion Questions:

1. From the information presented here, would you say that age diversity could be considered a source of competitive advantage for a company in the computer industry? Please explain.

2. The computer industry is somewhat well-known for its lack of gender and racial diversity as well as possible ageism. For example, the CEO of Facebook, Mark Zuckerberg, received much media attention for saying, "Young people are just smarter" in 2007 at the age of 22 while speaking to a group at Stanford University (Ross, 2013). Do you think the image of lacking diversity and favoring young people presents a strategic business problem for the computer industry? Why or why not?

3. If you were the CEO of a computer company, what message would you give to your employees, and what types of norms would you set in your organization with respect to diversity? How would you do it?

Learning Objectives

After reading this chapter, you should be able to:

- Name the various generations that are currently in the workforce
- Understand the challenges and opportunities of an age-diverse workforce
- Roughly define to whom "older" and "younger" employee labels are typically applied
- Understand age stereotypes and the impact they have on employees
- Describe research findings on the validity of age stereotypes which demonstrate almost all the stereotypes are false
- Know what an age diversity climate is and why it matters to organizations
- Articulate best-known methods for managing age diversity in organizations

This chapter explains that there are currently four generations of employees who work side by side in the workforce, which presents both opportunities and challenges. We examine what is generally meant by "older" and "younger" employees as well as age stereotypes and the impact they have on employees. The chapter presents research findings on age stereotypes, the majority of which do not find empirical support for age stereotypes. Finally, the chapter concludes with a discussion on age diversity climate in organizations and best-known methods to manage age diversity.

There are currently four generations of employees working together in the workforce. Employees in their twenties may be working alongside coworkers in their seventies. According to the Society for Human Resource Management (SHRM), the four generations are as follows. Traditionalists are those employees born between the years of 1922 and 1945, and they comprise approximately 8% of the workforce. Baby Boomers were born between 1946 and 1964, and they comprise 44% of the workforce. Generation X refers to people born between 1965 and 1980, and this group comprises about 34% of the workforce. Millennials (also referred to as Generation Y) were born between 1981 and 2000, and this group comprises about 14% of the workforce, a number which is growing over the years (SHRM, 2009).

Researchers have described that developed countries are experiencing a demographic shift and an aging workforce because of lower birth rates and longer life expectancies (Tempest, Barnatt, & Coupland, 2002). Presently, more than half of the United States' workforce is age 40 or older (U.S. Bureau of Labor Statistics, 2008). Germany is witnessing a similar demographic shift, where the 50–64 age cohort will become the largest by 2020 (Statistisches Bundesamt, 2006). Within the European Union, the percentage of employees age 50 or older was expected to increase by almost 25% by the year 2016 (*Economist*, 2006). The EU-27 (a group of 27 countries in the European Union)[1] employment rate for persons aged 55–64 increased from 36.9% to 46% between 2000 and 2009 (European Network of Heads of PES, 2011). In the United Kingdom, there are almost 1.5 million people in the 85 and older age category, and this number is expected to grow to 5 million by 2050 (BBC, 2014). Therefore, there is an aging trend in the population of many countries. This demographic shift raises questions such as:

How do we help people remain independent and active as they age? How can we strengthen health promotion and prevention policies, especially those directed to older people? As people are living longer, how can the quality of life in old age be improved? Will large numbers of older people bankrupt our health care and social security systems? How do we best balance the role of the family and the state when it comes to caring for people who need assistance, as they grow older? How do we acknowledge and support the major role that people play as they age in caring for others?

(World Health Organization, 2002)

In an effort to find answers to these questions and to prepare for the challenges associated with an aging population, the World Health Organization presented a policy framework on aging at the Second United Nations World Assembly in Madrid, Spain, on April 2002, in which it adopted and defined the term **active aging** (World Health Organization, 2002). Active aging is "the process for optimizing opportunities for health, participation, and security in order to enhance quality of life as people age. This definition includes continuing activity in the labour force" (European Network of Heads of PES, 2011, p. 2).

As older employees transition to retirement, or semi-retirement, many people are also engaging in **bridge employment**, which refers to workers who have retired from long-term positions but are still engaged in the workforce (Kim & Feldman, 2000; Wang, Olson, & Shultz, 2012). Such employees are helpful for both organizations and the economy because they are experienced workers who can fill important roles and prevent labor shortages. They also are more flexible than typical full-time workers with respect to scheduling, assignments, and benefits.

As workplaces become increasingly diverse with respect to age, research findings show that both the youngest and the oldest employees can perceive age discrimination and feel they are "never the right age" (Duncan & Loretto, 2004). There is a substantial amount of evidence that older employees at work can face stereotypes, prejudice, and discrimination (Posthuma & Campion, 2009). For example, in "Ryther v. KARE (1997), a supervisor told his 53-year-old sportscaster that he 'had bags under his eyes,' was 'an old fart,' 'wasn't able to grasp the new computer system,' and 'couldn't handle the new technology'" (Dipboye & Colella, 2005, p. 208). Likewise, young employees may be seen as inexperienced and/or lacking the capacity to take on leadership roles (Flint, 2001). As one young employee stated: "During my job search, I had much more of a challenge making myself look older, since I am often mistaken for 16. I tried my hardest to look older—using everything from fake reading glasses (to) more conservative clothing and carrying a briefcase" (Armour, 2003, para. 39). Snape and Redman (2003) found that age discrimination is reported as often for the young as for the old. **Age discrimination**, or **ageism**, is defined as treating people in a less desirable manner and denying them opportunities on the basis of their age (Allport, 1954). Age discrimination is seen in all age groups (Hassell & Perrewé, 1993; Wood, Wilkinson, & Harcourt, 2008), but reports of it are greatest among both older and younger age groups (Duncan & Loretto, 2004; Garstka, Hummert, & Branscombe, 2005). Although both the younger and older age cohorts report discrimination, stereotypes against older workers are the more prevalent in the workplace (Posthuma & Campion, 2009).

What Does It Mean to Be an "Older" or "Younger" Worker?

There is no consensus on this matter. For example, in the United States the Age Discrimination in Employment Act (ADEA) of 1967 protects employees 40 or over from employment discrimination on the basis of their age. This law must be followed by all employers with 20 or more employees, employment agencies, labor organizations, and state and local governments (Equal Employment Opportunity Commission, 2015). However, Ng and Feldman (2010) pointed out that it may be inappropriate to consider employees 40 and over to be "old." They reasoned that the largest segment of the working population in the world is between the ages of 45 and 49, which would mean that the average of the world's working population would be in the "old" category if we used a cutoff of 40. In another research article published by Finkelstein, Burke, and Raju (1995), they used 55 as the cutoff age for the older worker category to be in line with a research program about "Americans Over 55 at Work." In sum, different researchers have used different cutoffs to define what an "older" worker is. Some have used the legal definition following the law of their country (e.g., ADEA in the United States protects people 40 and older) while others have used a cutoff of 55, or some other number, based on demographic data. For more information on how ADEA protects older workers please visit the following link, where the EEOC has posted a selected list of pending and resolved age discrimination cases: https://www.eeoc.gov/eeoc/litigation/selected/adea.cfm.

In addition, there has also been some speculation about a prime age for workers. The **prime age** refers to an age group of employees who are the most preferred employees, specifically those between the ages of 25 and 35 (Duncan & Loretto, 2004; Loretto, Duncan, & White, 2000).

Age Stereotypes

Biases about different age groups are typically driven by **age stereotypes,** or over-generalizations about individuals based on the age group to which they belong. As with other stereotypes, age stereotypes may or may not have any basis in fact with respect to any particular individual.

Stereotypes About Older and Younger Workers

Research reviews related to older workers have identified both negative and positive stereotypes associated with older workers. Posthuma and Campion (2009) conducted an extensive review of the literature where they presented the overall findings of their review of 117 articles. They identified several patterns in the stereotypes that tend to be associated with older workers. For example, negative stereotypes about older employees include that they are less capable of learning new things, that they are less motivated, that they can have lower performance than younger employees, that they are resistant to change and learning new technology, and that they may stay with the organization for a shorter period of time because they have fewer years to work (Posthuma & Campion, 2009).

There are also positive characteristics associated with older employees. For example, people tend to associate older employees with being dependable, more emotionally stable than young employees, more reliable, and also more likely to be helpful and perform **organizational citizenship behavior,** defined as discretionary behavior which is not part of one's formal job requirements but helps the functioning of the organization (Bertolino, Truxillo, & Fraccaroli, 2013; Organ, 1988; Truxillo, McCune, Bertolino, & Fraccaroli, 2012).

Some research also shows stereotypes about older employees which could be seen as both positive and negative. For example, the idea that older workers are experienced could have positive connotations because experienced individuals know how to handle their jobs very well. However, "experienced" may also be seen as a euphemism for being old (Finkelstein, Kulas, & Dages, 2003). The question of being overqualified has been raised in employment discrimination cases (Lamber, 1993). Courts have implied that "overqualified" may be a "code word for too old" (Lamber, 1993, p. 348).

Less research has been conducted about younger employees compared to older ones (Deal, Altman, & Rogelberg, 2010). However, some stereotypes that have been associated with younger employees are that they have a sense of entitlement, are narcissistic, and are not loyal (Twenge, 2006). Communicating with Millennials has also been associated with a lack of comfort, trust, and respect by some (Myers & Sadaghiani, 2010).

Global View: Northern Ireland

In Northern Ireland, the Employment Equality (Age) Regulations (Northern Ireland) 2006, enforced by the Equality Commission for Northern Ireland, is a law that makes discrimination on the basis of age illegal with respect to employment, occupations, higher education, and vocational training. It covers people of all ages. The law defines six ways in which unlawful discrimination could take place. **Direct discrimination** is where an employer treats someone less favorably than they do another person of a different age group. **Indirect discrimination** refers to using a practice which is applied to everyone but results in some groups having an advantage over others. **Age victimization** means treating people less favorably because either they have complained about age discrimination or have aided someone else in doing so. **Age harassment** means to be treated in a way that is humiliating or offensive because of one's age group. **Discrimination for failing to carry out an age discriminatory instruction** is when people are treated less favorably for refusing to do something that would be against the age discrimination law. Finally, **discrimination after a relationship has come to an end** means the individual is treated less favorably or harassed because he or she has left the employer. An example would be if the employer refuses to provide a letter of reference for a former employee (Equality Commission for Northern Ireland, 2015).

The regulation prohibits all employers, no matter the size of the company, from subjecting job applicants or current employees, including contract workers and former employees, to age discrimination and harassment. This covers all aspects of the employment relationship, including recruiting, selection, terms of employment such as the employment environment and access to benefits, termination, and post-employment situations (Equality Commission for Northern Ireland, 2015).

Research Findings

Do Jobs Have a Correct Age?

In a review of age in the workplace, Posthuma and Campion (2009) found that some jobs are indeed associated with people of different ages. For instance, one study found that the number of tasks that are associated with older persons as well as the number of job incumbents who are older persons increases the likelihood that this is seen as an older person's job (Cleveland & Hollman, 1990). Moreover, negative stereotypes associated with older persons are more likely to be activated when older people apply for jobs that are not seen as being appropriate for their age (Perry, Kulik, & Bourhis, 1996). The authors concluded that evaluators are most likely to discriminate against older workers when they are biased against older workers, when they are cognitively distracted and do not have the mental resources to inhibit age bias, and when applicants are applying for stereotypically age-incongruent jobs (Perry et al., 1996).

Age Stereotypes and Research About Job Performance

Posthuma and Campion (2009) concluded that most stereotypes about older workers have no basis in fact. They also found evidence refuting the stereotype that older workers are weaker performers. Overall, they found that performance tends to increase with age and that, when declines are seen, they tend to be small (Posthuma & Campion, 2009).

Ng and Feldman (2008) conducted a **meta-analysis** (a procedure where results from all studies on a particular topic are statistically aggregated to arrive at the true population effect of the relationship in question) to examine the **correlation** (the linear relationship between two variables) between employee age and job performance. The authors concluded that age was largely unrelated to core task performance, creativity, and performance in training programs. However, they found evidence that age demonstrated a stronger relationship with seven other dimensions of performance. These dimensions were: organizational citizenship behavior, workplace safety, counterproductive work behavior, workplace aggression, substance abuse, tardiness, and absenteeism. The results showed that age was positively associated with citizenship behavior and workplace safety, but negatively associated with counterproductive work behavior, workplace aggression, substance abuse, tardiness, and absenteeism. The effect sizes were small to moderate in magnitude.

One caveat to the findings between employee age and task performance reported by Ng and Feldman (2008) is evidence that the relationship may be curvilinear, or an inverted U shape. The overall linear relationship reported in the meta-analysis for the relationship between age and supervisor-reported task performance was a correlation of 0.03. This is a very small positive correlation. However, in a subsequent analysis they tested for a curvilinear effect and found that the magnitude of this relationship is slightly different based on age category. Specifically, the correlation between employee age and supervisor-rated task performance is 0.04 for workers less than 30 years of age, 0.09 for workers between 31–35 years of age, 0.06 for workers from 36–40 years of age, and −0.05 for workers over 40. This means that peak performance was observed, with a small effect size, for employees ages 31–35 while a small performance decrement was observed for the over 40 group.

Age Stereotypes and Research About Training and Return on Investment

Data from both the United States and Hong Kong show that older employees are less likely to receive training than younger employees (Heywood, Ho, & Wei, 1999; Maurer & Rafuse, 2001). Organizations may believe they will get better returns on investment if they train younger workers because they may see them as being easier to train, less expensive, more willing to learn new things, and more likely to have a long organizational tenure (Posthuma & Campion, 2009). However, there is very little evidence of this. Research shows that older workers tend to have more employment stability and are less likely to quit than younger employees (Hedge, Borman, & Lammlein, 2006). Part of the reason for this may be because when older workers are laid off from organizations, it usually takes them longer to find new employment compared to younger workers (Posthuma & Campion, 2009). The end result is that older employees typically do not represent a lower return on investment for training because they are less likely to quit working at the organization, and the organization will recoup those training costs in the short-run (Posthuma & Campion, 2009).

With respect to cost, there is also no evidence that older employees cost more than younger ones. Although employee salaries increase steadily until employees are about 50 years old, older workers are also less likely to be absent from work (Broadbridge, 2001; Hedge et al., 2006), more likely to stay at the organization longer (Posthuma & Campion, 2009), and typically require less training on how to do their jobs because of their years of work experience. A study conducted by Ng and Feldman (2008) found older employees are less likely to exhibit counterproductive work behavior and more likely to perform organizational citizenship behavior (Ng & Feldman, 2008). There is also no evidence that older employees cost more due to accidents or injuries at work than younger employees. Salminen (2004) reviewed studies on workplace injuries and found that younger employees (defined as those less than 25 years of age) were more likely to be involved in nonfatal injuries at work, with 56% of studies showing a higher injury rate among younger employees, 27% of studies showing no difference, and 17% of studies showing a higher injury rate among older employees. However, in the studies where there were job fatalities, 64% of the studies showed that younger employees had a lower rate of fatalities, 20% of the studies showed no difference between age groups, and 16% of the studies showed that the young employees had a higher percentage of fatalities (Salminen, 2004). In sum, there are reasons to believe that older workers would cost companies either more or less money. They may get paid higher salaries on the one hand, but they also exhibit more stable and longer periods of employment with more helpful behavior, which offsets the cost of the higher salaries. Overall, there is no evidence that there is a substantial difference in cost between older and younger employees.

In addition, Ng and Feldman (2012) also conducted a meta-analysis that set out to examine six common stereotypes about older workers. Specifically, they investigated the stereotypes: (a) that older workers are less motivated, (b) that they are less eager to participate in training and career development, (c) that they are more resistant to change, (d) that they are less trusting in others, (e) that they are less healthy, and (f) that they are more vulnerable to work–family imbalance. The study included 418 empirical studies representing a sample size of 208,204 participants. Ng and Feldman found no support for five out of the six stereotypes about older workers. They found support for only the stereotype that older workers have a lower desire to partake in developmental activities compared to their younger counterparts. Therefore, Ng and Feldman concluded that most stereotypes about older employees are false.

Research Findings About Employee Age and Job Attitudes

Costanza, Badger, Fraser, Severt, and Gade (2012) conducted a meta-analysis to examine the differences in job attitudes of older and younger workers. They examined three job attitudes: job satisfaction, organizational commitment, and turnover intent. Their analyses aggregated effect sizes from 20 studies drawing from 19,961 participants and spanning the four generations: Traditionals, Baby Boomers, Generation X, and Millennials. Overall, they found that the differences between the four generations on job attitudes were either not statistically different from zero or very close to zero effect size. The authors concluded that there are no meaningful differences between the generations with respect to job attitudes (Costanza et al., 2012).

At the same time, there is some evidence that age is positively correlated with overall work attitudes. Ng and Feldman (2010) conducted a meta-analysis where they examined age as a continuous variable and measured the correlation between age and various aspects of job attitudes. Their meta-analysis was based on 802 empirical studies, 56% of which were conducted in the United States. They categorized the job attitudes into three categories: task-based attitudes, people-based attitudes, and organization-based attitudes. They found the most evidence that age is positively correlated to task-based attitudes. In other words, older employees reported more positive task-based attitudes about their jobs than younger employees. The size of these effects was small to medium in magnitude. For example, age was positively associated with overall job satisfaction, satisfaction with the work itself, satisfaction with pay, and work involvement. Age was also negatively associated with stressors including role conflict, role ambiguity, and role overload. The only exception, where older workers reported being less satisfied, was with respect to satisfaction with promotions.

The meta-analysis conducted by Ng and Feldman (2010) also found some evidence with respect to the correlation between age and people-based job attitudes as well as organization-based job attitudes. For people-based attitudes, they found a small correlation showing that age was positively related to satisfaction with coworkers, satisfaction with supervisor, and interpersonal trust and negatively related to relationship conflict. The correlations with interaction fairness, coworker support, supervisor support, and perceived politics were very small or zero in magnitude, which means there is virtually no relationship between age and those job attitudes. For organization-based job attitudes, there was a small positive correlation between age and commitment to the organization, organizational identification, loyalty to the organization, person-organizational fit, and trust in the organization (Ng & Feldman, 2010). Therefore, overall this meta-analysis found a positive association between employee age and most forms of job attitudes.

Taken together, the two meta-analyses conducted by Costanza et al. (2012) and Ng and Feldman (2010) suggest that while there may not be significant differences in job attitudes between different generational groups, there is an overall trend such that as employee age goes up job attitudes tend to become slightly more positive.

The Impact of Age Stereotypes

Despite the lack of evidence that older workers exhibit weaker performance, the review conducted by Posthuma and Campion (2009) referred to over 60 articles showing that age-related stereotypes have influenced a number of decisions in employment settings, such as interviews and performance appraisals. The authors explain that "research has shown that as a result of age stereotypes, older persons with the same or similar qualifications or attributes as younger persons commonly receive lower ratings in interviews and performance appraisals" (Avolio & Barrett, 1987; Finkelstein et al., 1995; Gordon, Rozelle, & Baxter, 1988; Haefner, 1977; Levin, 1988), (Posthuma & Campion, 2009, p. 171). For example, in one study participants were asked to rate what they thought the average 30-year-old person and the average 60-year-old person would be like with respect to job-related characteristics. The authors reported that the 60-year-old person was rated lower on performance capability as well as development capability, while the 30-year-old was rated lower on stability (Rosen & Jerdee, 1976). There were no differences reported on interpersonal skills (Rosen & Jerdee, 1976). A meta-analysis of ratings of applicants and workers in both experimental and field settings found a small effect size favoring younger workers over older workers (Gordon & Arvey, 1986).

Perhaps one of the most striking findings was that older workers themselves often have these biases about their own group (i.e., older employees). Posthuma and Campion (2009) described that although there is some evidence that older workers are less likely to have biases about older workers compared to their younger worker counterparts (Rupp, Vodanovich, & Crede, 2005), the majority of the evidence points out that both older and younger workers share the same stereotypes regarding older employees (Glover & Branine, 2001; Schwab & Heneman, 1978). For example, two research studies reported that older supervisors gave other older employees lower performance evaluations (Ferris, Yates, Gilmore, & Rowland, 1985; Shore, Cleveland, & Goldberg, 2003). Furthermore, a meta-analysis investigating age bias demonstrated that older adults are biased against people of their own age group in that they believe older individuals are less competent (Kite, Stockdale, Whitley, & Johnson, 2005).

One possible explanation for the pervasiveness of these age stereotypes is that people have been repeatedly exposed to these misconceptions, and this information has subconsciously embedded in most people's minds. In a study examining subconscious bias against various groups, Nosek et al. (2007) aggregated the results of over 2,500,000 participants who took the Implicit Association Test (the most validated and generally accepted technique for testing subconscious bias) and found that 80% of the participants were more readily able to associate young people with positive characteristics and older people with negative characteristics. If these stereotypes are common and can be recalled very quickly and automatically, that would explain the pervasiveness of age stereotypes. It would also explain why even older persons have these stereotypes against their own group—it has been in their minds for many years, possibly decades.

Challenges Faced by Younger Employees

One challenge faced by younger employees is whether they are legally protected under their countries' employment laws. For example, the major age discrimination law in the United States is the **Age Discrimination in Employment Act (ADEA)**, which covers employees ages 40 and older. Although some of the 50 states within the United States have an employment law which covers younger workers, the majority do not, and there is no federal law protecting employees under age 40. This makes it easier for employers to discriminate against younger workers without facing penalties. Research shows that younger employees with little seniority are most likely to be laid off during economic downturns (Kim & Feldman, 2000). In a research study of younger workers conducted by Loretto, Duncan, and White (2000), 35% of participants felt that age influenced them both positively and negatively in their employment. Younger workers simultaneously expressed the feeling that they had gotten the job because of their youth but also stated the negative impression of being seen as untrustworthy and given less responsibility because of their age, as well as being paid less than other workers with similar jobs (Loretto et al., 2000).

Global View: Australia

The Age Discrimination Act of 2004 is an Australian law that prohibits employment discrimination against employees of all ages, younger or older. The Australian government defines discrimination in one of three ways: **direct discrimination**, **indirect discrimination**, and **acts committed because of age and for some other reason**. Direct discrimination refers to treating another person less favorably than one would treat someone of a different age, and doing so because of (a) the age of the aggrieved person, (b) the characteristics that pertain to the age of the aggrieved person, or (c) the characteristics that are generally imputed to persons in the age group of the aggrieved person. Indirect discrimination is where the discriminator imposes conditions, requires practices that are not reasonable under the circumstances, or requires practices that are likely to disadvantage persons of some age groups. The burden of proof to show that a practice is reasonable under the circumstances is on the discriminator. Acts committed because of age and other reasons include discriminating against a person due to his or her age, due to the characteristics that generally pertain to individuals of that age, or on the basis of traits generally imputed to persons of a specific age group (Australian Government, 2015).

Furthermore, unlawful discrimination is prohibited in all of the following contexts: employment; education; access to premises; provision of goods, services, and facilities; accommodations; disposal of land; administration of Commonwealth programs and laws; and requests for information on which age discrimination could be based (Australian Government, 2015).

Challenges Faced by Young Supervisors

As age diversity increases in the workplace, it is inevitable that employees will find themselves in situations that are **incongruent**, or opposite, to what traditional stereotypes would hold. For example, supervisors may be younger than their subordinates, or mentors may be asked to work with mentees who are older than they are. Work by Lawrence (1996) on **age norms** describes that in organizations there are informal expectations about the age groups that should occupy various jobs. The older, more experienced people should typically manage the younger, less experienced ones.

Only a few studies have examined age-incongruent situations where the supervisor is younger than the subordinate. Collins, Hair, and Rocco (2009) reported that older subordinates had lower expectations from younger supervisors compared to younger subordinates. Some have described that older employees dislike taking instructions from supervisors who are younger than they are (Hirsch, 1990; Shellenbarger & Hymowitz, 1994). Sometimes younger supervisors may also be uncomfortable giving directions to subordinates who are older than they are (Hirsch, 1990). Perry, Kulik, & Zhou (1999) suggest that perhaps younger supervisors with older subordinates create discomfort because they contradict age norms (Lawrence, 1996).

Perry et al. (1999) found evidence that age incongruence between supervisors and subordinates was sometimes problematic and sometimes not. They noted that older subordinates reporting to younger supervisors were more likely to exhibit work change behavior, or "adaptive behavior which is motivated by negative work affect" (Perry et al., 1999, p. 347). However, older subordinates were also more likely to engage in organizational citizenship behavior. Perry et al. (1999) reasoned that if older workers feel they have a lower level of training and knowledge relative to their younger supervisors, the former might engage in more citizenship behavior to compensate for the lack of information or skills.

In a study about mentoring, Finkelstein, Allen, and Rhoton (2003) examined the role of age in mentoring relationships. They found that, on average, older protégés received less career-related mentoring, had shorter relationships with their mentors, were closer in job level to their mentors, and reported more mutual learning from the mentoring relationships than their younger counterparts. The authors conducted a content analysis of qualitative statements made by participants in order to understand their findings more fully. Of the protégés in the study, 33% reported being mentored by someone similar to their age while 8% reported being mentored by someone younger than they were.

Participants reported both advantages and disadvantages of being mentored by people similar to their age or younger than themselves. Regarding mentors similar to their age, advantages included similar life experiences and opportunities for learning and relationship building. Disadvantages to mentors who were the same age included concerns about the mentor's knowledge and experience as well as relationship boundaries between the two. With respect to mentors who were younger, the overwhelming benefit listed was that the younger mentor could provide new knowledge. The major disadvantage mentioned was the mentor's knowledge and experience (Finkelstein et al., 2003).

Investigating Tension Between Age Groups

Other potential sources of tension between different age groups were examined by North and Fiske (2013) in a study to create an intergenerational tension ageism measurement instrument. The study proposes and provides some evidence that younger people sometimes express concerns (unease or displeasure) with older people in regards to succession, identity, and consumption. **Succession** refers to older people making way for younger people to have political power and to determine how organizations and society should function. **Identity** refers to disliking that older persons enter the turf that is normally reserved for younger people. Expressing disapproval of older individuals who participate in activities or social media groups like Facebook, Twitter, or Snapchat that are usually dominated by younger people is an example of identity concern. Finally, **consumption** refers to the concern that older people may be using up more than their fair share of government and social resources. This is accompanied by the fear that there will not be enough resources left when the younger generation reaches their retirement age. In this study, participant age significantly and negatively predicted succession, identity, and consumption, with succession having the strongest effect and consumption having the weakest effect (North & Fiske, 2013). Thus, there is some evidence that younger employees think their older counterparts need to make way for the younger generation to lead.

Global View: The United Kingdom

The United Kingdom passed the 2010 Equality Act, which superseded and extended the Employment Equality (Age) Regulations of 2006. The guidelines pertaining to this act include that it is unlawful to directly discriminate against anyone by treating them less favorably than someone else because of their age. It is also unlawful to discriminate indirectly against anyone by applying a practice that disadvantages any particular age group. It is illegal to subject someone to harassment because of their age and to victimize someone because they have made or intend to make an age discrimination claim either for themselves or to provide evidence in someone else's claim. It is illegal to discriminate against someone in certain circumstances after employment has ended unless there is a justifiable reason for that. It is also illegal to force someone to retire unless it can be objectively justified (Advisory, Conciliation and Arbitration Service (ACAS) 2015a, 2015b; Government of the United Kingdom, 2015).

The 2010 Equality Act covers employees of all ages, not just older employees. It protects current employees, applicants, trainees, and employees who no longer work for the organization under some circumstances. It applies to employers of all types and pertains to all stages of the employment relationship including: recruiting, selection, training, pay, benefits, promotion, performance appraisal, dismissal, retirement, pensions, and work-related social activities (ACAS, 2015a, 2015b; Government of the United Kingdom, 2015).

The Importance of a Positive Age Diversity Climate

Recent research studies are in consensus showing that a positive and inclusive age diversity climate is important for organizations. Kunze, Boehm, and Bruch (2011) conducted a study that included 128 companies with 8,651 employees and assessed age diversity, age discrimination climate, employee commitment to the organization, and firm performance. The study reported that age diversity was positively and significantly associated with an age discrimination climate in the organizations, which speaks to one of the challenges of an age-diverse workforce. On one hand, one might expect that age diversity would demonstrate there is little or no age discrimination because employees of all ages are present. On the other hand, it is only when there is a diversity of ages that people can also be discriminated against because of their age. This sample supported the latter argument since age diversity and age discrimination climate were positive associated. Age discrimination climate was then negatively and significantly related to employee commitment. This was problematic because commitment was then positively related to firm performance. In other words, the model they investigated looked like this:

Age diversity → age discrimination climate → employee commitment → firm performance

Age diversity makes it more likely that employees will perceive an age discrimination climate in the organization. Age discrimination climate reduces employee commitment, which reduces firm performance. Therefore, this first study cautions us that when the workforce is age diverse we must be careful that diversity does not lead to perceptions of age discrimination.

In a second study published by Kunze, Boehm, and Bruch (2013), the authors examined important workplace factors which could mitigate or exacerbate the relationship between age diversity and climate for age discrimination which they found in their previous paper (Kunze et al., 2011). The study revealed that age diversity is positively related to age discrimination climate, which in turn is negatively related to organizational performance. The authors found that diversity-friendly human resource policies mitigate the effects between age diversity and a climate for age discrimination. In other words, diversity-friendly human resource practices are helpful in mitigating the potential for age-diverse employees to perceive that there is a climate of age discrimination in their company. However, the authors also found that negative age stereotypes among the top managers exacerbated the effects of age diversity on perceived climate for age discrimination and made that relationship stronger. In sum, diversity-friendly human resources practices improve the working environment in age-diverse workplaces and reduce the likelihood that employees will perceive a climate for age discrimination in the organization. Having senior leaders who hold age stereotypes does the opposite.

A different study published by Rabl and Triana (2014) experimentally examined the relationships among organizational age diversity, organizational age diversity management practices, and applicants' attitudes toward age diversity to predict both organizational attractiveness and expected age discrimination. The results showed that organizational age diversity and age diversity management practices were positively associated with organizational attractiveness and negatively associated with expected age discrimination in the organization. Results also demonstrated that an organization's age diversity, an organization's age diversity management practices, and potential applicants' attitudes toward age diversity jointly affect both organizational attractiveness and expected age discrimination. Participants with a positive attitude toward age diversity responded the most positively to organizational age diversity and diversity management practices. Specifically, they showed the greatest increase in organizational attractiveness and the greatest decrease in anticipated age discrimination in the organization when organizations were diverse and also had age diversity management practices.

In another study published by Boehm, Kunze, and Bruch (2014), the authors found that age-inclusive human resources practices are positively associated with an age diversity climate, which, in turn, is positively associated with collective employee reports of **social exchange** with their employer. Employees' sense of social exchange with the employer is defined as confidence in the employer–employee relationship where if the employees work hard on behalf of the employer, the employer will reciprocate and provide benefits to the employees in the future. This variable (employee social exchange with the employer) was then positively associated with company performance and negatively associated with collective turnover intentions among the employees. In other words, the model they found looks like this:

> Inclusive HR practices ➔ age diversity climate ➔ social exchange with employer ➔ company performance and reduced turnover intent

Inclusive HR practices lead to a positive age diversity climate which leads to feelings of social exchange with the employer. The social exchange with the employer then leads to both better company performance and lower turnover intentions among employees.

In sum, the evidence is clear that a positive age diversity climate and positive human resources practices that support an environment inclusive of all age groups improves employee attitudes, which subsequently improves company performance. Having a positive age diversity climate should also make it easier to attract employees, particularly those who have personal value for diversity.

Recommendations for Practice From Reviews of Age Research

The review of the age discrimination literature conducted by Posthuma and Campion (2009) culminated in several recommendations for organizations. These are summarized here:

- Identify reasonable factors: When older workers will be negatively affected by a decision, the law requires managers to provide justification for these decisions based on reasonable factors that do not have anything to do with the employee age. Otherwise, this could result in lawsuits.
- Avoid erroneous decisions: Managers must avoid making decisions based on erroneous stereotypes associated with older employees. Excluding qualified older employees from hiring, promotion, and training decisions can result in less productivity and may be more costly for organizations in the long run.
- Use job-related information: One of the best ways to avoid using stereotypical information in job-related processes is to focus discussions on job-related information.

- Use training and development: In organizational training, managers should learn to identify the common stereotypes against older workers and also be aware of the evidence that refutes these stereotypes so they can avoid using such stereotypes in future decision-making. Managers should also be made aware of the positive characteristics associated with older employees (e.g., stable, loyal) to avoid managers relying on negative stereotypical information to make decisions.
- Target high-risk settings: Because there are stereotypes associating employees of certain ages with certain types of jobs, employers should be especially mindful to allow equal opportunity to people of all ages in those specific jobs.
- Use older workers as a competitive advantage: Employee knowledge, skills, and abilities are much better predictors of performance than employee age. Managers who recognize this will be able to identify the most qualified employees, irrespective of how old they are.
- Consider adding complexity: Sometimes supervisors stereotype older employees, assume their cognitive resources are limited, and simplify their tasks in an attempt to make them more productive. To the contrary, giving older employees cognitively challenging tasks can help prevent the loss of cognitive function and keep them engaged, motivated, and productive.

In addition to a zero-tolerance policy for age discrimination, organizations must be careful to consistently and clearly endorse age-neutral policies. Employees of all ages (older, younger, and those in between) must feel like the organization provides them equal access to opportunities. Organizations should be mindful of providing opportunities, including training and development as well as job assignments, to employees who are qualified regardless of their age. As discussed in previous chapters, all human resources–related decisions including selection, evaluation, compensation, termination, training, project assignments, and all other aspects of the employment relationship should be based on the employees' knowledge, skills, and abilities to do the job irrespective of age. It is also important for organizations to acknowledge and celebrate the qualifications and accomplishments of employees of all ages. Accomplishments for younger and older workers alike should be praised to avoid the appearance of favoritism with some age groups over others. Finally, as was discussed in some of the previous chapters, it is important to make employees, especially those with managerial responsibilities, aware of the biases people hold about age as well as the fact that these biases are not correct according to the research data. It should be helpful to train managers and those who have decision-making authority over any aspect of human resources decisions about age stereotypes and the detrimental effects they can have on organizations. In addition, such training must explain that we all hold biases and are capable of stereotyping others, which leads to discriminatory actions. Therefore, actions taken pertaining to human resources decisions should be based on the job-related qualifications of the employee to fulfill the duties required for the job irrespective of age.

Closing Case

Recommendations for Making Jobs More Inclusive of All Age Groups

Recognizing the need for age diversity in the workplace, several organizations are examining business practice and making recommendations to make jobs more inclusive. The following recommendations are from ACAS (2015a, 2015b) and Target Jobs (2015) in the United Kingdom.

- Avoid making references to age in the job description. Remove terms such as "recent graduate" which could discourage older applicants. Likewise, think carefully about the minimum work experience requirements. Asking for too many years of experience could unnecessarily remove young applicants who have the skills to do the job but have not had enough time to demonstrate those skills over a long period of time.
- Use images and recruiting campaigns that reflect a diverse group of people. Presenting only one type of demographic in an advertisement could give the impression that other groups are not welcome.
- Remove language that could be considered ageist in advertising and recruiting campaigns. For example, using the phrase "young and enthusiastic" discourages older applicants.
- Recruit from various sources that will provide a diverse applicant pool. This may include advertising and recruiting in various geographic locations and organizations that have a diverse pool of qualified candidates.
- Carefully consider the requirements listed in the job description. Are all of the requirements listed necessary? If the requirements are too specific or too many, that will narrow the pool of candidates from which you can choose.
- Provide training to those involved in the decision-making process. Those who are creating the short list of applicants and interviewing candidates should base their decisions on the knowledge, skills, and abilities of the candidates.
- Avoid asking interview questions related to age. For example, avoid asking people if they are comfortable working with older or younger persons, and avoid making comments about the suitability of the candidate's fit for a certain job given his or her age. The conversation should center around job requirements and the candidate's ability to meet them.

- Accept equivalent qualifications. For instance, in fields where knowledge or technology changes over time, consider that graduates from different decades studied different courses and earned different credits. If candidates of different ages have comparable qualifications and can demonstrate they have the skills to do the current job, accepting those equivalent qualifications would ensure that some age groups are not excluded from consideration.

Discussion Questions:

1. The suggestions provided here seem straightforward. Yet many people perceive age discrimination, and many thousands of age discrimination lawsuits are filed every year. In what ways might it be easy for employers to implement the aforementioned guidelines? In what ways might it be difficult for employers to implement these guidelines?
2. In your own experience as a job applicant or as someone involved in the interviewing and selection process, have you witnessed age bias in the selection process? If so, how could it have been prevented?
3. Can you think of other suggestions for organizations to be more inclusive of all age groups?

Note

1. EU-27 member states are: Austria, Belgium, Bulgaria, Cyprus, Czech Republic, Denmark, Estonia, Finland, France, Germany, Greece, Hungary, Ireland, Italy, Latvia, Lithuania, Luxembourg, Malta, the Netherlands, Poland, Portugal, Romania, Slovak Republic, Slovenia, Spain, Sweden, and the United Kingdom.

References

ACAS. (2015a). Age and the workplace: A guide for employers and employees. Retrieved from http://www.acas.org.uk/media/pdf/e/4/Age-and-the-workplace-guide.pdf
ACAS. (2015b). Equality and discrimination: Understand the basics. Retrieved from http://www.acas.org.uk/media/pdf/d/8/Equality-and-discrimination-understand-the-basics.pdf
Allport, G. (1954). *The nature of prejudice*. Boston, MA: Beacon Press.
Armour, S. (2003, October 7). Young workers say their age holds them back. *USA Today*. Retrieved from http://www.usatoday.com/money/workplace/2003-10-07-reversage_x.htm
Australian Government. (2015). Age Discrimination Act 2004. No. 68, 2004. Compilation No. 31. Compilation date June 18, 2015. Retrieved from https://www.comlaw.gov.au/Details/C2015C00256
Avolio, B. J., & Barrett, G. V. (1987). Effects of age stereotyping in a simulated interview. *Psychology and Aging, 2*, 56–63.

BBC. (2014, December 15). Carr, Catherine, producer. "The age bomb." *The Invisible Age.* Retrieved from http://www.bbc.co.uk/programmes/b04v328c

Bertolino, M., Truxillo, D. M., & Fraccaroli, F. (2013). Age effects on perceived personality and job performance. *Journal of Managerial Psychology, 7/8,* 867–885.

Boehm, S. A., Kunze, F., & Bruch, H. (2014). Spotlight on age-diversity climate: The impact of age-inclusive HR practices on firm-level outcomes. *Personnel Psychology, 67*(3), 667–704.

Broadbridge, A. (2001). Ageism in retailing: Myth or reality? In I. Golver & M. Branine (Eds.), *Ageism in work and employment* (pp. 153–174). Burlington, VT: Ashgate.

Cleveland, J. N., & Hollman, G. (1990). The effects of the age-type of tasks and incumbent age composition on job perceptions. *Journal of Vocational Behavior, 36,* 181–194.

Collins, M. H., Hair, J. F., Jr., & Rocco, T. S. (2009). The older-worker-younger-supervisor dyad: A test of the Reverse Pygmalion effect. *Human Resource Development Quarterly, 20*(1), 21–41.

Costanza, D., Badger, J. M., Fraser, R. L., Severt, J. B., & Gade, P. A. (2012). Generational differences in work-related attitudes: A meta-analysis. *Journal of Business and Psychology, 27,* 375–394.

Deal, J. J., Altman, D. G., & Rogelberg, S. G. (2010). Millenials at work: What we know and what we need to do (if anything). *Journal of Business and Psychology, 25,* 191–199.

Dipboye, R. L., & Colella, A. (2005). *Discrimination at work: The psychological and organizational bases.* Mahwah, NJ: Lawrence Erlbaum Associates.

Duncan, C., & Loretto, W. (2004). Never the right age? Gender and age-based discrimination in employment. *Gender, Work & Organization, 11,* 95–115.

Economist. (2006, February 16). Turning boomers into boomerangs, *378,* 65–67.

Equal Employment Opportunity Commission. (2015). The Age Discrimination in Employment Act of 1967. Retrieved from http://www.eeoc.gov/laws/statutes/adea.cfm

Equality Commission for Northern Ireland. (2015). Age Discrimination Law in Northern Ireland. Retrieved from http://www.equalityni.org/ECNI/media/ECNI/Publications/Individuals/AgediscriminationlawShortguide2011.pdf

European Network of Heads of PES. (2011, December 8). Meeting the challenges of Europe's aging workforce: The Public Employment Service response. Issues paper adopted during the 29th meeting of European Heads of Public Employment Services, Warsaw.

Ferris, G. R., Yates, V. L., Gilmore, D. C., & Rowland, K. M. (1985). The influence of subordinate age on performance ratings and causal attributions. *Personnel Psychology, 38,* 545–557.

Finkelstein, L. M., Allen, T. D., & Rhoton, L. A. (2003). An examination of the role of age in mentoring relationships. *Group and Organization Management, 28,* 249–281.

Finkelstein, L. M., Burke, M. J., & Raju, N. S. (1995). Age discrimination in simulated employment contexts: An integrative analysis. *Journal of Applied Psychology, 80,* 652–663.

Finkelstein, L. M., Kulas, J. T., & Dages, K. D. (2003). Age differences in proactive newcomer socialization strategies in two populations. *Journal of Business and Psychology, 17,* 473–502.

Flint, J. (2001, June 1). Young losers. *Ward's AutoWorld.* Retrieved from http://wardsautoworld.com/ar/auto_young_losers/

Garstka, T., Hummert, M., & Branscombe, N. (2005). Perceiving age discrimination in response to intergenerational inequity. *Journal of Social Issues, 61,* 321–342.

Glover, I., & Branine, M. (2001). "Do not go gentle into that good night": Some thoughts on paternalism, ageism, management and society. In I. Golver & M. Branine (Eds.), *Ageism in work and employment* (pp. 47–64). Burlington, VT: Ashgate.

Gordon, R. A., & Arvey, R. D. (1986). Perceived and actual ages of workers. *Journal of Vocational Behavior, 28,* 21–28.

Gordon, R. A., Rozelle, R. M., & Baxter, J. C. (1988). The effect of applicant age, job level, and accountability on the evaluation of job applicants. *Organizational Behavior and Human Decision Processes, 41*, 20–33.

Government of the United Kingdom. (2015). Equality Act 2010. Chapter 15. Retrieved from http://www.legislation.gov.uk/ukpga/2010/15/pdfs/ukpga_20100015_en.pdf

HackerRank. (2015). The inevitable return of COBOL. Retrieved from http://blog.hacker rank.com/the-inevitable-return-of-cobol/

Haefner, J. E. (1977). Race, age, sex, and competence as factors in employer selection of the disadvantaged. *Journal of Applied Psychology, 62*, 199–202.

Hassell, B. L., & Perrewé, P. L. (1993). An examination of the relationship between older workers' perceptions of age discrimination and employee psychological states. *Journal of Managerial Issues, 5*, 109–120.

Hedge, J. W., Borman, W. C., & Lammlein, S. E. (2006). *The aging workforce: Realities, myths, and implications for organizations*. Washington, DC: American Psychological Association.

Heywood, J. S., Ho, L. S., & Wei, X. (1999). The determinants of hiring older workers: Evidence from Hong Kong. *Industrial & Labor Relations Review, 52*(3), 444–459.

Hirsch, J. S. (1990, February 26). Older workers chafe under young managers. *Wall Street Journal*, p. B1.

Kim, S., & Feldman, D. C. (2000). Working in retirement: The antecedents of bridge employment and its consequences for quality of life in retirement. *Academy of Management Journal, 43*(6), 1195–1210.

Kite, M. E., Stockdale, G. D., Whitley, B. E., & Johnson, B. T. (2005). Attitudes toward younger and older adults: An updated meta-analytic review. *Journal of Social Issues, 61*, 241–266.

Kunze, F., Boehm, S. A., & Bruch, H. (2011). Age diversity, age discrimination climate and performance consequences—a cross organizational study. *Journal of Organizational Behavior, 32*(2), 264–290.

Kunze, F., Boehm, S. A., & Bruch, H. (2013). Organizational performance consequences of age diversity: Inspecting the role of diversity-friendly HR policies and top managers' negative age stereotypes. *Journal of Management Studies, 50*(3), 413–442.

Lamber, J. C. (1993). Overqualified, unqualified or just right: Thinking about age discrimination and Taggart v. Time. *Brooklyn Law Review, 58*, 347–367.

Lawrence, B. S. (1996). Organizational age norms: Why is it so hard to know one when you see one? *Gerontologist, 36*(2), 209–220.

Levin, W. C. (1988). Age stereotyping: College student evaluations. *Research on Aging, 10*, 134–148.

Loretto, W., Duncan, C., & White, P. J. (2000). Ageism and employment: Controversies, ambiguities and younger people's perceptions. *Ageing and Society, 20*(3), 279–302.

Maurer, T. J., & Rafuse, N. E. (2001). Learning, not litigating: Managing employee development and avoiding claims of age discrimination. *Academy of Management Executive, 15*(4), 110–121.

Myers, K. K., & Sadaghiani, K. (2010). Millenials in the workplace: A communication perspective on Millenials' organizational relationships and performance. *Journal of Business and Psychology, 25*, 225–238.

Ng, T. W. H., & Feldman, D. C. (2008). The relationship of age to ten dimensions of job performance. *Journal of Applied Psychology, 93*, 392–423.

Ng, T. W. H., & Feldman, D. C. (2010). The relationships of age with job attitudes: A meta-analysis. *Personnel Psychology, 63*, 677–718.

Ng, T. W. H., & Feldman, D. C. (2012). Evaluating six common stereotypes about older workers with meta-analytical data. *Personnel Psychology, 65*, 821–858.

North, M. S., & Fiske, S. T. (2013). A prescriptive intergenerational-tension ageism scale: Succession, identity, and consumption (SIC). *Psychological Assessment*, *25*(3), 706.

Nosek, B. A., Smyth, F. L., Hansen, J. J., Devos, T., Lindner, N. M., Ranganath, K. A., Smith, C. T., Olson, K. R., Chugh, D., Greenwald, A. G., & Banaji, M. R. (2007). Pervasiveness and correlates of implicit attitudes and stereotypes. *European Review of Social Psychology*, *18*(1), 36–88.

Organ, D. W. (1988). *Organizational citizenship behavior: The good soldier syndrome*. Lexington, MA: Lexington Books.

Perry, E. L., Kulik, C. T., & Bourhis, A. C. (1996). Moderating effects of personal and contextual factors in age discrimination. *Journal of Applied Psychology*, *81*, 628–647.

Perry, E. L., Kulik, C. T., & Zhou, J. (1999). A closer look at the effects of subordinate— supervisor age differences. *Journal of Organizational Behavior*, *20*(3), 341–357.

Posthuma, R. A., & Campion, M. A. (2009). Age stereotypes in the workplace: Common stereotypes, moderators, and future research directions. *Journal of Management*, *35*, 158–188.

Rabl, T., & Triana, M. (2014). Organizational value for age diversity and potential applicants' organizational attraction: Individual attitudes matter. *Journal of Business Ethics*, *121*, 403–417.

Rosen, B., & Jerdee, T. H. (1976). The nature of job-related age stereotypes. *Journal of Applied Psychology*, *61*(2), 180.

Ross, A. S. (2013, August 20). In Silicon Valley, age can be a curse. Retrieved from http://www.sfgate.com/business/bottomline/article/In-Silicon-Valley-age-can-be-a-curse-4742365.php

Rupp, D. E., Vodanovich, S. J., & Crede, M. (2005). The multidimensional nature of ageism: Construct validity and group differences. *Journal of Social Psychology*, *145*, 335–362.

Salminen, S. (2004). Have young workers more injuries than older ones? An international literature review. *Journal of Safety Research*, *35*(5), 513–521.

Schwab, D. P., & Heneman, H. G. (1978). Age stereotyping in performance appraisal. *Journal of Applied Psychology*, *63*, 573–578.

Shead, M. (2013, March 7). Universities won't teach 'uncool' Cobol anymore–but should they? *ZDNet*. Retrieved from http://www.zdnet.com/article/universities-wont-teach-uncool-cobol-anymore-but-should-they/

Shellenbarger, S., & Hymowitz, C. (1994, June 13). Over the hill? As population ages, older workers clash with younger bosses. *Wall Street Journal*, p. A1.

Shore, L. M., Cleveland, J. N., & Goldberg, C. B. (2003). Work attitudes and decisions as a function of manager age and employee age. *Journal of Applied Psychology*, *88*, 529–537.

Snape, E., & Redman, T. (2003). Too old or too young? The impact of perceived age discrimination. *Human Resources Management Journal*, *13*, 78–83.

Society for Human Resource Management (SHRM). (2009). The multigenerational workforce: Opportunity for competitive success. Retrieved from http://www.shrm.org/research/articles/articles/documents/09-0027_rq_march_2009_final_no%20ad.pdf

Statistisches Bundesamt. (2006). Bevölkerung Deutschlands bis 2050. 11. Koordinierte Bevölkerungsvorausberechnung [Germany's population until 2050. 11th coordinated population projection]. Retrieved from http://www.destatis.de/jetspeed/ portal/cms/Sites/destatis/Internet/DE/Presse/pk/2006/Bevoelkerungsentwicklung/bevoelkerungsprojektion2050,property=file.pdf

Target Jobs. (2015). Age diversity matters. Finding age-positive employers. Retrieved from https://targetjobs.co.uk/careers-advice/equality-and-diversity/320133-age-diversity-matters

Tempest, S., Barnatt, C., & Coupland, C. (2002). Grey advantage: New strategies for the old. *Long Range Planning*, *35*, 475–492. doi:10.1016/S0024-6301(02)00102-4.

Truxillo, D. M., McCune, E. A., Bertolino, M., & Fraccaroli, F. (2012). Perceptions of older versus younger workers in terms of big five facets, proactive personality, cognitive ability, and job performance. *Journal of Applied Social Psychology, 42*, 2607–2639.

Twenge, J. (2006). *Generation me: Why today's young Americans are more confident, assertive, entitled—and more miserable than ever before.* New York: Free Press.

U.S. Bureau of Labor Statistics. (2008). *Older workers.* Retrieved from http://www.bls.gov/spotlight/2008/older_workers

Wang, M., Olson, D. A., & Shultz, K. S. (2012). *Mid and late career issues: An integrative perspective.* London: Routledge.

Wenz, J. (2015, October 29). Why NASA needs a programmer fluent in 60-year-old languages. Retrieved from http://www.popularmechanics.com/space/a17991/voyager-1-voyager-2-retiring-engineer/

Wood, G., Wilkinson, A., & Harcourt, M. (2008). Age discrimination and working life: Perspectives and contestations—a review of the contemporary literature. *International Journal of Management Reviews, 10*, 425–442.

World Health Organization. (2002, April). Active aging. A policy framework. Presented at the Second United Nations World Assembly on Ageing. Spain. Retrieved from http://apps.who.int/iris/bitstream/10665/67215/1/WHO_NMH_NPH_02.8.pdf

nine
Ability

Opening Case

Derrick Coleman: First Legally Deaf Professional Football Player to Win a Super Bowl

In 2014, Derrick Coleman and the Seattle Seahawks won the Super Bowl (the national championship game for the National Football League). Coleman is hard of hearing and legally Deaf. "On a scale of 0–10, normal people range from about a seven, eight, or nine," Coleman said. "Without my hearing aids, I'm about a one or two" (Bresnahan, 2015).

Coleman, who lost his hearing at an early age, quickly distinguished himself as having a high level of ability for the game of football. He does not remember hearing because he became Deaf at the age of three. Nonetheless, he had a passion for playing football and quickly developed and demonstrated his expertise. Coleman played football in middle school, high school, and college, where he played at the University of California, Los Angeles (UCLA). He went on to become a professional football player, first joining the Minnesota Vikings and then the Seattle Seahawks (biography.com, 2016).

In spite of his loss of hearing, Coleman and his fellow team members, primarily the quarterback, follow a quick and simple procedure on the football field which allows the Seahawks' fullback to successfully execute plays. Coleman is able to hear with the assistance of his hearing aids, and he is also able to read lips (Friend, 2014). On the field, when Russell Wilson, the team's quarterback, calls a play, Coleman requests that Wilson look at him so he can both hear and/or read the quarterback's lips (Friend, 2014). This quick eye contact allows Coleman to play the game expertly and seamlessly.

Coleman is the third Deaf professional football player to join the National Football League. The first Deaf player in the National Football League was Bonnie Sloan, who joined the St. Louis Cardinals in 1973. The second Deaf player was Kenny Walker, who joined the Denver Broncos in 1991. However, Derrick Coleman is the first legally Deaf player to win a Super Bowl championship (Friend, 2014).

Coleman is an inspiration to many people, demonstrating that individuals with a disability in one aspect have many abilities and can achieve the highest levels of success within their profession. Coleman has been tremendously successful but says the path was not always easy. For example, at school he was teased and called "Four Ears" because he wore a hearing aid. To help children who are dealing with disabilities (Bresnahan, 2015), Coleman started the No Excuse Foundation. This is a nonprofit organization which provides financial and educational support for children, teenagers, and adults who are hearing impaired. The organization advocates on behalf of the hearing impaired and creates awareness among the hearing through education in order to reduce instances of bullying of hearing impaired individuals. The vision of the organization is to have a world in which people are accepting of individuals with hearing impairments (http://derricklcoleman.com/?p=26).

Discussion Questions:

1. We have just considered an example of the Seattle Seahawks successfully integrating its team's diversity on the basis of hearing ability and going on to win a Super Bowl. How open do you believe professional sports teams are to hiring persons with disabilities?
2. Is there any evidence that having someone with a disability on the team has in any way diminished the team's ability to play the sport well?
3. What things can professional sports teams and other organizations do to be more welcoming of people with a disability who demonstrate high levels of ability to perform the job?

Learning Objectives

After reading this chapter you should be able to:

- Define disability
- Explain the essential functions of a job
- Understand reasonable accommodation and undue hardship

- Know roughly what percentage of the population has a disability
- Understand how disability varies by age
- Be aware of educational attainment of people who have a disability
- Be aware of discrimination against people who have a disability
- Be aware of recommendations for organizations to provide equal opportunity to people with disabilities

The purpose of this chapter is to discuss diversity among people on the basis of ability. There are over one billion people in the world who have a disability (United Nations World Health Organization, 2011). It is important to keep in mind that having a disability in one dimension out of many dimensions in one's life does not detract from the fact that individuals have many other abilities. In a recent review article written by Baldridge, Beatty, Boehm, Kulkarni, and Moore (in press), they stress that "viewing disability as a naturally occurring form of human diversity and an emphasis on human rights are important precursors for reducing workplace disability discrimination, as is a focus on ability rather than disability."

In this chapter, we discuss how disability is defined in the United States by the Americans with Disabilities Act of 1990. We also examine how disability is defined and seen in other parts of the world based on recent research on this topic. This chapter describes the types of discrimination people with disabilities have faced as well as their employment statistics relative to persons without a disability. Finally, suggestions from the United Nations for handling disabilities in a fair manner and providing equal opportunity in the workplace are discussed.

What Is a Disability?

According to Colella and Bruyère (2011), there is no universally accepted definition of the word "disability." Disability has been described as a socially constructed concept where differences between people become disabling when some individuals are not fully integrated into society (Oliver, 1990). Part of the difficulty with defining disability globally is that disability rights are somewhat new in many nations, and the definition of disability and workplace discrimination laws pertaining to disability remain fluid due to changes in social opinion, legislation, and court decisions. Because the definition of disability and the conditions covered under disability law can change over time, employers are sometimes confused about who qualifies as having a disability (Ren, Paetzold, & Colella, 2008).

The World Health Organization describes **disability** as "the umbrella term for impairments, activity limitations and participation restrictions, referring to the negative aspects of the interaction between an individual (with a health condition) and that individual's contextual factors (environmental and personal factors)" (World Health Organization, 2011, p. 4).

Disability in the United States is defined by the Americans with Disabilities Act of 1990 (ADA), a piece of civil rights legislation which prohibits discrimination and is intended to provide persons with disabilities the same opportunities and rights as everyone else with respect to employment, buying goods and services, and participating in local government as well as public services (ADA, 2016). A **disability** is defined by the ADA as "a physical or mental impairment that substantially limits one or more major life activities, a person who has a history or record of such an impairment, or a person who is perceived by others as having such an impairment. The ADA does not specifically name all of the impairments that are covered" (ADA, 2016). **Major life activities** include things such as walking, speaking, breathing, hearing, seeing, learning, working, and being able to take care of oneself, among many others. Thus a few examples of conditions that are considered a loss of major life activities include loss of hearing, loss of vision, mobility impairment, and mental disabilities.

There are many different types of disabilities. In fact, the ADA covers conditions too numerous to list. A **mobility impairment** is associated with the loss of physical function such as the inability to walk. A **mental impairment** may include a psychological disorder, emotional or mental illnesses, and learning disabilities.

The portion of the ADA which specifically handles employment-related discrimination is Title I. "Title I of the Americans with Disabilities Act of 1990 prohibits private employers, State and local governments, employment agencies and labor unions from discriminating against qualified individuals with disabilities in job application procedures, hiring, firing, advancement, compensation, job training, and other terms, conditions, and privileges of employment. The ADA covers employers with 15 or more employees, including State and local governments. It also applies to employment agencies and to labor organizations" (ADA, 2016).

In 2008, the Americans with Disabilities Amendments Act (ADAAA, 2008) was passed to emphasize that the definition of a disability should be broad and typically should not require extensive analysis. According to the Equal Employment Opportunity Commission (EEOC) (2016a) the law also expanded the definition of "major life activities" to include chronic illnesses which had not been covered in the past, including multiple sclerosis and cancer. Chronic illnesses which are episodic and may be in remission are included if they substantially limit major life activities when these illnesses are active. According to the language of the ADAAA of 2008, it expands the definition of "major life activities" by including two non-exhaustive lists. The first list details many activities which the EEOC has recognized for many years (e.g., walking) as well as activities which the EEOC has not explicitly recognized (e.g., bending, reading, and communicating). The second list includes major bodily functions such as "functions of the immune system, normal cell growth, digestive, bowel, bladder, neurological, brain, respiratory, circulatory, endocrine, and reproductive functions" (EEOC, 2016a).

The purpose of the Americans with Disabilities Act is to level the playing field and provide equal opportunities to people with a disability compared to people without a disability. This includes employment, whereby a qualified individual is one who can carry out the **essential functions** of the job with or without reasonable accommodation. It is important for employers to define the essential functions of all jobs because these are the functions that are critical for the existence of the job, and applicants must be able to carry out these functions with or without accommodation to be considered qualified. The non-essential functions of the job are tasks which are secondary to that particular position.

What Is a Reasonable Accommodation and an Undue Hardship?

A **reasonable accommodation** refers to an adjustment which an employer can make to enable a qualified person to perform the job without causing an undue hardship to the employer. Defining an **undue hardship** depends on the size of the employer. If providing an accommodation requires a significant expense or difficulty relative to the employer's size and financial resources, then the employer does not have to provide the accommodation because it is not reasonable for them. The following are examples from the EEOC that exemplify this point.

Example: A store clerk with a disability asks to work part-time as a reasonable accommodation, which would leave part of one shift staffed by one clerk instead of two. This arrangement poses an undue hardship if it causes untimely customer service.

Example: An employee with a disability asks to change her scheduled arrival time from 9:00 a.m. to 10:00 a.m. to attend physical therapy appointments and to stay an hour later. If this accommodation would not affect her ability to complete work in a timely manner or disrupt service to clients or the performance of other workers, it does not pose an undue hardship (EEOC, 2016b).

In reality, most employee accommodations do not cause an undue hardship. According to the language in the ADA (2016), there are four considerations when determining if something causes an undue hardship to an employer (see Figure 9.1).

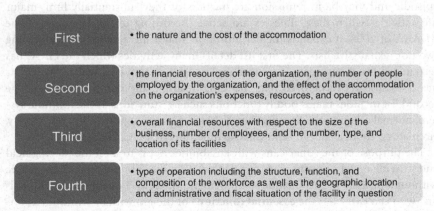

First	• the nature and the cost of the accommodation
Second	• the financial resources of the organization, the number of people employed by the organization, and the effect of the accommodation on the organization's expenses, resources, and operation
Third	• overall financial resources with respect to the size of the business, number of employees, and the number, type, and location of its facilities
Fourth	• type of operation including the structure, function, and composition of the workforce as well as the geographic location and administrative and fiscal situation of the facility in question

FIGURE 9.1. Four Considerations When Determining Undue Hardship to an Employer

Source: Americans with Disabilities Act (2016).

Employers sometimes express concerns about the cost of accommodating employees with disabilities (Colella & Bruyère, 2011), but research shows that most accommodations cost nothing or a modest sum. Reports show that 58% of accommodations cost employers nothing, while 37% of employers experienced a one-time cost, 4% indicated that the accommodation resulted in an ongoing annual cost, and 1% said that the accommodation required an ongoing annual cost as well as a one-time cost. Of those employers with accommodations that required a one-time cost, the average cost was $500. When asked how much an accommodation for a disabled worker cost above the cost of providing equipment for a non-disabled worker in the same position, the average reported was $400 (Job Accommodation Network, 2015). In sum, the average cost of an accommodation is modest. Employers who made accommodations also reported several benefits as a result, including: retaining valued employees, increasing employee productivity, eliminating the cost of training a new employee, and increasing workplace diversity (Job Accommodation Network, 2015). Examples of reasonable accommodations include making existing facilities used by employees usable by people with disabilities, restructuring jobs, acquiring modification equipment or devices, modifying training materials or policies, and providing part-time or modified work schedules (ADA, 2016).

Global View: Spain

In Spain, the LISMI, or law of Social Integration of Disabled People, requires that employers with a more than 50 employees hire individuals with disabilities at no less than 2% of its workforce (LISMI, 2017). However, the reality is that few businesses comply with the law, including the transportation system in that country (http://www.lismi.es). For example, in Madrid public transportation is not 100% wheelchair accessible. A common complaint is that of the buses that have wheelchair lifts, many do not work. Unsafe wheelchair ramps, lack of funds to update older buildings to the new code compliance regulations, and poorly planned subway stations such as Estación del Sol, in Madrid, which was built without an elevator to connect the subway's platform to the street above, represent daily hurdles disabled people in Madrid must face (Santana, 2015).

How Many People Have a Disability?

Over one billion people, or about 15% of the world's population, have a disability (United Nations World Health Organization, 2011). The World Health Organization (2015a) estimates that 360 million people worldwide, or over 5% of the world's population, have a disabling hearing loss. With respect to visual impairment and blindness, the World Health Organization (2014) estimates that 285 million people are visually impaired worldwide. Of these, 39 million are blind while 246 million have low vision. While an estimated 82% of people living with blindness are aged 50 or older, 80% of all visual impairments can be cured or prevented (World Health Organization, 2014). With respect to mental disabilities, the World Health Organization (2015b) describes that there are many different mental disorders and that they include "a combination of abnormal thoughts, perceptions, emotions, behaviour and relationships with others." Such disorders include depression, bipolar disorder, schizophrenia and other psychoses, dementia, intellectual disabilities, and developmental disabilities such as autism. Worldwide, an estimated 350 million people are affected by depression, 60 million are affected by bipolar disorder, 21 million are affected by schizophrenia, and 47.5 million have dementia (World Health Organization, 2015b).

According to the United States Census Bureau (Brault, 2012), about 56.7 million people, or 18.7% of the population in the United States, have a disability. Of these 56.7 million people with a disability, 38.3% are considered severe disabilities, and 12.3% need assistance. The prevalence of a disability increases with age. The percentages of people with a disability in various age brackets are as follows: 8.4% of the population aged 15 or under, 10.2% of the population aged 15 to 24, 11% of the population aged 24 to 44, 19.7% of the population aged 45 to 54, 28.7% of the population aged 55 to 64, 35% of the population aged 65 to 69, 42.6% of the population aged 70 to 74, 53.6% of the population aged 75 to 79, and 70.5% of the population aged 80 or over (Brault, 2012).

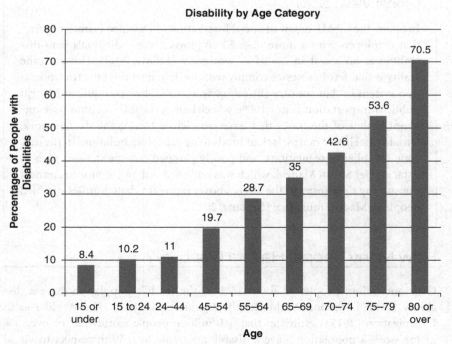

FIGURE 9.2. Disability by Age Category

Source: Brault (2012): United States Census Bureau.

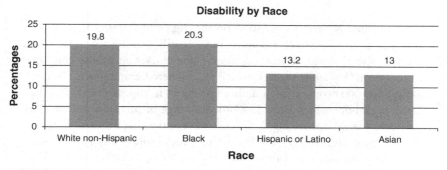

FIGURE 9.3. Disability by Race

Source: Brault (2012): United States Census Bureau.

Broken down by race, 19.8% of the White non-Hispanic population has a disability while 20.3% of the Black population has a disability, 13.2% of the Hispanic or Latino population has a disability, and 13% of the Asian population has a disability (Brault, 2012).

Global View: Germany

Germany has generally adopted a medical definition of disability, defining disability as a person whose physical, cognitive, or psychological health deviates from the typical average for someone of similar age for a period of more than six months, thus having a negative impact on their inclusion in society (SGB IX). Disability status is diagnosed by a medical doctor, who assigns a degree of disability ranging from 0% to 100%. This disability score is documented on an official disability identification card which can then be used by the cardholder to obtain selected benefits in their private or professional lives (Baldridge et al., 2016).

German organizations employing over 20 employees must fill 5% of their positions with applicants who have a disability. If they fail to do so, they must pay a monthly penalty ranging from 115€ to 290€ for each job which should have been occupied by someone with a disability (Baldridge et al., 2016). The revenues generated from these fines totaled 486 million Euros in the year 2012 and were used to provide vocational integration efforts for the disabled (BIH, 2013; Kock, 2004).

Germany has not always endorsed practices that allow the disabled to fully participate in social institutions. For example, Germany had a practice of separation in the past which included having special schools for children with disabilities. These institutions separated children with disabilities from their peers, thus creating stigmatization and inequality for persons with disabilities both early and later in life (Powell, 2003).

The United Nations Convention on the Rights of Persons with Disabilities was enacted in 2009. However, there is still a difference in Germany between those employed in the general labor market and those employed in the secondary labor market, which has sheltered employment. In 2011, almost 300,000 people with disabilities held jobs in approximately 700 sheltered workshops which provide a broader range of products and services. Sheltered workshops are highly specialized facilities that provide vocational rehabilitation to persons with disabilities. People voluntarily participate in sheltered workshops, and these sheltered workshops currently provide an opportunity for approximately 300,000 people to work at more than 2,600 locations (Völker, 2014). However, only 2.7% of persons employed in the secondary labor market were successful in transferring into the general labor market (BIH, 2013). Unemployment rates are also higher for persons with disabilities in Germany, with the unemployment rate of disabled persons at 14.8% in the year 2012 compared to 6.8% for persons without a disability (Völker, 2014).

Disability and Employment Status

Worldwide, the data show that people with disabilities have lower employment rates than people without disabilities. Switzerland, Mexico, Norway, and Canada have some of the highest employment ratios for people with disabilities (employment rate of people with disabilities divided by employment rate of the overall population). Their employment ratios are 0.81, 0.79, 0.76, and 0.75, respectively. South Africa, Poland, Peru, Japan, and Spain have some of the lowest employment ratios for people with disabilities. Their employment ratios are 0.30, 0.33, 0.37, 0.38, and 0.44 respectively (United Nations World Health Report, 2011).

According to the United States Bureau of Labor Statistics (2016) the overall unemployment rate for the civilian labor force in the United States was 6.2% for the year 2014. Among persons with a disability, the unemployment rate was 12.5% for 2014. Unemployment rates for persons with disabilities also vary by race. For example, 11.2% of White non-Hispanic persons with a disability were unemployed compared to 8.6% of Asians, 21.6% of Blacks, and 16.1% of Hispanics. By comparison, the unemployment rates for persons with no disability are as follows: 5.1% of White non-Hispanic persons with a disability were unemployed compared to 4.9% of Asians, 11% of Blacks, and 7.2% of Hispanics. Unemployment rates for disabled persons also vary by their level of education, as follows: 16% for those having less than a high school diploma, 11.3% for high school graduates, 10.7% for those with some college or an associate's degree, and 8.3% for those with a bachelor's degree or higher. In all categories, the unemployment rate for disabled persons is higher than their non-disabled counterparts, whose unemployment rates by education level are as follows: 8.6% for those having less

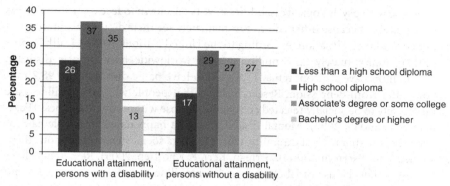

FIGURE 9.4. Educational Attainment of People With and Without a Disability

Source: United States Census Bureau (2016).

than a high school diploma, 5.8% for high school graduates, 5.2% for those with some college or an associate's degree, and 3% for those with a bachelor's degree or higher.

With respect to education, the United States Census Bureau (2016) reports that as of the year 2008, 26% of persons with a disability had less than a high school diploma, while 37% had a high school diploma, 35% had an associate's degree or some college, and 13% had a bachelor's degree or higher. Therefore, educational attainment is somewhat lower than that of people without a disability in the United States for 2008, where 17% had less than a high school diploma, 29% had a high school diploma, 27% had an associate's degree or some college, and 27% had a bachelor's degree or higher (United States Census Bureau, 2016).

Discrimination Against Persons With Disabilities

Research shows that observers can categorize persons with disabilities, which triggers stereotyping and can lead to discriminatory behavior (Stone & Colella, 1996). For example, job applicants in wheelchairs have faced discrimination, with employers believing they might be difficult to accommodate (Johnson & Heal, 1976; Lyth, 1973). One research study found that job applicants without a physical mobility impairment were 3.2 times more likely to obtain a positive reaction compared to qualified applicants who had a mobility impairment (Ravaud, Madiot, & Ville, 1992). Another study (Bowe, McMahon, Chang, & Louvi, 2005) reported that people with hearing loss often complain about not being hired for positions, receiving equal training for jobs, receiving promotions, being discharged from their jobs, and not receiving needed accommodations, as well as being teased by coworkers because of their speech or pronunciation of words. Research shows that job applicants with a visual impairment can be at a disadvantage if their résumés are not seen as aesthetically pleasing compared to those of applicants who do not have a disability (Wang, Barron, & Hebl, 2010).

People with psychological disabilities have been shown to face discrimination as well, possibly because others do not immediately see their disability and may not understand their situation. According to the United Nations World Health Report (2011), approximately 22.2 million people worldwide have bipolar disorder, 16.7 million have schizophrenia, 13.8 million have panic disorder, and 98.7 million suffer from depression. Research shows that people with mental illness are more likely to be socially rejected compared to those without mental illness (Feldman & Crandall, 2007). Mental disability stigma happens when people categorize others with a mental disability, which triggers social stereotypes about them and leads to discrimination (Corrigan, Kerr, & Knudsen, 2005). Researchers have suggested that the use of labels such as "mental illness" activates stereotypes and leads to social rejection of people with mental disability (Link, Cullen, Struening, Shrout, & Dohrenwend, 1989).

In addition, research shows that being discriminated against can lead to a lack of employment and adequate housing for people with disabilities (Corrigan & Kleinlein, 2005). Therefore, it is important to be mindful of the language that is used when describing people with disabilities to avoid triggering stereotypes that can lead to such damaging effects. Stereotyping can also lead to more interactions between people with mental disabilities and the police or criminal justice system (Watson, Corrigan, & Ottati, 2004). Further, social stereotyping associated with diagnoses can lead people without disabilities to perceive the disabled as being more different. Additionally, individuals with disabilities may internalize these stereotypes, which can be damaging to self-esteem if they anticipate social rejection (Corrigan, 2007). Research shows that such stereotyping of people with disabilities has led many who have invisible disabilities or chronic illnesses that are not always apparent to others to "pass" and not reveal their condition to employers or coworkers for fear of being stigmatized (Beatty, 2012; Clair, Beatty, & MacLean, 2005).

Global View: India

In India, the Department of Empowerment of Persons with Disabilities describes that a person with a disability is someone who experiences no less than 40% of any disability as certified by a doctor. A number of conditions are covered including blindness, low vision, leprosy, hearing impairment, loco-motor disability, autism, mental retardation, mental illness, and cerebral palsy, among other conditions and combinations of these conditions (Department of Empowerment of Persons with Disabilities, 2016).

To increase employment rates among disabled persons, the Ministry of Social Justice and Empowerment provides monetary awards and recognition to outstanding employers of people with disabilities. Also, small quotas have been implemented to employ people with disabilities in selected jobs within public sector organizations. However, only 34% of people with disabilities are employed (Baldridge et al., 2016). This may be due, in part, to lenient enforcement whereby failure to comply with the quota system is not met with government sanctions (Dawn, 2012). Cultural barriers also exist for persons with disabilities in India, where disability is associated with sin, shame (Peters, Gabel, & Symeonidou, 2009), and past karmas (World Bank Report, 2007). There is also limited infrastructure in some parts of India with respect to providing accessibility for persons with mobility impairments. Overall, persons with disabilities in India face employment uncertainty and are not represented in trade unions, and thereby they have little voice in important employment forums (Confederation of Indian Industry Report on Disability, 2009; Diversity and Equal Opportunity Centre Report, 2009; World Bank Report, 2007).

Employee Reactions to Coworkers With Disabilities and Accommodations

Research findings in the area of employee reactions to those with disabilities present some results that are favorable for people with disabilities and some that are not. One experimental study shows that stigma about persons with disabilities is negatively associated with attitudes toward one's coworkers with a disability, negatively associated with perceived fairness of accommodations for the disabled at work, and positively associated with discriminatory employment judgments (McLaughlin, Bell, & Stringer, 2004). This research study found that women were less likely to make discriminatory employment judgments compared to men and that minorities were more likely to judge an accommodation for their coworkers as fair compared to Whites (McLaughlin et al., 2004). It is possible that people who have personally experienced minority status on one or more dimensions are more sympathetic to those who also experience minority status on the basis of ability.

In another experimental study examining the effects of emotional disability and performance standards on performance ratings, Czajka and DeNisi (1988) found that at all proficiency levels, employees with a disability received more favorable ratings than employees without a disability. When performance standards were not specified, disabled workers were given higher performance ratings than non-disabled workers across all proficiency levels. However, when performance standards were specified, these performance rating differences disappeared, and non-disabled workers were rated slightly higher than disabled workers at all proficiency levels. The authors described that perhaps they found evidence of the norm to be kind toward people with disabilities. The authors explained that most people are emotionally ambivalent toward the disabled and that many people may hold a belief that people with disabilities may be less capable of doing a job, yet deserve a break because of their disability (Czajka & DeNisi, 1988).

One other finding that has been demonstrated across two experimental studies is that participants react more negatively to others with a disability when their own personal rewards are somehow connected to those of the disabled person. Colella, DeNisi, and Varma (1998) conducted an experiment where a confederate (a student who appears to be one of the participants but is in fact working as part of the research team) either had dyslexia or had no disability and was either working independently or interdependently with a partner. The results of the study showed that only in the interdependent condition where the participant's rewards were dependent upon the dyslexic student's performance did the participants have a negative reaction toward the disabled student as their partner. When interdependence of rewards was not an issue, there were no negative effects of the confederate's disability status on the performance ratings or expectations others had of them. That is to say, the other participants accurately rated the dyslexic confederate's current performance and expectation of future performance as reflected by that person's current performance. However, there was a negative effect for the dyslexic confederate's disability status on the desirability of him or her as a partner when the chances for obtaining the reward were dependent upon a partner's performance. The authors concluded that negative bias is most likely to occur only under conditions where the other person's action has a consequence for the participant (Colella et al., 1998).

These findings are consistent with another study published by Paetzold et al. (2008) that experimentally examined fairness perceptions of accommodating people with disabilities. In the experiment, a confederate who pretended to have dyslexia was either granted an accommodation of receiving a few more minutes to finish the task or not. The authors found that granting an accommodation was seen as less fair than not granting it and that fairness perceptions were lowest when the person with a disability received an accommodation and excelled in his or her performance and won the largest cash prize. Results showed a paradox: the intent of the Americans with Disabilities Act is to level the playing field for people with disabilities, but others perceive an accommodation as unfair when it helps the requester outperform the competition.

Global View: China

The 1990 Law of the People's Republic of China on the Protection of Disabled Persons defines a person with a disability as a "... person who suffers from abnormalities or loss of a certain organ or function, psychologically or physiologically, or in anatomical structure and has lost wholly or in part the ability to perform an activity in the way considered normal ..." (International Labour Office, 2003, p. 13).

Before 1980, people with disabilities in China were frequently referred to as "can fei," meaning "the handicapped and useless" (Liu, 2001). Through the work of disability rights advocates and government support, this has slowly changed, and now the term "can ji ren," which means "disabled persons" or "persons with disabilities," is more often used by the public as well as on official state documents (Disabled World, 2010).

One challenge to disability rights in China is cultural because in a number of areas disability is viewed as a punishment for the sins of one's parents or one's own past life sins (Liu, 2001). Feelings of shame or guilt sometimes create barriers to acceptance of a disability among family members (Lam, 1992). Further, mental health is often associated with self-discipline in China while emotional problems are associated with weakness of character (Lee, 1996).

Some research suggests Chinese people have more positive attitudes toward people with physical disabilities compared to people with developmental disabilities and mental disorders (Wang, Chan, Thomas, Lin, & Larson, 1997). Results from a Chinese sample also showed that participants were more sympathetic toward people with disabilities that were acquired rather than congenital (Wang et al., 1997).

According to the China Labour Bulletin (2017), of the disabled people who could care for themselves in 2010, 34% of those living in urban areas were employed and 49% of those living in rural areas were employed. Those who did find employment were often working in low-wage positions. In an effort to increase employment opportunities for the disabled, Regulations on the Employment of People with Disabilities were introduced in 2007 and required that firms should have 1.5% of their workforce comprised of persons with disabilities, otherwise they shall pay a fee which will go into employment fund for the disabled (China Labour Bulletin, 2017). However, it appears this regulation has not been enforced. A survey of government entities across 30 cities in China showed that the largest percentage of disabled employees in any of the government agencies surveyed was .39%. Also, an audit of the penalty fees which are supposed to be used as an employment fund for the disabled found that only 13.7% of those funds were used for that purpose (Fang, 2011).

Recommendations for Organizations

Research shows that educational interventions which inform people about disability can be successful. Hunt and Hunt (2004) implemented a brief educational intervention to examine whether this training would improve knowledge and attitudes of participants toward disabled persons. The research showed an effect of the educational intervention such that the presentation significantly increased both the respondents' knowledge about persons with disabilities as well as their attitudes toward persons with disabilities. Overall, women reported having higher knowledge about people with disabilities compared to men, and they also reported having more positive attitudes toward disabled people than men. Nevertheless, the training was effective.

According to the United Nations World Health Report (2011), disability is a human rights issue because throughout the world people with disabilities are denied equal access to employment, health care, education, and political partici-pation and are sometimes denied autonomy or subject to the violation of dignity. The United Nations recommends the following:

- Respect for the dignity and individual autonomy of all people, including the ability to make one's own choices
- No tolerance for discrimination
- Inclusion of people with disability in society so they have effective and full participation
- Acceptance of people with disabilities as a natural part of human diversity and respect for these differences
- Providing equality of opportunity for all
- Providing accessibility for the disabled
- Promoting equality between women and men with disabilities
- Respecting the capacities of children with disabilities and the right of these children to preserve their identities

As discussed earlier, according to the Americans with Disabilities Act in the U.S., it is very important for organizations to know the essential functions of a job from the time they create the job description and post it. If a job description clearly outlines the essential functions of the job that candidates must meet, this can help organizations avoid discrimination against qualified individuals who have a dis-ability. Employees who participate in the interview/selection process to fill jobs should conduct **structured interviews**, whereby they ask the same questions of all candidates and evaluate the answers based on consistent pre-determined cri-teria to provide a consistent interview experience and candidate evaluation. Also, the interview questions should be based on the job description and should focus on ascertaining whether the candidates have the knowledge, skills, and abilities to perform the job. The purpose of the interview is to select candidates who are capable of performing the essential functions of the job with or without reason-able accommodation.[1]

Employees with disabilities should be compensated equitably compared to employees without disabilities, based on their skills, education, and experience, just like any other employee. People with disabilities should also be provided the same opportunities for training and development as employees without disabilities. Further, employees with disabilities should be provided with developmental feedback during performance appraisal processes, the same as other employees would be, to help them further develop their professional skills. The performance standards applied to evaluate performance for the essential functions of the job should also be the same for employees with and without disabilities.

There are several organizations that provide assistance for employers seeking to hire workers with disabilities or provide accommodations. One example is the Job Accommodation Network (https://askjan.org), which answers questions about workplace accommodations as well as the Americans with Disabilities Act and related legislation. The U.S. Department of Labor (https://www.dol.gov/odep/resources/earn.htm) also provides resources to help organizations hire and retain disabled employees through the Employer Assistance and Resource Network on Disability Inclusion (EARN).

Closing Case
Chiropractic College and Accommodations for the Blind

In a significant success for the rights of blind students, the Iowa Supreme Court voted in favor of a blind student plaintiff and ordered Palmer Chiropractic College to provide accommodations which allow disabled students to finish their degrees (Nelson, 2014). Palmer Chiropractic College was founded in 1897 and is considered the birthplace of the field of chiropractic (Foley, 2014). The court refused to accept the college's argument that "eyesight is a requirement for the profession, which involves adjusting patients' spines to treat pain" (Foley, 2014). Palmer Chiropractic College argued that chiropractors need to read X-rays in order to deliver effective and safe adjustments and that it was not feasible for blind students to rely on sighted assistants.

Speaking on behalf of the majority, Justice Daryl Hecht argued that the college discriminated when it did not allow Aaron Cannon to complete his degree with help from a sighted reader. He said that Palmer has had blind graduates in the past and that 20% or more of chiropractors' offices do not provide medical imaging. The dissenting opinion was delivered by Justice Thomas Waterman, who expressed that political correctness was being elevated over common sense in the ruling (Nelson, 2014).

Palmer Chiropractic College said it would continue making "reasonable academic accommodations" for disabled students. The president of the National Board of Chiropractic Examiners said in a statement: "We share the concerns expressed in the dissenting opinion regarding the potential adverse effects the ruling may have on health and public safety" (Foley, 2014). The decision reinstates the ruling of the Davenport Civil Rights Commission ordering Palmer Chiropractic College to readmit Cannon with the use of a sighted assistant and pay him $100,000 in damages and legal fees. Palmer Chiropractic College appealed the decision, but the appeal was unsuccessful (Foley, 2014).

Discussion Questions:

1. Do you agree or disagree with the decision of the Davenport Civil Rights Commission? Why?
2. Do you think that chiropractors must have good vision in order to do their work?
3. According to the Americans with Disabilities Act, organizations are required to provide reasonable accommodations that do not cause them an undue hardship. Does it seem like providing a sighted assistant to read X-rays meets the definition of a reasonable accommodation for Palmer Chiropractic College?

Note

1. This is the requirement according to the Americans with Disabilities Act in the U.S., and it will vary across countries.

References

ADA. (2016). Information and technical assistance on the Americans with Disabilities Act. Retrieved from http://www.ada.gov/

ADAAA. (2008). ADA Amendments Act of 2008. Equal Employment Opportunity Commission. Retrieved from http://www.eeoc.gov/laws/statutes/adaaa.cfm

Baldridge, D., Beatty, J., Boehm, S. A., Kulkarni, M., & Moore, M. (in press). Persons with (dis)abilities. In A. Colella & E. King (Eds.), *The Oxford handbook of workplace discrimination*. New York: Oxford University Press.

Beatty, J. E. (2012). Career barriers experienced by people with chronic illness: A U.S. study. *Employee Responsibilities and Rights Journal, 24*, 91–110.

BIH. (2013). *Jahresbericht der Bundesarbeitsgemeinschaft der Integrationsämter und Hauptfürsorgestellen*. Wiesbaden: Universum.

Biography.com. (2016, February 5). Derrick Coleman. A&E Television Networks. Retrieved from http://www.biography.com/people/derrick-coleman

Bowe, F. G., McMahon, B. T., Chang, T., & Louvi, I. (2005). Workplace discrimination, deafness and hearing impairment: The national EEOC ADA research project. *Work, 25*(1), 19–25.

Brault, M. W. (2012, July 27). Americans with disabilities: 2010. United States Census Bureau. Retrieved from https://www.census.gov/newsroom/cspan/disability/20120726_cspan_disability_slides.pdf

Bresnahan, S. (2015, August 6). Derrick Coleman: The deaf Super Bowl champion who broke the sound barrier. *CNN*. Retrieved from http://www.cnn.com/2015/08/06/health/derrick-coleman-seahawks-deaf/

China Labour Bulletin. (2017). Workplace Discrimination. Retrieved from http://www.clb.org.hk/content/workplace-discrimination#disability

Clair, J. A., Beatty, J. E., & MacLean, T. L. (2005). Out of sight but not out of mind: Managing invisible social identities in the workplace. *Academy of Management Review, 30*, 78–95.

Colella, A., & Bruyère, S. M. (2011). Disability and employment: New directions for industrial and organizational psychology. In S. Zedek (Ed.), *APA handbook of industrial/organizational psychology* (pp. 473–503). Washington, DC: American Psychological Association.

Colella, A., DeNisi, A. S., & Varma, A. (1998). The impact of ratee's disability on performance judgments and choice as partner: The role of disability—job fit stereotypes and interdependence of rewards. *Journal of Applied Psychology, 83*, 102–111.

Confederation of Indian Industry. (2009). *A values route to business success: The why and how of employing persons with disability*. Bangalore, India: Diversity and Equal Opportunity Center.

Corrigan, P. W. (2007). How clinical diagnosis might exacerbate the stigma of mental illness. *Social Work, 52*(1), 31–39.

Corrigan, P. W., Kerr, A., & Knudsen, L. (2005). The stigma of mental illness: Explanatory models and methods for change. *Applied and Preventive Psychology, 11*, 179–190.

Corrigan, P. W., & Kleinlein, P. (2005). The impact of mental illness stigma. In P. W. Corrigan (Ed.), *On the stigma of mental illness: Practical strategies for research and social change* (pp. 11–44). Washington, DC: American Psychological Association.

Czajka, J. M., & DeNisi, A. S. (1988). Effects of emotional disability and clear performance standards on performance ratings. *Academy of Management Journal, 31*, 394–404.

Dawn, R. (2012). Challenges in the employment of persons with disabilities. *Economic and Political Weekly, 47*(36), 20–22.

Department of Empowerment of Persons with Disabilities. (2016). Annual Report 2015-16. Ministry of Social Justice and Empowerment. Government of India. Retrieved from http://www.disabilityaffairs.gov.in/upload/57301ed5a347fDisabilities_AR_2015-16_%20English.pdf

Disabled World. (2010, March 16). Overview of Disability in China. Retrieved from https://www.disabled-world.com/news/asia/china/disability-china.php

Diversity and Equal Opportunity Centre. (2009). Employment of disabled people in India. Retrieved from http://www.dnis.org/Employment.pdf

Equal Employment Opportunity Commission. (2016a). Notice concerning the Americans with Disabilities Act (ADA) Amendments Act of 2008. Retrieved from http://www.eeoc.gov/laws/statutes/adaaa_notice.cfm

Equal Employment Opportunity Commission. (2016b). The Americans with Disabilities Act: A primer for small business. Retrieved from https://www.eeoc.gov/eeoc/publications/adahandbook.cfm

Fang, L. (2011, September 9). Denied Access to China's Disability Fund. *Caixin Online*. Retrieved from http://english.caixin.com/2011-09-09/100302298.html

Feldman, D. B., & Crandall, C. S. (2007). Dimensions of mental illness stigma: What about mental illness stigma causes social rejection? *Journal of Social and Clinical Psychology, 26*(2), 137–154.

Foley, R. J. (2014, June 28). Ruling: College must accommodate blind chiropractic students. Associated Press. Des Moines Register. Retrieved from http://www.desmoinesregister.com/story/news/crime-and-courts/2014/06/28/palmer-chiropractic-college-blind-students/11581557/

Friend, T. (2014, January 31). Derrick Coleman misses nothing. *ESPN*. Retrieved from http://espn.go.com/nfl/playoffs/2013/story/_/id/10372203/super-bowl-xlviii-deafness-deter-seattle-derrick-coleman

Hunt, C. S., & Hunt, B. (2004). Changing attitudes toward people with disabilities: Experimenting with an educational intervention. *Journal of Managerial Issues*, *16*, 266–281.

International Labour Organization. (2003, January 17). *Legislation, Policy and Programmes Concerning the Employment of People with Disabilities in Selected Countries of Asia and the Pacific: Background Document*. Bangkok: International Labour Organization. Retrieved from http://www.ilo.org/wcmsp5/groups/public/—asia/—ro-bangkok/documents/publication/wcms_bk_pb_90_en.pdf

Job Accommodation Network. (2015, September 1). Workplace accommodations: Low cost, high impact. Retrieved from http://askjan.org/media/downloads/LowCostHighImpact.pdf

Johnson, R., & Heal, L. W. (1976). Private employment agency responses to the physically handicapped applicant in a wheelchair. *Journal of Applied Rehabilitation Counseling*, *7*(1), 12–21.

Kock, M. (2004). Disability law in Germany: An overview of employment, education and access rights. *German Law Journal*, *5*(11), 1373–1392.

Lam, C. (1992). *Vocational rehabilitation development in Hong Kong: A cross-cultural perspective*. Stillwater, OK: National Clearing House of Rehabilitation Training Materials.

Lee, E. (1996). Chinese families. In M. McGoldrick, J. Giordano, & J. Pearce (Eds.), *Ethnicity family therapy* (2nd ed., pp. 248–267). New York: Guilford Press.

Link, B. G., Cullen, F. T., Struening, E., Shrout, P. E., & Dohrenwend, B. P. (1989). A modified labeling theory approach to mental disorders: An empirical assessment. *American Sociological Review*, *54*(3), 400–423.

LISMI. (2017). LISMI – Ley de Integración Social del Minusválido. Retrieved from http://www.lismi.es/

Liu, G. Z. (2001). Chinese culture and disability: Information for US service providers. Center for International Rehabilitation Research Information and Exchange (CIRRIE). Retrieved from http://cirrie.buffalo.edu/culture/monographs/china.php

Lyth, M. (1973). Employers' attitudes to the employment of the disabled. *Occupational Psychology*, *47*(1/2), 67–70.

McLaughlin, M. E., Bell, M. P., & Stringer, D. Y. (2004). Stigma and acceptance of coworkers with disabilities: Understudied aspects of workforce diversity. *Group and Organization Management*, *29*, 302–333.

Nelson, S. (2014, June 27). Iowa Supreme Court rules blind student should be allowed at Palmer. WQAD. Retrieved from http://wqad.com/2014/06/27/iowa-supreme-court-rules-blind-student-should-be-allowed-at-palmer/

Oliver, M. (1990). *The politics of disablement*. London: Palgrave Macmillan.

Paetzold, R., García, M. F., Colella, A., Ren, R., Triana, M., & Ziebro, M. (2008). Perceptions of people with disabilities: When is "reasonable" accommodation fair? *Basic and Applied Social Psychology*, *30*, 27–35.

Peters, S., Gabel, S., & Symeonidou, S. (2009). Resistance, transformation and the politics of hope: Imagining a way forward for the disabled people's movement. *Disability & Society*, *24*(5), 543–556.

Powell, J. J. W. (2003). Constructing disability and social inequality early in the life course: The case of special education in Germany and the United States. *Disability Studies Quarterly*, *23*(2), 57–75.

Ravaud, J., Madiot, B., & Ville, I. (1992). Discrimination towards disabled people seeking employment. *Social Science & Medicine*, *35*(8), 951–958.

Ren, L. R., Paetzold, R. L., & Colella, A. (2008). A meta-analysis of experimental studies on the effects of disability on human resource judgments. *Human Resource Management Review, 18*(3), 191–203.

Santana, C. (2015, December 3). La ciudad está diseñada para que al discapacitado lo empujen. *El País*. Retrieved from http://politica.elpais.com/politica/2015/11/12/actual idad/1447351553_586661.html

SGB IX. Sozialgesetzbuch (SGB). (2001). Neuntes Buch (IX)—Rehabilitation und Teil-habe behinderter Menschen. Retrieved from http://www.gesetze-im-internet.de/sgb_9/index.html

Stone, D. L., & Colella, A. (1996). A model of factors affecting the treatment of disabled individuals in organizations. *Academy of Management Review, 21*, 352–401.

United Nations. (2009). Convention of the rights of persons with disabilities. Retrieved from http://www.un.org/disabilities/convention/conventionfull.shtml

United States Bureau of Labor Statistics. (2016). Table 1. Employment status of the civil-ian noninstitutional population by disability status and selected characteristics, 2014 annual averages. Retrieved from http://www.bls.gov/news.release/disabl.t01.htm

United States Census Bureau. (2016). Table 1. Selected characteristics of civilians 16 to 74 years old with a work disability, by educational attainment and sex for 2008. Retrieved from https://www.census.gov/people/disability/data/cps.html

Völker, K. (2014, June 20). Work and employment for persons with disabilities in Germany. BAG WfbM. Bundesarbeitsgemeinschaft. Werkstätten für behinderte Menschen e.V. Special board and standing committee meeting on employment event, Brussels.

Wang, K., Barron, L. G., & Hebl, M. R. (2010). Making those who cannot see look best: Effects of visual resume formatting on ratings of job applicants with blindness. *Rehabil-itation Psychology, 55*(1), 68–73.

Wang, M. H., Chan, F., Thomas, K. R., Lin, S. H., & Larson, P. (1997). Coping style and per-sonal responsibility as factors in the perception of individuals with physical disabilities by Chinese international students. *Rehabilitation Psychology, 42*(4), 303.

Watson, A. C., Corrigan, P. W., & Ottati, V. (2004). Police responses to persons with mental illness: Does the label matter? *Journal of the American Academy of Psychiatry and the Law, 32*, 378–385.

World Bank Report. (2007). People with disabilities in India: From commitments to out comes. Retrieved from http://www.worldbank.org.in/WBSITE/EXTERNAL/COUNTRIES/SOUTHASIAEXT/INDIAEXTN/0,,contentMDK:21557057~pagePK:1497618~piP K:217854~theSitePK:295584,00.html

World Health Organization. (2011). World report on disability. Geneva: World Health Orga-nization. Retrieved from http://www.who.int/disabilities/world_report/2011/report.pdf

World Health Organization. (2014). Visual impairment and blindness. Retrieved from http://www.who.int/mediacentre/factsheets/fs282/en/

World Health Organization. (2015a). Deafness and hearing loss. Retrieved from http://www.who.int/mediacentre/factsheets/fs300/en/

World Health Organization. (2015b). Mental disorders. Retrieved from http://www.who.int/mediacentre/factsheets/fs396/en/

ten
National Origin and Immigration

Opening Case

America, the Melting Pot

The **melting pot** is a metaphor to describe how a society develops, whereby people of different cultures, races, and religions are combined to create a diverse, multi-ethnic society. The term originated in the United States and is often used to describe societies experiencing large-scale immigration from a number of different countries.

The writings of J. Hector St. John de Crevecoeur in his *Letters from an American Farmer* (St. John de Crèvecoeur, 1792; reprinted in 1981) are an example from American literature of the concept of immigrants "melting" into the new home country. He writes, "Here individuals of all nations are *melted* into a new race of men, whose labors and posterity will one day cause great changes in the world."

> . . . whence came all these people? They are a mixture of English, Scotch, Irish, French, Dutch, Germans, and Swedes . . . What, then, is the American, this new man? He is neither a European nor the descendant of a European; hence that strange mixture of blood, which you will find in no other country. I could point out to you a family whose grandfather was an Englishman, whose wife was Dutch, whose son married a French woman, and whose present four sons have now four wives of different nations. He is an American, who, leaving behind him all his ancient prejudices and manners, receives new ones from

the new mode of life he has embraced, the new government he obeys, and the new rank he holds . . . The Americans were once scattered all over Europe; here they are incorporated into one of the finest systems of population which has ever appeared (St. John de Crèvecoeur, 1792; reprinted in 1981).

The Statue of Liberty is one of the most distinctive landmarks in the United States. She is associated with immigrants because she stands on Ellis Island in New York Harbor, a place where many thousands of immigrants first set foot on U.S. soil in search of a new and better life. There is a poem called "The New Colossus" which is engraved on the pedestal where Lady Liberty stands. The poem was written by Emma Lazarus, and it ends like this: "Give me your tired, your poor, Your huddled masses yearning to breathe free, The wretched refuse of your teeming shore. Send these, the homeless, tempest-tost to me, I lift my lamp beside the golden door!" (Liberty State Park, 2017)

1. America is a nation full of immigrants and descendants of immigrants. In what ways do you think this shapes Americans' views on immigration and acceptance of immigrants today?
2. America has the idea of being a melting pot. In countries that have no such idea that they are a melting pot of immigrants, how do you think they view immigrants?

Learning Objectives
After reading this chapter, you should be able to:

- Be familiar with the term "melting pot" and why it is applied to America
- Know about discrimination against immigrant groups and why it happens
- Be aware of Title VII employment law, which prohibits national origin discrimination
- Name some prominent immigrants to the United States who have made great contributions to society
- Know why immigration is influenced by the economy and politics
- Understand the economic impact of immigration
- Understand how immigrant groups become part of the larger society through processes such as recategorization, contact, segregation, assimilation, and acculturation
- List a few suggestions for organizations to be inclusive and avoid national origin discrimination

The purpose of this chapter is to define immigration and discuss research findings on immigration, primarily in the United States but including other parts of the world as well. According to the United Nations (2013), more people immigrate to the United States than any other country in the world. This makes the United States a great context in which to examine immigration and its outcomes. We begin by defining immigration and discussing research findings about immigration in organizations. We delve into topics including discrimination against immigrants and its root causes. The chapter also examines the economic impact of immigration in the United States. We then turn to a discussion of things that can be done to reduce the bias against immigrants and present a discussion about acculturation, assimilation, and integration of immigrants into the new host country. Finally, recommendations for organizations with regard to immigration are presented.

America is a nation of immigrants (Hirschman & Snipp, 2001, p. 623). With the exception of American Indians, who are the first known human inhabitants of the area that is now the United States, every other group has immigrated to the United States. Ever since Christopher Columbus reached America in 1492, immigrants have been coming to the United States in search of a new life with more freedom and better opportunity. Yet there is little research on discrimination in the workplace due to immigration status. While much research has examined sex discrimination, race discrimination, and to a lesser extent age discrimination (Dipboye & Colella, 2005), research in the area of immigration discrimination at work is very limited (Bell, Kwesiga, & Berry, 2010). In fact, immigrants have been called the invisible minority (Bell et al., 2010). The omission of immigrants in research is problematic because immigrants made up approximately 16.7% of the U.S. labor force in 2015 (Bureau of Labor Statistics, 2016). There is also a high level of immigration worldwide (Schwartz, Unger, Zamboanga, & Szapocznik, 2010). According to the United Nations, 232 million people currently live abroad; this represents an increase of 32.57% from 175 million in the year 2000 (United Nations, 2013). Therefore, it is valuable to learn more about immigrants and their experiences.

Global View: Albert Einstein, a German-Born American Physicist

One of the most famous people ever to immigrate to the United States is Albert Einstein. Albert Einstein was born in Germany to a Jewish family and went to school in Germany and then in Switzerland. Einstein became a professor at the University of Berlin, winning the Nobel Prize in 1921. Einstein is widely regarded as one of the greatest scientific minds of all time, if not the greatest, because he made groundbreaking findings and predictions decades ago which are still being proven to be true to this day (biography.com, 2017).

Einstein is also an example of an immigrant who came to the United States and made contributions to national security. With the onset of Adolf Hitler's Nazi regime and increasing anti-Semitism in Germany, Einstein and his wife immigrated to the United States in 1933, around the same time that Adolf Hitler became the chancellor of Germany. Einstein authored a famous letter to President Franklin D. Roosevelt in 1939, advising him of the possibility of developing an atomic bomb and warning him that the Nazi regime was likely working on their own atomic weapons, as they had started stockpiling uranium (Bromberg, 2016). The closing statements of the letter are as follows:

> I understand that Germany has actually stopped the sale of uranium from the Czechoslovakian mines, which she has taken over. That she should have taken such early action might perhaps be understood on the ground that the son of the German Under-Secretary of State, Von Weishlicker [sic], is attached to the Kaiser Wilheim Institute in Berlin where some of the American work on uranium is now being repeated.
>   Yours very truly,
>   (Albert Einstein)
>
>   (PBS, 2016)

After World War II ended, Albert Einstein was an advocate for nuclear disarmament. He died in Princeton, New Jersey, in 1955 (Bromberg, 2016).

Immigrants and the Immigrant Experience

Although immigrants have made many contributions to the United States, "not all immigrant groups have experienced the same reception and opportunities or have been accorded the same influence" (Hirschman & Snipp, 2001, p. 623). Many groups including African-Americans, Jews, Irish, Italians, Chinese, Japanese, and Hispanics, among others, have faced discrimination in the United States (Feagin & Feagin, 1993). One challenge with studying discrimination against immigrants is that immigrant status is confounded with other potentially stigmatizing characteristics such as ethnicity, race, language, speaking accent, and religion.

Employment Laws Pertaining to Immigration

There are two major employment laws in the United States which were passed to protect immigrants from discrimination in employment. Title VII of the Civil Rights Act of 1964 protects against discrimination based on national origin (U.S. National Archives, 2016). In 2015, almost 10.6% of the 89,385 charges which sought protection under Title VII of the Civil Rights Act (a total of 9,438 charges) were related to national origin (EEOC, 2016a). The second major law, the Immigration Reform and Control Act of 1986 (IRCA), prohibits discrimination in employment based on national origin or citizenship status for those authorized to work in the United States. The IRCA requires that employers with four or more employees must not discriminate on the basis of national origin against people who are U.S. citizens, U.S. nationals, or aliens authorized to work in the United States. Also, employers must not discriminate on the basis of U.S. citizenship against people who are U.S. citizens, U.S. nationals, or the following categories of aliens who have work authorization: permanent residents, temporary residents, refugees, and asylees (Society for Human Resource Management, 2008).

An example of national origin discrimination is as follows, whereby J&R Baker Farms paid $205,000 to settle an Equal Employment Opportunity Commission (EEOC) race and national origin discrimination lawsuit:

> EEOC filed suit on Aug. 28, 2014, alleging that Baker Farms violated Title VII of the Civil Rights Act of 1964 when it subjected American and African-American workers to disparate terms and conditions of employment based on their national origin and/or race, including segregated buses, segregated work crews, and differences in production standards, work assignments, and other conditions of work. The complaint further alleged since at least the fall of 2010, Baker Farms engaged in a pattern or practice of unlawfully terminating qualified American and/or African-American workers and replacing them with foreign-born workers (EEOC, 2016b).

Research Findings

A study conducted by Avery, Tonidandel, Volpone, and Raghuram (2010) examined work overload among immigrants compared to non-immigrants. They found no correlation between immigrant status and hours worked. They did find effects between hours worked and reported work overload such that the results were modified by the amount of interpersonal justice (i.e., whether they were treated with dignity and respect). Specifically, for immigrants there was no association between hours worked and self-reported work overload when they were treated in an interpersonally fair way, but there was a positive association between hours worked and work overload when they did not receive interpersonally fair treatment. For non-immigrants, the relationship between hours worked and work overload was positive whether they received high or low interpersonally fair treatment.

Several studies have also examined discrimination against immigrants in a personnel selection context. Hosoda, Nguyen, and Stone-Romero (2012) reported that job applicants who spoke with a Mexican-Spanish accent were seen as less suitable and were less likely to be promoted to a software engineering position compared to comparable applicants with an American-English accent. In another study, Hosoda and Stone-Romero (2010) examined responses to applicants in different job contexts (high or low status and high or low communication demands). Results showed that applicants with Japanese accents were evaluated less favorably than applicants with French accents, especially for jobs with high communication demands. In a different study conducted by Wright and Dwyer (2003), the authors studied employment during the period from 1994–2000 and found that 64% of the growth in the bottom quintile of employment was occupied by immigrants, indicating that immigrants often accept lower-level jobs which native-born workers may not desire. While immigrants to the United States are more likely to be employed than native-born citizens, they tend to have lower incomes, live in poverty more often, and are less likely to have health care (Grieco, Acosta, de la Cruz, Gambino, Gryn, Larsen, & Walters, 2012). Similar results were found in a sample from Germany. Baltes and Rudolph (2010) examined stereotypes about Turkish job candidates among a group of German college students in an experimental study. The authors had the study participants evaluate four male candidates for a position, two of whom were Turkish and two of whom were German. Results showed that the endorsement of negative Turkish stereotypes significantly reduced the evaluations of highly qualified Turkish candidates.

Another challenge that immigrants face in the workforce is that employers with English-only policies can increase the salience of their immigrant status (Bradley-Geist & Schmidtke, in press). In a recent lawsuit represented by the U.S. Equal Employment Opportunity Commission, Filipino-American hospital employees in California were threatened by their coworkers for not speaking English. According to the EEOC, their coworkers "constantly made fun of their accents, ordering them to speak English even when they were already speaking English." The Filipino-American employees were also harassed if they did not speak English (EEOC, 2012). Thus, the English-only policies encouraged people to pay attention to language differences, emphasizing employees' immigrant status. These policies may have also primed employees to see immigrant groups as a threat to the majority group's way of life (Bradley-Geist & Schmidtke, in press).

Further, another difficulty immigrants face in the workforce is that job credentials earned in their native country may not be recognized in their new host country (e.g., Aycan & Berry, 1996). Employers are often unfamiliar with degrees and certificates awarded by organizations and schools from other countries and may have difficulty judging the equivalence of foreign-issued credentials compared to those of their own country. Also, some professions require that those who practice (e.g., medicine, law) have earned those credentials in the United States or have passed the requisite exam in English and in the United States. In other words, immigrants' education and skills may sometimes be devalued relative to those of native-born citizens (Hakak, Holzinger, & Zikic, 2010). Other times, language may present a barrier to entry until the immigrant in question has mastered the English skills necessary to pass the required licensure exams in English.

Why Do Immigrants Experience Discrimination?

Social Categorization

Social categorization theory maintains that individuals put themselves and others into categories based on individual characteristics, including race, sex, age, and nationality, among others. They categorize people into in-groups (meaning that they belong to their own group) and out-groups (meaning that they belong to different groups). Positive characteristics are commonly ascribed to one's in-group while negative characteristics are ascribed to the out-group members (Tajfel & Turner, 1986; Turner, 1985). This process is problematic for immigrants to the United States because, if they are categorized into the out-group and negative characteristics are ascribed to them, this can lead to discrimination.

People tend to view members of the out-group as being more homogeneous than members of their own in-group (Jones, Wood, & Quattrone, 1981; Mullen & Hu, 1989). Because of this tendency to categorize and over-simplify out-groups, native-born citizens may generalize their views and attitudes about one group of immigrants toward other immigrants (Pettigrew, 1998).

Indeed, waves of immigration to the United States in the late nineteenth century prompted warnings by those groups already established in the United States about the "mongrelization" of the Nordic and Anglo-Saxon races in the United States as immigrants from Southeastern Europe and Central America arrived in the United States (Sacks, 2003). This is a common attitude toward newly arrived immigrants by higher status ethnic groups in the United States (Lee & Fiske, 2006).

One point of contention with immigrants and minority groups has often been language. The national language in the United States is English, and this helps facilitate communication, commerce, and travel between the 50 states. However, there are examples in U.S. history where language has been used by the English-speaking majority in a forceful way to exert control over non-English-speaking minority groups. Gonzalez (2000) describes that American Indians in Oklahoma had public school systems around 1850s where 90% of the children learned their native language in addition to English. By the late 1800s, however, the government initiated a policy to Americanize American Indians by removing thousands of children from their families and sending them to boarding schools to learn English (Gonzalez, 2000, p. 210). Something similar happened in Puerto Rico after the U.S. occupation of the island in 1898, when the U.S. Congress declared the island bilingual. While Puerto Ricans spoke Spanish almost exclusively, the military governor from the United States ordered all public school teachers to become fluent in English and instituted an English-proficiency test for high school graduation (Gonzalez, 2000, p. 210).

Stereotyping

The stereotype content model developed by Fiske, Cuddy, Glick, and Xu (2002) is helpful to understand stereotyping of immigrants. The model proposes that perceptions of others can be conceptualized by a two-dimensional framework with competence on one dimension and warmth on the other dimension. Lee and Fiske (2006) report that while people do distinguish between immigrants from different regions, they also hold a generic image of an "immigrant" which is associated with low warmth and low competence. Using the stereotype content model to study perceptions of immigrants among U.S. college students, Lee and Fiske (2006) reported the least favorable perceptions of competence and warmth for undocumented immigrants, regardless of their country of origin. Other groups that received low ratings on competence and warmth were migrant farm workers, Africans, Latinos, Mexicans, and South Americans. Several groups were seen ambivalently, with competence and warmth being high-low or low-high. For example, Irish and Italian immigrants were seen as high in warmth but low in competence. Asian immigrants (Chinese, Japanese, and Korean) were perceived the opposite way, as being high on competence but low on warmth. Indian immigrants, Canadian immigrants, and third-generation immigrants were grouped in the same cluster as Americans and college students.

Some research has reported that employers may simultaneously praise immigrant groups while discriminating against them. Bell et al. (2010) described some employers who praised Asians and Hispanics for having a strong immigrant work ethic. Nevertheless, those same employers who praised the immigrant work ethic paid immigrants significantly lower wages than other employers. Praise of immigrants could function as a type of moral credentialing (Monin & Miller, 2001), whereby people are freed up to discriminate against immigrants by diminishing their concern of appearing prejudiced (Bradley-Geist & Schmidtke, in press).

Threat

According to **realistic group conflict theory**, one important factor leading to intergroup competition is the threat that another group is competing with one's own group for scarce resources (Sherif & Sherif, 1969). Perceptions of threat tend to be associated with economic conditions. When economic conditions are strong and resources are plentiful, people are more welcoming of immigrants. When the economy is poor, people are more leery of immigrants and may even fear that immigrants are taking their jobs. Quillian (1995) reported that during poor economic conditions, more prejudice was exhibited when the proportion of immigrants in the country was larger. According to Gallup, the percentage of Americans believing that immigration hurts the U.S. economy increased from 40% to 49% between 2000 and 2005 (Bradley-Geist & Schmidtke, in press), which corresponds with an economic decline.

An extensive review of the immigration literature conducted by Bradley-Geist and Schmidtke (in press) summarized that those who have the most to fear from immigrants will have the most negative attitudes toward them. For example, Haubert and Fussell (2006) proposed that most of the research observing anti-immigrant attitudes has sampled blue-collar workers and minorities, the groups who would experience the most competition from immigrants. Analyzing different data from the General Social Survey, Haubert and Fussell (2006) explained that a cosmopolitan world view, defined as having a white-collar occupation, having a college education, holding liberal values, rejecting ethnocentrism, and having lived abroad, was strongly associated with pro-immigrant attitudes. A different study conducted by Malhotra, Margalit, and Mo (2013) proposed that some research fails to find an association between threat and attitudes toward immigrants because the samples in those studies include participants who would not personally be threatened by immigrants. To overcome this limitation, Malhotra et al. (2013) sampled employees in the U.S. high-tech industry where high-skilled foreign workers directly compete with native workers. Consistent with the authors' expectations, native employees in the high-tech industry were more likely than employees from other industries to oppose the extension of H-1B visas to high-tech foreign workers.

In addition to threats related to scarce resources, **symbolic threat** is another source of threat which can make people nervous about immigration. Symbolic threat refers to the majority group's concerns that the immigrant groups will challenge their values or way of life (Stephan, Ybarra, & Bachman, 1999).

Global View: Las Patronas (The Bosses)—Mexican Women Helping Migrants

Called "Las Patronas," this group of women work together to provide light meals and bottled water to the hundreds of migrants that speed past their town atop freight trains headed north to the United States (Bonello, 2014). Named after their hometown of Guadalupe, La Patrona, which translates to English as Guadalupe, the Patron Saint, these charitable protectors, who live in poverty, have nourished tens of thousands of migrants since they began this compassionate mission in 1995. When the Romero sisters were returning from the supermarket 21 years ago, they heard the voices of people calling to them from the train top: "Mother, we are hungry" (Grant, 2014). Without a second thought the girls tossed the passersby the bread and milk they had just purchased. Since then, the sisters, encouraged by their mother and with the help of numerous other local women, have been feeding migrants, providing a "potentially life-saving donation" (Grant, 2014) to men, women, and children.

Criticized by some and even threatened by drug dealers, Las Patronas are relentless in their support of immigrant human rights. For their humanitarian work, Las Patronas have been recognized worldwide. They have been featured in two documentaries and a movie (Sierra, 2016). In 2013, Norma Romero Vázquez, who heads Las Patronas, was awarded the National Prize for Human Rights in Mexico.

Politics

The political climate toward immigrants in a particular country will also be indicative of how they are treated. Pettigrew (1998) examined immigration in Western Europe and stated that, unlike the United States where immigration is common historically, some countries have no such conceptualization of being a melting pot and are not as welcoming to immigrants (Pettigrew, 1998). Countries that support immigration tend to have commensurate laws and policies that allow immigration, and they are less likely to force either assimilation or segregation upon immigrants (Berry, 1997).

Even in the United States, the population is divided about immigration reform and what to do with respect to the millions of illegal immigrants who either entered the country illegally or, in most cases, overstayed visas. During the 2016 U.S. presidential elections, many different views on immigration reform emerged. Views on immigration tend to divide along political party lines, with Democratic candidates and moderate Republican candidates largely advocating for a path to citizenship for illegal immigrants who have lived in the United States and demonstrated good civic duty (i.e., worked, paid taxes, not been convicted of any crime). The more conservative Republicans, including leading candidates for the Republican Party, advocated a harder stance on immigration, including deporting the 11–12 million illegal immigrants living in the United States, erecting a large wall along the U.S./Mexico border, and calling for a temporary ban on Muslims coming into the United States.

Global View: Google Co-Founder, Sergey Brin, Is a Russian-Born Immigrant

One of the largest and most well-regarded technology companies in Silicon Valley and worldwide is Google. The company was cofounded by Larry Page and Sergey Brin, who met at Stanford University in 1995. Brin was born in Moscow, Russia, to a Jewish family. He and his family immigrated to the United States in 1979 to escape persecution against Jews. After obtaining a degree in math and computer science from the University of Maryland, Brin went to Stanford University for a Ph.D. in computer science (Biography.com, 2016). Larry was considering attending Stanford, and Sergey, who was already a student there, was assigned to show him around (Google.com, 2016). Therefore, they began the collaboration that would become Google when they were computer science doctoral students at Stanford University.

Since they launched Google in 1998, Google has become the most popular search engine in the world. In fact, the saying "Google it" implies their search engine is the standard for Internet web searching. The company held its initial public offering in 2004, making both Brin and Page billionaires. In 2016, Larry Page was 12th on the *Forbes* list of The World's Billionaires (net worth of $35.2 billion), and Sergey Brin was 13th on the list (net worth of $34.4 billion) (*Forbes*, 2016). As of July 2015, Google, which is headquartered in Mountain View, California, employed 57,100 people (Bort, 2015).

What Is the Economic Impact of Immigration in the United States?

According to several sources, the overall economic impact of immigration on the U.S. economy is positive. According to the American Immigration Council (2012), (a) there is no correlation between immigration and unemployment,

(b) immigrants create jobs both because they are consumers who demand goods and services and because they are often entrepreneurs who create businesses, and (c) immigrants and native-born workers are usually in different jobs and do not compete with one another. According to a report by the Kauffman Foundation (Fairlie, 2013), immigrants were nearly twice as likely to start businesses compared to their native-born counterparts in each month of the year 2012. According to a report by the Congressional Budget Office (2010), almost one-third (30%) of native-born workers ages 25 and older had some college education short of a bachelor's degree in the year 2009 compared to 17% of foreign-born workers. More than one-quarter (27%) of foreign-born workers did not have a high school diploma compared to 6% of native-born workers. Further, the top occupations of foreign-born workers ages 25 to 64 were construction and extraction (8.8% of the foreign-born labor force), production occupations (8.7% of the foreign-born labor force), building and grounds cleaning and maintenance (8.5% of the foreign-born labor force), and sales (8.4% of the foreign-born labor force). Meanwhile, the most common occupations for native-born employees ages 25 to 64 were as follows: office and administrative support (13.8% of the native-born labor force), management (12.9% of the native-born labor force), sales (10.5% of the native-born labor force), and education, training, and library occupations (7% of the native-born labor force). Overall, the American Immigration Council (2012) concludes that immigrants mostly do not compete with native-born workers for jobs.

Different data reported by the Center for Immigration Studies (Camarota, 2013) largely corroborates the results presented by the American Immigration Council. The Center for Immigration Studies cites data and reports presented by several authors including George Borjas, an immigration economist and professor at Harvard University. According to Borjas (2013), the presence of legal and illegal immigrants in the labor market increases the U.S. economy gross domestic product (GDP) by about 11% ($1.6 trillion) annually. This contribution to the overall economy does not represent a large contribution to the native-born population because 97.8% of the increase in GDP goes to the immigrants in the form of wages and benefits. Borjas estimates that the net gain of legal and illegal immigration to native-born people is 0.2% of the total GDP in the United States. This results in a surplus of $35 billion per year, which on the one hand reduces the wages of the native-born citizens who are in competition with the immigrants for jobs by $402 billion per year but on the other hand increases the income of employers who hire immigrant labor by an estimated $437 billion per year. Overall, the data indicate that the native-born who lose from immigration are those without a high school diploma, that is to say, a significant proportion of the working poor. By increasing the supply of workers, immigration reduces the wages of the portion of the native-born population who compete with immigrants for those jobs. The studies that have found a negative impact on the native-born population find that it reduces employment for the less educated, for the young, and for minorities (Camarota, 2013).

Global View: Immigration Tests a Tradition of Openness in Sweden

Sweden is a country that has traditionally been open to immigration. However, the conversation about immigration within Sweden has become more heated and contentious in recent years because the volume of people seeking to enter this country has grown. According to Crouch (2014), a reporter with the *New York Times*, the number of people seeking asylum, primarily from Syria and Iraq, was approximately 80,000 in 2014, an increase of 57,000 refugees from 2013. Sweden had not seen such a large number of asylum seekers since 1992 when 60,000 Kosovar Albanians left for Sweden fleeing war in Yugoslavia. As a result of Sweden's open policy toward immigrants, 15% of the country's population was foreign born as of 2014 (Crouch, 2014).

This increase in immigration has prompted discussions both against and for immigration. On the anti-immigrant side of the debate, a group known as the Sweden Democrats, which is a right-wing party that points out the short-term costs of accepting immigrants into the country and the fact that they may bring change with them (Crouch, 2014). One man, Kurt-Olof, who worked at Saab for 47 years, including on an assembly line, said he would vote for the Sweden Democrats because "refugees come here and get a smorgasbord of benefits . . . They cost too much, and there are too many cultures" (Crouch, 2014).

On the pro-immigrant side of the debate, Fredrik Reinfeldt, who was prime minister of Sweden until 2014, appealed to the people to be sympathetic, saying, "I appeal to the Swedish people to open their hearts . . . These are people who come into Swedish society to build it together with us. Together we are building a better Sweden." Reinfeldt is a member of the Moderate Party in Sweden (Crouch, 2014).

This exchange took place shortly before the national election of Sweden in 2014. The results of the election showed that Sweden shifted somewhat to the left in its political preference. Stefan Löfven of the Social Democratic Party was elected to be the new prime minister. Reinfeldt and his Moderate Party received the second highest number of votes. The Sweden Democrats received the third largest number of votes in the election (Electionresources.org, 2016).

Nevertheless, by 2016 Sweden tightened its rules on immigration. Legislation proposed by the Social Democrat minority to limit the number of people granted permanent resident status was approved in a 240 to 45 vote. The government explained that the legislation "was necessary to prevent the country from becoming overstretched by the surge of migration to Europe that began last year." Sweden accepted 160,000 asylum-seekers in the year 2015 (Bilefsky, 2016).

What Can Be Done About Bias Against Immigrant Groups?

It is important for organizations to be aware of the possibility of discrimination toward immigrants to the United States because it can result in illegal employment discrimination. However, there is some evidence that discrimination on the basis of immigration status may be mitigated if the social categorization process that would lead individuals to ascribe out-group status to immigrant groups were modified such that those individuals are reminded of their own immigrant status, thereby allowing them to see similarities between themselves and the immigrant groups. If we know that the process of discrimination in employment begins via an individual's social categorization process whereby they assign immigrants to the out-group, see them as lower status individuals, and discriminate (Dovidio & Hebl, 2005; Tajfel & Turner, 1986; Turner, 1985), then the way to stop the root cause of discrimination would be by overriding the social categorization that puts immigrants in the out-group through a process called recategorization.

Recategorization

There is evidence that a **recategorization process** is possible if people can be made aware that the out-group members are also members of one's own group on a different dimension (Gaertner & Dovidio, 2000; Urban & Miller, 1998). For example, if dominant group members are reminded that they (or their ancestors) are (were) also immigrants, and hence have something in common with the immigrants, they may recategorize the immigrants into their own in-group on this immigration dimension. Further, because people ascribe positive characteristics to their own in-groups (Tajfel & Turner, 1986; Turner, 1985), if the majority group members realize they share things in common with immigrants, they may be more sympathetic to those immigrants than they would otherwise.

Contact

One idea, known as the **contact hypothesis**, proposes that the more contact people from different groups have with one another over time, the more the tensions between those groups will subside as they begin to know and understand one another better. Pettigrew and Tropp (2006) conducted a meta-analysis and found support for the contact hypothesis such that intergroup contact was negatively associated with prejudice. However, not all studies show that contact reduces prejudice. For instance, a different study found that anti-Hispanic hate crimes were higher in states with higher levels of recent Hispanic immigration (Stacey, Carbone-López, & Rosenfeld, 2011). However, hate crimes were not related to the relative size or economic position of the Hispanic population. In fact, in areas that were more heavily populated by Hispanics, hate crimes against them were lower. This means that it is not only contact, but the context surrounding that contact, which tends to predict how much intergroup tensions will decline.

According to Thompson (2011), in addition to contact, the right conditions must be present in order for intergroup conflict to decline. In fact, contact under the wrong conditions may exacerbate the negative relationships between groups. In order for contact to work, the following characteristics should be present:

1. Social support and institutional support such that the leaders have been clear in their endorsement of integration of the different groups
2. Acquaintance potential so that people have the opportunity to develop meaningful relationships with members of the other group
3. Equal status whereby members of the different groups are on an equal footing when they interact with one another; if contact involves unequal status, prejudice may be reinforced rather than reduced
4. Shared goals so the team has an overarching, clear, and shared group goal in order for them to find some common ground and put aside their differences
5. Cross-group friendships, meaning that it is ideal if group members know that one of their own friends has a relationship with a member of the out-group, which makes the out-group seem friendlier and tends to reduce tensions between the groups (Thompson, 2011).

Segregation, Assimilation, Acculturation

Another factor that is likely to influence levels of contact is segregation (Bradley-Geist & Schmidtke, in press). Immigrants are often segregated from native-born citizens both socially and in employment. For instance, Hispanic immigrants in the U.S are over-represented in labor-intensive jobs like agriculture, grounds maintenance, housekeeping, and food processing (Passel & Cohn, 2009; Rivera-Batiz, 1999). These jobs tend to be very physically demanding and are often dangerous. According to the U.S. Occupational Safety and Health Administration (OSHA), immigrants, and especially Hispanic immigrants, are over-represented in dangerous industries and are more likely to experience workplace injuries (including fatalities) than the general population (OSHA, 2011).

A research study by Rivera-Batiz (1999) studying undocumented workers in the labor market found that the lower wages of Mexican illegal immigrants in the United States are associated, in part, with exploitation and/or discrimination based on their illegal status. Undocumented workers are often hiding and have no legal status, which makes them targets for exploitation. The legalization of undocumented workers provides a substantial and direct positive effect on the earnings of these immigrants. For example, the wages of male Mexican legal immigrants were 41.8% higher than those of undocumented workers. Similarly, female legal immigrants earned 40.8% more than their undocumented counterparts. Further, an analysis of undocumented immigrants who were legalized after the 1986 Immigration Reform and Control Act (IRCA) of 1986 showed a significant wage increase in the four years following legalization, specifically 15% for men and 21% for women (Rivera-Batiz, 1999).

Culture is another important factor on which immigrants may differ from native-born citizens (Bradley-Geist & Schmidtke, in press). Immigrants and their descendants vary greatly in the degree to which they retain cultural norms, values, and traditions associated with their home country versus adopting those of the culture in their new host country. **Assimilation** is the process of becoming more like the majority in the new host country. For example, some immigrants change their name because they think it will help them fit in better in the new country (e.g., an Irish family named O'Reilly changing their name to Reilly would be a common example). Although it is sometimes confused with assimilation, **acculturation** is a broader term which can include assimilation as well as resistance to change by both the dominant and non-dominant group and the creation of new cultural forms as the groups interact and blend (Berry, 1997; Bradley-Geist & Schmidtke, 2016). Research related to acculturation has examined the psychological, sociocultural, and economic adaptation of immigrants and has suggested that, in addition to individual differences such as personality and cultural knowledge, the extent to which a society accepts immigrants and multiculturalism can impact adaptation (Aycan & Berry, 1996; Berry, 1997). Therefore, the more the immigrant groups stand out and appear to have salient differences with native-born people in the host country, the more difficult it will be for them to adapt. For example, Sniderman, Hagendoorn, and Prior (2004) found that reactions toward immigrants were more strongly associated with the immigrants fitting in culturally than economically.

Suggestions for Organizations

In order to ensure organizational policies are legally compliant, employers must first verify that the people they are hiring are legally authorized to work in a given country. In the United States, employers must not discriminate against people on the basis of national origin or U.S. citizenship status. However, they must also take precautions to not knowingly hire people who are not authorized to work in the country. Therefore, employers should establish a policy of hiring only individuals who are authorized to work in the United States. It is important to note that establishing a U.S. citizen–only hiring policy is illegal, and employers may do this only if it is required by federal, state, or local laws or a government contract (Society for Human Resource Management, 2008). Employers must also complete an I-9 form for all employees hired. This form is the Employment Eligibility Verification Form and requires employees to present valid documentation demonstrating their identity and legal authorization to work in the United States (U.S. Citizenship and Immigration Services, 2013). Finally, employers must allow employees to present any combination of documents that are permitted for employment verification purposes under the law. They must not require one form of documentation over another because not all aliens who are legally authorized to work in the United States have the same types of paperwork. Therefore, as long as the documents are allowable by law and appear to be valid when they are examined visually, they should be accepted (Society for Human Resource Management, 2008; U.S. Citizenship and Immigration Services, 2013).

Employers must also be careful with English-only workplace policies. The Equal Employment Opportunity Commission has actively pursued discrimination cases against companies with English-only policies which have been accused of being discriminatory under Title VII of the Civil Rights Act of 1964. Title VII prohibits discrimination on the basis of national origin. An English-only policy should be used only if there is a business necessity for it, and employers seeking to establish English-only policies are advised to seek legal counsel before doing so (Society for Human Resource Management, 2014). The following examples from the EEOC clarify this point by presenting one example where an English-only rule was found to be discriminatory and one example where it was not determined to be discriminatory.

Evidence Establishes that Policy was Adopted for Discriminatory Reasons

John, a Latino man who is bilingual in Spanish and English, works in a warehouse for Factory, Inc. John works on an assembly line and has job duties that do not require him to speak English. Factory decides to adopt a rule that requires all workplace communications to be conducted in English after a complaint is received objecting to John speaking Spanish during a break. In practice, the English-only rule is applied at all times on company property, even though its text says that it should not be applied during breaks and personal time.

John files a Title VII charge challenging the rule. Based on the evidence, the EEOC finds reasonable cause to believe that John was subjected to unlawful disparate treatment. In particular, the evidence reveals that Factory, Inc., had no work-related reasons for the rule, and a manager expressed concern prior to the rule's adoption that other warehouse employees were likely to taunt Latinos if they knew about the rule. Finally, Factory, Inc.'s chief executive referred to the Spanish language as "garbage" in a public interview. The evidence establishes reasonable cause to believe that the English-only rule was adopted because of anti-Latino bias (EEOC, 2016c, Example 28).

Policy Narrowly Tailored to Promote Safe and Efficient Job Performance

Claudia, a Honduran-born U.S. immigrant who is fluent in Spanish and English, is employed by County hospital as a housekeeper, and she is assigned to clean operating rooms. She files a charge of discrimination alleging that she was subjected to unlawful national origin discrimination when the hospital adopted an English-only rule. The respondent produces evidence showing that the rule applies to all workers, including cleaning staff, but only for job-related discussions when they are working in the operating room. The evidence shows that most of the medical staff in the operating room only speak English.

Clear and precise communication between the medical staff and the cleaning staff is essential in the operating room because cleanliness is of paramount importance to patients' health and safety. The rule only applies to job-related discussions in the operating room and does not apply in any other circumstances. Based on this evidence, the EEOC does not find reasonable cause to believe that County Hospital's English-only rule violates Title VII (EEOC, 2016c, Example 29).

To avoid discrimination and be inclusive toward foreign-born applicants, employers should also have clearly documented job descriptions with the knowledge, skills, and abilities required for the job. This will allow employers to identify qualified candidates, regardless of their national origin. Employers must avoid singling out candidates who appear to be foreign-born or speak with an accent and must not ask them to provide documents that are not required of other employees. Finally, employers should complete the I-9 form and review the appropriate documentation after the employee has been hired for the job, not before (Duong & Park, 2013). This prevents any appearance that a candidate was not selected for a job because of his or her national origin. It also keeps the employer from asking the candidates for personal information that may be unrelated to the job requirements until they reach a point in the process where that information is necessary.

Closing Case

Requirements Keep Young Immigrants Out of Long Island Classrooms

Carlos Garcia Lobo, age 8, left Honduras and headed to meet his mother in Long Island, New York, accompanied by his 15-year-old cousin. Carlos, who had been living with his grandmother in Honduras, was sent to New York to live with his mother after a machete-bearing gang robbed his grandmother's home. The journey to New York took weeks, and they rode on buses day and night. Carlos, however, encountered an unforeseen obstacle which his family says seems insurmountable (Mueller, 2014). In New York, children whose families cannot provide the requisite documents to prove either that they live in the district or that they have guardianship of the child are excluded from attending school. The legal enrollment procedures adopted by the New York State Education Department in September of 2014) present a problem not only for Carlos and his mother, but for many other children like Carlos who are staying with relatives (Mueller, 2014).

Carlos arrived in Long Island, New York, on July 10, 2014, and was able to join his mother after seven years of separation. Since his arrival, his mother, Ms. Lobo, has gone to the local school at least 10 times to provide his immunization records, her address, and the name of a fellow tenant to whom she pays rent. However, she feels that her efforts have been in vain (Mueller, 2014). The school says they must have a statement from the home's absentee owner. When Ms. Lobo sent a letter to the homeowner to request such a statement, her letter was returned marked "return to sender." A school secretary once suggested that Ms. Lobo move in the hopes that she could get the required letter from a new landlord so that Carlos could be enrolled in school (Mueller, 2014).

Ms. Lobo and other families who sublease rooms in a house need to present a notarized lease or owner's affidavit, the residential deed or mortgage statement from the homeowner(s), and two home bills. This has led activists to say that such rules undermine a federal law that provides access to schools. In fact, according to the American Immigration Council (2012), "In June 1982, the Supreme Court issued *Plyler v. Doe*, a landmark decision holding that states could not constitutionally deny students a free public education on account of their immigration status. By a 5–4 vote, the Court found that any resources which might be saved from excluding undocumented children from public schools were far outweighed by the harms imposed on society at large from denying them an education." However, "In the three decades since the *Plyler* ruling was issued, states and localities have passed numerous measures and adopted unofficial policies that violate the spirit if not the letter of the decision."

In 2015, a review conducted by New York's State Education Department and the Attorney General's office found that 20 school districts in New York were asking for documentation which created barriers that prevented undocumented students from attending school. "The investigation found that schools were requiring illegal enrollment materials from families, including copies of Social Security cards and visa expiration dates, which illegal immigrants generally would not have" (Mueller, 2015). Therefore, the state compelled the schools to change their documentation requirements for enrollment and report instances where children were denied admission until June of 2018 (Mueller, 2015).

Discussion Questions:

1.   There are different perspectives on how to handle undocumented immigrants, in part because of the tension between humanitarian views and economic views. What are some arguments for and against providing social services to undocumented immigrants?

2.   Why do you suppose states and schools have challenged the 1982 Supreme Court decision which ruled that states cannot deny a child free education on the basis of his/her immigration status by requiring undocumented immigrants to present documents that would be difficult for them to obtain?

References

American Immigration Council. (2012, June 15). Public education for immigrant students: States challenge Supreme Court's decision in Plyler v. Doe. Retrieved from http://www. immigrationpolicy.org/just-facts/public-education-immigrant-students-states-chal lenge-supreme-court%E2%80%99s-decision-plyler-v-do

Avery, D. R., Tonidandel, S., Volpone, S. D., & Raghuram, A. (2010). Overworked in America? How work hours, immigrant status, and interpersonal justice affect perceived work overload. *Journal of Managerial Psychology, 25,* 133–147.

Aycan, Z., & Berry, J. W. (1996). Impact of employment-related experiences on immigrants' psychological well-being and adaptation to Canada. *Canadian Journal of Behavioural Science/Revue canadienne des sciences du comportement, 28*(3), 240.

Baltes, B. B., & Rudolph, C. W. (2010). Examining the effect of negative Turkish stereotypes on evaluative workplace outcomes in Germany. *Journal of Managerial Psychology, 25*(2), 148–158.

Bell, M. P., Kwesiga, E. N., & Berry, D. P. (2010). The new "invisible men and women" in diversity research. *Journal of Managerial Psychology, 25,* 177–188.

Berry, J. W. (1997). Immigration, acculturation, and adaptation. *Applied Psychology, 46*(1), 5–34.

Bilefsky, D. (2016, June 21). Sweden Toughens Rules for Refugees Seeking Asylum. *The New York Times.* Retrieved from https://www.nytimes.com/2016/06/22/world/europe/ sweden-immigrant-restrictions.html

Biography.com. (2016). Sergey Brin. Retrieved from http://www.biography.com/people/ sergey-brin-12103333

Biography.com. (2017). Albert Einstein. Retrieved from http://www.biography.com/people/ albert-einstein-9285408#synopsis

Bonello, D. (2014, July 17). 'Las Patronas:' Mexican Women Help Border Kids Reach U.S. *NBC News.* Retrieved from http://www.nbcnews.com/storyline/immigration-border-crisis/ las-patronas-mexican-women-help-border-kids-reach-u-s-n158241

Borjas, G. (2013, April). Immigration and the American worker: A review of the academic literature. Center for Immigration Studies. Retrieved from http://www.hks.harvard. edu/fs/gborjas/publications/popular/CIS2013.pdf

Bort, J. (2015, July 17). Google's hiring may have slowed, but it's still adding thousands of new employees. *Business Insider*. Retrieved from http://www.businessinsider.com/google-has-57000-employees-2015-7

Bradley-Geist, J. C., & Schmidtke, J. M. (in press). Immigrants in the workplace: Stereotyping and discrimination. In A. Colella & E. King (Eds.), *The Oxford handbook of workplace discrimination*. New York: Oxford University Press.

Bromberg, H. (2016). Albert Einstein. Retrieved from http://immigrationtounitedstates.org/473-albert-einstein.html

Bureau of Labor Statistics. (2016, May 19). Foreign-born workers: Labor force characteristics—2015. Bureau of Labor Statistics. U.S. Department of Labor. Retrieved from http://www.bls.gov/news.release/pdf/forbrn.pdf

Camarota, S. A. (2013, May). The fiscal and economic impact of immigration on the United States. Center for Immigration Studies. Retrieved from http://cis.org/node/4573#4

Congressional Budget Office. (2010, July). The role of immigrants in the U.S. Labor Market: An update. The Congress of the United States. Retrieved from https://www.cbo.gov/sites/default/files/111th-congress-2009-2010/reports/07-23-immigrants_in_labor_force.pdf

Crouch, D. (2014, September 13). Rift emerges before vote in Sweden as immigration tests a tradition of openness. *New York Times*. Retrieved from http://www.nytimes.com/2014/09/13/world/europe/rift-emerges-in-sweden-over-immigration.html

Dipboye, R. L., & Colella, A. (2005). *Discrimination at work: The psychological and organizational bases*. Mahwah, NJ: Lawrence Erlbaum Associates.

Dovidio, J. F., & Hebl, M. R. (2005). Discrimination at the level of the individual: Cognitive and affective factors. In R. L. Dipboye & A. Colella (Eds.), *Discrimination at work: The psychological and organizational bases* (pp. 11–35). Mahwah, NJ: Lawrence Erlbaum Associates.

Duong, V., & Park, J. J. (2013, March 20). March 2013: Discrimination and immigration. Society for Human Resource Management. Retrieved from https://www.shrm.org/legalissues/legalreport/pages/discriminationinimmigration.aspx

Electionresources.org. (2016). Election resources on the Internet: Elections to the Swedish Riksdag - Results Lookup. Retrieved from http://www.electionresources.org/se/riksdag.php?election=2014

Equal Employment Opportunity Commission. (2016a). Charge statistics FY 1997 through FY 2015. Retrieved from https://www.eeoc.gov/eeoc/statistics/enforcement/charges.cfm

Equal Employment Opportunity Commission. (2016b, July 6). J&R Baker Farms to pay $205,000 to settle EEOC race and national origin discrimination lawsuit. Retrieved from https://www.eeoc.gov/eeoc/newsroom/release/7-6-16.cfm

Equal Employment Opportunity Commission. (2016c, November 18). EEOC Enforcement Guidance on National Origin Discrimination. Example 28: Evidence Establishes That Policy Was Adopted for Discriminatory Reasons. Example 29: Policy Narrowly Tailored to Promote Safe and efficient Job Performance. Retrieved from https://www.eeoc.gov/laws/guidance/national-origin-guidance.cfm

Fairlie, R. W. (2013, April). Kauffman index of entrepreneurial activity 1996–2012. Kauffman Foundation. Retrieved from http://www.kauffman.org/~/media/kauffman_org/research%20reports%20and%20covers/2013/04/kiea_2013_report.pdf

Feagin, J. R., & Feagin, C. B. (1993). *Racial and ethnic relations* (4th ed.). Englewood Cliffs, NJ: Prentice Hall.

Fiske, S. T., Cuddy, A. J. C., Glick, P., & Xu, J. (2002). A model of (often mixed) stereotype content: Competence and warmth respectively follow from perceived status and competence. *Journal of Personality and Social Psychology, 82*, 878–902.

Forbes. (2016). The world's billionaires. Retrieved from http://www.forbes.com/billionaires/list/#version:static

Gaertner, S., & Dovidio, J. F. (2000). *Reducing intergroup bias: The common ingroup identity model.* Philadelphia, PA: The Psychology Press.

Gonzalez, J. (2000). *Harvest of empire: A history of Latinos in America.* New York: Penguin Books.

Google.com. (2016). Our history in depth. Retrieved from https://www.google.com/about/company/history

Grant, W. (2014, July 31). Las Patronas: The Mexican women helping migrants. *BBC Mundo.* Retrieved from http://www.bbc.com/news/world-latin-america-28193230

Grieco, E. M., Acosta, Y. D., de la Cruz, G. P., Gambino, C., Gryn, T., Larsen, L. J., & Walters, N. P. (2012). *The foreign-born population in the United States: 2010. American community survey reports.* Washington, DC: Census Bureau.

Hakak, L. T., Holzinger, I., & Zikic, J. (2010). Barriers and paths to success: Latin American MBAs' views of employment in Canada. *Journal of Managerial Psychology, 25,* 159–176.

Haubert, J., & Fussell, E. (2006). Explaining pro-immigrant sentiment in the US: Social class, cosmopolitanism, and perceptions of immigrants. *International Migration Review, 40,* 489–507.

Hirschman, C., & Snipp, C. M. (2001). The state of the American dream: Race and ethnic socioeconomic inequality in the United States, 1970–1990. In D. B. Grusky (Ed.), *Social stratification* (2nd ed., pp. 623–636). Boulder, CO: Westview Press.

Hosoda, M., Nguyen, L. T., & Stone-Romero, E. (2012). The effect of Hispanic accents on employment decisions. *Journal of Managerial Psychology, 27,* 347–364.

Hosoda, M., & Stone-Romero, E. F. (2010). The effects of foreign accents on employment-related decisions. *Journal of Managerial Psychology, 25,* 113–132.

Huntington, S. P. (2004, March/April). The Hispanic challenge. *Foreign Policy,* 30–45.

Jones, E. E., Wood, G. C., & Quattrone, G. A. (1981). Perceived variability of personal characteristics in ingroups and outgroups: The role of knowledge and evaluation. *Personality and Social Psychology Bulletin, 7,* 523–528.

Lee, T. L., & Fiske, S. T. (2006). Not an outgroup, not yet an ingroup: Immigrants in the stereotype content model. *International Journal of Intercultural Relations, 30*(6), 751–768.

Liberty State Park. (2017). *The New Colossus.* Status of Liberty National Monument. Emma Lazarus' Famous Poem. Retrieved from http://libertystatepark.com/emma.htm

Lippi-Greene, R. (2004). *English with an accent: Language, ideology, and discrimination in the United States.* New York: Routledge.

Malhotra, N., Margalit, Y., & Mo, C. (2013). Economic explanations for opposition to immigration: Distinguishing between prevalence and conditional impact. *American Journal of Political Science, 57*(2), 391–410.

Monin, B., & Miller, D. T. (2001). Moral credentials and the expression of prejudice. *Journal of Personality and Social Psychology, 81*(1), 33.

Mueller, B. (2014, October 21). Requirements keep young immigrants out of long island classrooms. *New York Times.* Retrieved from http://www.nytimes.com/2014/10/22/nyregion/rules-and-paperwork-keep-long-islands-immigrant-children-from-classroom.html

Mueller, B. (2015, February 18). New York Compels 20 School Districts to Lower Barriers to Immigrants. *New York Times.* Retrieved from https://www.nytimes.com/2015/02/19/nyregion/new-york-compels-20-school-districts-to-lower-barriers-to-immigrants.html

Mullen, B., & Hu, L. T. (1989). Perceptions of ingroup and outgroup variability: A meta-analytic integration. *Basic and Applied Social Psychology, 10*(3), 233–252.

Occupational Safety and Health Administration (OSHA). (2011). Immigrant worker health and safety: A guide for front-line advocates. Retrieved from https://www.osha.gov/dte/grant_materials/fy10/sh-20830-10/Advocate_Guide.pdf

Passel, J. S., & Cohn, D. (2009, April 14). A portrait of unauthorized immigrants in the United States Pew Hispanic Center. Retrieved from http://pewhispanic.org/files/reports/107.pdf

PBS. (2016). Letter from Albert Einstein to FDR, 8/2/39. Source: Argonne National Laboratory. American Experience. Produced by WGBH for PBS. Retrieved from http://www.pbs.org/wgbh/americanexperience/features/primary-resources/truman-ein39/

Pettigrew, T. F. (1998). Reactions toward the new minorities of Western Europe. *Annual Review of Sociology, 24*, 77–103.

Pettigrew, T. F., & Tropp, L. R. (2006). A meta-analytic test of intergroup contact theory. *Journal of Personality and Social Psychology, 90*(5), 751–783.

Quillian, L. (1995). Prejudice as a response to perceived group threat: Population composition and anti-immigrant and racial prejudice in Europe. *American Sociological Review, 60*, 586–611.

Rivera-Batiz, F. L. (1999). Undocumented workers in the labor market: An analysis of the earnings of legal and illegal Mexican immigrants in the United States. *Journal of Population Economics, 12*, 91–116.

Sacks, K. B. (2003). How Jews became white. In R. E. Ore (Ed.), *The social construction of difference & inequality* (pp. 55–69). Boston, MA: McGraw-Hill.

Schwartz, S. J., Unger, J. B., Zamboanga, B. L., & Szapocznik, J. (2010). Rethinking the concept of acculturation implications for theory and research. *American Psychologist, 65*(4), 237–251.

Sherif, M., & Sherif, C. W. (1969). Ingroup and intergroup relations: Experimental analysis. In M. Sherif & C. W. Sherif (Eds.), *Social Psychology* (pp. 221 – 266). New York: Harper & Row.

Sierra, G. (2016, May 20). Las Patronas alimentan a inmigrantes ilegales montados en trenes de carga en Veracruz. *Clarín Noticias.* Retrieved from http://www.clarin.com/zona/Inmigrantes-odisea-llegar-EEUU_3_456584338.html

Sniderman, P. M., Hagendoorn, L., & Prior, M. (2004). Predisposing factors and situational triggers: Exclusionary reactions to immigrant minorities. *American Political Science Review, 98*, 35–49.

Society for Human Resource Management. (2008). Immigration Reform and Control Act of 1986 (IRCA). Retrieved from https://www.shrm.org/legalissues/federalresources/federalstatutesregulationsandguidanc/pages/immigrationreformandcontrolactof1986(irca).aspx

Society for Human Resource Management. (2014). English-only language policy. Retrieved from https://www.shrm.org/templatestools/samples/policies/pages/cms_013464.aspx

St. John de Crèvecouer, J. H. (1792). Letters from an American farmer. Philadelphia: Matthew Carey.

St. John de Crèvecoeur, J. H. (1981). Letters from an American farmer and sketches of eighteenth-century America. Ed. Albert E. Stone. New York: Penguin Classics.

Stacey, M., Carbone-López, K., & Rosenfeld, R. (2011). Demographic change and ethnically motivated crime: The impact of immigration on anti-Hispanic hate crime in the United States. *Journal of Contemporary Criminal Justice, 27*(3), 278–298.

Stephan, W. G., Ybarra, O., & Bachman, G. (1999). Prejudice toward immigrants. *Journal of Applied Social Psychology, 29*(11), 2221–2237.

Tajfel, H., & Turner, J. (1986). The social identity theory of intergroup behavior. In S. Worchel & W. G. Austin (Eds.), *Psychology of intergroup relations* (pp. 7–24). Chicago: Nelson-Hall.

Thompson, L. L. (2011). *Making the team: A guide for managers* (4th ed.). Upper Saddle River, NJ: Pearson Prentice-Hall.

Turner, J. (1985). *Social categorization and the self concept: A social cognitive theory of group behavior* (Vol. 2). Greenwich, CT: JAI Press.

United Nations. (2013, September 11). Number of international migrants rises about 232 million. Retrieved from http://www.un.org/en/development/desa/news/population/number-of-international-migrants-rises.html

Urban, L. M., & Miller, N. (1998). A theoretical analysis of crossed categorization effects: A meta-analysis. *Journal of Personality and Social Psychology, 74*, 894–908.

U.S. Citizenship and Immigration Services. (2013). Handbook for employers: Guidance for completing Form I-9 (Employment Eligibility Verification Form). Retrieved from https://www.uscis.gov/sites/default/files/files/form/m-274.pdf

U.S. Equal Employment Opportunity Commission. (2012, September 17). Delano Regional Medical Center to pay nearly $1 million in EEOC national origin discrimination suit. Retrieved from https://www1.eeoc.gov/eeoc/newsroom/release/9-17-12a.cfm?renderforprint=1

U.S. National Archives. (2016). The Civil Rights Act of 1964 and the Equal Employment Opportunity Commission. Retrieved from http://www.archives.gov/education/lessons/civil-rights-act

Wright, E. O., & Dwyer, R. E. (2003). The patterns of job expansions in the USA: A comparison of the 1960s and 1990s. *Socio-Economic Review, 1*(3), 289–325.

eleven
Appearance, Family Responsibility, Pregnancy, and Genetics

Opening Case

Meghan Trainor: Stop Modifying My Appearance to Make Me Look Thinner

Meghan Trainor is a singer and songwriter who makes it a point that her image not be modified using software such as Photoshop to make her body look thinner. She aspires to be different from other performers and to be a role model for young women to let them know that talent comes in all shapes and sizes. Trainor is a Grammy Award–winning artist who has performed very popular singles such as "All About That Bass" and "Lips Are Moving." Her music encourages women to embrace their curves and shape.

In May of 2015, Trainor became upset when she noticed that the video of her latest single, "Me Too," showed an altered image of her, with a smaller waist than her actual waist size. She demanded that the video producers take the video down and put the unaltered video back online. Trainor says, "I took down the Me Too video because they Photoshopped the crap out of me and I am so sick of it . . . So I took it down until they fix it" (CBSN, 2016; Quinn, 2016). The video producers did as she requested, and the original, unaltered video was then released.

Discussion Questions:

1. Why would the video producers have Photoshopped Meghan Trainor's waist to make it look smaller? What does that say about the culture that is consuming the video?

2. What do you think people can learn from Trainor's confrontation and demand that her original video and body appearance be restored?
3. In what ways might Trainor's confrontation and the restoration of the original video online be beneficial for both women and men?

Learning Objectives
After reading this chapter, you should be able to:

- Understand major forms of appearance diversity in the workplace, including attractiveness, weight, and height
- Be familiar with weight discrimination and its outcomes
- Define family responsibility discrimination
- Know about the motherhood penalty
- Be aware of the challenges pregnant women face in the workplace
- Define GINA

This is the final chapter in Section 2 of this textbook presenting major types of human differences that result in diversity. The purpose of this chapter is threefold. First, we will discuss appearance including weight and height, forms of diversity which have not yet been discussed in this textbook. Second, we will revisit family responsibility and pregnancy to supplement the sections on maternity and paternity leave which can be found in Chapters 3 and 5. Third, the chapter ends with a short section on the Genetic Information Nondiscrimination Act (GINA), which is the newest form of employment discrimination covered under Title VII of the Civil Rights Act of 1964.

Weight and Appearance

Attractive people have been defined as "those who conform to norms for attractiveness on both mutable facets of appearance, such as dress and grooming, and relatively immutable facets, such as facial features, body weight, and stature" (Dipboye, 2005, p. 282). Studies have shown that attractiveness is correlated to occupational success (Langlois, Kalakanis, Rubenstein, Larson, Hallam, & Smoot, 2000), more positive appraisals in selection and promotion decisions (Hosoda, Stone-Romero, & Stone, 2003; Stone, Stone, & Dipboye, 1992), higher levels of education, higher occupational status, higher life satisfaction (Umberson & Hughes, 1987), and higher income (Roszell, Kennedy, & Grabb, 1989). Furthermore, studies have also shown a consensus in people's ratings of others' attractiveness, and this consensus has been observed across various rater characteristics including sex, age, race, socioeconomic status, and cultural background

(Jackson, 1992). In sum, attractive people seem to enjoy certain advantages, and there seems to be a consensus about who is considered attractive. However, one unresolved issue is "whether the target person's sex moderates the effects of attractiveness" (Dipboye, 2005, p. 287). The findings in this area have been mixed, with no consensus in the literature on how much attractiveness matters for men versus women (Heilman & Saruwatari, 1979, Heilman & Stopeck, 1985a, 1985b; Maccarone, 2003).

The Relationship Between Attractiveness Outcomes

The physical attractiveness stereotype is very simple: what is beautiful is good (Dion, Berscheid, & Walster, 1972). The human bias toward attractive individuals seems to be embedded early in life, with studies showing that children are biased toward attractive children (Dion, 1973; Dion & Berscheid, 1974; Langlois & Stephan, 1981) and that babies prefer more attractive faces (Langlois et al., 1987). This is consistent with the literature showing that attractive people have more favorable career outcomes (Hosoda, Stone-Romero, & Coats, 2003; Langlois et al., 2000; Roszell et al., 1989; Stone et al., 1992; Umberson & Hughes, 1987). Although effect sizes tend to be small, with only 1% to 5% of variance attributable to attractiveness, these effects have been shown to be persistent (Dipboye, 2005).

In a study conducted by Cunningham, Roberts, Barbee, Druen, and Wu (1995), the authors report that the human ideal of a pretty face varies relatively little from culture to culture. The authors conducted three studies to examine the consistency of physical attractiveness across cultural groups. In Studies 1 and 2 they focused on faces, and in Study 3 they focused on bodies. Findings showed that Asian, Hispanic, and White judges were strikingly consistent in their judgments of attractiveness, providing similar ratings of Hispanic, Asian, and White female faces. All groups gave higher ratings to faces with large eyes, greater distance between the eyes, and small noses. People generally preferred faces that appeared sexually mature (which may convey strength, dominance, status, and competency according to the authors) and narrower female faces with smaller chins, as well as expressive, higher eyebrows; dilated pupils; larger lower lips; larger smiles; and well-groomed, full hair. Across Studies 1 and 2, there was some evidence that Asian judges appreciated female faces that appeared slightly less sexually mature and less expressive than the facial ideal in America. Asian judges were slightly more accepting than White judges of women with lower cheekbones and wide cheeks. They were more negative toward women with wide chins, and they were also less positive to a wide smile and higher set eyebrows, suggesting less interest in sexual maturity and expressiveness than their American counterparts. Study 3 examined the preferences of Blacks. Blacks and Whites made highly similar judgments about most aspects of the face but differed with regard to body preferences. Blacks were more likely than Whites to select the larger of the two silhouettes as being more attractive (Cunningham et al., 1995).

In a different study conducted by Dipboye, Arvey, and Terpstra (1977), the authors conducted an experiment and found that the candidate who was perceived to be the most qualified for a managerial position was highly qualified, physically attractive, and male. The authors conducted a laboratory experiment where applicant sex, attractiveness, and qualifications were manipulated. Results showed that highly qualified applicants were preferred over poorly qualified applicants, regardless of sex and attractiveness. Male applicants were preferred over female applicants, and attractive applicants were preferred over unattractive candidates. Also, attractive male applicants were rated significantly higher than attractive female applicants, and unattractive male applicants were also rated higher than unattractive female applicants.

Studies examining the effects of attractiveness have also been conducted at the labor market level. In a study on beauty and the labor market, Hamermesh and Biddle (1994) found evidence of earnings differentials based on beauty. The authors examined the impact of looks on earnings using interviewers' ratings of respondents' physical appearance. They reported that the wages of people with below-average looks were lower than those of average-looking workers, and there was also a premium in wages for good-looking people which was slightly smaller in magnitude than the difference between the below-average and average-looking workers. The penalty and premium may be higher for men, but these gender differences are not large according to Hamermesh and Biddle (1994). In sum, the authors explained that plain (less attractive) people earned less than average-looking people, who earned less than good-looking people. This plainness penalty was about 5%, slightly larger than the beauty premium, which was about 4%. Further, the effects for men were at least as great as for women. Other findings from this study include that unattractive women had lower labor force participation rates. These women also married men with less human capital than more attractive women. Further, better-looking people tended to sort into occupations where beauty may be more beneficial. The authors also found that the impact of individuals' looks was mostly independent of occupations, which suggests the existence of employer discrimination whereby the market filters more attractive people into positions where that may be advantageous (Hamermesh & Biddle, 1994).

In a meta-analytic study which aggregated the results of many other empirical studies, Hosoda, Stone-Romero, and Coats (2003) found a medium effect size ($d = 0.37$) across the 62 studies included in their meta-analytic investigation such that attractive people fared better than unattractive people on various job-related outcomes including selection, performance evaluation, and promotion. The authors reported that the attractiveness bias was due to the fact that positive expectations were associated with attractiveness and that physical attractiveness is beneficial for individuals' job outcomes (Hosoda et al., 2003).

Some papers have also examined whether attractiveness may ever be a disadvantage, referred to as the "beauty is beastly" effect. Johnson, Podratz, Dipboye, and Gibbons (2010) examined both the "beauty is beastly" effect and the "what is beautiful is good" effect. The "beauty is beastly" effect suggests that attractiveness can be detrimental to women when attractive women apply for masculine sex-typed jobs (Heilman & Saruwatari, 1979; Heilman & Stopeck, 1985a, 1985b). This idea is based on Heilman's (1983) lack of fit model, which describes that "occupational sex bias is a result of an incongruity between one's perceived skills and attributes, which are associated with gender, and the perceived nature of the job's requirements" (Heilman & Saruwatari, 1979, p. 203). In other words, in masculine types of jobs, attractiveness may be a detriment for women if they seem to not be a good fit for the job. The "what is beautiful is good" effect suggests that physically attractive persons benefit from their attractiveness across many situations, including employment outcomes. This perspective has been supported in many studies, including the meta-analysis of 62 studies by Hosoda et al. (2003) referenced earlier.

The major conclusion of the Johnson et al. (2010) study is that the "beauty is beastly" effect appears to be limited and occurs for masculine jobs where physical appearance is rated as unimportant. The "what is beautiful is good" effect is robust over a wide range of stimuli and jobs. Findings from their first study showed that attractive applicants were rated as more suitable for employment. Attractive women were rated as more suitable than unattractive women for feminine jobs. Attractiveness was also related to employment suitability for masculine sex-typed jobs. Attractive applicants were rated as more suitable for jobs for which physical appearance was important than jobs for which physical appearance was unimportant. Findings from the second study presented in the Johnson et al. (2010) research showed that compared to unattractive women, attractive women were rated as significantly more suitable for the masculine job for which physical appearance was important (car salesperson) and for the feminine jobs (social worker and secretary), but they were rated as being significantly less suitable for the masculine job for which physical appearance was unimportant (prison guard) (Johnson et al., 2010). Therefore, attractiveness seems to be beneficial for women in most (but not all) circumstances.

Finally, in a meta-analytic study aggregating the effects of height on workplace success and income, Judge and Cable (2004) found that tall individuals have advantages in several important aspects of their careers and organizational lives. We have seen examples of the influence of height in U.S. presidential elections for many years. According to Judge and Cable (2004, p. 428), U.S. citizens have not elected a president who was below average in height since 1896, and U.S. president "William McKinley at 5 ft 7 in. (1.7 m) was ridiculed in the press as a 'little boy.'"

Judge and Cable (2004) proposed a process model describing that height is positively associated with self-esteem and social esteem (how positively an individual is evaluated or regarded by others in society), which are positively related to both objective and subjective job performance, and this ultimately is positively associated with career success and income. The main study findings show that physical height is positively associated with social esteem, emerging as a leader, and performance. Height was more strongly associated with success for men than for women, but this difference was not statistically significant. Height was positively related to income after controlling for sex, age, and weight. The meta-analytic results showed that, across all outcome variables examined, height had a correlation of 0.26 with favorable employment outcomes, which is considered a medium effect size. The authors also conducted four studies in addition to the meta-analysis and found that height significantly predicted earnings with effect sizes in the small to medium range. Judge and Cable (2004) further discussed that height is positively associated with several job outcomes, and this advantage does not appear to be driven by a possible link between height and intelligence. Indeed, the largest meta-analytic estimate reported in their study was a corrected correlation of 0.41 for the association between height and social status, which implies that the height advantage is likely being driven by the positive way in which society reacts to tall people (Judge & Cable, 2004).

Weight

What Is Considered to be Underweight, Average Weight, Overweight, and Obese?

According to the National Institutes of Health, the way to assess one's weight is with the body mass index (BMI). The BMI is a measure of body fat based on weight and height which applies to adults (National Institutes of Health, 2016a). The BMI formula in pounds is computed as follows:

$$BMI = (703 * \text{weight in pounds})/\text{height in inches}^2$$

The metric formula is as follows:

$$BMI = \text{weight in kilograms}/\text{height in meters}^2$$

BMI categories are interpreted as follows:

Underweight = < 18.50
Normal weight = 18.50–24.9
Overweight = 25–29.9
Obese = 30 or higher

An online calculator may be found at this National Institutes of Health web site: http://www.nhlbi.nih.gov/health/educational/lose_wt/BMI/bmicalc.htm.

According to the U.S. National Institutes of Health, data from the National Health and Nutrition Examination Survey for the period from 2009–2010 show that over two-thirds of adults are overweight or obese, with one-third of adults being obese. Over 1 in 20 adults have extreme obesity. Among children and adolescents, about one-third of children are overweight or obese, and one in six children are obese (National Institutes of Health, 2016b).

Global View: Chile

In a push to reduce the country's childhood obesity rate, the Chilean government recently implemented new nutrition standards that are touted as a "pioneer worldwide" (Vergara & Henao, 2016). The Chilean president, Michelle Bachelet, describes it as "historic for the country and ... unheard of in the world" (Informador.mx, 2016). It took nine years to produce this legislation (Informador.mx, 2016), but this unprecedented law adheres to recommendations by the World Health Organization which stipulate specific amounts of sugar, fats, and salt to be consumed in one's diet. According to the World Health Organization and Chile's new food labeling law, for every 100 grams of solid food, the nutritional value must not exceed a maximum of 275 calories, 400 milligrams of sodium, 10 grams of sugar, and 4 grams of saturated fats (Ramirez, Sternsdorff & Pastor, 2016; Vergara & Henao, 2016). For comparison purposes, consider a 43-gram Hershey's milk chocolate bar, which contains 220 calories, 8 grams of saturated fat, 24 grams of sugar, and 35 milligrams of sodium (Hersheys.com, 2016).

Chilean public health officials and government officials alike hope that the new nutrition standards will alleviate the obesity problem the country faces. Currently, Chile has one of the highest rates of overweight and obese citizens among Latin American and Caribbean countries. Also, 10% of its children have been deemed to be overweight for each of the last eight years (Ramirez et al., 2016).

Research Findings on Weight

Research showing that overweight people face employment discrimination was presented by Pingitore, Dugoni, Tindale, and Spring (1994). This investigation reported that overweight adults, particularly women, are likely to suffer employment discrimination. In this study, a professional actor performed the roles of a normal weight and an overweight applicant. The researchers asked participants questions to determine whether overweight applicants were subject to bias in interview evaluations, whether this bias was greater for women, who would be most likely not to hire an overweight adult, whether employment bias against overweight people was higher in jobs with public contact, whether negative personality dispositions were attributed to overweight applicants, and whether negative personality attributions mediated the relationship between obesity and hiring judgments made. The findings showed that bias against hiring overweight job applicants existed, especially for female applicants. The applicant's body weight was thus a significant predictor in the hiring decision. Unexpectedly, overweight applicants were no more likely to be hired for a job requiring minimal public contact than they were for a position requiring extensive public contact, which implies that appearance and job requirements were not associated. The decision not to hire an obese applicant was only partially mediated by personality attributions about the obese applicant. In sum, the research mostly shows that overweight individuals may face discrimination and experience disadvantages on the job market, but that evidence is not consistent across all studies.

More research corroborating the finding that overweight people face employment discrimination was conducted by Pagán and Dávila (1997), who reported that occupational segregation observed for obese women may be caused mostly by labor market discrimination whereas occupational sorting of obese males into various occupations may be the result of the low barriers they face when moving across occupations. The authors examined the occupational selection of obese individuals using a national longitudinal data set from the United States. They found that obesity does not seem to play a role in predicting the probability of labor force participation for males but that obesity among women is associated with a lower probability of holding a job in some occupations. They conclude that women pay a penalty for being obese and that this obesity wage penalty varies little across occupations. Obese females are largely employed in relatively low-paying occupations and are mostly excluded from the high-paying managerial/professional and technical occupations. Overweight males sort themselves into jobs through occupational mobility to offset this penalty. Specifically, overweight men appear to choose jobs where they have a productivity advantage over the non-obese, and they often accept a premium for undertaking more employment-related risks (e.g., sales). For example, males employed in the service industry are more likely to be obese. Pagán and Dávila (1997) explain that men prone to obesity may choose to work in the service industry because this occupation affords them a higher wage in exchange for accepting greater stress-related risk. Pagán and Dávila (1997) also noted that BMI may not be the best measure of obesity because it does not measure actual body fat. It is possible that a large BMI for males could capture strength and size for bulky men, for instance.

Global View: Egypt

Egypt's state broadcasting company suspended eight of its female employees who regularly appear on television (Youssef, 2016) because they were perceived to be too heavy to be on television (Youssef, 2016). The Egyptian Radio and Television Union, which is headed by a woman who used to be a television presenter herself, informed the eight women that they were being given one month to lose weight before they could appear on television again with a more "appropriate appearance" (*BBC News*, 2016; Youssef, 2016). The Women's Centre for Guidance and Legal Awareness has condemned the decision, saying that it is a violation against the constitution and women. On social media, some have supported the women while others have made fun of them and called them "bakabouzas," a term Egyptians use to describe overweight girls (*BBC News*, 2016). Waheed Abdul Majid, an author and academic who was interviewed about the story, suggested the channel should focus on improving its content as opposed to the appearance of its presenters (*BBC News*, 2016).

Stereotypes About Overweight Employees

In an investigation about the validity of stereotypes about overweight employees, Roehling, Roehling, and Odland (2008) examined associations between body weight and personality traits, including conscientiousness, agreeableness, emotional stability, and extraversion. The impetus for the study was to test commonly held stereotypes that overweight job applicants and employees are less conscientiousness, less agreeable, less emotionally stable, and less extraverted than others who are not overweight. The authors measured the relationship between body weight (BMI and percentage of body fat) and these personality traits in two samples, one large sample of adults from the United States and one smaller sample of college students from the Midwest region of the United States. Results from Study 1 showed that BMI was negatively and significantly associated with extraversion and conscientiousness, but effect sizes were very small and accounted for little variance in the personality measures. There was no association between BMI and agreeableness or emotional stability. Study 2 results showed no association between BMI and any of the four personality traits. Study 2 also measured weight by body fat in addition to BMI, and the results for body fat showed no association with any of the four personality traits. Overall, results refuted stereotypic beliefs about overweight employees. There was no evidence that BMI or fat had any association with agreeableness and emotional stability, and there was little (mostly no) evidence that BMI or body fat had an association with extraversion and conscientiousness. Roehling et al. (2008) conclude that body weight is not a practically significant predictor of personality traits and should not be used as a predictor of personality in employment decisions.

Little Recourse in the Event of Weight Discrimination

Roehling (1999) concludes that much of the weight-based discrimination that occurs is not likely to be considered illegal because current laws provide little protection against weight-based discrimination. Title VII of the Civil Rights Act of 1964 does not identify weight as a protected class. Two general circumstances where use of employee weight may result in illegal discrimination include **disparate treatment**, where an employer treats some applicants less favorably than others because of some characteristic (e.g., race, color, religion, sex, national origin), and **disparate impact**, in which a selection method results in disproportionately ruling out some groups of candidates more so than others. If an employer applies an illegal weight rule as part of their selection process, and the rule has a significant disparate impact on a protected class, that would be evidence of disparate impact. For example, if an employer provides a hip measurement standard as part of the selection process for female servers at a restaurant, that could have a disproportionate effect on African-American or Hispanic women since weight may increase with age and has been found to be higher in certain groups, including African-Americans and Hispanics (Roehling, 1999).

When overweight persons seek legal protection for weight discrimination, they generally do so under one of two laws in the U.S which protect against disability. The **Rehabilitation Act of 1973 (RHA)** prohibits employment discrimination against qualified individuals with disabilities by organizations that hold government contracts, receive federal grants, or are government agencies or departments. This law was further augmented by the **Americans with Disabilities Act of 1990 (ADA)**, which extends this prohibition to private employers and state and local entities. Under these laws, a disability representing a physical impairment must substantially limit one or more major life activities such as taking care of oneself, performing manual tasks, walking, seeing, hearing, speaking, breathing, learning, and working. To be classified as having a disability that substantially limits the major life activity of working, plaintiffs need to demonstrate they are seriously restricted in their ability to perform either a class of jobs or a range of jobs in various job classes (Roehling, 1999).

According to Roehling, Posthuma, and Dulebohn (2007), plaintiffs have a high burden in order to establish obesity-related perceived disability claims under federal law. The Americans with Disabilities Act protects workers who are regarded or perceived as disabled in addition to those with actual disabilities. Overweight plaintiffs tend to file perceived disability claims and experience greater success compared to other disability claims. According to the ADA and the Rehabilitation Act of 1973, a **disability** refers to a person with a physical or mental impairment that substantially limits one or more of the individual's major life activities. Obesity is considered a disability only in rare circumstances. For instance, if someone is morbidly obese (100% over ideal weight) or suffering from a physiological condition (thyroid condition), or if obesity limits major life activity such as walking, hearing, or speaking, that person may be covered under the ADA. However, the ADA does not cover conditions that are medically correctable (Roehling et al., 2007).

According to Equal Employment Opportunity Commission (EEOC) regulations, perceived discrimination can be covered under the ADA if the person in question has: (a) a physical or mental impairment which does not substantially limit major life activities but is treated by the employer as constituting such a limitation; (b) a physical or mental impairment which substantially limits major life activities only as a consequence of the attitudes of others toward such impairment; or (c) no impairment at all but is treated by the employer as having a substantially limiting impairment (Roehling et al., 2007).

A major court case, **Cook v. State of Rhode Island Department of Mental Health**, took place in 1993. It marked the first time a court considered an obesity-related perceived discrimination claim covered under the ADA or RHA. The court's focus was on whether the employer perceived the employee's weight as a substantial impairment to one or more major life activities. In this case the plaintiff was Bonnie Cook, a 5-foot 2-inch, 320-pound woman with an excellent work record at the organization in question. She claimed the organization would not rehire her a few years after she had left voluntarily because of her weight. Ms. Cook filed a lawsuit claiming that she had been discriminated against because of a disability covered by the RHA Section 504. A jury ruled that discrimination against severely obese people violates federal disability law and awarded her $100,000 in compensatory damages. Further, a judge ruled that the organization needed to reinstate Ms. Cook in her position (Lewin, 1993).

According to Roehling et al. (2007), when obesity-related discrimination claims are made, there tend to be factors that would provide evidence supporting the plaintiff as well as evidence supporting the defense. Evidence supporting obesity-related perceived disability claims include the level of the plaintiff's obesity (with those who are morbidly obese being more successful in their claims), evidence of derogatory obesity-related remarks made by the employer, biased medical assessments made by company physicians, and deficient human resources practices. Evidence that contributes to successful employer defenses include failure to demonstrate the "substantial impairment of major life activity" requirement, meaning the plaintiff must show that the employer had a perception the plaintiff was unable to perform a class or broad range of jobs. Other defenses include the presence of a legitimate, non-discriminatory reason for the behavior being challenged in the lawsuit (Roehling et al., 2007).

Recommendations for Organizations About Appearance and Weight

The best policy for organizations to follow is to focus on employees' job-related qualifications as they pertain to the job in question when making human resources decisions. If particular characteristics have nothing to do with one's knowledge, skills, and ability to get the job done, then employers should avoid focusing on those characteristics. It is reasonable for employers to expect employees to report to work clean and well groomed. If uniforms or particular attire are required on the job, then job candidates should be informed of this job requirement in advance. Otherwise, employers should avoid taking actions which could be perceived as discriminatory on the basis of a person's appearance or weight. Employers should also be flexible with employee requirements about appearance at work, particularly if aspects of employee appearance are related to their religious beliefs, cultural values, or (dis)ability status. The emphasis should be on employees' abilities to perform the job, not the way they look (Uniform Guidelines on Employee Selection Procedures, 1979).

With respect to appearance and weight, it is important to note that some states are passing legislation which begins to address the matter of bullying in the workplace. Since 2015, California businesses have been required to train their managers to identify abusive conduct and bullying at work in an effort to curb sexual harassment. The Fair Employment and Housing Council in California regulations instruct employers to provide employee training on abusive conduct and workplace bullying behavior (Bell, 2016). They define abusive conduct as malicious behavior including derogatory remarks, insults, or behavior a reasonable person would consider threatening or humiliating (Bell, 2016). Although being a mean person is not illegal, actions which could be construed as workplace bullying and harassment could lead to perceived discrimination, reprimands for employees, and potentially legal action for organizations. Organizations should set a respectful and professional tone among employees and emphasize working toward meeting the organization's goals rather than other irrelevant topics that could lead to perceived discrimination.

Employers should also focus on having healthy employees. Organizations can provide environments conducive to employee health based on the way organizational facilities are structured and on the types of food offered in the organizational cafeteria, such as a variety of fruits and vegetables, whole grains, and other healthy offerings. Encouraging employees to exercise can be done by providing a campus exercise room where employees may go during their breaks or lunch periods or by maintaining grounds with sidewalks for employees to go for walks during breaks or after having lunch. Along these lines, wellness programs have become popular to promote employee health. Such programs can save organizations money in the long-term if they reduce the cost of health care by lowering employee illness. One caveat for employers in the United States to be aware of is that they should only collect information about employee health that is essential. This information needs to be kept confidential, and employees must be notified in advance of such data collection. According to recent guidance from the EEOC, if employers collect information about employee health as part of their wellness programs, employees must be informed clearly and in advance about how the information collected will be used (Nagele-Piazza, 2016). The EEOC issued two rules which take effect in 2017 for employer wellness plans to meet the requirements of the ADA and the Genetic Information Nondiscrimination Act (GINA— discussed in the following). Under the ADA, employers must provide notice to participants of wellness programs if they will collect health information through screenings and assessments (Nagele-Piazza, 2016). GINA and its requirements will be discussed at the end of this chapter.

Regarding weight, Roehling and colleagues (2007) provide some recommendations for organizations. They suggest having formal policies against weight discrimination and also educating employees about examples of insensitive weight-related comments/behaviors that must be avoided. Another recommendation is to review job descriptions to determine if weight requirements presented are related to essential requirements of the job, as well as discussing weight loss with employees only if it is relevant to the job they perform. Further, companies should provide employee training to help employees understand the ADA. In jobs that require physical capabilities, employees should be referred to medical professionals who can provide an unbiased examination. Finally, employee wellness programs that encourage exercise and provide employees opportunities to use fitness and wellness facilities can help promote overall health (Roehling et al., 2007).

Family Responsibility and Pregnancy

Family responsibility discrimination is discrimination that occurs on the basis of employee responsibilities to care for family members, such as their children, disabled family members, and elderly parents (Von Bergen, 2008). Family responsibility discrimination is a relatively new form of employment discrimination (Dickson, 2008) that has received recent attention due to the increasing number of lawsuits and their associated costs (Scott, 2007). Moreover, research on family responsibility discrimination has been described as exploratory since few researchers have examined this topic (Dickson, 2008). For example, in Dipboye and Colella's (2005) comprehensive book on employment discrimination, family responsibility discrimination was discussed on only two pages.

Employee lawsuits related to family responsibility discrimination increased almost 400% between the years 2000 and 2010 (Calvert, 2010). Women comprise 46.9% of the American labor force (Bureau of Labor Statistics, 2012) and are the majority of plaintiffs in family responsibility discrimination cases (Scott, 2007). However, family responsibility discrimination has also become a concern for men (Bond, Thompson, Galinsky, & Prottas, 2003). In comparison to employment discrimination cases based on race, sex, disability, national origin, and religion, family responsibility discrimination cases show a greater than 50% win rate, with no significant difference between men and women in the likelihood of success (Still, 2006).

In response to the rise in family responsibility discrimination claims and the associated costs of litigation, the EEOC published the "Unlawful Disparate Treatment of Workers with Caregiving Responsibilities" enforcement guidelines (EEOC, 2007). According to the EEOC, caregiving responsibility discrimination, or family responsibility discrimination, occurs when an employer's decision affecting a caregiver unlawfully discriminates on the basis of a protected characteristic under Title VII of the Civil Rights Act of 1964 and the Americans with Disabilities Act of 1990. Other laws that have been used in family responsibility discrimination cases include, but are not limited to, the Pregnancy Discrimination Act of 1975, the Family and Medical Leave Act of 1993, and the Employee Retirement Income Security Act of 1974 (Williams & Bornstein, 2008).

Research shows negative consequences of perceived family responsibility discrimination, including lower job satisfaction (Anderson, Coffey, & Byerly, 2002; Dickson, 2008), lower organizational attachment (Dickson, 2008), and lower benefit usage (Butler, Gasser, & Smart, 2004; Dickson, 2008), as well as higher turnover intentions and higher work–family conflict (Anderson et al., 2002; Dickson, 2008; Thompson, Beauvais, & Lyness, 1999). The EEOC "Employer Best Practices for Workers with Caregiving Responsibilities" guide (EEOC, 2011) suggests that employers adopt new practices to reduce the chance of equal employment opportunity (EEO) violations against caregivers and to remove barriers to equal employment opportunity.

Mother(Father)hood and Pregnancy

We now turn our attention to studies examining the presence of a motherhood penalty, a fatherhood premium, and a bias toward pregnant women. A study conducted by Budig and England (2001) examined the wage penalty for motherhood. They concluded that the wage penalty for motherhood is equal to about 7% per child among young American women. The authors summarized reasons that have been proposed to explain why working mothers may earn less than other women, including that having children causes them to lose job experience, be less productive at work, trade off higher wages for mother-friendly jobs, and possibly also be discriminated against by employers. Research is somewhat unclear about what part of the child penalty is explained by work experience because some authors/ studies report penalties controlling for work experience while other studies have not controlled for experience. This makes it impossible to precisely compare the findings across research studies. Losing job experience adversely affects mothers' wages because more experienced workers are more productive and therefore are paid more. Another explanation for the motherhood penalty is Becker's (1991) "new home economics," which argues that mothers may be less productive on the job than non-mothers because they are tired from home duties or because they are saving their energy for anticipated work at home. The assumption is that non-mothers spend more of their time outside of work in leisure instead of in childcare or other household work and that leisure takes less energy—thus leaving more energy for paid work. Another possibility is that mothers may seek mother-friendly jobs (e.g., work part-time, have flexible hours, on-site day care, etc.). The features of these jobs make them easier to combine with motherhood but also result in lower earnings. Finally, it is possible that discrimination is taking place if employers assume that mothers, on average, may be less productive than non-mothers or if employers simply do not have a desire to employ mothers (Budig & England, 2001).

Studies Attempting to Explain the Motherhood Penalty

To test where the wage penalty for motherhood comes from, Budig and England (2001) conducted a study using the 1982–1993 U.S. National Longitudinal Survey of Youth and distinguished among years of full-time experience, years of part-time experience, and seniority. Roughly one-third of the penalty is explained by years of past job experience and seniority, including whether past work was part-time. The analyses showed indirect evidence that at least part of the child penalty may result from mothers being less productive in a given hour of paid work because they are more exhausted or distracted than others. The amount of discrimination varies by number of children and marital status because those factors affect decisions about how time and energy is allocated between child rearing and jobs (Budig & England, 2001).

Results from Budig and England (2001) showed that penalties are larger for married women than for unmarried women, while married and divorced women had similarly high child penalties. This does not mean there is a marriage penalty. In fact, marriage had positive effects in all analyses/statistical models that did not include children. Further, second children reduce wages more than a first child, especially for married women. Women with more children have fewer years of job experience, and after controlling for experience, a penalty of 5% per child remains. "Mother-friendly" characteristics of the jobs held by mothers explain little of the penalty beyond the tendency of more mothers than non-mothers to work part-time. The authors explain that the portion of the motherhood penalty that is unexplained probably results from the effect of motherhood on productivity and/ or from discrimination by employers against mothers. While the benefits of mothering diffuse widely—to employers, neighbors, friends, spouses, and the children who received the mothering, the costs of child rearing are borne disproportionately by mothers. Findings showed that Black women and Latinas had smaller penalties, but only for the third and subsequent births (Budig & England, 2001).

In a different study assessing the motherhood penalty in getting a job, Correll, Benard, and Paik (2007) report that mothers are rated as less hirable, less suitable for promotion and management training, and more deserving of lower salaries because they are believed to be less competent and less committed to paid work. The authors conducted a laboratory experiment to evaluate the hypothesis that status-based discrimination plays an important role in explaining the motherhood penalty, and they also conducted an audit study of actual employers to assess its real-world implications. In the laboratory study sampling undergraduate students, the experiment manipulated the race and gender of the applicant by changing first names on the applications. They also manipulated parental status on résumés and in a memo by adding a statement that the applicant was the parent-teacher association coordinator. The outcome variables, or dependent measures, included competence and commitment, standards for ability/job proficiency, evaluation measures (salary recommended for each applicant, promotability, management training course recommendation, recommended for hire). In both studies, participants evaluated application materials for a pair of same-gender, equally qualified job candidates who differed on parental status. In the audit study, the authors measured positive responses to applicants based on the number of callbacks from actual employers. The authors found support for status-based discrimination mechanisms of motherhood penalty over a broad range of measures, (i.e., motherhood is a status characteristic and/or a trait with differentially valued states that impacts performance expectations; Correll et al., 2007).

Correll and coauthors expected that job applicants who were presented as mothers would be rated as less competent, less committed to paid work, less suitable for hire and promotion, and deserving of lower starting salaries compared with otherwise equal women who were not mothers. They predicted that competence and commitment ratings would mediate, or transmit, the effects of motherhood status to the outcome variables. Finally, they expected that mothers would be judged by a harsher standard than non-mothers. Findings from the laboratory study showed that mothers were penalized on a host of measures, including perceived competence and recommended starting salary by approximately $12,000 (7.9%) less than was offered to non-mothers. Mothers were also rated as significantly less promotable, were less likely to be recommended for management, and were also held to stricter performance standards. Childless women were recommended for hire 1.8 times more frequently than were mothers. Compared to fathers, mothers were offered approximately 8.6% lower salaries (Correll et al., 2007). By comparison, men were not penalized for, and sometimes benefited from, being a parent. For example, supporting the idea of a fatherhood bonus (Orloff, 1996), they were more likely to be allowed to be late and were offered higher salaries. Fathers were offered salaries of approximately $152,000 while childless men were offered approximately $148,000. Mothers were offered approximately $139,000 while childless women were offered approximately $151,000 (Correll et al., 2007).

In the audit study of employers conducted by Correll et al. (2007), findings showed that employers discriminate against mothers, but not against fathers or childless women. Interestingly, childless women were 3.35 times more likely to be recommended for hire than childless men. Childless women were especially advantaged compared to mothers, as they were over six times more likely to be recommended for hire. African-American women and White women both experience a motherhood penalty, and the magnitude of that penalty is largely the same for both groups. Consistent with the authors' theoretical predictions, competence and commitment were found to at least partially mediate, or transmit, the negative effect of motherhood status on workplace evaluations. In other words, motherhood leads to a penalty because it leads people to associate the applicant with less competence and commitment to the job (Correll et al., 2007).

In an attempt to understand the mechanisms that result in the motherhood penalty, Cuddy, Fiske, and Glick (2004) examined ratings of warmth versus competency when professional women become mothers. The authors conceptually differentiated groups along two dimensions, competence and warmth, resulting in four combinations: high warmth/high competence, high warmth/low competency, high competence/low warmth, low competence/low warmth. The authors explain that only groups perceived as both warm and competent (e.g., middle-class people) enjoy both assistance from and cooperation with other groups. Homemakers are viewed as low status and cooperative, resulting in them being characterized as warm but not competent; this results in condescending affection toward them (Bridges, Etaugh, & Barnes-Farrell, 2002; Cuddy et al., 2004; Eagly & Steffen, 1984, 1986; Eckes, 2002; Etaugh & Poertner, 1992). By contrast, female professionals are seen as high status, and this elicits envy, which results in them being characterized as competent but cold; this results in begrudging respect and resentment (Bridges et al., 2002; Cuddy et al., 2004; Eckes, 2002; Etaugh & Poertner, 1992; Etaugh & Study, 1989).

Cuddy et al. (2004) conducted a laboratory study with college students to investigate how working mothers were perceived compared to childless working women and men, and working fathers. They found that working mothers risked being reduced to one of two subtypes: homemakers (seen as warm but incompetent) or female professionals (seen as competent but cold). The gain that working mothers achieved in perceived warmth did not help them, but their loss in perceived competence did hurt them. Findings suggested that when working women become mothers, they traded perceived competence for perceived warmth and were not rated as being both warm and competent. By contrast, working men did not make this trade-off. When they became fathers, they gained perceived warmth but maintained perceived competence. Childless men were rated as being more competent than warm. People reported less interest in hiring, promoting, and educating working mothers relative to working fathers and childless employees. Also, competence ratings predict interest in hiring, promoting, and educating workers. Finally, parents were rated as significantly warmer than non-parents (Cuddy et al., 2004). In sum, working women with children are not immune from stereotypes and discrimination. When working women become mothers, they make a trade-off in perceived warmth for perceived competence. This trade-off unjustly costs them professional credibility and hinders their odds of being hired, promoted, and generally supported in the workplace (Cuddy et al., 2004).

Pregnancy

A study conducted by Hebl, King, Glick, Singletary, and Kazama (2007) endeavored to understand whether pregnant women would experience backlash for certain types of non-traditional female behaviors. They predicted that when pregnant women pursue traditional (as compared with non-traditional) roles, they will elicit greater benevolence, but that when pregnant women pursue non-traditional (as compared with traditional) roles, they will elicit greater hostility. The authors conducted two studies. In Study 1, they had visibly pregnant versus non-pregnant confederates wearing prosthetics to make them appear pregnant apply for jobs (non-traditional role) versus act as customers (traditional role) at retail stores. In Study 2, the authors examined working adults' reactions to fictitious pregnant or non-pregnant job applicants for a variety of masculine and feminine jobs. This experiment manipulated pregnancy (pregnant, non-pregnant), gender type of position (feminine, masculine), and participant's gender (male, female) to examine gender type of the job and gender of the participant as potential moderators of discrimination.

Overall, the findings showed that pregnant women evoke hostile reactions in situations in which they stray from traditional feminine gender roles. Store employees exhibited more hostile behavior (e.g., rudeness) toward pregnant applicants compared to non-pregnant applicants and more benevolent behavior (e.g., touching, overfriendliness) toward pregnant customers versus non-pregnant customers. However, the results showed no evidence of formal discrimination. The second experiment revealed that pregnant women were especially likely to encounter hostility (from both men and women) when applying for masculine as compared with feminine jobs. Both men and women are susceptible to bias toward pregnant applicants. Pregnant women were penalized by both men and women when considered for positions that were incongruent with a traditional feminine role (Eagly & Karau, 2002; Hebl et al., 2007).

Global View: Spain

In Spain, fewer women are having children, and 25%–30% of women between the ages of 35 and 40 will not bear children (Perez-Lanzac, 2016a, 2016b). Dr. Albert Esteve of the Center for Demographic Studies at the University of Barcelona affirms three main causes for the decrease: 2% is due to infertility, 5% is due to couples choosing not to have children, and the rest is primarily attributed to women waiting until their thirties to become mothers (Perez-Lanzac, 2016a, 2016b). Statistics reveal that in the 1980s the average age for new mothers was approximately 28 years. By 2014, the average had increased to 32 years. In fact, Spain leads Europe in this trend of delayed maternity (Perez-Lanzac, 2016a, 2016b).

Women seem to be postponing maternity for several reasons. According to a study conducted by Dr. Irene Lapuerta, professor at the Public University of Navarra, approximately 60% of women are able to maintain their work status after childbirth. Of the remaining 40%, 19% become unemployed or are not actively employed, 11% reduce their working hours, and 2% take a leave of absence (Carbajosa, 2016). The director for the Women's Watch, Business, and Economy of the Chamber of Commerce in Barcelona explains that work "pressure is brutal" (Carbajosa, 2016). She adds that, when women request a reduction in hours, they are "condemned" to jobs for which they are overqualified. Next is stringent work schedules. A study by the Institute of Family Policy revealed that only one in nine Spaniards has flexible work hours and that telecommuting is nearly non-existent. Only 7 out of 100 employees in Spain currently have the option to telecommute (Veganzones, 2016).

Work–Family Benefits Use

Finally, in a study conducted by Thompson, Beauvais, and Lyness (1999), the authors examined the association between work–family benefits and work–family culture in organizations and employee benefit utilization, organizational attachment, and work–family conflict. In this paper, the authors defined **work–family culture** as shared assumptions, beliefs, and values about the extent to which the organization supports and values the integration of employees' work and family lives. The findings showed that perceptions of a supportive work–family culture are significantly related to whether or not employees will use work–family benefits, how committed they are to the organization, whether they intend to stay with the organization, and how much work–family conflict they experience, even after controlling for the availability of work–family benefits (Thompson et al., 1999).

Specifically, the authors found that three dimensions of work–family culture were associated with behaviors and attitudes: (a) managerial support for work–family balance, (b) career consequences linked to utilizing work–family benefits, and (c) organizational time expectations that could interfere with family responsibilities. The more employees perceived a supportive work–family culture, the more likely they were to use work–family benefits. Both work–family benefit availability and supportive work–family culture were positively related to commitment toward the organization and negatively related to work–family conflict and intentions to leave the organization. Perceptions of a supportive work–family culture were positively and significantly associated with work attitudes beyond the effect of the availability of work–family benefits. Perceptions of a supportive work–family culture were also negatively related to work–family conflict. Further, employees who were married, were female, or had children were more likely to utilize work–family benefits than other employees. The authors concluded that no matter how many and what kinds of work–family programs are offered, the culture in the organization will determine not only whether people will use the benefits, but also their general attitudes toward the organization. Managerial support on a daily basis may be the most critical cultural variable in employees' decisions to use family-friendly benefits and programs (Thompson et al., 1999).

Legislation and Recommendations Regarding Family Responsibility and Pregnancy

Regarding pregnancy in the United States, the guidance from the EEOC pertaining to the Pregnancy Discrimination Act of 1978 advises the following. The Pregnancy Discrimination Act covers current, past, and potential pregnancy. It is illegal to terminate or refuse to hire someone because she is pregnant. The Pregnancy Discrimination Act covers lactation and breastfeeding and prohibits forced leave policies. It also requires organizations to treat men and women the same in parental leave policies. The Act also requires that pregnant employees have access to health insurance benefits just as any other non-pregnant employee would have (EEOC, 2015). Under the Fair Labor Standards Act (FLSA), employers are required to provide nursing mothers with "reasonable break time and a private space for expressing breast milk while at work" for up to one year after the birth of a child (EEOC, 2012). The law states that the room cannot be the bathroom and that it should be a private space that is shielded from view and will not be entered by others while the lactating mother is using the room (EEOC, 2012).

Regarding caregiving, in the United States, the Family Medical Leave Act (FMLA) applies to employers with 50 or more employees during 20 or more workweeks in the current or preceding calendar year. Employees are entitled to up to 12 weeks of unpaid, job-protected leave during a 12-month period for specific family and medical reasons including childbirth, adoption, to take care of a spouse, child, or parent with a serious medical condition, or to take care of a serious medical condition they have themselves. While on FMLA leave, employers are required to maintain coverage for the employee on their group health insurance plan, and they must also restore the employee to the same or an equivalent job upon their return to work (EEOC, 2012).

GINA

The newest category under Title II of the Civil Rights Act of 1964 is called the Genetic Information Nondiscrimination Act of 2008. This act prohibits discrimination in employment on the basis of genetic information and took effect on November 21, 2009. GINA is enforced by the Equal Employment Opportunity Commission (EEOC).

Under Title II of GINA, it is illegal for employers to discriminate against employees or job applicants based on genetic information. GINA prohibits employers from using genetic information to make employment decisions, and it restricts employers and other organizations covered by Title II (called covered entities), including employment agencies, labor organizations, and joint labor-management training and apprenticeship programs, from "requesting, requiring or purchasing genetic information, and strictly limits the disclosure of genetic information" (EEOC, 2016).

Genetic information refers to data about an individual's genetic tests or those of that individual's family members, in addition to information about the person's family medical history and manifestation of a disease or disorder in an individual's family members. "Family medical history is included in the definition of genetic information because it is often used to determine whether someone has an increased risk of getting a disease, disorder, or condition in the future. Genetic information also includes an individual's request for, or receipt of, genetic services, or the participation in clinical research that includes genetic services by the individual or a family member of the individual, and the genetic information of a fetus carried by an individual or by a pregnant woman who is a family member of the individual and the genetic information of any embryo legally held by the individual or family member using an assisted reproductive technology" (EEOC, 2016).

Under GINA, genetic information may not be used to discriminate against anyone on the basis of hiring, firing, compensation, promotion, job assignments, layoffs, training opportunities, benefits, or any condition of employment. "An employer may never use genetic information to make an employment decision because genetic information is not relevant to an individual's current ability to work" (EEOC, 2016). It is also illegal to harass an individual because of his or her genetic information. Harassment may include offensive or derogatory remarks about an applicant or employee in relation to their genetic information. Harassment may come from a supervisor, a coworker, or other individuals who are not employees, including clients or customers (EEOC, 2016).

According to GINA, it is also illegal to "fire, demote, harass, or otherwise 'retaliate' against an applicant or employee for filing a charge of discrimination, participating in a discrimination proceeding (such as a discrimination investigation or lawsuit), or otherwise opposing discrimination" (EEOC, 2016). Further, it is illegal for covered entities to reveal genetic information about applicants or employees. Covered entities are required to keep genetic information confidential and in separate medical files. For example, genetic information may be stored together with other medical information to comply with the Americans with Disabilities Act.

It is usually unlawful for a covered entity to obtain genetic information. There are six narrow exceptions to this prohibition according to the EEOC (2016):

- Inadvertent acquisition of genetic information can occur. For example, a manager or supervisor may hear others talking about a family member's illness.
- Genetic information (including family medical history) may be learned during health or genetic services, such as wellness programs provided by the employer in which employees participate voluntarily.
- Family medical history may be obtained during the certification process for FMLA leave (or leave under similar state or local laws). This results from an employee requesting leave to care for a family member with a serious health condition.
- Genetic information may be obtained via publicly available documents, including newspapers, provided the employer did not seek out the information with the intention of finding genetic information or accessing sources from which they are likely to acquire genetic information.
- Genetic information may be obtained via a genetic monitoring program to monitor the biological effects of toxic substances in the workplace if the monitoring is required by law or under carefully defined conditions, assuming the program is voluntary.
- Genetic information may be acquired for employees by employers who participate in DNA testing for legally required reasons such as a forensic lab or for purposes of human remains identification. However, the genetic information obtained can only be used for analysis of DNA markers for quality control to detect contamination of the sample (EEOC, 2016).

Closing Case

Pregnancy and Accommodation: A Lawsuit at UPS

In 2008, Peggy Young sued United Parcel Service (UPS), a package delivery service, claiming discrimination on the basis of her pregnancy. When Young became pregnant, her doctor instructed her not to lift packages over 20 pounds. When Young requested this of UPS, she was denied this accommodation (Barnes & Schulte, 2015). "They told me basically to go home and come back when I was no longer pregnant," Young said in an interview with the Associated Press. "I couldn't believe it" (Sherman, 2014). She sued UPS in 2008, left the company in 2009, and then lost the discrimination case in two lower courts prior to the case going before the Supreme Court in 2014 (Harkins, Knapp, Kaplan, & Park, 2015; Sherman, 2014).

Young's case hinged on the Pregnancy Discrimination Act. This law was passed by Congress in 1978 to include pregnancy discrimination as a violation of the 1964 Civil Rights Act. The Pregnancy Discrimination Act has two clauses which are critical to the case. First, it states that protections against sex discrimination under Title VII of the Civil Rights Act of 1964 must also apply to pregnancy, childbirth, and related medical conditions. Second, the law says that employers must treat "women affected by pregnancy . . . the same for all employment-related purposes . . . as other persons not so affected but similar in their ability or inability to work" (EEOC, 1978; Harkins et al., 2015).

The matter in Young's case was whether UPS discriminated via its policy to provide temporary light-duty work for employees who (a) had on-the-job injuries, (b) were considered disabled under federal law, or (c) lost their federal driver certification. "If you were painting your house and fell off a ladder, or if you had a ski accident, that wouldn't qualify for restricted light duty. That's where pregnancy fell at that time. It was not covered in any state law except California's," stated Ross, spokeswoman for UPS (Sherman, 2014).

UPS had hired Young as a part-time driver whose primary task was to deliver overnight letters by 8:30 a.m. UPS requires people in these positions to have the ability to lift packages as heavy as 70 pounds. Young explained that she rarely handled packages over 20 pounds and that her job typically involved handling letters that sat on the passenger seat of her van. UPS told Young she could not continue in her job and did not qualify for a temporary assignment (Harkins et al., 2015; Sherman, 2014).

The Supreme Court agreed to hear this case and ruled on the case in 2015, as the case would aid in the interpretation of the Pregnancy Discrimination Act of 1978. The wording in question in the Pregnancy Discrimination Act of 1978 says that employers need to treat pregnant women the same way they treat "other persons not so affected [by pregnancy] but similar in their ability or inability to work" (Zillman, 2015). The Supreme Court ruled in favor of Young in March of 2015 with six justices voting for Young and three justices siding with UPS. Justice Breyer wrote the majority opinion and explained that if an employer does not accommodate a pregnant woman but does accommodate other employees "similar in their ability or inability to work" that employer must have a valid and non-discriminatory reason for doing so (Barnes & Schulte, 2015). The three dissenting justices explained that they thought the majority ruling not only went beyond the intention of the Pregnancy Discrimination Act but that it also placed new restrictions on employers (Zillman, 2015).

Discussion Questions:

1. According to Katherine Kimpel, an employment discrimination expert, 75% of women joining the workforce today will become pregnant at least one time while they are working, and many of them will keep working during their pregnancies (Zillman, 2015). In what ways does this ruling help these women?
2. How could UPS have responded differently to Young's request to avoid the discrimination lawsuit?
3. In what ways is pregnancy similar to and different from other temporary conditions that can diminish an employee's ability to do his/her job?

References

Anderson, S. E., Coffey, B. S., & Byerly, R. T. (2002). Formal organizational initiatives and informal workplace practice: Links to work-family conflict and job-related outcomes. *Journal of Management, 173*, 1–24.

Barnes, R., & Schulte, B. (2015, March 25). Justices revive case claiming UPS discriminated against pregnant worker. The Washington Post. Retrieved from https://www.washingtonpost.com/national/justices-revive-case-claiming-ups-discriminated-against-pregnant-worker/2015/03/25/217223aa-d317-11e4-a62f-ee745911a4ff_story.html?utm_term=.86b0654c0809

BBC News. (2016, August 17). Egypt state TV orders female hosts to lose weight. Retrieved from http://www.bbc.com/news/blogs-news-from-elsewhere-37100676

Becker, Gary S. (1991). A *treatise on the family*. Cambridge, MA: Harvard University Press.

Bell, J. (2016, March 30). California offers guidance on educating employees about workplace bullying. Society for Human Resource Management. Retrieved from https://www.shrm.org/resourcesandtools/legal-and-compliance/state-and-local-updates/pages/california-offers-guidance-on-educating-employees-about-workplace-bullying.aspx

Bond, J., Thompson, C., Galinsky, E., & Prottas, D. (2003). Highlights of the national study of the changing workforce. Retrieved from http://www.familiesandwork.org/summary/nscw2002.pdf

Bridges, J. S., Etaugh, C., & Barnes-Farrell, J. (2002). Trait judgments of stay-at-home and employed parents: A function of social role and/or shifting standards? *Psychology of Women Quarterly, 26*, 140–150.

Budig, M. J., & England, P. (2001). The wage penalty for motherhood. *American Sociological Review, 66*, 204–225.

Bureau of Labor Statistics. (2012). Current population survey. "Table 3: Employment status of the civilian noninstitutional population by age, sex and race." Annual Averages 2011. Retrieved from http://www.bls.gov/cps/cpsaat03.pdf

Butler, A., Gasser, M., & Smart, L. (2004). A social cognitive perspective on using family-friendly benefits. *Journal of Vocational Behavior, 65*, 57–70.

Calvert, C. T. (2010). Family responsibilities discrimination: Litigation update 2010. Center for WorkLife Law. Retrieved from http://www.worklifelaw.org/pubs/FRDupdate.pdf

Carbajosa, A. (2016, June). Con hijos, todo menos iguales. Las mujeres estudian tanto o más que los hombres y acceden en masa al mercado laboral, pero cuando nacen los niños, la frágil igualdad se quiebra y el país se resiente. *El Pais*. Retrieved from http://politica. elpais.com/politica/2016/06/23/actualidad/1466688284_152123.html

CBSN. (2016, May 10). Meghan Trainor pulls new music video. CBS News. Retrieved from http://www.cbsnews.com/videos/meghan-trainor-says-waist-was-photoshopped-in-video/

Correll, S. J., Benard, S., & Paik, I. (2007). Getting a job: Is there a motherhood penalty? *American Journal of Sociology, 112*, 1297–1338.

Cuddy, A. J. C., Fiske, S. T., & Glick, P. (2004). When professionals become mothers, warmth doesn't cut the ice. *Journal of Social Issues, 60*, 701–718.

Cunningham, M. R., Roberts, A. R., Barbee, A. P., Druen, P. B., & Wu, C.-H. (1995). Their ideas of beauty are, on the whole, the same as ours: Consistency and variability in the cross-cultural perception of female physical attractiveness. *Journal of Personality and Social Psychology, 68*(2), 261–279.

Dickson, C. E. (2008). Antecedents and consequences of perceived family responsibilities discrimination in the workplace. *Psychologist-Manager Journal, 11*, 113–140.

Dion, K. K. (1973). Young children's stereotyping of facial attractiveness. *Developmental Psychology, 9*, 183–188.

Dion, K. K., & Berscheid, E. (1974). Physical attractiveness and peer perception among children. *Sociometry, 37*, 1–12.

Dion, K. K., Berscheid, E., & Walster, E. (1972). What is beautiful is good. *Journal of Personality and Social Psychology, 24*, 285–290.

Dipboye, R. L. (2005). Physically unattractive bias. In R. L. Dipboye & A. Colella (Eds.), *Discrimination at work: The psychological and organizational bases* (pp. 281–301). Mahwah, NJ: Lawrence Erlbaum Associates.

Dipboye, R. L., Arvey, R. D., & Terpstra, D. E. (1977). Sex and physical attractiveness of raters and applicants as determinants of resumé evaluations. *Journal of Applied Psychology, 62*(3), 288–294.

Dipboye, R. L., & Colella, A. (2005). *Discrimination at work: The psychological and organizational bases*. Mahwah, NJ: Lawrence Erlbaum Associates.

Eagly, A. H., & Karau, S. J. (2002). Role congruity theory of prejudice toward female leaders. *Psychological Review, 109*, 573–598.

Eagly, A. H., & Steffen, V. J. (1984). Gender stereotypes stem from the distribution of women and men into social roles. *Journal of Personality and Social Psychology, 46*, 735–754.

Eagly, A. H., & Steffen, V. J. (1986). Gender and aggressive behavior: A meta-analytic review of the social psychological literature. *Psychological Bulletin, 100*, 309–330.

Eckes, T. (2002). Paternalistic and envious gender stereotypes: Testing predictions from the stereotype content model. *Sex Roles, 47*, 99–114.

Equal Employment Opportunity Commission (EEOC). (1978). The Pregnancy Discrimination Act of 1978. https://www.eeoc.gov/laws/statutes/pregnancy.cfm

Equal Employment Opportunity Commission. (2007). Enforcement guidance: Unlawful disparate treatment of workers with caregiving responsibilities. Retrieved from http://www.eeoc.gov/policy/docs/caregiving.pdf

Equal Employment Opportunity Commission. (2011). Employer best practices for workers with caregiving responsibilities. Retrieved from http://www.eeoc.gov/policy/docs/care giver-best-practices.html

Equal Employment Opportunity Commission. (2012, February 15). Written testimony of Melvina C. Ford senior policy advisor wage & hour division U.S. Department of Labor. Retrieved from https://www.eeoc.gov/eeoc/meetings/2-15-12/ford.cfm

Equal Employment Opportunity Commission. (2015, June 25). EEOC issues updated pregnancy discrimination guidance. Retrieved from https://www.eeoc.gov/eeoc/newsroom/release/6-25-15.cfm

Equal Employment Opportunity Commission. (2016). Genetic information discrimination. Retrieved from https://www.eeoc.gov/laws/types/genetic.cfm

Etaugh, C., & Poertner, P. (1992). Perceptions of women: Influence of performance, marital and Parental variables. *Sex Roles*, *26*, 311–321.

Etaugh, C., & Study, G. G. (1989). Perceptions of mothers: Effects of employment status, marital status, and age of child. *Sex Roles*, *20*, 59–70.

Hamermesh, D. S., & Biddle, J. E. (1994). Beauty and the labor market. *American Economic Review*, *84*, 1174–1194.

Harkins, J. P., Knapp, A. C., Kaplan, S. E., & Park, E. (2015). The heavy burden of light duty: Young v. UPS. Littler. Retrieved from https://www.littler.com/heavy-burden-light-duty-young-v-ups

Hebl, M. R., King, E. B., Glick, P., Singletary, S. L., & Kazama, S. (2007). Hostile and benevolent reactions toward pregnant women: Complementary interpersonal punishments and rewards that maintain traditional roles. *Journal of Applied Psychology*, *92*, 1499–1511.

Heilman, M. E. (1983). Sex bias in work settings: The lack of fit model. *Research in Organizational Behavior*, *5*, 269–298.

Heilman, M. E., & Saruwatari, L. R. (1979). When beauty is beastly: The effects of appearance and sex on evaluations of job applicants for managerial and nonmanagerial jobs. *Organizational Behavior and Human Performance*, *23*, 360–372.

Heilman, M. E., & Stopeck, M. H. (1985a). Being attractive, advantage or disadvantage? Performance based evaluations and recommended personnel actions as a function of appearance, sex, and job type. *Organizational Behavior and Human Performance*, *35*, 202–215.

Heilman, M. E., & Stopeck, M. H. (1985b). Attractiveness and corporate success: Different causal attributions for males and females. *Journal of Applied Psychology*, *70*, 379–388.

Hersheys.com. (2016). Hershey's milk chocolate bar. Retrieved from https://www.hersheys.com/en_us/products/product/bars/hersheys-milk-chocolate-bar-1-point-55-ounce-bars.html

Hosoda, M., Stone-Romero, E. F., & Coats, G. (2003). The effects of physical attractiveness on job-related outcomes: A meta-analysis of experimental studies. *Personnel Psychology*, *52*, 431–463.

Hosoda, M., Stone-Romero, E. F., & Stone, D. L. (2003). The effects of co-worker race and task demand on task-related outcomes as mediated by evoked affect. *Journal of Applied Social Psychology*, *33*, 145–178.

Informador.mx. (2016, July 4). Chile aplica la ley 'más exigente del mundo' contra la obesidad. Informador.Mx: Guadalajara, Jalisco. Retrieved from http://www.informador.com.mx/internacional/2016/670233/6/chile-aplica-la-ley-mas-exigente-del-mundo-contra-la-obesidad.htm

Jackson, L. A. (1992). *Physical appearance and gender: Sociological and sociocultural perspectives.* Albany, NY: State University of New York Press.

Johnson, S. K., Podratz, K. E., Dipboye, R. L., & Gibbons, E. (2010). Physical attractiveness biases in ratings of employment suitability: Tracking down the "beauty is beastly" effect. *Journal of Social Psychology, 150,* 301–318.

Judge, T. A., & Cable, D. M. (2004). The effect of physical height on workplace success and income: A preliminary test of a theoretical model. *Journal of Applied Psychology, 89,* 428–441.

Langlois, J. H., Kalakanis, L., Rubenstein, A. J., Larson, A., Hallam, M., & Smoot, M. (2000). Maxims or myths of beauty? A meta-analytic and theoretical review. *Psychological Bulletin, 126,* 390–423.

Langlois, J. H., Roggman, L. A., Casey, R. J., Ritter, J. M., Rieser-Danner, L. A., & Jenkins, V. Y. (1987). Infant preferences for attractive faces: Rudiments of a stereotype? *Developmental Psychology, 23,* 363–369.

Langlois, J. H., & Stephan, C. W. (1981). Beauty and the beast: The role of physical attractiveness in the development of peer relations and social behavior. In S. S. Brehm, S. M. Kassin, & F. X. Gibbons (Eds.), *Developmental social psychology: Theory and Research,* (pp. 152–168). New York: Oxford University Press.

Lewin, T. (1993, November 24). Workplace bias tied to obesity is ruled illegal. *New York Times.* Retrieved from http://www.nytimes.com/1993/11/24/us/workplace-bias-tied-to-obesity-is-ruled-illegal.html

Maccarone, D. (2003). Affirmative action for the attractive? *Psychology Today, 36,* 18.

Nagele-Piazza, L. (2016, July 15). EEOC issues model notice for employer wellness programs. Society for Human Resource Management. Retrieved from https://www.shrm.org/resourcesandtools/legal-and-compliance/employment-law/pages/eeoc-wellness-notice.aspx

National Institutes of Health. (2016a). Calculate your body mass index. Retrieved from http://www.nhlbi.nih.gov/health/educational/lose_wt/BMI/bmi-m.htm

National Institutes of Health. (2016b). Overweight and obesity statistics. Retrieved from http://www.niddk.nih.gov/health-information/health-statistics/Pages/overweight-obesity-statistics.aspx

Orloff, A. (1996). Gender and the welfare state. *Annual Review of Sociology, 22,* 51–78.

Pagán, J. A., & Dávila, A. (1997). Obesity, occupational attainment, and earnings. *Social Science Quarterly, 78,* 756–770.

Perez-Lanzac, C. (2016a, January). Demasiado tarde para ser madre. El retraso de la maternidad aboca a los interesados a tratamientos de fertilidad; un 10% no lo logra. *El País.* Retrieved from http://politica.elpais.com/politica/2016/01/27/actualidad/1453904610_786378.html

Perez-Lanzac, C. (2016b, June). Una de cada cuatro mujeres nacidas en 1975 no tendrá hijos. *El País.* Retrieved from http://politica.elpais.com/politica/2016/02/10/actualidad/1455120637_611269.html

Pingitore, R., Dugoni, B. L., Tindale, R. S., & Spring, B. (1994). Bias against overweight job applicants in a simulated employment interview. *Journal of Applied Psychology, 79,* 949–959.

Quinn, D. (2016, May 13). Meghan Trainor reveals why she was so angry about Photoshop scandal: "I don't know why you would shave my waist . . . I'm the 'all about that bass' girl." Retrieved from http://www.people.com/article/meghan-trainor-angry-photoshop-scandal

Ramirez, R., Sternsdorff, N., & Pastor, C. (2016, May). Chile's Law on Food Labelling and Advertising: A Replicable Model for Latin America? Santiago: Llorente &

Cuenca. Retrieved from http://www.desarrollando-ideas.com/wp-content/uploads/sites/5/2016/05/160504_DI_report_food_chile_ENG.pdf

Roehling, M. V. (1999). Weight-based discrimination in employment: Psychological and legal aspects. *Personnel Psychology, 52*, 969–1016.

Roehling, M. V., Posthuma, R. A., & Dulebohn, J. (2007). Obesity-related "perceived disability" claims: Legal standards and human resource implications. *Employee Relations Law Journal, 32*, 30–51.

Roehling, M. V., Roehling, P. V., & Odland, L. M. (2008). Investigating the validity of stereotypes about overweight employees: The investigation of body weight and normal personality traits. *Group & Organization Management, 33*, 392–424.

Roszell, P., Kennedy, D., & Grabb, E. (1989). Physical attractiveness and attainment among Canadians. *Journal of Psychology, 123*, 547–559.

Scott, A. M. (2007). Family responsibility discrimination—regulatory update. *Employee Benefit Plan Review*, 35–37. Retrieved from http://www.klgates.com/files/tempFiles/b84b6bee-b677-439c-91ae-faecdb7d2b3c/Article_Scott_Responsibility_Discrimination.pdf

Sherman, M. (2014, November 29). Ex-UPS driver's pregnancy bias claim at high court. *Yahoo News*. Retrieved from https://www.yahoo.com/news/ex-ups-drivers-pregnancy-bias-claim-high-court-130759759-finance.html?ref=gs

Still, M. (2006). Litigating the maternal wall: U.S. lawsuits charging discrimination against workers with family responsibilities. Center for WorkLife Law. Retrieved from http://www.law.yale.edu/documents/pdf/FRD_report_FINAL1.pdf

Stone, E. F., Stone, D. L., & Dipboye, R. L. (1992). Stigmas in organizations: Race, handicaps, and physical attractiveness. In K. Kelley (Ed.), *Issues, theory, and research in industrial/organizational psychology* (pp. 385–457). Amsterdam, Netherlands: Elsevier.

Thompson, C. A., Beauvais, L. L., & Lyness, K. S. (1999). When work-family benefits are not enough: The influence of work-family culture on benefit utilization, organizational attachment, and work-family conflict. *Journal of Vocational Behavior, 54*, 392–415.

Umberson, D., & Hughes, M. (1987). The impact of physical attractiveness on achievement and psychological well-being. *Social Psychology Quarterly, 50*, 227–236.

Uniform guidelines on employee selection procedures—Part 1607. (1979, March 2). *Federal Register, 44*, 11996–12009.

Veganzones, C. (2016, June). La conciliación laboral, entre los criterios más importantes para escoger un trabajo. *ABC Sociedad*. Retrieved from http://www.abc.es/sociedad/abci-conciliacion-laboral-entre-criterios-mas-importantes-para-escoger-trabajo-201605271103_noticia.html

Vergara, E., & Henao, L. (2016, June). Chile seeks to fight obesity with new food labeling law. Associated Press The Big Story. Retrieved from http://bigstory.ap.org/article/f9b43cf296a546a09ef1c11d5e3fec01/chile-seeks-fight-obesity-new-food-labeling-law

Von Bergen, C. W. (2008). "The times they are a-changin": Family responsibilities discrimination and the EEOC. *Employee Responsibilities and Rights Journal, 20*, 177–194.

Williams, J. C., & Bornstein, S. (2008). The evolution of "FReD": Family responsibilities discrimination and developments in the law of stereotyping and implicit bias. *Hastings Law Journal, 59*, 1311–1358.

Youssef, N. (2016, August 17). Egypt suspends 8 female TV anchors, saying they are overweight. *New York Times*. Retrieved from https://www.google.com/amp/mobile.nytimes.com/2016/08/18/world/middleeast/egypt-suspends-8-female-tv-anchors-saying-they-are-overweight.amp.html?client=safari

Zillman, C. (2015, March 25). UPS loses Supreme Court pregnancy discrimination case. *Fortune*. Retrieved from http://fortune.com/2015/03/25/ups-pregnancy-discrimination/

twelve
Intersectionality

Opening Case
President Barack Obama

President Obama is a good example of someone who has many different identity intersections in his life. He was born to a White mother from the United States and an African father from Kenya. Therefore, he identifies as a son and as both White and African. He is married to Michelle Obama and thus also identifies with being a husband. They have two daughters, which means he also identifies with being a father. He spent part of his childhood with his maternal grandparents in Hawaii. Therefore, he identifies as being a grandson and someone who has lived on the U.S. mainland as well as in Hawaii. Professionally, President Obama is an Ivy League–educated lawyer from Chicago, Illinois, who served in the U.S. Senate and then joined the small group of people who have had the experience of being President of the United States. He is also a person of the Christian faith. This is one example of the complexity of identity which illustrates how numerous one person's different sources of identity can be.

Discussion Questions:

1.   Like President Obama, we all have many different characteristics with which we identify. What are some characteristics you identify with?

2. Are the characteristics that you identify with always in agreement? What are some identities that fit together harmoniously? Do you have other identities that are in direct conflict with one another?

Learning Objectives

After reading this chapter, you should be able to:

- Define intersectionality
- Be familiar with research findings on intersectionality including gendered race, intersectional invisibility, and double jeopardy
- Understand the historic origins of intersectionality with respect to Black women
- Know the difference between intersectionality and faultlines
- Be aware of different characteristics that can intersect, including social class, religion, and sexual orientation, among others
- Name a few things companies can do to be inclusive toward employees who experience intersections of various dimensions, especially those that can be stigmatizing

The purpose of this chapter is to examine the topic of intersectionality, or experiencing the intersection of multiple identity characteristics at once. There is relatively little research on intersectionality within the diversity literature; nevertheless, this is an area that is gaining more attention. While studying individual characteristics is important, the reasoning behind intersectionality attempts to acknowledge that it is also important to study some characteristics together rather than in isolation.

If it is important to study multiple characteristics together, you may wonder why this research isn't more common. From my own experience as a researcher, it is sometimes difficult to cleanly present research papers with multiple characteristics being examined. In order to make a theoretical contribution, one must have a good reason for analyzing the variables within the study design. If too many variables are included, the theory of the paper may be unclear and the contribution diminished. There is also a limitation as to how many characteristics can be measured, analyzed, and presented for certain types of statistical analyses. Further, if one picks a few characteristics to examine in a research project, that means that some characteristics have been included while others have been excluded. This can give the impression that the study is incomplete and that the authors place less value on the characteristics which were excluded from the study. In one instance, my research team was encouraged by journal reviewers to drop a second form of diversity from a paper and present only one type of diversity for simplicity. Therefore, sometimes it is more practical and conceptually simpler to publish research with only one form of demographic characteristic, which also limits work on intersectionality.

In this chapter, intersectionality is defined and a summary of the limited research we have in this area is presented. Much of the research that has been conducted on this topic is at the intersection of race and sex, the two most commonly studied characteristics in the field of diversity and discrimination.

What Is Intersectionality?

Intersectionality refers to an approach that simultaneously takes multiple categories of identity into account such as gender, race, social class, and sexual orientation (Cole, 2009; Hyde, 2014). This indicates that the effect of one identity category should not be examined in isolation but instead should be understood in the context of other social identities.

What Do We Know About the Outcomes of Intersectionality for People in Organizations?

The intersection of race and gender has received the most attention in intersectionality research, probably because more research has been conducted about race and gender than any other characteristics. One stream of research is on **gendered race**, or the notion that some racial groups tend to be associated with masculine or feminine traits (Galinsky, Hall, & Cuddy, 2013). Freeman and Ambady (2011) propose and test that stereotypes of men and women are aligned with Blacks and Asians respectively, indicating that people associate Blacks with masculinity and Asians with femininity. In the investigation conducted by Galinsky et al. (2013), they conducted six studies, and their findings were as follows. In the first two studies, they found that compared to the White stereotype, the Black stereotype was associated with more masculinity and the Asian stereotype was associated with more femininity. In their third study, they found that heterosexual White males had a preference for Asian females over Black females and that these effects were driven by preferences for femininity versus masculinity. In the fourth study, they analyzed U.S. Census data from the year 2000 and found that the majority of interracial marriages followed the pattern found in the third study. The fifth study found that gendered race stereotypes had some effect on personnel decisions such that Blacks are preferred over Asians (but still preferred less than Whites) for a masculine leadership position, and thus Asians were disadvantaged the most. The sixth study analyzed college sports data and found that Blacks were more likely to be associated with masculine sports relative to Asians (Galinsky et al., 2013). Overall, these authors conclude that race tends to be associated with masculinity/femininity and that this has consequences in life.

Another result of the race and gender intersection that adversely affects people in organizations is **intersectional invisibility** (Purdie-Vaughns & Eibach, 2008). Intersectional invisibility refers to individuals with multiple lower status identities being neglected because they are not prototypical of any of their identity groups.

According to a theory paper published by Purdie-Vaughns and Eibach (2008), because people with multiple minority group identities (e.g., ethnic minority women) do not fully fit the prototype of their identity groups, they will experience intersectional invisibility. Thus, Black women (or any other minority women) are more likely to be unnoticed and unheard, and their opinions in group discussions are more likely to be misattributed to other Black women, implying that people perceive them to be relatively more interchangeable (Sesko & Biernat, 2010).

A different type of intersectionality that has consequences for people in organizations is that of biracial individuals. In one study, biracial people (Black/White in one study and Asian/White in another study) were perceived to be colder and sometimes less competent than both Whites and minorities of the corresponding racial group, indicating that biracial people are vulnerable to racial biases and discrimination (Sanchez & Bonam, 2009). Further, those who are biracial people (White and minority) are less likely to be viewed as minorities and are considered to be less appropriate beneficiaries of minority resources or programs such as affirmative action, compared to biracial people from two minority groups or monoracial minorities (Good, Sanchez, & Chavez, 2013).

Double Jeopardy

Double jeopardy represents the intersection of race and sex and the disadvantages that women of color can face because of their sex and racial/ethnic group membership. Because women and racial minorities are both lower status groups in society (Glick & Fiske, 1996; Goldman et al., 2006; McKay et al., 2007; Sidanius & Pratto, 1999), there is a potential for women from racial/ethnic minority groups to face bias on the basis of both sex and race. The double jeopardy hypothesis predicts that minority women could be at a double disadvantage on account of both their sex and their race (Barnum, Liden, & Ditomaso, 1995; Beale, 1970; Berdahl & Moore, 2006; Bond & Perry, 1970; Chow, 1987; Epstein, 1973; Garcia, 1989; Jackson, 1973; King, 1975; Lorber, 1998; Reid, 1984). For example, while a White woman in the United States might experience discrimination on the basis of her sex, she would still enjoy the privileges of being in the dominant racial group. On the other hand, an African-American woman in the United States has higher chances of experiencing discrimination on the basis of her sex, her race, or both forms of minority status.

Origins of Double Jeopardy in the United States

The book *Black Feminist Thought* by Patricia Hill Collins describes what double jeopardy is with extensive and clear examples. The author sheds light on the injustice that Black women have historically faced because they are at the intersection of race, sex, and sometimes also social class. The history of injustice against Black women in the United States begins with slavery. Collins (2000) describes how Black women's bodies were used during slavery as a means of production to benefit White slaveholders via slave labor, reproduction, and labor as wet nurses.

According to Collins, Black women have been treated as "mules" and assigned hard physical labor (Collins, 2000, p. 11). Sojourner Truth, a woman who experienced slavery, described this harsh reality very eloquently in her 1851 speech at a women's rights convention in Ohio when she described that, "Nobody ever helps me into carriages, or over mud puddles . . . I have plowed, and planted. I could work as much and eat as much as any man . . . and bear the lash as well . . ." (Truth, 1851). During slavery, Black women's bodies were exploited as units of production because they gave birth to children, which then increased the slave owners' property and labor force (Collins, 2000). Sojourner Truth attested to this when she said, "I have born 13 children, and seen them most all sold off to slavery . . ." (Truth, 1851).

Patricia Hill Collins successfully portrays the dilemmas that Black women face because they are at the intersection of race and sex. On one hand, Black women want equality for all Black people. On the other hand, sometimes this means that Black women experience pressure (either internal or external) to not discuss their problems openly (Cole & Guy-Sheftall, 2003), including when they experience poor treatment from Black men. According to these authors, Black women may prefer not to speak about the struggles for equality within their community and their relationships for fear that somehow their words might result in a negative portrayal of Black people which would, in turn, be counterproductive for their equal rights (Collins, 2000). It is also possible that Black women may remain silent about poor treatment from Black men in order to protect them, given the stereotypes about Black men, the high incarceration rates of Black men, and the police violence that has resulted in the deaths of Black men both historically and in recent years as a result of police use of deadly force in the United States.

There are several examples showing how the discrimination faced by Black women can come from within the Black community as well as the outside community. When Black women expressed an interest in serving as leaders during civil rights movements, they were sometimes not taken seriously by Black men. For example, a Black female activist, Septima Clark, tried to influence the male-dominated Southern Christian Leadership Conference during the civil rights movement. She "sent a letter to Dr. King asking him not to lead all the marches himself, but instead to develop leaders who could lead their own marches. Dr. King read that letter before the staff. It just tickled them; they just laughed" (Collins, 2000, p. 218). According to Cole and Guy-Sheftall (2003, p. 87), who also wrote extensively about the struggles of Black women for equality, "the women pleaded to be included" and allowed to speak at the March on Washington, but they were largely relegated to "sitting off to the side, invisible to the public." After the March on Washington, a Black feminist, Pauli Murray, wrote an essay about Black male oppression of Black women: "It was bitterly humiliating for Negro women on August 28 to see themselves accorded little more than token recognition in the historic March on Washington. Not a single woman was invited to make one of the major speeches or to be part of the delegation of leaders who went to the White House. This omission was deliberate" (Cole & Guy-Sheftall, 2003, p. 89).

Women faced similar kinds of sexism even in the more radical Black organizations. The Black Panther party found it difficult to accept women as leaders (Collins, 2000). Elaine Brown, speaking about what she witnessed and experienced as a Black Panther, said that some Panther men called assertive women, including herself, who defied male control "smart bitches" who "needed to be silenced" (Cole & Guy-Sheftall, 2003, p. 92). In a different example, Maulana Ron Karenga, a prominent civil rights leader and the founder of Kwanzaa (a cultural holiday), simultaneously advocated for Black civil rights but endorsed unequal roles for Black men and women in the 1960s (Story, 2008) by stating, "What makes a woman appealing is femininity, and she can't be feminine without being submissive . . . The role of women is to inspire men, educate their children, and participate in social development . . . We say male supremacy is based on three things: tradition, acceptance, and reason. Equality is false; it's the Devil's concept" (Halisi & Mtume, 1967). Cole and Guy-Sheftall (2003) conclude: "We will fare much better when we commit ourselves to dealing openly and honestly with what harms us—whether it is racism in the majority culture or sexism in our own backyards" (Cole & Guy-Sheftall, 2003, p. 101). While double jeopardy research originates with Black women, the same types of issues can be experienced by women of all other racial/ethnic minority groups because sexism exists across racial/ethnic groups.

What Do We Know About Double Jeopardy in Organizations?

The double jeopardy hypothesis maintains that women of color are likely to be at a greater disadvantage compared to White women or men of color, having minority identities on both gender and race (Beale, 1970). Several empirical studies support this hypothesis on various work-related outcomes. Studies show that Hispanic and Black women earn the lowest wages, have the least workplace authority (Browne, 2000; Browne, Hewitt, Tigges, & Green, 2001; Maume, 1999), and are the most highly segregated into undesirable positions (Aldridge, 1999; Spalter-Roth & Deitch, 1999). Regarding pay, Latina and Black females earn the least (Browne, 2000), and people who identify with multiple stigmatized identities suffer from greater pay penalty than those who identify with just one (Woodhams, Lupton, & Cowling, 2015). Barnum et al. (1995) did not find evidence of double jeopardy on the basis of sex and race in their study when investigating pay as their dependent variable. Berdahl and Moore (2006) did find evidence that women experienced more sexual harassment than men and that racial minorities experienced more racial harassment than Whites. Further, minority women experienced higher levels of harassment (i.e., sexual and ethnic harassment combined) overall than majority men, majority women, and minority men (Berdahl & Moore, 2006).

Moreover, sexual and racial harassment jointly predict employee satisfaction with a supervisor and perceived organizational tolerance of harassment for minority women (Buchanan & Fitzgerald, 2008). Providing a nuanced perspective on double jeopardy with respect to harassment, Raver and Nishii (2010) proposed and found an inurement effect of multiple types of harassment on work-related outcomes. Specifically, different types of harassment did not have additive or multiplicative effects on organizational commitment and turnover intentions. This inurement effect suggests that once individuals experience one form of harassment, other forms may not add much negative impact because they become accustomed to the environment of discrimination and stigmatization.

In personnel selection, support for the double jeopardy hypothesis may depend on other contextual factors. For instance, Derous, Ryan, and Nguyen (2012) found that in résumé screening for high status jobs, Arab women were evaluated as less suitable than Arab men, Dutch women, and Dutch men, but that was not the case for low status jobs. Occupational stereotypes also play a role such that Arab women were more positively evaluated than Arab men when job requirements were stereotypically feminine (Derous, Ryan, & Serlie, 2015).

Global View: Pakistan

The modern world sometimes clashes with culture and tradition, and in some instances women have been killed as a result. According to the Human Rights Commission of Pakistan, they have confirmed 1,276 incidents of honor killings between February 2014 and February 2016. These numbers may be underestimated, because most instances go unreported due to cultural acceptance of these acts or an unwillingness of police or the judicial system to investigate (Inayat, 2016). In these honor crimes, the law is often ignored and women are put to death if they are perceived to have dishonored the family. In May 2014, a young pregnant woman by the name of Farzana Parveen was stoned to death by her family members because she married a man she was in love with instead of the man the family had selected for her (Hakim, 2014). In November 2014, following a worldwide outcry, Farzana Parveen's father, brother, cousin, and former fiancé were found guilty of murder and sentenced to death, while another one of her brothers was sentenced to 10 years in jail. "But more often than not, those who commit these brutal acts against women are never charged, protected by tribal laws" (Hakim, 2014). According to Hakim (2014), "Some hard-line religious scholars believe that only through the killing of an offending family member— usually a woman—can honour be restored to the rest of the family and tribe."

After several high-profile killings of young women fueled international outrage, Pakistan passed a law requiring killers to serve 12.5 years in prison if convicted of an honor killing. In the past, killers would go free if they were forgiven by relatives (Inayat, 2016).

Is it multiple identities that enable a father to stone his daughter to death because she has dishonored the family by marrying the man she loved instead of the one chosen for her? Is it multiple identities that allow the victim's brothers to participate in the killing? There is a lot to be said here about the power and turmoil at the intersection of family, tradition, and culture.

What Do We Know About Some of the Less Studied Aspects of Diversity (Including Social Class and Religion) as They Intersect With Other Forms of Identity?

Among the less studied aspects of diversity, a few studies have examined sexual orientation, social class, and religion. Sexual orientation, as it intersects with gendered race, affects people's perceptions. According to a study by Johnson and Ghavami (2011), when individuals are asked to judge the sexual orientation of certain people, they are more likely to be correct if the people are aligned in terms of race and gender such as an Asian female (stereotypically feminine for being both Asian and female) or a Black male (stereotypically masculine for being both Black and male). They are also more likely to perceive people whose race and gender have misaligned stereotypes (e.g., Black females and Asian males) as being lesbian or gay. In this study, both gay and heterosexual participants in the United States were more likely to judge people as being gay when their race was associated with characteristics that were contrary to their gender (e.g., Asian males). Perceivers made the most accurate judgments when judging the sexual orientation of the groups with the strongest gender stereotypes (e.g., Black men and Asian women), and they made the most mistakes when judging the sexual orientation of counter-stereotypical groups (e.g., Black women and Asian men). In a different study, findings show that for African-American gays, lesbians, and bisexuals, racism and anti-gay discrimination have an additive influence on depression (Thoma & Huebner, 2013).

Social class, or socioeconomic status (SES), also intersects with race and gender, yielding unique consequences. For instance, for Blacks and Latino/as, although they experience racism regardless of their SES, those of lower SES report greater lifetime exposure to discrimination and more recent discrimination experiences while those of higher SES report greater workplace discrimination (Brondolo et al., 2009). Especially in organizations, scholars argue that gender and social class hierarchies are reproduced, reinforcing inequality between males and females, and among different levels of social class (Acker, 2006). In line with this argument, Wasserman and Frenkel (2015) show that organizational spaces, both physical and psychological, and expectations for ideal workers are masculine. However, while women of higher social class feel relatively more comfortable and understand how to fit in with such masculinity, women from lower social classes perceive the masculine spaces as more marginalizing and have difficulty adapting.

Pertaining to the intersection of religion and gender, religion presents both challenges and benefits for women. Muslim women, for instance, are expected to behave according to the guidelines of Shariah law and to be modest. A study conducted by Essers and Benschop (2009) examined how Muslim businesswomen respond to those rules. They generally showed compromise, albeit in varying levels and ways. Some women kept a symbolic boundary between male clients and themselves, some disregarded rules they perceived as overly dogmatic, and some focused on specific parts of the Qur'an emphasizing work morals and female role models. Chong (2011) also showed that religion reinforces patriarchal norms. However, other studies demonstrated that women found support from niche aspects of male-oriented religion to cope with social problems (Avishai, Jafar, & Rinaldo, 2015). Similarly, for Jewish women in Israel, religion was a way to show and feel agency (Avishai, 2008).

Global View: Gay Asian Men Forced to Marry Women to Please Their Families

In England and other places around the world, gay Asians are marrying other gay Asians of the opposite sex to keep up the appearance of being heterosexual for the sake of their families. For example, Amara (2014) describes a situation where a gay man is married to a lesbian woman and they live in different places. "All around his home are all the signs of a happy marriage, despite his wife living a few miles away. It's a deception she willingly goes along with, however. She is a lesbian, he is gay, and neither can bear to tell their families—opting instead for the pretence of life as a straight couple through a marriage of convenience" (Amara, 2014). The husband admits it is a farce but adds that this may prevent his wife's parents from killing her (Amara, 2014).

According to Asif Quraishi, an openly gay Asian man who lives in England, "There isn't actually a word for gay or lesbian in our mother languages. The only words that there are, are totally derogatory." A different man who is also openly gay said that when he explained to his family that he was homosexual, his brother took him to a strip club to try and cure him of the situation.

He said that if his family knew he was at a gay nightclub, they would kill him for "honour" (Razzall, 2014).

One woman who was interviewed anonymously said that she was forced to marry her cousin at the age of 19. On their wedding night, he told her that he was gay. "When we were left alone and it was time to go to bed, he said 'Is it alright if I sleep next door because I'm not into women?'" According to this woman, her family told her she should have tried harder to salvage the marriage. Her mother said that if she "had done everything right, he wouldn't have been gay" (Razzall, 2014).

In sum, these are several examples of people facing challenges because they are at the intersection of multiple (sometimes conflicting) identities including sexual orientation, family, and culture which require them to be something they are not with respect to one identity in order to feel acceptance with respect to another identity.

The Difference Between Intersectionality and Team Faultlines

In the beginning of this chapter, we examined some challenges of conducting research at the intersection of multiple characteristics both theoretically and statistically. One area of study within the diversity literature which has attempted, and succeeded, in measuring multiple characteristics of a team at the same time is the study of faultlines.

Faultlines are defined as hypothetical lines that divide a team into subgroups based on different demographic attributes such as gender and race (Lau & Murnighan, 1998, 2005), and they are often characterized by their strength or how homogeneous these subgroups are. For instance, let us assume we have two teams with six people each. Team 1 has three Asian men and three White women. Team 2 has two Asian men, one White man, two White women, and one Asian woman. Although the level of dispersion is equal across the two teams (i.e., three men, three women, three Asians, three Whites), Team 1 has a stronger faultline because the subgroups are more homogeneous with both race and gender aligned.

Faultlines, therefore, are similar to intersectionality in that they both consider multiple attributes on which people could be distinguished at the same time. In the current example, both race and gender are taken into account. However, faultlines are different from intersectionality in that the former is a team-level construct while the latter is an individual-level construct. That is, faultlines reflect how similar or different team members are on various dimensions whereas intersectionality is concerned with the focal individual having multiple identities and how these identities jointly affect the person.

What Combinations of Characteristics, or Intersections, May Best Explain Human Interactions in Organizations?

As mentioned in the opening remarks of this chapter, the research on intersectionality is somewhat limited. Based on the argument that organizations reproduce and reinforce the social hierarchy (Acker, 2006), some salient forms of identity associated with hierarchy, such as gender, race, and social class, would be highly relevant for organizational behavior. While other characteristics such as sexual orientation can be kept private, gender and race, in particular, are easily observable, and because of this, they automatically elicit stereotypes, positive or negative, that are heavily ingrained in society.

Acker (2006) argues that work in organizations has developed around the role of prototypical White men. Although it is changing, typical job requirements such as fixed work hours from 9 a.m. to 5 p.m. may not fit with the general expectations women must fulfill. High-level jobs may allow more flexibility, but men, racial majority members, and those with high socioeconomic status are usually the ones occupying such positions (Acker, 2006). As demonstrated by studies on gendered race (Galinsky et al., 2013), intersectional invisibility (Purdie-Vaughns & Eibach, 2008), and double jeopardy (Beale, 1970), race and gender are closely intertwined, affecting individuals with multiple lower status identities in unique ways. This shows that race and gender together may explain various dynamics of not only formal organizational structures but also informal interactions among employees.

Race and Sex: Which Characteristic Tends to Be a Stronger Predictor of Discrimination?

Only a few research papers have measured sex and race at the same time, thereby allowing us to glean information about intersectionality with respect to discrimination. The findings of a few of those studies are as follows.

In a study conducted by Wicher (2008) the researcher instructed participants to evaluate the performance of a manager who was either a Black man, a Black woman, or a White woman and measured participants' negative stereotypes of both Black and women managers. Sexist attitudes were negatively and significantly associated with evaluations of White women's performance ratings but not Black women's performance ratings. However, racist attitudes were negatively and significantly associated with performance evaluations of both Black men and Black women managers. Therefore, in this study, racism seemed to be a more direct predictor of discrimination against Black women managers than sexism.

A theoretical paper published by Kulik, Roberson, and Perry (2007) proposed that research does not tend to support the double jeopardy hypothesis predicting that discrimination has an additive or multiplicative effect for people who belong to multiple minority groups. Instead, they propose that group membership in one category will likely dominate impressions others form about the person in question while the other categories will likely be ignored. Kulik et al. (2007) proposed that the category salience (i.e., the most visible group membership) and the characteristics of the perceiver (i.e., their attitudes about race, sex, ability, etc.) will drive the way the perceiver judges the person being observed and which characteristic dominates his or her judgments. This is more evidence to support the majority of research that has been conducted in the area of diversity and discrimination, which typically considers one characteristic at a time and statistically controls for other characteristics rather than studying an intersection of several characteristics as the main focus of the study.

Global View: Intersection of Gay Rights, Family, and the Legal System in Chile

An icon of the fight for sexual orientation diversity, Chilean judge Karen Atala experienced firsthand what it is like to be lesbian in a country where divorce became legal in 2004. In May of 2004, the Chilean Supreme Court found Atala unfit to care for her children because she was lesbian and lived with her partner. The girls, who were three, four, and eight years of age at the time, were to be raised by their father, the plaintiff of the case. In 2011, Atala brought a successful suit against the State of Chile in the Inter-American Court of Human Rights, where she spoke of the "dolor que no se puede explicar," the unspeakable pain, of being deprived of raising your children (Montes, 2016). In 2012, the Inter-American Court of Human Rights condemned the State of Chile for Atala's case and ordered that the State provide restitution to Atala and her daughters (Montes, 2016).

Suggestions for Organizations

As we have seen through the research on intersectionality, all employees in organizations identify with multiple groups and have multiple identities. There is also potential for people to be discriminated against on the basis of multiple identities, as we see in the double jeopardy situation. Employers should be aware of this possibility and should be sensitive to the needs of people who could be in these double minority situations because they may need more support than other employees if they could face bias from multiple sources. Maintaining zero-tolerance policies for all forms of discrimination and providing mentoring programs, especially for women, minorities, and those who fall into both demographics, could be especially important to retain talent.

It is also essential for organizations to be supportive of those who might be struggling with multiple identities, especially conflicting identities. Particularly with identities which could be stigmatizing, some employees may be in a position of actively "passing," or concealing those identities. Organizations should strive to create an inclusive environment where employees do not have to worry about hiding their identity. Modeling inclusion from leadership to the lower levels of the organization will be helpful in this regard. It would also be beneficial for organizations to sponsor affinity groups for people with various minority identities so that they find a source of emotional and moral support within the organization. Sponsoring such groups of social support can help employees feel valued and able to bring their whole selves to work, which ultimately should increase morale and productivity.

Closing Case

Art as an Expression of Multiple Identities and Minority Status

Anida Yoeu Ali is a performing artist who believes art can help people understand religion, identity, and minority status. Ali is a Muslim Khmer woman who was born in Cambodia but raised in Chicago (Studio Revolt, 2011). Her family was part of Cambodia's minority Cham community, which faced persecution from the Khmer Rouge during the 1970s (Nghiem, 2014).

Ali describes in an interview that her family was able to flee Cambodia and move to the United States, where her grandfather lived. He sponsored the family to move to the United States, and because of this, Ali was able to avoid being recruited by the Khmer Rouge as a child soldier because she was too young to be enlisted. She has many identities including Malaysian, Cham, and Thai in her family background. Growing up, she says she identified with being Muslim more so than being Cambodian. "For me issues of identity have always been something I've been struggling with," says Ali (Nghiem, 2014). Her performances are aimed at including humor and science fiction in order to depict the challenge of multiple identities and what it feels like to be the one who is different (Nghiem, 2014).

Discussion Questions:

1.   There is a saying that a picture is worth 1,000 words. Do you believe that art could be a good way to communicate complicated diversity issues such as intersectionality?

2. Think of one or two examples you have seen in the past of some form of art (whether it was a painting, a play, a movie, music, photography, or some other example) which conveyed a complex meaning in a clear and distinct way. What are these examples?
3. In what ways do organizations currently use art to convey meaning with respect to diversity?
4. In what ways can organizations expand their use of art to improve diversity management?

References

Acker, J. (2006). Inequality regimes gender, class, and race in organizations. *Gender & Society, 20*(4), 441–464.

Aldridge, D. (1999). Black women and the new world order: Toward a fit in the economic marketplace. In I. Browne (Ed.), *Latinas and African American women at work: Race, gender and economic inequality* (pp. 357–379). New York: Russell Sage Foundation.

Amara, P. (2014, September 22). The sham marriages of convenience protecting gay Asians. *Independent*. Retrieved from http://www.independent.co.uk/news/uk/home-news/the-sham-marriages-of-convenience-protecting-gay-asians-9749338.html

Avishai, O. (2008). Halakhic Niddah consultants and the orthodox women's movement in Israel: Evaluating the story of enlightened progress. *Journal of Modern Jewish Studies, 7*(2), 195–216.

Avishai, O., Jafar, A., & Rinaldo, R. (2015). A gender lens on religion. *Gender & Society, 29*(1), 5–25.

Barnum, P., Liden, R. C., & Ditomaso, N. (1995). Double jeopardy for women and minorities: Pay differences with age. *Academy of Management Journal, 38*, 863–880.

Beale, F. (1970). Double jeopardy: To be black and female. In T. Cade (Ed.), *The Black woman: An anthology* (pp. 90–110). New York: Signet.

Berdahl, J. L., & Moore, C. (2006). Workplace harassment: Double jeopardy for minority women. *Journal of Applied Psychology, 91*, 426–436.

Bond, J. C., & Perry, P. (1970). Is the Black male castrated? In T. Cade (Ed.), *The Black woman* (pp. 113–118). New York: New American Library.

Brondolo, E., Beatty, D. L., Cubbin, C., Pencille, M., Saegert, S., Wellington, R., Tobin, J., Cassells, A., & Schwartz, J. (2009). Sociodemographic variations in self-reported racism in a community sample of Blacks and Latino (a) s. *Journal of Applied Social Psychology, 39*(2), 407–429.

Browne, I. (Ed.). (2000). *Latinas and African American women at work: Race, gender, and economic inequality: Race, gender, and economic inequality.* New York: Russell Sage Foundation.

Browne, I., Hewitt, C., Tigges, L., & Green, G. (2001). Why does job segregation lead to wage inequality among African Americans? Person, place, sector, or skills? *Social Science Research, 30*(3), 473–495.

Buchanan, N. T., & Fitzgerald, L. F. (2008). Effects of racial and sexual harassment on work and the psychological well-being of African American women. *Journal of Occupational Health Psychology, 13*(2), 137.

Chong, K. H. (2011). *Deliverance and submission: Evangelical women and the negotiation of patriarchy in South Korea.* Harvard East Asian Monographs. Cambridge, MA: Harvard University Press.

Chow, E. N. (1987). The development of feminist consciousness among Asian American women. *Gender and Society, 3*, 284–299.

Cole, E. R. (2009). Intersectionality and research in psychology. *American Psychologist, 64*(3), 170.

Cole, J. B., & Guy-Sheftall, B. (2003). *Gender talk: The struggle for women's equality in African American communities.* New York: Random House.

Collins, P. H. (2000). *Black feminist thought* (2nd ed.). New York: Routledge.

Derous, E., Ryan, A. M., & Nguyen, H. H. D. (2012). Multiple categorization in resume screening: Examining effects on hiring discrimination against Arab applicants in field and lab settings. *Journal of Organizational Behavior, 33*(4), 544–570.

Derous, E., Ryan, A. M., & Serlie, A. W. (2015). Double jeopardy upon resume screening: When Achmed is less employable than Aisha. *Personnel Psychology, 68*, 659–696.

Epstein, C. F. (1973, August). Black and female: The double whammy. *Psychology Today, 3*, 57–61.

Essers, C., & Benschop, Y. (2009). Muslim businesswomen doing boundary work: The negotiation of Islam, gender and ethnicity within entrepreneurial contexts. *Human Relations, 62*(3), 403–423.

Freeman, J. B., & Ambady, N. (2011). A dynamic interactive theory of person construal. *Psychological Review, 118*(2), 247.

Galinsky, A. D., Hall, E. V., & Cuddy, A. J. (2013). Gendered races implications for interracial marriage, leadership selection, and athletic participation. *Psychological Science, 24*, 498–506. doi:10.1177/0956797612457783.

Garcia, A. M. (1989). The development of Chicana feminist discourse, 1970–1980. *Gender and Society, 3*, 217–238.

Gilrane, V. L., Jones, K. P., Speights, S., & King, E. B. (2011, April). Is beautiful good for everyone? Race, gender, and attractiveness bias. Paper presented at the 26th Annual Conference for the Society of Industrial and Organizational Psychology, Chicago, IL.

Glick, P., & Fiske, S. T. (1996). The ambivalent sexism inventory: Differentiating hostile and benevolent sexism. *Journal of Personality and Social Psychology, 40*, 491–512.

Goldman, B. M., Gutek, B., Stein, J. H., & Lewis, K. (2006). Employment discrimination in organizations: Antecedents and consequences. *Journal of Management, 32*, 786–830.

Good, J. J., Sanchez, D. T., & Chavez, G. F. (2013). White ancestry in perceptions of Black/White biracial individuals: Implications for affirmative-action contexts. *Journal of Applied Social Psychology, 43*(S2), E276–E286.

Hakim, Y. (2014, December 12). The Pakistani women punished for love. *BBC News.* Retrieved from http://www.bbc.com/news/world-asia-30400690

Halisi, C., & Mtume, J. (1967). *The quotable Karenga.* Los Angeles: US Organization.

Hyde, J. S. (2014). Gender similarities and differences. *Annual Review of Psychology, 65*, 373–398.

Inayat, N. (2016, October 6). Pakistan law cracks down on 'honor killings'. *USA Today.* Retrieved from http://www.usatoday.com/story/news/world/2016/10/06/pakistani-law-cracks-down-honor-killing/91677520/

Jackson, J. (1973). Black women in a racist society. In C. Willie, B. Kramer, & B. Brown (Eds.), *Racism and mental health* (pp. 185–268). Pittsburgh, PA: University of Pittsburgh Press.

Johnson, K. L., & Ghavami, N. (2011). At the crossroads of conspicuous and concealable: What race categories communicate about sexual orientation. *PLoS One, 6*(3), e18025. doi:10.1371/journal.pone.0018025.

King, M. (1975). Oppression and power: The unique status of the Black woman in the American political system. *Social Science Quarterly, 56*, 123–133.

Kulik, C. T., Roberson, L., & Perry, E. L. (2007). The multiple-category problem: Category activation and inhibition in the hiring process. *Academy of Management Review, 32*(2), 529–548.

Lau, D. C., & Murnighan, J. K. (1998). Demographic diversity and faultlines: The compositional dynamics of organizational groups. *Academy of Management Review, 23*(2), 325–340.

Lau, D. C., & Murnighan, J. K. (2005). Interactions within groups and subgroups: The effects of demographic faultlines. *Academy of Management Journal, 48*(4), 645–659.

Lorber, J. (1998). *Gender inequality: Feminist theories and politics*. Los Angeles, CA: Roxbury.

Maume, D. J., Jr. (1999). Glass ceilings and glass escalators: Occupational segregation and race and sex differences in managerial promotions. *Work and Occupations, 26*, 483–509.

McKay, P. F., Avery, D. R., Tonidandel, S., Morris, M. A., Hernandez, M., & Hebl, M. R. (2007). Racial differences in employee retention: Are diversity climate perceptions the key? *Personnel Psychology, 60*, 35–62.

Montes, R. (2016, February 15). Chile debe ahora aprobar el matrimonio y adopción igualitatios. *El País*. Retrieved from http://internacional.elpais.com

Nghiem, A. (2014, December 17). "Buddhist bug" art explores difference. *BBC News*. Retrieved from http://www.bbc.com/news/world-asia-30521845

Purdie-Vaughns, V., & Eibach, R. P. (2008). Intersectional invisibility: The distinctive advantages and disadvantages of multiple subordinate-group identities. *Sex Roles, 59*(5–6), 377–391.

Raver, J. L., & Nishii, L. H. (2010). Once, twice, or three times as harmful? Ethnic harassment, gender harassment, and generalized workplace harassment. *Journal of Applied Psychology, 95*(2), 236.

Razzall, K. (2014, December 14). The gay Asian men living a lie. *BBC News*. Retrieved from http://www.bbc.com/news/uk-30433831

Reid, P. T. (1984). Feminism versus minority group identity: Not for Black women only. *Sex Roles, 10*, 247–255.

Sabat, I. E., Lindsey, A. P., Ahmad, A. S., Membere, A. A., King, E. B., & Arena, D. (2015, April). Prior knowledge of disclosures and interpersonal discrimination in the workplace. Paper presented at the 30th Annual Conference of the Society for Industrial Organizational Psychology, Philadelphia, PA.

Sanchez, D. T., & Bonam, C. M. (2009). To disclose or not to disclose biracial identity: The effect of biracial disclosure on perceiver evaluations and target responses. *Journal of Social Issues, 65*(1), 129–149.

Sesko, A. K., & Biernat, M. (2010). Prototypes of race and gender: The invisibility of Black women. *Journal of Experimental Social Psychology, 46*(2), 356–360.

Sidanius, J., & Pratto, F. (1999). *Social dominance: An intergroup theory of social hierarchy and oppression*. Cambridge, UK: Cambridge University Press.

Spalter-Roth, R., & Deitch, C. (1999). "I don't feel right sized; I feel out-of-work sized" gender, race, ethnicity, and the unequal costs of displacement. *Work and Occupations, 26*(4), 446–482.

Story, K. A. (2008). There's No Place like "Home": Mining the Theoretical Terrain of Black Women's Studies, Black Queer Studies and Black Studies. *The Journal of Pan African Studies*, 2, 44–57.

Thoma, B. C., & Huebner, D. M. (2013). Health consequences of racist and antigay discrimination for multiple minority adolescents. *Cultural Diversity and Ethnic Minority Psychology, 19*(4), 404–413.

Truth, S. (1851). *Ain't I a Woman? Modern History Sourcebook: Sojourner Truth*. Transcript of a speech Truth delivered at the Women's Convention, Akron, Ohio. Fordham University. Retrieved from https://sourcebooks.fordham.edu/mod/sojtruth-woman.asp

Wasserman, V., & Frenkel, M. (2015). Spatial work in between glass ceilings and glass walls: Gender-class intersectionality and organizational aesthetics. *Organization Studies, 36*(11), 1485–1505.

Wicher, E. W. (2008). *Double jeopardy of race and gender in performance ratings* (Unpublished doctoral dissertation). Wayne State University, Wayne, MI.

Woodhams, C., Lupton, B., & Cowling, M. (2015). The snowballing penalty effect: Multiple disadvantage and pay. *British Journal of Management, 26*(1), 63–77.

thirteen
Team Diversity

Opening Case

Diversity at Twitter: Thoughts on Diversity From an Ex-Employee

In November 2015, Leslie Miley, an African-American engineering manager at Twitter, posted a note about the company's diversity profile prior to his departure from the social media firm. Miley explained that he loved using Twitter and that he still loved the company because the platform had enabled several movements such as #BlackLivesMatter in response to the shootings of African-Americans at the hands of (primarily) White police officers (Dickie, 2015; Miley, 2015).

However, he also described that Twitter, along with many other Silicon Valley high-tech companies, has a diversity problem: namely, a lack of diversity. Miley explained that while Twitter users in 2014 included 27% African-Americans, 25% Hispanic-Americans, and 21% women, the employees inside Twitter's engineering and product group were 3% African-American and Hispanic and less than 15% women. Miley stated: "There were moments that caused me to question how and why a company whose product has been used as an agent of revolutionary social change did not reflect the diversity of thought, conversation, and people in its ranks" (Miley, 2015).

In 2015, a report of the demographic breakdown of major Silicon Valley companies showed that Twitter's demographics included 56% White, 37% Asian, 3% Hispanic, 1% Black, 1% mixed race, and 2% unidentified (Heer,

2015). This is similar to other major technology companies including Apple, Google, and Facebook.

Miley further explained that he had to do a lot of lobbying during the selection process to advocate on behalf of minority candidates. He described that minority candidates were often criticized by hiring committees for not being fast enough to solve problems, not having internships at prestigious companies, or taking too long to complete their college degrees. Only after hours of lobbying his colleagues would the minority candidates be hired, and then, Miley adds, those minority employees went on to perform well on the job (Bates, 2015; Miley, 2015).

During a company meeting, Miley asked what the engineering groups at Twitter were doing to increase the diversity of the organization. The response he received from the senior vice president of engineering was that "diversity is important, but we can't lower the bar" (Dickie, 2015; Mohan, 2015). He realized at that time that he was the only African-American in engineering leadership (Bates, 2015; Miley, 2015).

After several weeks, Miley decided to present a job proposal to the senior vice president of engineering about increasing diversity. While Miley and the senior vice president agreed on the importance of tracking the racial background of candidates in the pipeline to investigate why these minority employees were not reaching the higher leadership levels at Twitter, they disagreed on how to do this. According to Miley, the senior vice president of engineering suggested that they create a computer program to analyze the last names of the applicants and determine the likelihood of them being from a particular racial/ethnic background. Miley was disappointed with this answer, explaining that a computer program could not take into account nuances caused by colonization, slavery, or identity, and he cited how a similar tool failed to recognize the ethnicity of the Jewish and African-American employees within the engineering groups at Twitter (Dickie, 2015; Miley, 2015).

Miley closed his statement as follows: "To quote Mark S. Luckie 'Without a variety of voices contributing ideas, the workplace becomes a homogenized environment where potential brilliance may never be achieved. Diversity should rightly be seen as a benefit to growth, not an obstruction to avoid.' For some at Twitter, diversity is an obstruction to avoid. With my departure, Twitter no longer has any managers, directors, or VP's of color in engineering or product management. From *this* position, Twitter may find it difficult to make the changes to culture and product" (Miley, 2015).

Discussion Questions:

1. How common do you think it is to associate new hires who add to organizational diversity with lowering company standards? Why do you believe people make this association?

2. Do you think the Twitter senior vice president of engineering responded to Miley's questions about diversity in an appropriate manner? Why or why not?

3. What do you think Twitter and other high-tech companies can do to increase their representation of racial minority and women employees in engineering?

Learning Objectives

After reading this chapter, you should be able to:

-   Understand why team diversity presents both opportunities and challenges
-   Describe phenomena that may help explain why team diversity can have either positive or negative effects in teams including information elaboration, diversity beliefs of the team members, and complex situational/contextual factors
-   Know that diversity effects in teams tend to be nuanced and affected by the power of the individual team members as well as the differences between team members
-   Understand that bias in teams may be subconsciously driven
-   Be aware of the effects of team longevity on the performance of demographically diverse teams
-   List a few tips for managing team diversity

Team Diversity

Diversity researchers refer to diversity as the "double-edged sword" because research consistently shows that in some instances diversity helps teams and in other instances it presents challenges. This is intriguing and concerning at the same time, because organizations both in the U.S and in many other countries are increasingly becoming more diverse as global companies operate in multiple countries and people immigrate across country boundaries for educational and professional work opportunities. Diversity is a fact of life and an organizational reality. Therefore, many researchers devote their careers to understanding the intricacies around the relationship between diversity and team outcomes as well as the contextual factors that can influence that relationship to become more positive or more negative.

In this chapter, we will examine research findings on the advantages of diversity as well as the challenges of diversity in teams. The chapter presents the major findings around the relationship between diversity and both team and organizational performance. Finally, the chapter concludes with suggestions for managing diversity in teams based on best-known methods from diversity research.

What Phenomena May Explain the Inconsistent Effects of Diversity on Teams?

Information Elaboration

A number of studies have begun to uncover possible explanations and situations under which diversity is and is not helpful to team performance. One recent theory, the **categorization-elaboration model** (van Dick, van Knippenberg, Hägele, Guillaume, & Brodbeck, 2008; van Knippenberg, De Dreu, & Homan, 2004), proposes that biases stemming from social categorization effects that take place in a diverse team may impede groups in using informational resources. However, that same team diversity may introduce a process of group information elaboration, meaning that there is an information exchange, discussion, and integration of task-relevant information and perspectives which ultimately help the team perform better. Homan, van Knippenberg, Van Kleef, and De Dreu (2007) tested the categorization-elaboration model and found a positive effect between team information diversity and information elaboration, meaning that team members shared more information.

This reasoning is consistent with research on faultlines within teams. Although lack of cohesion and increased conflict are usually considered to have negative effects in teams, faultlines could be leveraged to help team members voice their differences and share information (Lau & Murnighan, 2005; Thatcher, Jehn, & Zanutto, 2003). Research shows that people are more likely to express their perspectives if there are like-minded teammates who can support them (Asch, 1954, 1956; Azzi, 1993; Wittenbaum and Stasser, 1996). In experiments conducted by Asch (1954), the presence of members with similar demographic characteristics in one's subgroup increased the likelihood of the participants expressing their opinions. Research on boards of directors also shows that cliques can form on a board based on relationships among directors; these cliques can influence the board's decisions (Stevenson & Radin, 2009). Recall that faultlines represent subgroups in teams. Informational faultlines include subgroups along task-related attributes such as education, functional area, and tenure. Teams with informational faultlines should produce a broader range of ideas because they have a diverse body of knowledge (Amason & Sapienza, 1997; Milliken & Vollrath, 1991; Schweiger, Sandberg, & Ragan, 1996). In sum, this research suggests that subgroups in teams can increase team members' participation, which then promotes discussion among team members.

Beliefs About Diversity

Studies have also revealed that the diversity beliefs of team members have an important influence on the team diversity–team performance relationship. Van Dick et al. (2008) found that team diversity is not a problem, but problems are more likely to arise in diverse teams when the team members have a low value of diversity. Having team members who value diversity and see it as an opportunity as well as having an environment that promotes learning from diversity (Kochan et al., 2003) helps facilitate the positive outcomes of diversity. Further, a study by Shin, Kim, Lee, and Bian (2012) tested conditions under which team diversity was positively related to team member creativity. The results showed that the relationship between cognitive team diversity and individual creativity was positive when creative self-efficacy was high. Therefore, when team members believe in their ability to get the work done and have a diversity of ideas, they can reap the benefits of a diverse team.

Complex Situational Effects

Another theme which is clearly emerging from the literature is that team diversity effects are complex and situationally driven. Some have concluded that past research took a simplified approach to diversity and that team diversity research today needs to examine more complex relationships (Bell, Villado, Lukasik, Belau, & Briggs, 2010; van Knippenberg & Schippers, 2007). Jehn, Northcraft, and Neale (1999) found results which demonstrate why a more nuanced approach to studying team diversity may be fruitful. They found that different types of diversity result in different forms of conflict and that conflict affects perceived performance, actual performance, satisfaction, commitment, and intent to remain. Overall, they concluded that informational diversity is likely to improve team performance and that for a team to be effective it should have high information diversity coupled with low value diversity (meaning that they share values and should not experience disputes based on their deeply held beliefs), which should reduce conflict.

The Effects of Power, Demographics, and Contextual Factors Together

In a recent study about diversity and power on boards of directors, Triana, Miller, and Trzebiatowski (2014) found that firm strategic changes were predicted jointly by gender diversity on the board of directors, the firm's past performance, and director power. Diverse boards have been seen as initiators of change. However, diversity may introduce conflict and impede decision-making, which could make it more difficult to implement strategic changes, particularly when firm performance is low. Triana et al. (2014) examined how board gender diversity, firm performance, and the power of women directors (e.g., chair of a powerful committee) combined influenced the amount of strategic change made by the firms in our sample. Results support a three-way interaction (of three predictor variables together), indicating that when the board is not under threat because performance has been good and women directors are in powerful positions, the relationship between board gender diversity and amount of strategic change is the most positive. However, when the board is under threat due to low firm performance and women directors have high power, the relationship between board gender diversity and amount of strategic change is the most negative. "Results suggest that diversity is double-edged in nature because it can propel or impede strategic change depending on firm performance and the power of women directors" (Triana et al., 2014, p. 609).

It makes sense that boards would favor safe choices—and be less open to trying new things—during times of trouble. It also makes sense that the more diverse perspectives a board has, the harder it will be to reach consensus and take action. However, some of the best ideas are born out of conflict, debate, and discussion. The Triana et al. (2014) findings imply that firms are least likely to consider new ideas precisely when they need them the most: at times when the company has not been performing well. During times of stress, people's mental faculties narrow, and they enter survival mode; this is referred to as **threat rigidity** (Staw, Sandelands, & Dutton, 1981). When threat rigidity happens, people tend to stop thinking creatively and absorbing new information. Instead, they rely on old routines and ways of doing things they know well because this requires minimal cognitive processing when their mental energy is already taxed. The same thing can happen to boards and other types of teams, preventing them from considering the very ideas that might help their organization's performance improve.

Instead of taking this study's results to mean that companies should tamp down diversity during tough times to allow them to move forward, Triana et al. (2014) hope the business world will interpret these findings to mean that companies need diverse perspectives during times of adversity. Board of director chairs could combat rigidity and narrow-mindedness by actively seeking to draw out new ideas and differing opinions. For example, instead of a free-form discussion, in which conventional ideas might dominate, the chair or meeting leader might ask each board member to submit comments in writing beforehand so all members have the opportunity to express their thoughts. Alternatively, establishing group norms that allow each member a turn to speak would promote a more open-minded environment in which different ideas could surface.

Global View: Canada

Justin Trudeau, the newly elected prime minister of Canada, has made headlines within his first few days of office by forming a Cabinet that is gender-balanced between men and women. He will have a 31-person Cabinet, and it will be made up of 16 men, 15 women, 2 Aboriginals, and 5 visible minorities. The regional breakdown of his Cabinet members is also diverse, coming from several different provinces across Canada. Overall, the prime minister's new Cabinet is much more demographically diverse than that of his predecessor. In fact, this is the first gender-balanced Cabinet in Canadian history (Ditchbum, 2015; Murphy, 2015).

The 15 women will hold important positions in the Canadian government, including: minister of justice and attorney general of Canada, leader of the Environment and Climate Change Portfolio, trade minister, minister of indigenous and northern affairs, workforce development and labour minister, head of democratic institutions, chief of staff, and minister of employment, workforce development, and labour, among others (Ditchbum, 2015).

This is a large contrast to 1969 when the late Cabinet minister, Judy LaMarsh, lamented being the only woman in the Cabinet and was quoted as saying that "they made no effort to disguise the fact that they regarded me as a curiosity and stared whenever I could be seen" (Ditchbum, 2015). When asked why gender parity in the Cabinet was important to him, Trudeau responded, "Because it's 2015." The crowd cheered the statement (Ditchbum, 2015; Murphy, 2015).

The Effects of Demographic Distance and Contextual Factors

In another study, Triana, Porter, DeGrassi, and Bergman (2013) found that helping behavior in teams is influenced jointly by racial distance (i.e., differences) between team members, the workload distribution among the team members, and performance feedback given to the team members. In this study, one person on the team was randomly assigned to receive performance feedback during the task. The researchers examined how a team member's performance feedback on their handling of a disproportionately heavy share of the team's workload, together with their racial distance from the rest of their teammates, affected the amount of help that person received from their teammates. Results from a laboratory study where 79 teams worked on a decision-making computer simulation showed that performance feedback on the way a feedback recipient handled a disproportionately heavy share of the work modified the effects of workload on helping. This effect was further modified by the feedback recipient's racial distance from the rest of his or her teammates. Racially distant (i.e., dissimilar) negative feedback recipients who had a disproportionately heavy share of their team's workload received less help from teammates than their racially similar counterparts. The results happened irrespective of whether the feedback recipient was a racial majority or minority group member; the main driver of the effects was how dissimilar they were from the rest of their team irrespective of their race. The authors proposed that these interactive effects of workload, feedback, and racial distance of a feedback recipient on the amount of help received might be a result of teammates making negative attributions about the feedback recipients. The authors only found partial support for this hypothesis, which suggests only slight evidence that other teammates make conscious negative attributions about their teammates. This implies that some of the effects observed may be subconsciously driven.

Possible Subconscious Bias Effects

Perhaps one of the most interesting ideas for future research to help tease out the complex effects of diversity in teams has to do with subconscious bias and the effects it may have in teams. Triana et al. (2013) concluded that the lack of helping they observed in their study might be attributed to subconscious bias among participants who reacted negatively to others who were different from their own racial background. Research indeed suggests that ". . . most of a person's everyday life is determined not by their conscious intentions and deliberate choices but by mental processes that . . . operate outside of conscious awareness and guidance" (Bargh & Chartrand, 1999, p. 462). For example, McConnell and Leibold (2001) found that White participants with subconscious biases against Blacks and in favor of Whites were less likely to smile at, speak to, and be friendly toward Black experimenters compared to White experimenters. Two studies also show that being cognitively distracted is linked to more discriminatory behavior. Hofmann, Gschwendner, Castelli, and Schmitt (2008) reported that subconscious racial prejudice was a stronger positive predictor of overt discrimination when their participants were cognitively taxed (after doing a distractor task that made them mentally tired) compared to when they did not complete the extra task. If the conscious part of the mind is tired or busy, subconscious bias is more likely to emerge because less cognitive control is available to prevent the biased behavior. Since research shows that subconscious bias favoring the dominant groups in society and disfavoring the minority groups in society is very common (Greenwald, McGhee, & Schwartz, 1998; Greenwald, Nosek, & Banaji, 2003; Greenwald, Nosek, & Sriram, 2006; Greenwald, Poehlman, Uhlmann, & Banaji, 2009; Greenwald, Rudman, & Nosek, 2002; Greenwald, Mellott, & Schwartz, 1999), it seems reasonable and practical to investigate how subconscious bias can affect diversity in teams.

Things Seem to Improve With Time

The relationship between team diversity and team performance may also depend on timing effects. Harrison, Price, Gavin, and Florey (2002) found that deep-level diversity (i.e., diversity on the basis of personality, attitudes, values, beliefs) has stronger consequences for groups than demographic diversity over time. This is because as group members spend more time together stereotypes are replaced with more accurate knowledge, which may help decrease prejudice, reduce conflict, and increase team cohesion. Watson, Kumar, and Michaelsen (1993) found that demographically diverse teams initially underperformed compared to homogenous teams, but over time (after about three months) they matched and then exceeded the performance of the homogenous teams. By the end of the Watson et al. (1993) experiment, they found that overall performance between the demographically homogenous and diverse teams was similar but that the diverse groups scored higher on two task measures including the range of perspective and alternatives generated.

Furthering this line of research on the effects of time in teams, Barkema and Shvyrkov (2007) found that top management team diversity is associated with the formation of subgroups that hamper communication but that these effects were attenuated with overlapping tenure among top management team members. Therefore, once again, shared tenure among teammates seems to improve adaptiveness (O'Reilly, Snyder, & Boothe, 1993) and lower conflict (Pfeffer, 1983), which promotes cooperation and helps the team perform better.

Then What Are the Overall Findings?

When there are conflicting findings about a particular relationship being examined, the best course of action is to look at any **meta-analyses** that have been conducted in that area of study. A meta-analysis is a study of studies, meaning that the authors collect all studies that have ever been conducted to test the relationship in question (Hunter & Schmidt, 2004). The authors code the effect sizes (often a correlation coefficient) of all the studies and then statistically aggregate those effects into one meta-analytic estimate, applying corrections for the unreliability of the measures used in the original studies and for sampling error or sample size (more weight is assigned to larger samples). The end result of the meta-analytic computation is an estimate of the true population effect for the variables in question; this estimated true population effect is referred to as the Greek letter, rho (ρ).

Therefore, given all of the divergent findings in the relationship between team diversity and its outcomes, we now turn to a discussion of the recent meta-analytic estimates in this area of study. Overall, meta-analyses of team demographic diversity show small effects of demographic diversity on team cohesion and team performance. Webber and Donahue (2001) reported that demographic diversity had a small negative relationship with cohesion ($\rho = -0.03$) as well as performance ($\rho = -0.07$). Horwitz and Horwitz (2007) found small negative relationships between demographic diversity and the quality of team performance ($\rho = -0.006$) as well as the quantity of team performance ($\rho = -0.02$). Joshi and Roh (2009) reported a small negative correlation between team demographic diversity and team performance ($r = -0.03$). Overall, the literature on the relationship between team demographic diversity and firm performance is inconsistent but slightly supports the pessimistic view of diversity, with very small effect sizes.

However, meta-analyses show that the effects between team diversity and both team attitudes and team performance tend to be more positive when the diversity in question is task related. Webber and Donahue (2001) found a small positive effect of job-related diversity on cohesion ($\rho = 0.10$)[1] and team performance ($\rho = 0.02$). In a different meta-analysis, Horwitz and Horwitz (2007) reported that task-related diversity was positively associated with the quality of team performance ($\rho = 0.13$) and the quantity of team performance ($\rho = 0.07$). Joshi and Roh (2009) also reported a positive correlation between task-related diversity and team performance ($r = 0.04$).[2] Therefore, with respect to task-related diversity and team performance, the literature seems to support the optimistic view of diversity, with small effect sizes. This means that diversity effects are typically driven by contextual factors and that more research is needed to tease apart those situations that can help teams reap the benefits of their diversity and mitigate the possible challenges of their differences.

Global View: United Kingdom

A report has concluded that more officers of minority backgrounds must be recruited by the Metropolitan Police in order to reflect London's diversity. The London Assembly determined that while 40% of Londoners are of Black, Asian, and other minority groups, only 11% of the Metropolitan Police force are of those ethnic backgrounds. Furthermore, the report found that a growing number of women are leaving the Metropolitan Police over the past few years in light of "longer shifts, more night shifts and reduced flexible hours" (*BBC News*, 2014; Melville, 2014).

The chair of the committee which produced the report explained that the Metropolitan Police have made progress in recruiting a more diverse workforce and appreciating diversity. However, as the population becomes more diverse over time the Metropolitan Police have a challenge to reflect this diversity.

Overall, the report made four main recommendations, including (a) implementing a legal change if the police force is unable to recruit more minority officers by 2016, (b) reviewing its flexible work practices, (c) carrying out exit interviews for all females leaving the police force, and (d) identifying the barriers keeping women from joining specialist teams (*BBC News*, 2014). The Metropolitan Police also plan to place a lower emphasis on the written aspect of its entrance exam after 2013 data showed that this step of the selection process lowered the percentage of Black, Asian, and minority employees in the applicant pool from 35% to 24% (*BBC News*, 2014).

Finally, the Metropolitan Police have also stated that they will only be recruiting from London in an effort to reflect the city's diversity in its workforce (Melville, 2014).

Tips for Leading Diverse Teams

Given the mixed research findings about diversity in teams, project managers should be aware of the level of diversity in their teams and the types of diversity in order to mitigate performance risks and enhance performance opportunities. Is there too much diversity? Too little diversity? Either way, it can present challenges for teams and should be considered during the initiation stages of a project when the team is being formed as well as during the risk management process when risks are identified and strategies for mitigating those risks are formed.

If products are being designed, marketed, and sold across different countries with different cultures and languages, it will be important to have the right level of diversity on one's team to prevent embarrassing or costly mistakes. Too little diversity could present a problem in such a situation, and project managers could mitigate the risk by ensuring they have the right skill sets on their team from the project initiation phase. Similarly, if a task is straightforward and diversity of information is not as critical, having a high level of personality diversity on a team could create problems and delays in an otherwise easy project. Project managers do not always pick their teams, but rather, they often get the people who are available. If project managers sense they have too much deep-level diversity and it is leading to conflict, they could initiate team building and conflict management early to mitigate this problem.

Closing Case

Diversity at Twitter: Manager's Response to Thoughts on Diversity From an Ex-Employee

A couple of days after Leslie Miley posted his message about the lack of demographic diversity at Twitter (described in the opening case of this chapter), the senior vice president of engineering, Alex Roetter, posted a response. He began by admitting that many people, himself included, have blind spots and that one of his is to resort to engineering-driven and quantitative solutions to solve problems. He says the statements attributed to him were not accurate or complete and represent something far from his intention, which means that he miscommunicated, and for that he said he was sorry (Guynn, 2015; Mohan, 2015; Roetter, 2015).

Roetter then turned his attention to the action plan that Twitter is taking in order to improve diversity within the organization. He outlined several specific goals for the coming year which Twitter has made public, and he explained that the company has shared its gender and ethnic numbers publicly so that they can be held accountable (Mohan, 2015). Here are the specific items he outlined, some of which had been made public earlier in

2015 in an announcement made by Twitter about its diversity goals for 2016 (Ungerleider, 2015).

First, Twitter will require inclusion training of their workforce starting in January. The training, including subsequent booster sessions, will continue throughout the lifecycle of the employee or intern, including during new hire orientation, interviewer training, manager training, and promotion committee training. Second, they are increasing the clarity in their ability to view representation of underrepresented minorities at all stages, from hiring to promotion, and reviewing their employment practices. They will also analyze retention rates. Third, they were developing actions related to diversity which managers at all levels of the engineering team would be expected to implement, not just top-level representation goals. Finally, through the collaboration of employee resource groups, their recruiting team, and their diversity and inclusion team, they are reaching out to both new and experienced graduates from minority groups. Roetter stated, "We are and will be recruiting the best talent from Hispanic-Serving Institutions and Historically Black Colleges and Universities. We are also supporting professional gatherings that serve underrepresented groups, like the Society of Hispanic Professional Engineers" (Roetter, 2015).

Discussion Questions:

1. Do you think the senior vice president's response to the diversity issues raised in the opening case of the chapter was appropriate? Why or why not?
2. Does the four-part action plan outlined by the senior vice president seem like a reasonable approach to handling the lack of diversity at Twitter? Why or why not?
3. Twitter plans to recruit the best talent from Hispanic-Serving Institutions and Historically Black Colleges and Universities. If this is a new recruiting outlet for Twitter, do you think this could be seen by some employees as lowering the bar for recruitment? What could Twitter do to avoid perceptions that standards have been lowered?

Notes

1. Please note that the ρ symbol (called rho) refers to a corrected correlation coefficient. The correlation between two variables has been corrected for the unreliability of the measurement instruments used to measure the two variables and for sampling error.
2. Please note that the r symbol represents a correlation coefficient. Correlations are statistics which represent the linear relationship between two variables. Positive correlations mean the two variables move together (when one goes up, so does the other;

when one goes down, so does the other). Correlations range from -1 to 1, with a relationship of 0 representing no relationship, a relationship of +1 representing a perfect positive relationship, and a relationship of -1 representing a perfect negative relationship.

References

Amason, A. C., & Sapienza, H. J. (1997). The effects of top management team size and inter-action norms on cognitive and affective conflict. *Journal of Management, 23*(4), 495–516.

Asch, S. E. (1954). *Social psychology.* Englewood Cliffs, NJ: Prentice-Hall.

Asch, S. E. (1956). Studies of independence and conformity: A minority of one against a unanimous majority. *Psychological Monographs, 70*(9) (No. 416).

Azzi, A. E. (1993). Implicit and category-based allocations of decision-making power in majority-minority relations. *Journal of Experimental Social Psychology, 29,* 203–228.

Bargh, J. A., & Chartrand. T. L. (1999). The unbearable automaticity of being. *American Psychologist, 54,* 462–479.

Barkema, H., & Shvyrkov, O. (2007). Does top management team diversity promote or hamper foreign expansion? *Strategic Management Journal, 28*(7), 663–680.

Bates, K.G. (2015, November 6). Q&A With The Black Twitter Engineer Who Left Over Diversity Problems. NPR. Retrieved from http://www.npr.org/sections/codeswitch/2015/11/06/454949422/a-q-a-with-lesley-miley-the-black-twitter-engineer-who-left-over-diversity-probl

BBC News. (2014, December 18). Metropolitan police "needs greater diversity." Retrieved from http://www.bbc.com/news/uk-england-london-30525701

Bell, S. T., Villado, A. J., Lukasik, M. A., Belau, L., & Briggs, A. L. (2010). Getting specific about demographic diversity variable and team performance relationships: A meta-analysis. *Journal of Management, 37,* 709–743.

Dickie, M.R. (2015, November 3). Twitter Engineering Manager Leslie Miley Leaves Company Because Of Diversity Issues. *Tech Crunch.* Retrieved from https://techcrunch.com/2015/11/03/twitter-engineering-manager-leslie-miley-leaves-company-because-of-diversity-issues/

Ditchbum, J. (2015, November 4). "Because it's 2015": Trudeau forms Canada's 1st gender-balanced cabinet. *CBC News.* Retrieved from http://www.cbc.ca/news/politics/canada-trudeau-liberal-government-cabinet-1.3304590

Greenwald, A. G., McGhee, D. E., & Schwartz, J. L. K. (1998). Measuring individual dif-ferences in implicit cognition: The implicit association test. *Journal of Personality and Social Psychology, 74,* 1464–1480.

Greenwald, A. G., Nosek, B. A., & Banaji, M. R. (2003). Understanding and using the Implicit Association Test: I. An improved scoring algorithm. *Journal of Personality and Social Psychology, 85,* 197–216.

Greenwald, A. G., Poehlman, T. A., Uhlmann, E. L., & Banaji, M. R. (2009). Understanding and using the implicit association test: III. Meta-analysis of predictive validity. *Journal of Personality and Social Psychology, 97,* 17–41.

Greenwald, A. G., Rudman, L. A., & Nosek, B. A. (2002). A unified theory of implicit atti-tudes, stereotypes, self-esteem, and self-concept. *Psychological Review, 109*(1), 3–25.

Greenwald, A. G., Nosek, B. A., & Sriram, N. (2006). Consequential validity of the implicit association test. *American Psychologist, 61*(1), 56–61.

Greenwald, A. G., Mellott, D. S., & Schwartz, J. L. K. (1999). Measuring the automatic com-ponents of prejudice: Flexibility and generality of the implicit association test. *Social Cognition, 17*(4), 437–465.

Guynn, J. (2015, November 5). Twitter engineering chief pledges 'faster progress' on diversity. *USA Today*. Retrieved from http://www.usatoday.com/story/tech/2015/11/05/twitter-diveresity-leslie-miley-alex-roetter/75259454/

Harrison, D. A., Price, K. H., Gavin, J. H., & Florey, A. T. (2002). Time, teams, and task performance: Changing effects of surface- and deep-level diversity on group functioning. *Academy of Management Journal, 45*, 1029–1045.

Heer, N. (2015). Diversity of Tech Companies by the Numbers: 2015 Edition. Pixel Envy. Retrieved from http://pxlnv.com/blog/diversity-of-tech-companies-by-the-numbers-2015-edition

Hofmann, W., Gschwendner, T., Castelli, L., & Schmitt, M. (2008). Implicit and explicit attitudes and interracial interaction: The moderating role of situationally available control resources. *Group Processes & Intergroup Relations, 11*, 60–87.

Homan, A. C., Van Knippenberg, D., Van Kleef, G. A., & De Dreu, C. K. W. (2007). Bridging faultlines by valuing diversity: Diversity beliefs, information elaboration, and performance in diverse work groups. *Journal of Applied Psychology, 92*, 1189–1199.

Horwitz, S. K., & Horwitz, I. B. (2007). The effects of team diversity on team outcomes: A meta-analytic review of team demography. *Journal of Management, 33*, 987–1015.

Hunter, J. E., & Schmidt, F. L. (2004). *Methods of meta-analysis: Correcting error and bias in research findings* (2nd ed.). Thousand Oaks, CA: Sage.

Jehn, K. A., Northcraft, G. B., & Neale, M. A. (1999). Why differences make a difference: A field study of diversity, conflict and performance in workgroups. *Administrative Science Quarterly, 44*(4), 741–763.

Joshi, A., & Roh, H. (2009). The role of context in work team diversity research: A meta-analysis. *Academy of Management Journal, 52*(3), 599–627.

Kochan, T., Bezrukova, K., Ely, R., Jackson, S., Joshi, A., Jehn, K., Leonard, J., Levine, D., & Thomas, D. (2003). The effects of diversity on business performance: Report of the diversity research network. *Human Resource Management, 42*(1), 3–21.

Lau, D. C., & Murnighan, J. K. (2005). Interactions within groups and subgroups: The effects of demographic faultlines. *Academy of Management Journal, 48*(4), 645–659.

McConnell, A. R., & Leibold, J. M. (2001). Relations among the Implicit Association Test, discriminatory behavior, and explicit measures of racial attitudes. *Journal of Experimental Social Psychology, 37*, 435–442.

Melville, T. (2014, July 14). Metropolitan Police to 'reflect diversity' by recruiting only from London. Reuters. Retrieved from https://www.rt.com/uk/172700-metropolitan-police-recruit-londoners/

Miley, L. (2015). Thought on diversity part 2. Why diversity is difficult. Retrieved from https://medium.com/tech-diversity-files/thought-on-diversity-part-2-why-diversity-is-difficult-3dfd552fa1f7

Milliken, F., & Vollrath, D. (1991). Strategic decision-making tasks and group effectiveness: Insights from theory and research on small groups. *Human Relations, 44*, 1229–1253.

Mohan, P. (2015, November 6). Twitter Engineering SVP Alex Roetter on Diversity: "We Have Blind Spots". *Fast Company*. Retrieved from https://www.fastcompany.com/3053328/fast-feed/twitter-engineering-svp-alex-roetter-on-diversity-we-have-blind-spots

Murphy, J. (2015, November 4). Trudeau gives Canada first cabinet with equal number of men and women. *The Guardian*. Retrieved from https://www.theguardian.com/world/2015/nov/04/canada-cabinet-gender-diversity-justin-trudeau

O'Reilly, C. A., III, Snyder, R. C., & Boothe, J. N. (1993). Effects of executive team demography on organizational change. In G. P. Huber & W. H. Glick (Eds.), *Organizational change and redesign: Ideas and insights for improving performance* (pp. 147–175). New York: Oxford University Press.

Pfeffer, J. (1983). Organizational demography. In B. M. Staw & L. L. Cummings (Eds.), *Research in organizational behavior* (Vol. 5, pp. 299–357). Greenwich, CT: JAI Press.

Roetter, A. (2015). Re: Thought on diversity part 2. Retrieved from https://medium.com/@aroetter/re-thought-on-diversity-part-2-c15241452920

Schweiger, D. M., Sandberg, W. R., & Ragan, J. W. (1996). Group approaches for improving strategic decision making: A comparative analysis of dialectical inquiry, devil's advocacy, and consensus. *Academy of Management Journal, 29*, 51–72.

Shin, S. J., Kim, T. Y., Lee, J. Y., & Bian, L. (2012). Cognitive team diversity and individual team member creativity: A cross-level interaction. *Academy of Management Journal, 55*(1), 197–212.

Staw, B. M., Sandelands, L. E., & Dutton, J. E. (1981). Threat-rigidity effects in organizational behavior: A multilevel analysis. *Administrative Science Quarterly, 26*(4), 501–524.

Stevenson, W. B., & Radin, R. F. (2009). Social capital and social influence on the board of directors. *Journal of Management Studies, 46*, 16–44.

Thatcher, S. M. B., Jehn, K. A., & Zanutto, E. (2003). Cracks in diversity research: The effects of diversity faultlines on conflict and performance. *Group Decision and Negotiation, 12*(3), 217–241.

van Knippenberg, D., & Schippers, M. C. (2007). Work group diversity. *Annual Review of Psychology, 58*, 515–541.

Triana, M., Miller, T., & Trzebiatowski, T. (2014). The double-edged nature of board gender diversity: Diversity, firm performance, and the power of women directors as predictors of strategic change. *Organization Science, 25*, 609–632.

Triana, M., Porter, C. O. L. H., DeGrassi, S. W., & Bergman, M. E. (2013). We're all in this together, except for you: The effects of workload, performance feedback, and racial distance on helping behavior in teams. *Journal of Organizational Behavior, 34*, 1124–1144.

Ungerleider, N. (2015, August 28). Twitter Made its Diversity Goals Public, but They Aren't Very Drastic. *Fast Company*. Retrieved from https://www.fastcompany.com/3050524/fast-feed/twitter-made-its-diversity-goals-public-but-they-arent-very-drastic

van Dick, R., van Knippenberg, D., Hägele, S., Guillaume, Y. R. F., & Brodbeck, F. C. (2008). Group diversity and group identification: The moderating role of diversity beliefs. *Human Relations, 61*, 1463–1492.

van Knippenberg, D., De Dreu, C. K. W., & Homan, A. C. (2004). Work group diversity and group performance: An integrative model and research agenda. *Journal of Applied Psychology, 89*, 1008–1022.

van Knippenberg, D., & Schippers, M. C. (2007). Work group diversity. *Annual Review of Psychology, 58*, 515–541.

Watson, W. E., Kumar, K., & Michaelsen, L. K. (1993). Cultural diversity's impact on interaction process and performance: Comparing homogeneous and diverse task groups. *Academy of Management Journal, 36*, 590–602.

Webber, S. S., & Donahue, L. M. (2001). Impact of highly and less job-related diversity on work group cohesion and performance: A meta-analysis. *Journal of Management, 27*, 141–162.

Wittenbaum, G. M., & Stasser, G. (1996). Management of information in small groups. In J. L. Nye & A. M. Brower (Eds.), *What's social about social cognition? Research on socially shared cognition in small groups* (pp. 3–28). Thousand Oaks, CA: Sage.

fourteen
Subconscious/
Implicit Bias

Opening Case

Life on Auto-Pilot: The Automaticity of Living

Have you ever driven home from work or school and arrived at the driveway of your home only to realize you have no recollection of the drive home? Perhaps you were distracted and thinking about the events of the day. Somehow you managed to get into your automobile, follow the flow of traffic and the traffic signals, make all of the right turns and left turns necessary at the appropriate streets, and then arrive at your house. You did so without getting into a car accident and without being stopped by the police for not following the traffic laws. This represents a fairly sophisticated sequence of operations and a detailed set of steps that were performed to get you home. Yet there you are in the driveway of your home with no recollection of the process used to arrive there. How did that happen?

The answer is that you drove home subconsciously. Bargh and Chartrand (1999) explain that most of the events which take place in our daily lives are managed by our subconscious (as opposed to our conscious) mind. Think about other things that you might do subconsciously. For example, have there been times that you brushed your teeth, took a shower, or got dressed without putting much thought into it? Once again, you probably did most of those things subconsciously. For things that you have done repeatedly, seen repeatedly, or discussed or thought about repeatedly, that information has accumulated over time and been stored away in your subconscious mind. It is recalled quickly and automatically the next time you need that information.

Research shows that only a small fraction of what is in the mind is in conscious awareness at any given time (Bargh, 2005; Gollwitzer, 1990). The rest is in the subconscious mind. Consequently, we do not always realize what we are doing because "... most of a person's everyday life is determined not by their conscious intentions and deliberate choices but by mental processes that ... operate outside of conscious awareness and guidance" (Bargh & Chartrand, 1999, p. 462).

Discussion Questions:

1. If the majority of the things we do in a given day are governed by the subconscious mind, what other types of things that we do in a given day might be done subconsciously?

2. Experts agree that subconscious processing happens very quickly and relies on information which is accumulated in the mind over many years and can be called on automatically when needed. What does this mean about the way that we treat other people? As we encounter others throughout the day, in what ways might the biases and stereotypes we have about various social groups be manifested?

3. Let us consider individuals who are either distracted at the beginning of the day or tired at the end of the day and their mind is in subconscious mode. They are in a public place and come across a member of a different racial group they do not normally interact with very much on a given day. They instinctively avoid the person, do not make eye contact with the person, and do not smile at the person or address the person. Do these nonverbal gestures have any impact on the other person? Does the fact that they were likely subconsciously driven in the mind of the actor have any less impact on the other person than if they had been done consciously by the actor?

Learning Objectives

After reading this chapter, you should be able to:

- Define subconscious/implicit bias
- Know where subconscious/implicit bias comes from
- Understand that subconscious/implicit bias is triggered automatically and that most of people's daily activities are subconsciously driven
- Know what the Implicit Association Test is and where one can go to take it
- Realize that the majority of the population in the United States holds implicit biases for the majority groups and against the minority groups

- Understand conditions that can exacerbate biased reactions including having power and being tired
- List some things that combat subconscious/implicit bias, including:

  - Directions from leaders to focus on job-related qualifications
  - People with a motivation to respond without prejudice
  - Fostering value for diversity among employees
  - Presenting counter-stereotypical examples to reprogram subconscious bias

In this chapter, we examine subconscious/implicit bias and how it can affect people in organizations. This chapter examines research findings on implicit bias, explains the Implicit Association Test (IAT) that is used to measure implicit bias, and presents recommendations for mitigating implicit bias in organizations.

The interest in the subconscious has a long history. Sigmund Freud argued for the study of the subconscious, and he believed that most causes of human behavior are driven by the subconscious (Freud, 1915; Sulloway, 1992). Much research has been conducted in social and experimental psychology over the past two decades and examines how behavior can be both conscious and subconscious (Bargh, 2005; Bargh, Gollwitzer, Lee-Chai, Barndollar, & Trötschel, 2001; Chartrand & Bargh, 2002). The subconscious processes operate automatically and without intention and conscious effort, which means they can impede diversity and inclusion in organizations.

How Does Subconscious/Implicit Bias Form?

Research shows that when cognitive associations are made and reinforced based on past behaviors or information, that information gets stored in the subconscious and is ready to be primed into activation (Bargh & Chartrand, 1999; Bargh et al., 2001). The more a person is exposed to information that reinforces biases about particular groups, the more of it is stored in the subconscious mind, and the easier it is to activate that information in the future. A fast cognitive process, such information can be activated or primed through triggers (Gilbert, 1998; Gilbert, Pelham, & Krull, 1988). That is to say, when automatic information is primed, reinforced information (knowledge based on repeated exposure through the years) is invoked. For example, if the prime is related to the social categorization of another person or group, the observer will quickly access information they know about the group in question (e.g., women, men, Blacks, Whites, Hispanics, Muslims, immigrants, etc.) This process primes subconscious information about the focal person, which can then influence the observer's behavior toward the observed. **Subconscious/implicit bias** is this deeply embedded stereotypical information that can be stored in our minds from repeated exposure to stereotypes.

How Does Subconscious Bias Happen, Even if We Do Not Want It To?

People are not always in control of everything they do. There is a good explanation for this, as Chartrand (2001) clarified in an interview on this subject:

> Nonconscious pursuit is incredibly pervasive because it saves us cognitive resources. If we constantly had to think about what we want to accomplish in every particular situation, we would not be able to do anything else.
>
> (Chartrand, 2001, p. 3)

Associations formed over a long period of time are often stored in the section of the brain called the cerebellum (Sweeney, 2009; Wilson, 2002). This part of the brain primarily regulates automated functions, such as breathing, and is well-suited to handle deeply embedded information which has been deposited over time. For these deeply rooted associations in the cerebellum not to manifest in one's behavior, the neo-cortex, which is the part of the brain that allows you to think and reason, needs to be utilized. However, it is important to note that the neo-cortex has a much more limited processing capacity than the cerebellum. The conscious mind has a processing capacity of 80 bits of information per second through the neo-cortex while the subconscious mind can handle 11 million bits of information per second through the cerebellum (Csikszentmihalyi, 2003; Wilson, 2002). There is no comparison between what the conscious and subconscious parts of our brain can handle. This is why many of our daily life events are handled by the subconscious mind—out of necessity. Recall a time when you were taking a difficult exam, mathematics perhaps. If you felt tired and needed to take a break afterwards, that is probably because you focused so intently on performing the correct steps to arrive at the right solution that the conscious/thinking part of your brain was taxed and made you feel tired. Similarly, the neo-cortex is usually preoccupied with handling the situations and problems we encounter in our daily lives, and it has limited processing capacity.

This information suggests that if bias is collected in the subconscious mind over time due to an individual's life experiences, then bias can be deeply seated in the subconscious mind. This is what researchers refer to as **implicit bias**, or subconscious bias. Given the limited processing capacity of the neo-cortex, the conscious mind is unlikely to be able to stop every biased thought or action that gets primed from the subconscious mind. These biases can lead to **prejudice**, which is an unfavorable feeling or opinion about a group of people. Then prejudice can lead to **discrimination**, which is defined as treating people differently on the basis of their social group membership (Allport, 1954).

How Is Subconscious/Implicit Bias Measured?

The Implicit Association Test (Greenwald, McGhee, & Schwartz, 1998; Nosek, Banaji, & Greenwald, 2002) is a validated test of subconscious bias. The IAT is a rapid choice test, which means participants need to click on a computer keyboard as fast as they can to answer the questions on the screen. Participants take the test by categorizing words or pictures according to the instructions on the screen. The computer screen shows words that are both positive (i.e., good) and negative (i.e., bad), as well as various categories that need to be grouped according to the instructions. There are many different IAT tests that measure bias for or against many different groups. For example, there is a Black/White IAT, a gender and science/humanities IAT, and many more.

The IAT measures the milliseconds it takes the participant to correctly match the words on the screen, per the instructions. For example, the Black/White IAT measures the milliseconds that it takes participants to associate positive words with Black faces as opposed to White faces. The reasoning behind the IAT is that the longer it takes participants to associate Black faces with positive words, the harder they are working to suppress their implicit bias to complete the exercise (Greenwald, Nosek, & Banaji, 2003). The IAT test produces scores that range from −2 to +2, with positive numbers indicating preferences for Whites over Blacks (in the Black/White IAT), negative numbers indicating preferences for Blacks over Whites, and zero indicating no preference. There have been discussions about the validity of the IAT, with some criticizing it (Blanton et al., 2009; Landy, 2008) and others supporting it (McConnell & Leibold, 2009; Rudman, 2008; Ziegert & Hanges, 2009), but the IAT "is the dominant method for assessing implicit associations because of its robust psychometric features, flexibility, and resistance to faking" (Rudman, 2008, p. 426).

Research Findings Using the Implicit Association Test

Nosek et al. (2007) presented findings from a six-year data collection where the team administered the IAT to measure subconscious bias to over 2.5 million participants. These participants were mostly from the United States (85%), with 15% of participants from other countries. The results showed that 80% of participants who took the age IAT could more quickly associate older people with words that represent bad things and younger people with words that represent good things, while 6% showed the opposite pattern. For the Black/White IAT, 68% of participants were more able to quickly associate the required words when pictures of White people were associated with good words and pictures of Black people were associated with bad words, while 14% showed the opposite pattern. For the disability IAT, 76% showed a pro-abled implicit preference while 9% showed a pro-disabled preference. On the gender and science/humanities IAT, 72% of the sample more quickly associated males with science and females with humanities. Finally, on the gender and family/career IAT, 76% of the sample more quickly associated males with careers and females with family (Nosek et al., 2007).

Research shows that bias can be primed very quickly. Names that are difficult to pronounce are subconsciously deemed as risky and harmful (Song & Schwarz, 2009), leading to discriminatory treatment of people with such names. Also, if one has an ethnic-looking face (e.g., a Moroccan in this particular study), that person will likely be subconsciously categorized as an outsider (Dotsch, Wigboldus, Langner, & van Knippenberg, 2008). Stewart, von Hippel, and Radvansky (2009) found that older White adults displayed more implicit bias than younger White adults. After controlling for age-related inhibitory ability, White people also showed stronger implicit bias than Black people (Stewart et al., 2009).

Research shows that implicit bias is associated with behavior. McConnell and Leibold (2001) found that White participants with subconscious biases favoring Whites were less likely to smile at, spend time talking to, and behave in a friendly manner toward Black experimenters compared to White experimenters. Yogeeswaran and Dasgupta (2010) found that the more participants believed that the typical American is White, the less likely they were to select equally qualified Asian-Americans for national security jobs. This effect did not hold in identical jobs that had nothing to do with national security.

There is also evidence that the amount of implicit bias people exhibit can be adjusted somewhat. Blincoe and Harris (2009) found that participants who were subconsciously primed to be cooperative or respectful exhibited lower bias on the Black/White IAT compared to the people in the control group. There is also evidence that exposure to successful multiracial people can adjust levels of implicit bias toward Blacks (Plant et al., 2009). Bernstein, Young, and Claypool (2010) found that implicit prejudice toward Blacks on the Black/White IAT declined after President Obama was elected. Finally, there is some evidence that training can alter initial IAT scores. Wallaert, Ward, and Mann (2010) reported that instructions to avoid prejudice reduced implicit pro-White bias on the IAT.

No One Is Immune

It is possible for people to have implicit bias against their own group if there are negative social stereotypes about that group which have accumulated in one's mind. For example, the following quote from a famous African-American civil rights leader and activist, Jesse Jackson, explains that even he has bias buried in his mind. Jesse Jackson told an audience:

> There is nothing more painful to me at this stage of my life . . . than to walk down the street and hear footsteps and start thinking about robbery—then look around and see somebody White and feel relieved.
>
> (cited in Carpenter, 2008, p. 33)

This is an example of how the subconscious mind can form biased associations and recall them in a split second, despite consciously rejecting them as stereotypes. The author of the prior article states:

> Jackson's remark illustrates the basic fact of our social existence, one that even a committed black civil-rights leader cannot escape: ideas that we may not endorse—for example, that a black stranger might harm us but a white one probably would not—can nonetheless lodge themselves in our minds and, without our permission or awareness, color our perceptions, expectations and judgments.
>
> (Carpenter, 2008, p. 33)

Power Seems to Exacerbate Implicit Bias

Other research findings show that those in positions of power seem to demonstrate more implicit bias. Guinote, Willis, and Martellotta (2010) reported that participants who had power, compared to those with no power, expressed more positive words after seeing White faces than Black faces. In addition, those with power demonstrated more positive emotional reactions to photos of Chinese faces after seeing photos of White faces than after seeing Black faces. Another study conducted by Richeson and Ambady (2003) found that Whites assigned to the role of supervisor of a Black person displayed more racial bias than Whites assigned to the role of a subordinate. However, being assigned to a position of power made no difference in the implicit bias of Whites told to expect to interact with members of their same racial group. The authors state, "These results reveal the manner in which situational power hierarchies serve to reinforce existing social stratification" (Richeson & Ambady, 2003, p. 177).

Being Tired or Distracted Also Exacerbates Implicit Bias

Hofmann, Gschwendner, Castelli, and Schmitt (2008) found that implicit racial bias was more predictive of overt discrimination when participants were cognitively taxed than when they were not. It appears that when conscious processing is depleted, subconscious processing takes over and more biases emerge. Park, Glaser, and Knowles (2008) also found more evidence of prejudice when cognitive resources were depleted.

Might Implicit Biases Have Consequences in Organizations?

Managers make selection, compensation, promotion, training, and termination decisions. Is it possible that implicit bias can affect these decisions? Some studies have theorized a link between subconscious bias and employment discrimination (Bertrand, Chugh, & Mullainathan, 2005; Reskin, 2000) as well as discriminatory managerial behavior (Chugh, 2004). Chugh (2004, p. 203) describes that the

IAT demonstrates that social cognitive pitfalls threaten: a) managers' explicit commitments to egalitarianism and meritocracy, and b) managers' performance in their three primary roles of processing information, interacting with others, and making decisions (Mintzberg, 1973). Implicit bias influences managerial behavior in unexpected ways, and this influence is heightened in the messy, pressured, and distracting environments in which managers operate.

Workplace discrimination creates discrepancies in outcomes people tend to value at work (Goldman, Gutek, Stein, & Lewis, 2006; Tomaskovic-Devey, Thomas, & Johnson, 2005). A few examples of negative consequences for groups on the receiving end of bias include lost employment opportunities (Pager & Quillian, 2005; Pager, Western, & Bonikowski, 2009), lower salaries (Cohen & Huffman, 2003; Neckerman & Torche, 2007), and stifled promotions (Kalev, Dobbin, & Kelly, 2006; Stainback & Tomaskovic-Devey, 2009).

In addition, a study conducted by Pager and colleagues found that minority applicants without criminal backgrounds were no better off than White applicants with a criminal record (Pager et al., 2009). In the same study Blacks were guided into a position lower than the one for which they applied (Pager et al., 2009). Another study conducted by Bertrand and Mullainathan (2004) found that applicants with White-sounding names like Emily and Greg received 50% more callbacks from recruiters offering them interviews compared to African-American-sounding names like Lakisha and Jamal.

A study by Nosek et al. (2009) found an association between girls' scientific achievement in a country and the levels of gender-science implicit bias of that country. About 70% of the over half a million people who took the IAT from 34 different countries showed a bias associating men with science more so than women. When the authors examined the data at the country level, they found that national implicit bias associating men with science predicted national sex differences in math and science achievements between boys and girls (Nosek et al., 2009). Self-reported explicit stereotypes about gender and science did not provide any additional predictive power in explaining the achievement gap beyond the predictive power of national implicit biases. Therefore, the authors concluded that implicit stereotypes and the gender differences in scientific participation are mutually reinforcing and drive the persistent gender gap between men and women in science (Nosek et al., 2009).

How Can You Stop Implicit Bias from Having Negative Consequences?

The first step is to acknowledge that implicit bias exists and that almost everyone is biased in various ways. Research points to at least three helpful suggestions that can mitigate the consequences of implicit bias.

Provide Explicit Reminders to Focus on Job-Related Characteristics

In one study, the presence of directions from managers reminding participants to focus on job-related qualifications instead of irrelevant factors such as race or sex was shown to reduce discrimination in employment selection (Umphress, Simmons, Boswell, & Triana, 2008). This study assessed ways of reducing discrimination in the employment selection process to be more inclusive of qualified women and minorities. The authors analyzed the effects of **social dominance orientation**, defined as the belief that some groups in society are better than others and that power of "superior" groups over "inferior" groups is justified (Pratto, Sidanius, Stallworth, & Malle, 1994; Sidanius & Pratto, 1999). The researchers found that people high on social dominance orientation tend to discriminate against women and minorities, even when pre-tests of those individuals' qualifications (with no demographic information) show they are the best candidates for the job. However, when those people high on social dominance orientation are given directions from an authority figure to focus on job qualifications, the tendency to discriminate is reduced. Evidence from this study reveals that when leaders express that it is the qualifications of the individual to do the job that are critical to hiring the best person for the job, discrimination in the employment selection process is reduced. A different study conducted by Lepore and Brown (2002) found that subconsciously priming the category "Black" resulted in participants making more negative judgments. However, when participants were made aware of a connection between the priming and the judgments, they corrected their judgments. This implies that bias can be stopped from becoming behavior by calling attention to the situation and activating conscious mechanisms.

Seek Out People Who Are Motivated to Respond Without Prejudice

There are individual differences that make people less likely to exhibit prejudice. Some people who hold subconscious prejudice know that this is reprehensible and are motivated to respond without prejudice (Legault, Gutsell, & Inzlicht, 2011; Plant & Devine, 1998). Specifically, Plant and Devine (1998) created a measurement instrument to measure **motivation to respond without prejudice**. They determined that people who are internally motivated to respond without prejudice want to behave in a non-prejudiced way toward Black people and say that using stereotypes against Black people is wrong. People who are externally motivated to respond without prejudice try to appear non-prejudiced toward Black people in order to be politically correct and avoid negative reactions from others. As expected, people who have internal motivation to respond without prejudice are less likely to endorse stereotypes compared to those who are externally motivated to respond without prejudice. Having to make their opinions known publicly by saying them orally to the experimenter as opposed to writing them down privately and being assured of anonymity also had a large effect on the study results. Specifically, people with a low internal motivation to respond without prejudice but a high external motivation to respond without prejudice reported very little endorsement of stereotypes when they had to publicly give their opinion, but they reported eight times as much stereotype endorsement when their responses were written privately (Plant & Devine, 1998). This suggests two things. First, people in organizations who behave in an inclusive way may be masking a lot of stereotypical thoughts. Second, if there are strong company norms to be inclusive and people are held accountable by authority figures, it is possible to suppress people's stereotypic beliefs.

Another characteristic that is associated with more egalitarian behavior toward minority groups is personal value for diversity. Mor Barak, Cherin, and Berkman (1998) developed a measure of **personal value for diversity** which captures the belief that diverse viewpoints add value, that diversity is a business strategy, and that knowing more about diversity is helpful to make people more effective in their jobs. People with a high personal value for diversity in the workplace are more likely to be helpful to minorities and respond to them in less prejudicial ways (Triana, Kim, & García, 2011). Therefore, individuals whose personal beliefs and goals make them more mindful of bias and prevent them from acting on biased thoughts or impulses possess the characteristic of value for diversity. Dasgupta (2004, p. 143) points out:

> Implicit prejudices . . . often influence people's judgments, decisions, and behaviors in subtle but pernicious ways. However, the path from implicit bias to discriminatory action is not inevitable. People's awareness of potential bias, their motivation and opportunity to control it, and sometimes their consciously held beliefs can determine whether biases in the mind will manifest in action.

Recall Counter-Stereotypical Examples to Reprogram Stereotypical Associations in the Mind

In a study about implicit bias against female leaders, Dasgupta and Asgari (2004) reported that when female participants were exposed to information about famous female leaders, they were less likely to show automatic stereotyping of women in a subsequent experimental activity. In this study, exposure to counter-stereotypical examples of women reduced the automatic stereotyping of them.

Organizations may consider training employees about bias. For example, to prevent stereotyping against women in predominantly male fields, training could feature pictures of Marie Curie, the only woman to win a Nobel Prize twice (in two different fields, physics and chemistry) and other well-known female scientists, from different ethnic backgrounds, alongside their male counterparts. Other examples of prominent women are Sonia Sotomayor, who has a law degree from Yale Law School and is the first U.S. Supreme Court justice of Hispanic descent (and only the third woman on the Supreme Court), as well as Angela Merkel, the chancellor of Germany.

To avoid racial bias against minority groups in occupations that are predominantly White, people could be reminded of prominent minorities in those fields. Among many others, Neil deGrasse Tyson, an astrophysicist and Ph.D. from Columbia University, is an excellent example. Dr. DeGrasse Tyson is the director of the Hayden Planetarium at the American Museum of Natural History (http://www. haydenplanetarium.org/tyson) and has hosted multiple television shows including *Nova Science Now* and *Cosmos*. He is also African-American. Other examples of prominent African-Americans include Maya Angelou, a famous author and poet, as well as Colin Powell, a former U.S. secretary of state and retired four-star general of the U.S. Army. Being presented with counter-stereotypical information is an effective way of reducing stereotypical beliefs.

This logic is consistent with research conducted by Plant, Devine, Cox, Columb, Miller, Goplen, and Peruche (2009), who found that implicit bias against Blacks was lower at the same institution/university among the student body in the years after Barack Obama was elected president of the United States compared to the years before. They called it "the Obama effect" and reported that bias was lower, probably because of the repeated exposure the students had to a counter-stereotypic Black exemplar in the years leading up to the election and in the early years of the Obama Presidency.

In sum, there are at least three ways to reduce bias in decision-making processes that impact employment. First, remind employees that they are to focus on job-related qualifications rather than other factors. Second, work with people who are motivated to respond without prejudice and involve them in the decision-making process. Third, remind people of counter-stereotypical examples, or individuals from minority groups who have succeeded in contexts where they were in the statistical minority.

Recommended Materials

The Implicit Association Test is available free of charge at https://implicit.harvard.edu/implicit/takeatest.html. At this web site, you can take many different IATs to test automatic bias for or against several different groups including: Gender-Career IAT, Age IAT, Asian IAT, Skin-tone IAT, Weapons IAT, Presidents IAT, Weight IAT, Race IAT, Arab-Muslim IAT, Religion IAT, Native American IAT, Disability IAT, Sexuality IAT, and Gender-Science IAT. The test will give you a score at the end.

The Women in Science & Engineering Leadership Institute (WISELI) at The University of Wisconsin–Madison has developed an excellent collection of materials on implicit bias. "Searching for Excellence and Diversity: A Guide for Search Committee Chairs at the University of Wisconsin - Madison" is a guide for search committee chairs to raise awareness of unconscious biases and how they can influence the selection of candidates (Fine & Handelsman, 2012). There is also a brochure entitled "Reviewing Applicants: Research on Bias and Assumptions" (WISELI, 2012). These materials may be found at http://wiseli.engr.wisc.edu.

Closing Case

Iowa Court Rejects a Class-Action Lawsuit Based on Implicit Racial Bias

The Iowa District Court ruled in favor of the State of Iowa in Pippen v. Iowa (Haas, 2014). The decision brings an end to the first part of a class-action lawsuit claiming that the State of Iowa did not do enough to avoid implicit bias in making decisions—such as hiring and promotion—involving African-Americans. The plaintiffs' argued that implicit bias was present in decision-making and that the State of Iowa failed to comply with its rules and regulations designed to prevent adverse impact against African-Americans (Paulin, 2012; Smith, 2012).

The lawsuit represented about 6,000 employees, asked for over $70 million in damages, and alleged that 37 departments in the State of Iowa used hiring and promotion practices that created adverse impact toward African-Americans (Smith, 2012). A novel aspect of the lawsuit was that it used implicit bias as evidence for why White managers might be enacting bias in selection, compensation, and promotion decisions involving Black employees (Smith, 2012). As part of the case, psychologist Anthony Greenwald, one of the researchers who originated the Implicit Association Test described in this chapter, testified that people who hold pro-White/anti-Black implicit biases can discriminate against Black employees without realizing it (Paulin, 2012) and that, on average, 70% of people show an implicit preference for Whites over Blacks (Smith, 2012).

According to the Court, the plaintiffs could not support the most important element of the case. The Court explained that "plaintiffs could not challenge the State's decision-making process as a whole due to the myriad decision-makers and employment practices at issue" (Haas, 2014). Essentially, because there are so many decision-makers in the State of Iowa (37 departments, 700 job classifications, and about 2,000 supervisors with hiring and promotion authority), the Court did not believe it was appropriate to challenge the decision-making process of the state as a whole (Atherton, 2014; Haas, 2014).

In addition, the Court also stated that the plaintiffs were not able to show causation for their disparate impact claim (Atherton, 2014). According to the Court, data analysis by experts showed "better success rates for African-Americans than Whites among the different [state] agencies as between the different stages of the hiring process" (Haas, 2014). The Court reasoned that there was no evidence of adverse impact because the statistical evidence showed a Black advantage across various state agencies. The Court further stated that Iowa's public sector employs more African-Americans overall than the private sector (Haas, 2014).

In sum, this is the first case to rely on implicit bias as evidence of discrimination. The plaintiffs lost this case, but according to some (Haas, 2014; Smith, 2012), this is only the beginning and there will be more cases to make claims of implicit bias in the future. "Novel expert testimony is often rejected when it is first tried, but if plaintiff's lawyers keep trying, they ultimately may find a court that will admit such evidence. This type of testimony could be particularly damaging in a jury trial" (Smith, 2012).

Discussion Questions:

1. There is a discrepancy in this case. The Court points to evidence that there is no discrimination against African-Americans because they have a higher success rate than Whites in the hiring process. Yet African-Americans feel that implicit bias has impacted them in hiring and promotion. Is it possible that both of these two sides being presented are accurate?

2. What kinds of human resources processes could cause a situation where the hiring process is inclusive of African-Americans yet these same employees feel they do not advance in the organization? What might this say about process and accountability at the State of Iowa?

3. How could implicit biases be affecting all parties related to this case?

References

Allport, G. W. (1954). *The nature of prejudice*. Boston, MA: Beacon Press.

Atherton, A. (2014, July 25). Iowa Supreme Court Affirms Defense Ruling in Disparate-Impact Employment Discrimination Case Against State. On Brief: Iowa's Appellate Blog. Retrieved from https://www.iowaappeals.com/iowa-supreme-court-affirms-defense-verdict-in-disparate-impact-employment-discrimination-case-against-state/

Bargh, J. A. (2005). Bypassing the will: Toward demystifying the nonconscious control of social behavior. In R. R. Hassin, J. S. Uleman, & J. A. Bargh (Eds.), *The new unconscious* (pp. 37–58). Oxford: Oxford University Press.

Bargh, J. A., & Chartrand. T. L. (1999). The unbearable automaticity of being. *American Psychologist, 54*, 462–479.

Bargh, J. A., Gollwitzer, P. M., Lee-Chai, A., Barndollar, K., & Trötschel, R. (2001). The automated will: Nonconscious activation and pursuit of behavioral goals. *Journal of Personality and Social Psychology, 81*, 1014–1027.

Bernstein, M. J., Young, S. G., & Claypool, H. M. (2010). Is Obama's win a gain for Blacks? Changes in implicit racial prejudice following the 2008 election. *Social Psychology, 41*, 147–151.

Bertrand, M., Chugh, D., & Mullainathan, S. (2005). Implicit discrimination. *American Economic Review, 95,* 94–98.

Bertrand, M., & Mullainathan, S. (2004). Are Emily and Greg more employable than Lakisha and Jamal? A field experiment on labor market discrimination. *American Economic Review, 94,* 991–1013.

Blanton, H., Jaccard, J., Klick, J., Mellers, B., Mitchell, G., & Tetlock, P. E. (2009). Strong claims and weak evidence: Reassessing the predictive validity of the IAT. *Journal of Applied Psychology, 94,* 567–582.

Blincoe, S., & Harris, M. J. (2009). Prejudice reduction in white students: Comparing three conceptual approaches. *Journal of Diversity in Higher Education, 2,* 232–242.

Carpenter, S. (2008, April/May). Buried prejudice. *Scientific American Mind,* 32–39.

Chartrand, T. L. (2001, June 15). Interview with Tanya Chartrand. Ohio State University.

Chartrand, T. L., & Bargh, J. A. (2002). Nonconscious motivations: Their activation, operation, and consequences. In A. Tesser, D. A. Stapel, & J. V. Wood (Eds.), *Self and motivation* (pp. 13–41). Washington, DC: American Psychological Association.

Chugh, D. (2004). Societal and managerial implications of implicit social cognition: Why milliseconds matter. *Social Justice Research, 17,* 203–222.

Cohen, P. N., & Huffman, M. L. (2003). Individuals, jobs, and labor markets: The devaluation of women's work. *American Sociological Review, 68,* 443–463.

Csikszentmihalyi, M. (2003). *Good business: Leadership, flow, and the making of meaning.* New York: Penguin Books.

Dasgupta, N. (2004). Implicit ingroup favoritism, outgroup favoritism, and their behavioral manifestations. *Social Justice Research, 17,* 143–169.

Dasgupta, N., & Asgari, S. (2004). Seeing is believing: Exposure to counterstereotypic women leaders and its effect on the malleability of automatic gender stereotyping. *Journal of Experimental Social Psychology, 40*(5), 642–658.

Dotsch, R., Wigboldus, D. H. J., Langner, O., & van Knippenberg, A. (2008). Ethnic outgroup faces are biased in the prejudiced mind. *Psychological Science, 19,* 978–980.

Freud, S. (1915). *The unconscious.* New York: W. W. Norton & Co.

Fine. E., & Handelsman, J. (2012a). Searching for Excellence & Diversity: A guide for search committees at The University of Wisconsin - Madison, 2nd ed. Women in Science & Engineering Leadership Institute. Retrieved from http://wiseli.engr.wisc.edu/docs/SearchBook_Wisc.pdf

Fine. E., & Handelsman, J. (2012b). Reviewing applicants: Research on bias and assumptions. Women in Science & Engineering Leadership Institute. Retrieved from http://wiseli.engr.wisc.edu/docs/BiasBrochure_3rdEd.pdf

Gilbert, D. T. (1998). Ordinary personology. In D. T. Gilbert, S. T. Fiske, & G. Lindzey (Eds.), *The handbook of social psychology* (4th ed., Vols. 1 and 2, pp. 89–150). New York: McGraw-Hill.

Gilbert, D. T., Pelham, B. W., & Krull, D. S. (1988). On cognitive busyness: When person perceivers meet persons perceived. *Journal of Personality and Social Psychology, 54,* 733–740.

Goldman, B., Gutek, B., Stein, J. H., & Lewis, K. (2006). Employment discrimination in organizations: Antecedents and consequences. *Journal of Management, 32,* 786–830.

Gollwitzer, P. M. (1990). Action phases and mind-sets. In E. T. Higgins & R. M. Sorrentino (Eds.), *Handbook of motivation and cognition* (Vol. 2, pp. 53–92). New York: Guilford Press.

Greenwald, A. G., McGhee, D. E., & Schwartz, J. L. K. (1998). Measuring individual differences in implicit cognition: The Implicit Association Test. *Journal of Personality and Social Psychology, 74,* 1464–1480.

Greenwald, A. G., Nosek, B. A., & Banaji, M. R. (2003). Understanding and using the implicit association test: I. An improved scoring algorithm. *Journal of Personality and Social Psychology, 85,* 197–216.

Guinote, A., Willis, G. B., & Martellotta, C. (2010). Social power increases implicit prejudice. *Journal of Experimental Social Psychology, 46,* 299–307.

Haas, F. (2014). Iowa court rejects class action implicit bias race discrimination claim against the State of Iowa. Retrieved from http://www.nyemaster.com/blogs/iowa-court-rejects-class-action-implicit-bias-race-discrimination-claim-against-the-state-of-iowa/

Hofmann, W., Gschwendner, T., Castelli, L., & Schmitt, M. (2008). Implicit and explicit attitudes and interracial interaction: The moderating role of situationally available control resources. *Group Processes & Intergroup Relations, 11,* 60–87.

Kalev, A., Dobbin, F., & Kelly, E. (2006). Best practices or best guesses? Assessing the efficacy of corporate affirmative action and diversity policies. *American Sociological Review, 71,* 589–617.

Landy, F. (2008). Stereotypes, bias, and personnel decisions: Strange and stranger. *Industrial and Organizational Psychology, 1,* 379–392.

Legault, L., Gutsell, J. N., Inzlicht, M. (2011). Ironic effects of anti-prejudice messages: How motivational interventions can reduce (but also increase) prejudice. *Psychological Science, 22,* 1472-1477.

Lepore, L., & Brown, R. (2002). The role of awareness: Divergent automatic stereotype activation and implicit judgment correction. *Social Cognition, 20,* 321–351.

McConnell, A. R., & Leibold, J. M. (2001). Relations among the Implicit Association Test, discriminatory behavior, and explicit measures of racial attitudes. *Journal of Experimental Social Psychology, 37,* 435–442.

McConnell, A. R., & Leibold, J. M. (2009). Weak criticisms and selective evidence: Reply to Blanton et al. (2009). *Journal of Applied Psychology, 94,* 583–589.

Mintzberg, H. (1973). *The nature of managerial work.* New York: Harper and Row.

Neckerman, K. M., & Torche, F. (2007). Inequality: Causes and consequences. *Annual Review of Sociology, 33,* 335–357.

Nosek, B. A., Banaji, M. R., & Greenwald, A. G. (2002). Harvesting implicit group attitudes and beliefs from a demonstration web site. *Group Dynamics: Theory, Research, and Practice, 6,* 101–115.

Nosek, B. A., Smyth, F. L., Hansen, J. J., Devos, T., Lindner, N. M., Ranganath, K. A., Smith, C. T., Olson, K. R., Chugh, D., Greenwald, A. G., & Banaji, M. R. (2007). Pervasiveness and correlates of implicit attitudes and stereotypes. *European Review of Social Psychology, 18*(1), 36–88.

Nosek, B. A., Smyth, F. L., Sriram, N., Lindner, N. M., Devos, T., Ayala, A., Bar-Anan, Y., Bergh, R., Cai, H., Gonsalkorale, K., Kesebir, S., Maliszewskig, N., Netoh, F., Ollii, E., Parkj, J., Schnabelk, K., Shiomural, K., Tulbure, B., Wiersn, R., Somogyio, M., Akramid, N., Ekehammard, B., Vianellop, M., Banaji, M., & Greenwald, A. (2009). National differences in gender—science stereotypes predict national sex differences in science and math achievement. *Proceedings of the National Academy of Sciences, 106*(26), 10593–10597.

Pager, D., & Quillian, L. (2005). Walking the talk? What employers say and what they do. *American Sociological Review, 70,* 355–380.

Pager, D., Western, B., & Bonikowski, B. (2009). Discrimination in a low-wage labor market: A field experiment. *American Sociological Review, 74,* 777–799.

Park, S. H., Glaser, J., & Knowles, E. D. (2008). Implicit motivation to control prejudice moderates the effect of cognitive depletion on unintended discrimination. *Social Cognition, 26,* 401–419.

Paulin, D. (2012, April 18). Iowa judge rejects suit claiming blacks suffered 'implicit bias' in state hiring. *American Thinker.* Retrieved from http://www.americanthinker.com/blog/2012/04/iowa_judge_rejects_suit_claiming_blacks_suffered_implicit_bias_in_state_hiring.html

Plant, E. A., & Devine, P. G. (1998). Internal and external motivation to respond without prejudice. *Journal of Personality and Social Psychology, 75*, 811–832.

Plant, E. A., Devine, P. G., Cox, W. T. L., Columb, C., Miller, S. L., Goplen, J., & Peruche, B. M. (2009). The Obama effect: Decreasing implicit prejudice and stereotyping. *Journal of Experimental Social Psychology, 45*, 961–964.

Pratto, F., Sidanius, J., Stallworth, L. M., & Malle, B. F. (1994). Social dominance orientation: A personality variable predicting social and political attitudes. *Journal of Personality and Social Psychology, 67*, 741–763.

Reskin, B. F. (2000). The proximate causes of employment discrimination. *Contemporary Sociology, 29*, 319–328.

Richeson, J. A., & Ambady, N. (2003). Effects of situational power on automatic racial prejudice. *Journal of Experimental Social Psychology, 39*, 177–183.

Rudman, L. A. (2008). The validity of the Implicit Association Test is a scientific certainty. *Industrial and Organizational Psychology, 1*, 426–429.

Sidanius, J., & Pratto, F. (1999). *Social dominance: An intergroup theory of social hierarchy and oppression.* Cambridge: Cambridge University Press.

Smith, P. (2012, April 20). Implicit Bias, Disparate Impact, and Class Actions: Iowa District Court Rules in Favor of the State, but Employers Should Remain Wary. Iowa Employment Law Blog. Retrieved from http://www.iowaemploymentlawblog.com/2012/04/articles/title-vii/implicit-bias-disparate-impact-and-class-actions-iowa-district-court-rules-in-favor-of-the-state-but-employers-should-remain-wary/

Song, H., & Schwarz, N. (2009). If it's difficult to pronounce, it must be risky: Fluency, familiarity, and risk perception. *Psychological Science, 20*, 135–138.

Stainback, K., & Tomaskovic-Devey, D. (2009). Intersections of power and privilege: Long-term trends in managerial representation. *American Sociological Review, 74*, 800–820.

Stewart, B. D., von Hippel, W., & Radvansky, G. A. (2009). Age, race, and implicit prejudice. *Psychological Science, 20*, 164–168.

Sulloway, F. (1992). *Freud: Biologist of the mind.* Cambridge, MA: Harvard University Press.

Sweeney, M. S. (2009). *Brain.* Washington, DC: NGS Publishing.

Tomaskovic-Devey, D., Thomas, M., & Johnson, K. (2005). Race and the accumulation of human capital across the career: A theoretical model and fixed-effects application. *American Journal of Sociology, 111*, 58–89.

Triana, M., Kim, K., & García, F. (2011). To help or not to help? Personal value for diversity moderates the relationship between discrimination against minorities and citizenship behavior toward minorities. *Journal of Business Ethics, 102*, 333–342.

Umphress, E., Simmons, A., Boswell, W., & Triana, M. (2008). Managing discrimination in selection: The impact of directives from an authority and social dominance orientation. *Journal of Applied Psychology, 93*, 982–993.

Wallaert, M., Ward, A., & Mann, T. (2010). Explicit control of implicit responses: Simple directives can alter IAT performance. *Social Psychology, 41*, 152–157.

Wilson, T. D. (2002). *Strangers to ourselves: Discovering the adaptive unconscious.* Cambridge, MA: Harvard University Press.

Yogeeswaran, K., & Dasgupta, N. (2010). Will the "real" American please stand up? The effect of implicit national prototypes on discriminatory behavior and judgments. *Personality and Social Psychology Bulletin, 36*, 1332–1345.

Ziegert, J. C., & Hanges, P. J. (2009). Strong rebuttal for weak criticisms: Reply to Blanton et al. (2009). *Journal of Applied Psychology, 94*, 590–597.

fifteen
Diversity
Management

Opening Case

Businesswomen Navigate Traditions When Traveling to Saudi Arabia for Business

An increasing number of women are traveling to Saudi Arabia due to their careers. As they do so, they are encountering some laws and traditions that limit their physical mobility while in Saudi Arabia. For example, according to the U.S. Department of State (2017), women must be met by a sponsor when they arrive in Saudi Arabia. Otherwise they can experience long delays before being allowed to enter the country. Married women (including non-Saudis) must have permission from their husbands before they leave the country, and unmarried women must have permission from their father or male guardian (U.S. Department of State, 2017).

This raises the question of whether businesswomen from other parts of the world can work well in a society where laws are different. According to Nancy J. Ruddy, co-founder of the New York architectural firm CetraRuddy, the answer is yes, but it takes planning and agility. Ruddy has been working on a large project in Saudi Arabia to design a five-star business hotel and retail center. When asked if there were other hurdles for women to doing business in Saudi Arabia, Ruddy shared several examples of situations she encountered (Sharkey, 2015).

According to Ruddy, many of her business meetings with the client that hired her architecture firm to design the new hotel and retail center took place in a modern, 23-story office building (Sharkey, 2015). "But there was no ladies' room, which was totally shocking to me," she said.

Because there are almost no women in the Saudi Arabian workforce, there are no ladies' rooms in the office buildings. Whenever Ms. Ruddy needed to use the restroom, she had to take a 15-minute walk back to her hotel, accompanied by a man. The problem regarding the restroom was ultimately solved by placing a sign on one of the restrooms in the building for Ms. Ruddy's use. The male executives had private restrooms, and she asked if she could have one restroom designated for her use in the building (Sharkey, 2015).

The Saudi Embassy advises female travelers to dress conservatively, which means ankle-length dresses and long sleeves, not pants. In many areas, women should wear a full-length black covering called an abaya (McCombe, 2015). "A woman traveling with a man who is not her husband, sponsor or a male relative can be arrested" (Mann, 2017). According to the publisher of *Smart Women Travelers*, Carol Margolis, "Saudi women keep pushing for change and, as a result, travel into their country by Western women will become easier" (Sharkey, 2015).

Discussion Questions:

1. Do you think that the presence of Western women in Saudi Arabia will help obtain more freedom for the Saudi women? Please explain.
2. In what ways could Saudi Arabian companies make some changes to allow foreign businesswomen to conduct business more effectively while in their country?
3. Whose responsibility is it when women travel to Saudi Arabia to see to it that these women can do their jobs effectively? Should it be the responsibility of the women travelers to accommodate all traditions? Should the company seek some accommodations to accommodate female colleagues? Should the government intervene and make some concessions for companies in order to facilitate foreign business coming to their country?

Learning Objectives

After reading this chapter, you should be able to:

- Define diversity management
- Explain the arguments behind the business case for diversity
- Define diversity climate and the research findings associated with it

- Understand different approaches to diversity management and some pros and cons of each
- Know about diversity training and when it is most effective
- Describe best practices for managing diversity

The purpose of this chapter is to define diversity management and discuss the business case for diversity. The chapter then turns to a discussion of diversity climate and the research findings associated with diversity climate. We also examine different approaches to diversity management as well as diversity training and discuss their effectiveness. Finally, the chapter concludes with best practices for diversity management.

What Is Diversity Management?

Diversity management is defined as "planning and implementing organizational systems and practices to manage people so that the potential advantages of diversity are maximized while its potential disadvantages are minimized" (Cox, 1994, p. 11). Diversity management includes not only attracting and retaining a diverse workforce but also fostering an inclusive environment so that employees, regardless of their backgrounds, can work together toward organizational objectives. At a more practical level, managing diversity involves various organizational programs and human resource practices such as targeted recruiting, diversity training, mentoring programs, programs to aid advancement and promotion, and affirmative action (Kulik & Roberson, 2008).

The Business Case for Diversity

A seminal article by Cox and Blake (1991) provides a comprehensive framework that articulates the business case for diversity. The article reviews research findings and arguments to connect managing diversity with creating a competitive advantage for organizations. The authors present six major arguments that represent a business case for diversity.

- The **cost argument** explains that as organizations become more diverse, the consequences of having a poorly integrated workforce become more costly. Therefore, companies that are good at diversity management will ultimately save money in the long run.
- The **resource-acquisition argument** maintains that companies can develop a reputation for being a good place for women and minorities to work. Those companies that are known as a good place to work will ultimately be able to attract the best talent, which will give them a competitive advantage.

- The **marketing argument** maintains that for multinational companies, the insight that people of various backgrounds bring to the table can help improve marketing efforts in various countries, thereby leading to an advantage.
- The **creativity argument** explains that the more people you have from various different backgrounds, the more likely they are to think of new ways of solving problems and the less likely they are to simply follow the old ways of doing things. This should improve creativity.
- The **problem-solving argument** describes that people from diverse backgrounds have different ways of approaching problems and are more likely to discuss various approaches, thereby providing a rich pool of information and options in order to solve problems. This can produce better decisions through a wide range of options discussed.
- The **system flexibility argument** explains that a multicultural approach to diversity management will lead to a less rigid and less standardized organization. This will allow the organization to be more fluid in response to environmental changes, which can also improve firm performance and reduce cost.

Cox and Blake (1991) further explained that in order for these advantages to be realized in an organization, the organizational culture must be one that values diversity. Furthermore, cultural differences must be seen as an opportunity to learn, and diversity should be seen as more of an opportunity than a challenge. Moreover, the human resources system must be free from bias through all stages of the employment process (e.g., recruitment, training, performance appraisal, compensation and benefits, and promotion). Further, the company management must be educated about managing diversity, and company policies should facilitate the involvement of women in the workforce by reducing sexism and encouraging dual-career couples through the facilitation of work-life balance (Cox & Blake, 1991).

One critique and extension proposed to the business case for diversity is that perhaps practitioners and researchers are relying too much on building the business case for diversity. Bell, Connerley, and Cocchiara (2009) suggest that an unintended consequence of focusing too much on the business case for diversity is that it deemphasizes the fact that there is also a moral responsibility for diversity. In other words, it is possible that a diversity management approach could simultaneously be concerned with improving the bottom line as well as doing what is morally correct.

Summary of Research Findings on Diversity Management in Organizations

Diversity management research has generally shown positive effects of organizational diversity efforts on various employee outcomes. In a study conducted by

McKay, Avery, Tonidandel, Morris, Hernandez, and Hebl (2007), findings show that diversity climate perceptions can be useful in models examining organizational turnover. They found that diversity management is relevant to all employees, not just minorities, and that there are racial differences in the effects of diversity climate perceptions. Overall, diversity climate perceptions were significantly and negatively related to turnover intentions across all racial groups. A pro-diversity climate was associated with increased organizational commitment and reduced turnover intentions (McKay et al., 2007). Diversity climate was also negatively associated with turnover intentions, especially for Blacks (McKay et al., 2007).

This is consistent with other research findings that those who tend to experience the most discrimination (i.e., minorities and women) are also the most attentive to diversity efforts and value diversity efforts the most. Kossek and Zonia (1993) examined attitudes and beliefs about an organization's diversity climate among faculty at a large university. They found that White women and racioethnic minorities placed greater value on employer efforts to promote diversity than White men. Women and racioethnic minorities also held more favorable attitudes about the qualifications of women and racioethnic minorities. Gender heterogeneity in the organizational unit was positively associated with valuing diversity. Also, the greater the ratio of women in a unit, the more favorably diversity activities were viewed. Finally, perceptions of equal opportunity varied by demographic group. For instance, White respondents believed more strongly than racioethnic minorities that women have an equal chance to men of receiving department support. Men reported that women have equal opportunity whereas women were less likely to believe that women had equal opportunity (Kossek & Zonia, 1993).

Similar findings were reported by Mor Barak, Cherin, and Berkman (1998). They found that White men perceived the organization as more fair and inclusive than did White women or racial/ethnic minority men and women. White women and racial/ethnic minority men and women saw more value in and felt more comfortable with diversity than White men. Minorities attributed more value to diversity and reported feeling more comfortable with diversity than Whites. Female interviewees who were part of a minority group felt they were at a greater disadvantage than White men, women, or male minority members. A recurring theme the authors reported from their interviews with racial/ethnic minority men and women and with White women was their feeling that they lost job opportunities because their behavior did not conform to their supervisors' expectations. In contrast, White men thought there was fairness and inclusiveness in the formal organizational processes (Mor Barak, Cherin, & Berkman, 1998).

Research shows that diversity efforts can mitigate some of the harmful effects of perceived discrimination in the workplace. According to Triana, García, and Colella (2010), when employees perceive that their organization is promoting diversity, the negative impact of racial discrimination on organizational commitment is often ameliorated. Across three studies, they found that perceived racial discrimination was negatively related to organizational commitment, and in two of the three studies (mostly White and Hispanic samples) this negative relationship was weakened by perceived organizational diversity support. However, the African-American sample showed the reverse effect where the negative relationship between perceived racial discrimination and organizational commitment became stronger when organizational efforts to support diversity were high. The authors suggested that for groups experiencing higher amounts of discrimination, organizational diversity efforts may be seen as hypocritical if an employee has experienced discrimination in that organization.

Research also shows that diversity efforts are associated with increased performance among some groups of employees. In one study, the difference in performance between Whites and racial minorities (i.e., Hispanics or Blacks) is the smallest in organizations with high levels of diversity climate (McKay, Avery, & Morris, 2008). **Diversity climate** here refers to "the degree to which a firm advocates fair human resource policies and socially integrates underrepresented employees" (McKay et al., 2008, p. 352), capturing the quality of diversity management.

At the organizational level, several studies have found an association between diversity management and firm performance. Gonzalez and DeNisi (2009) found that racial diversity is positively related to return on income and productivity only when there is a supportive diversity climate, and it is negatively related to return on income and productivity under an adverse diversity climate. Similarly, McKay, Avery, and Morris (2009) demonstrate that unit sales improve the most when both managers and subordinates perceive high levels of diversity climate. McKay, Avery, Liao, and Morris (2011) found that customer satisfaction in major retail stores was highest when diversity management efforts were accompanied by a strong representation of minority employees. Furthermore, stock markets react to diversity management practices such that announcements of award-winning affirmative action programs are associated with high stock returns while discrimination settlements lead to negative returns (Wright, Ferris, Hiller, & Kroll, 1995).

From a policy-making standpoint, different diversity management programs vary in their effectiveness at increasing managerial diversity. Kalev, Dobbin, and Kelly (2006) conducted a comprehensive analysis on multiple diversity policies of private organizations from 1971 to 2002 and found that establishing responsibility for diversity in the organizational structure was the most effective way of increasing diversity in organizations.

Kalev et al. (2006) analyzed three approaches to promoting diversity: establishing organizational responsibility, using training and feedback, and reducing the social isolation of women and minority workers. They looked at seven diversity programs, including: affirmative action plans, diversity committees and task-forces, diversity managers, diversity training, diversity evaluations for managers, networking programs, and mentoring programs. They examined the impact of these programs on the representation of White men, White women, Black women, and Black men in the management ranks of private sector firms. Their results showed that moderating managerial bias through diversity training and diversity evaluations were least effective at increasing the number of White women, Black women, and Black men in management positions. Diversity training and evaluations for reducing perceptual biases were the least effective, but they worked better in organizations with structured responsibility for diversity. Addressing social isolation through mentoring and networking programs showed modest results. Establishing responsibility for diversity resulted in the broadest increase in managerial diversity, and units that increased managerial diversity saw better effects from training, evaluations, networking, and mentoring compared to units that did not (Kalev et al., 2006). In other words, diversity initiatives were most effective when managers were held accountable for considering diversity management efforts in their daily decision-making. Those initiatives include having diversity committees, diversity managers and departments, and affirmative action plans.

Further, the Kalev et al. (2006) results showed that diversity committees increased the odds of having Black women in management by 27% on average, White women in management by 19%, and Black men in management by 12%. Having full-time diversity staff raised the odds of having Black men in management by 14%, Black women in management by 13%, and White women in management by 11%. Firms that assigned responsibility for compliance with diversity management goals to a manager also saw stronger effects from some diversity management programs. Finally, the overall effects of initiatives varied across demographic groups, with White women benefiting most, followed by Black women, and Black men benefiting the least.

Different Approaches to Diversity Management

Thomas and Ely (1996) maintain that there are primarily two approaches that organizations take to diversity management—the discrimination-and-fairness paradigm and the access-and-legitimacy paradigm. The **discrimination-and-fairness paradigm** is concerned with equal opportunity and fairness in recruitment for all demographic groups, observing legal and political guidelines. This paradigm is a color- and gender-blind approach that does not tolerate differences among groups. In contrast, the **access-and-legitimacy paradigm** accepts differences across demographic groups but considers diversity as a source of business opportunity. Thus, for organizations adopting this approach, the main purpose of having a diverse workforce is to gain access to niche markets and to serve a diverse pool of customers effectively.

Under the discrimination-and-fairness paradigm, progress in diversity is measured by how well the company achieves its recruitment and retention goals. A limitation of this approach is that its colorblind, gender-blind ideal is somewhat predicated on the assumption that people are all the same and all aspire to being the same (Thomas & Ely, 1996). This puts pressure on employees to make sure the important differences among them (including demographic characteristics which define their identities) are not emphasized. Another limitation to this approach is that businesses may be too quick to ignore important differences between people in the interest of preserving harmony. Finally, the discrimination-and-fairness paradigm requires a theme of assimilation because its aim is to achieve a demographically representative workforce whose members treat one another exactly the same (Thomas & Ely, 1996).

Companies following the access-and-legitimacy paradigm almost always operate in a business environment where there is diversity among its customers, clients, or the labor pool. In other words, they have a market-based motivation for diversity (Thomas & Ely, 1996). There is a theme of differentiation in this approach, and the aim is to position employees where their demographic characteristics match those of important markets. There are some limitations to this approach. First, it emphasizes the role of cultural differences in a company without analyzing those differences to see how they influence the work that is completed. Second, the approach may be too quick to push staff with niche capabilities into differentiated roles without fully understanding those capabilities and how they could be integrated into the company's mainstream work. An example of this would be hiring minority employees who can speak Spanish to gain access and legitimacy within Spanish-speaking markets and then pigeonholing those employees into those roles without further thought for their career advancement elsewhere within the company.

Thomas and Ely (1996) proposed an alternative paradigm that attempts to overcome shortcomings of the discrimination-and-fairness paradigm and the access-and-legitimacy paradigm. They advocated for a **learning-and-effectiveness paradigm** that would promote equal opportunity, acknowledge cultural differences, and recognize the value in those differences. In doing so, firms would internalize differences among employees such that those firms would learn and grow because of employee diversity. Thomas and Ely further explain that they believe eight preconditions are needed for making the paradigm shift to becoming a learning-and-effectiveness organization, and most must be in place to make the shift effectively. The first two preconditions are related to leadership of the organization. The leadership must understand that a diverse workforce embodies various perspectives and approaches to work, and leaders must value that insight. Leaders must also recognize that expression of different perspectives represents both learning opportunities and challenges for organizations. The next four preconditions are related to the organizational culture. Organizational culture must expect high standards of performance from everyone, stimulate personal development, encourage openness, and make workers feel valued. Finally, the last two preconditions are that the organization must have a well-articulated and understood mission as well as a relatively egalitarian, non-bureaucratic structure (Thomas & Ely, 1996).

Since their introduction of approaches to diversity management based on case studies (Thomas & Ely, 1996), different approaches to diversity, how they manifest in diversity policies and structures, and how they influence employee and organizational outcomes have not yet been examined extensively. This may be, in part, due to a lack of a measurement instrument capturing different types of diversity perspectives in organizations. Such a measurement instrument capturing various diversity perspectives (e.g., integration and learning approach to diversity) was introduced in 2013 by Podsiadlowski, Gröschke, Kogler, Springer, and van der Zee. This will make future research on diversity approaches possible.

Global View: Singapore

Singapore is experiencing a dilemma because the diversity management practices of some of its major corporations do not agree with some of the country's laws. For example, Goldman Sachs's invitation to a group of LGBT (lesbian, gay, bisexual, and transgender) college students for a recruiting event stirred a bit of controversy (Wong, 2014). News about this event spurred the Singapore minister for social and family development, Chan Chun Sing, to publicly explain that although discrimination has no place in Singapore's society, companies that do business in Singapore should respect the local culture and rules and "not venture into public advocacy for causes that sow discord among Singaporeans" (Wong, 2014).

The minister's comments were made as an increasing number of multinational corporations are supporting Pink Dot, an annual gay rights event in Singapore. The mission of Pink Dot is to promote openness, understanding, and tolerance toward the LGBT community in Singapore (Pink Dot, 2017). Most LGBT people in Singapore are afraid to come out of the closet. Pink Dot has been hosting an annual event since 2009 to raise awareness about the prejudice that LGBT people face in Singapore and encourage support for LGBT rights (Pink Dot, 2017). Pink Dot had a record turnout in 2016 (Shen, 2016).

Tensions surrounding LGBT rights present a dilemma for the Singapore government, which would like to be perceived as pro international commerce and industry. Gay sex is banned in Singapore (Shen, 2016). However, major corporations doing business in Singapore such as JP Morgan, Goldman Sachs, Google, and British Petroleum are supportive of LGBT rights (Wong, 2014).

Diversity Training

Diversity training is defined as programs intended to facilitate positive intergroup interactions, reduce prejudice and discrimination, and enhance the skills, knowledge, and motivation of people to interact with diverse others (Pendry, Driscoll, &

Field, 2007). Many organizations invest in diversity training as a means of promoting harmony and inclusive behavior among a diverse workforce (Rynes & Rosen, 1995). There are different diversity training techniques including cultural simulation games, like Bafá Bafá, which create unique cultures as part of the simulation (Shirts, 1977) and interactive training sessions where people are exposed to members of other groups (Triandis, Kurowski, & Gelfand, 1994). The interactive training sessions often take the form of experiential training (where the goal is for members of different groups to interact and have good experiences) or exposure to the strengths of other groups (where each group learns to appreciate the strengths of the other group; Triandis, Kurowski, & Gelfand, 1994).

Even though diversity training is one of the most widely used diversity activities in organizations and has a high potential to be impactful (Bezrukova, Jehn, & Spell, 2012; Kulik & Roberson, 2008), research findings on its effectiveness are inconsistent (Briggs, 2002). According to a recent meta-analysis (Kalinoski et al., 2013), the overall relationship between diversity training and various employee outcomes is positive. Kalinoski et al. (2013) found that diversity training enhances employee attitudes, motivation, knowledge, and behaviors. In contrast, Kalev et al. (2006) found that diversity training resulted in a 7% decrease in the odds of having Black women in management and had no significant effect on other racial groups (i.e., White men and women and Black men). The inconsistencies between these two studies may be due to different outcomes measured in the two studies, with employee outcomes potentially being subject to socially desirable answers (Chung & Monroe, 2003). Another explanation for the differences in results is that employee attitudes and behaviors are more easily affected by diversity training than organizational outcomes to increase diversity, which are more difficult to change and require more time to change.

Diversity training seems to be most effective when the top-level managers in the organization make diversity initiatives a top priority (Rynes & Rosen, 1995). When this is not the case, however, diversity training efforts are less effective. The majority of human resources practitioners surveyed by Rynes and Rosen (1995) said their training efforts either had mixed results or were ineffective. Two other empirical studies assessing diversity training effectiveness have also found no significant effects from diversity training (Neville & Furlong, 1994; Pruegger & Rogers, 1994). In addition, several other researchers have noted that in the worst case, diversity training may produce backlash from males, reinforce negative stereotypes, or intensify hostility between groups (Beaver, 1995; Galen & Palmer, 1994; MacDonald, 1993; Mobley & Payne, 1992; Murray, 1993).

Scholars have pointed out that diversity training is not performing at its highest potential due to the misunderstanding or lack of consideration for various factors that mitigate its impact (Bezrukova et al., 2012). Bezrukova and colleagues (2012) conducted a review of the diversity training literature. They explained that the effectiveness of the training varies depending upon the type of diversity training. There are primarily two kinds of diversity training, namely awareness training and skill training (Kulik & Roberson, 2008). The purpose of **awareness training** is to enable employees to become aware of their stereotypes and processes underlying prejudice and discrimination. The goal is to bring about behavioral changes based on self-awareness. Awareness training often requests that participants share experiences with one another (Roberson, Kulik, & Pepper, 2001) and focuses on developing participants' self-awareness of diversity issues including cognitive biases that can affect their interpretation of others' behavior (Probst, 2003). **Skills training** is designed to teach employees new skills that may be helpful in dealing with diversity issues such as communication and conflict management skills (Holvino, Ferdman, & Merrill-Sands, 2004). For example, participants can focus on monitoring their actions and providing appropriate responses to workplace differences such as cross-cultural communication barriers.

Several studies have shown that awareness training does not increase trainees' knowledge or awareness (Chrobot-Mason, 2004; Sanchez & Medkik, 2004). Moreover, Sanchez and Medkik (2004) show that trainee knowledge and awareness are not related to post-training behaviors. This indicates that simply being aware of perceptual biases does not lead to behavioral changes. Because skills training is behavior oriented, it is more aligned with the ultimate goal of changing employee behaviors (Bezrukova et al., 2012; Kulik & Roberson, 2008). However, for more controversial issues such as LGBT rights in organizations, strong behavioral content may backfire (Kaplan, 2006).

According to the review conducted by Bezrukova et al. (2012), diversity training typically involves three outcomes. **Cognitive learning** refers to the extent to which trainees acquire knowledge. For example, the Multicultural Awareness Questionnaire (Law, 1998) measures knowledge about cultural diversity issues by calculating the total number of correct responses. **Affective learning** refers to changes in attitudes toward diversity and changes in trainees' self-efficacy to perform the topics discussed. Typical measures include self-assessments of attitudes toward ethnic groups. Trainee reactions to the training tend to be a mediating factor which influences how much participants take away from the training. **Behavioral learning** refers to the development of trainees' skills. This may include self-reported skills or implicitly identified skills, as well as objective behaviors and results. Commonly used self-reports are assessments of trainees' abilities to resolve conflict (Holladay & Quinones, 2008) or self-perceptions of behaviors that can be beneficial to diversity management.

Research has also argued that different trainee characteristics and environmental factors affect diversity training effectiveness. Kulik, Pepper, Roberson, and Parker (2007) demonstrate that trainees who show higher pre-training competence in diversity are more likely to take diversity training voluntarily. They posit that those who have low diversity competence are more likely to be unaware of their deficit, and even if they are aware of it, they may have low self-efficacy that the training will make a difference, potentially undermining the effect of training. Employee motivation after training is also important, as people need to be motivated to act upon their awareness and regulate their discriminatory behaviors (Kulik & Roberson, 2008). Thus, the working environment has to be supportive of knowledge transfer such that employees are provided with opportunities to utilize what they have learned and with adequate reinforcement for learned behaviors (Sanchez & Medkik, 2004). In a similar vein, diversity training is more effective when it is integrated with other diversity programs under a supportive culture promoted by the top management (Bezrukova et al., 2012). Therefore, organizations must undertake a needs assessment to judge if training is necessary, what critical skills are needed, whether they have a supportive climate, and if their employees are motivated and confident to learn during diversity training (Jayne & Dipboye, 2004). Diversity training programs that are tailored to the specific needs of the firm and implemented based on a thorough evaluation are more likely to succeed.

Considerations Around Mentoring

One commonly suggested reason for limited advancement of women and minorities in organizations is that they receive less mentoring (McDonald & Westphal, 2013; Noe, 1988). Because mentors are more likely to engage in a relationship with mentees who are similar to them, a limited number of minorities in leadership positions leads to a lack of mentors for minority subordinates (Noe, 1988). However, similarity in deep-level attributes such as personality, values, and interests may be more important than demographic similarity for protégés in getting quality mentoring (Lankau, Riordan, & Thomas, 2005). This may be especially applicable to long-term mentoring relationships.

Furthermore, drawing upon the queen bee effect (Dellasega, 2005), women may not necessarily benefit from female mentors. The **queen bee syndrome** refers to women who have achieved success within the organizational structure and then endorse traditional sex roles and deny there is discrimination against women (Abramson, 1975; Staines, Travis, & Jayerante, 1973). Consequently, these women show no sympathy or support toward other working women, especially their subordinates, and women do not like to work for these females (Gini, 2001). Managers may assign female mentors to other women thinking they will be helpful, but not all women are good mentors to other women. Therefore, female mentors' deep-level values about diversity and assisting other women should be better predictors of their behavior than their gender. This implies that more sophisticated ways of matching mentors with mentees (beyond gender similarity) should be considered. The best mentors are those who have a proven track record of supporting employees of all demographic backgrounds, including women and minorities who have gone on to advance in their organizations.

Best Practices for Managing Diversity

Research shows that for diversity management practices to be successful, they need to have the support of top management and managers need to be held responsible for diversity outcomes (Cox, 1994; Kalev et al., 2006; Kossek & Zonia, 1993). The way in which the organization's leadership approaches diversity is also important. Diversity practices that endorse **multiculturalism**, which acknowledges differences between different groups, have a more positive impact on social interactions than a **colorblind approach**, which attempts to ignore differences between groups (Vorauer, Gagnon, & Sasaki, 2009). The problem with the colorblind approach is that it encourages people to prevent problems by ignoring their differences and trying to avoid discussions that could offend others. However, this may inadvertently result in people becoming apprehensive and reducing communication between groups, which may lead to poor team dynamics. While emphasizing the similarities between team members could increase harmony in the team, it also discourages individuals from analyzing issues from multiple perspectives and from engaging in deeper and more complex discussions (Todd, Hanko, Galinsky, & Mussweiler, 2010). Instead, a more robust approach to diversity management could be to have a zero-tolerance policy for discriminatory or exclusive behavior combined with a mentality that multiculturalism is an advantage to a team and that differences are to be embraced and respected. A review of the efficacy of diversity management initiatives states that the best approaches are those that are inclusive of all groups (i.e., both minority and majority groups) and also provide opportunities for dissimilar individuals to communicate with and learn from one another (Stevens, Plaut, & Sanchez-Burks, 2008).

How, then, can organizations best develop an environment where differences between teammates are embraced and individuals experience the benefits of diversity without the down side of diversity (Cox, 1994)? According to research on biases between groups of people, one powerful way to reduce conflict between different groups of people is to have a **superordinate goal**. This means a goal that represents the greater good that all parties can agree to, regardless of their background (Sherif, 1958). For example, working toward the good of a project or the good of the organization is a uniting goal regardless of your background or personal beliefs.

Also, according to the work of Pettigrew and Tropp (2006), the **contact hypothesis**, or the idea that having contact between different groups of people also can reduce prejudice, is effective if implemented correctly. However, it is important to note that in order for contact between different groups of people to be effective in reducing prejudice, several conditions must be in place. First, the leadership must set the tone that they endorse the norm of inclusion and want different groups to be well integrated. Second, the different groups need to have enough contact with each other so they can have meaningful exchanges and learn about each other beyond a simple superficial interaction (Brewer & Brown, 1998). Short, infrequent interactions which do not provide sufficient opportunity for learning and understanding may actually worsen biases between groups if the participants only obtain limited information and walk away reaffirming the stereotypes with which they came into the discussion (Brewer & Brown, 1998). Further, the groups must feel like they have equal status in the discussion. If one group feels disadvantaged compared to another, stereotypes are likely to be reinforced probably because communication breaks down or the process feels hypocritical (Bradford & Cohen, 1984).

Finally, it is critical to implement any diversity management approach with sensitivity and respect. It is important to be sensitive to both the majority and minority group members. One must be sensitive to the needs of the majority group members because these group members are sometimes apprehensive about diversity programs if they feel guilt for the problems of minority groups, if they feel that diversity management is targeted at people other than themselves, or if they feel their group is being blamed for the problems of other groups (Feagin & O'Brien, 2003). If the majority group experiences these feelings, they are likely to withdraw from the situation or have a backlash effect against the diversity efforts (Beaver, 1995; Galen & Palmer, 1994; MacDonald, 1993; Mobley & Payne, 1992; Murray, 1993). Research shows that applying diversity-related pressure in organizations could increase biases among the people who resent the pressure (Kaiser et al., 2013). It is equally important to be sensitive to the needs of the minority group to avoid making anyone feel uncomfortable or offended. It is also critical to watch against perpetuating negative stereotypes about minority groups.

When discussing diversity topics in an organizational setting, it is just as important to know what *not* to do as it is to know what you should do. In a review of the fairness of diversity training, Gilliland and Gilliland (2001) provided an example of a poorly executed diversity program. According to their review, the U.S. Department of Transportation conducted training in the 1990s where "in an effort to expose racial and sexual prejudices ... men were 'ogled and fondled' by women ... Blacks and Whites were encouraged to exchange racial slurs" (Gilliland & Gilliland, 2001, p. 142). It is easy to see how this could be considered both offensive and discriminatory for all parties involved.

Taken together, the most robust approaches to discussing diversity openly would seem to include the following elements:

- Do not blame the problems of any group on any other group.
- Acknowledge that there are both similarities and differences between groups.
- Acknowledge that all groups and relationships between different groups are complex and nuanced for numerous reasons.
- Create a dialogue of sharing an understanding between the different groups.
- Encourage perspective taking to understand things from another group's point of view.
- Promote an understanding of the challenges minority groups can face in organizations by presenting research evidence about biases (including both conscious and subconscious/implicit biases) and the impact of those biases.
- Conduct discussions with professionalism and respect for all groups.

- Be informed. Those conducting diversity training and diversity management should read current research about diversity and keep up with current population information. Some good sources of information include:

    - Google Scholar: Go to http://www.scholar.google.com and search for "diversity" or "diversity management" as a keyword and browse the titles and abstracts for information. Full text articles are sometimes available, too.
    - Bureau of Labor Statistics (http://www.bls.gov) keeps a breakdown of employment broken down by sex, race, and age.
    - United States Census (http://www.census.gov) keeps information about current population breakdown by sex, race, and age.
    - United Nations (http://www.un.org/en/about-un/index.html) is an international organization of 193 members states which promotes peace, tolerance, and justice worldwide.
    - International Labour Organization (http://www.ilo.org/global/about-the-ilo/lang-en/index.htm) is an agency of the United Nations which brings together governments from 187 member states to set labour standards that promote decent work for all men and women.
    - The World Bank (http://www.worldbank.org/en/about/what-we-do) is a cooperative of 189 member countries whose goals are to end extreme poverty and foster income growth for the bottom 40% of people in every country.
    - World Economic Forum (https://www.weforum.org/system-initiatives/education-gender-and-work) publishes regular reports on the status of the gender gap worldwide.
    - Center for the Integration of Research, Teaching, and Learning (CIRTLE; http://www.cirtl.net/diversityresources) maintains a library of diversity resources including case studies, web links, and workshops.
    - ERIC (Education Resources Information Center; http://eric.ed.gov) maintains a great deal of information related to education. One can search for "diversity" to find research articles about classroom diversity.
    - Women in Science & Engineering Leadership Institute (WISELI) at the University of Wisconsin–Madison (http://wiseli.engr.wisc.edu/searchguidebooks.php#url) maintains an extensive page of resources regarding the glass ceiling, implicit bias, and recruiting for both diversity and excellence.
    - Other helpful databases which require a subscription and can be accessed from the library system of most universities include:

        - PsycInfo (Psychological Abstracts): http://www.apa.org/pubs/databases/psycinfo
        - Business Source Complete: http://www.ebscohost.com/academic/business-source-complete

- Education Full Text: http://www.ebscohost.com/academic/education-full-text
- Education Research Complete: http://www.ebscohost.com/academic/education-research-complete
- International Business Research Guide (information about cultures and news around the world): http://researchguides.library.wisc.edu/intbusiness
- Web of Science: http://wokinfo.com
- Diversity Inc. (current events related to diversity in the news): http://www.diversityinc.com
- Insight to Diversity (covers diversity issues in universities and other organizations): http://www.insightintodiversity.com

Closing Case

What Does Diversity Management Mean at the Country Level?

A Case of a Death Sentence in Sudan for Religious Conversion and Marriage

Research on diversity management focuses on diversity in organizations. But what does diversity management mean at the country level? More importantly, what should it mean at the country level? Consider the following example.

Meriam Ibrahim, a woman from Sudan who converted from Islam to Christianity, was condemned to death by hanging for apostasy, or desertion of one's religion and principles (*BBC News*, 2014; Leins, 2014). In Sudan, the sentence for apostasy is death (Povoledo, 2014). Although Ibrahim was ultimately set free and allowed to leave the country, the sentence was brought about when Ibrahim converted from Islam to Christianity and married a Christian man, Daniel Wani, an American citizen. According to the law of her native country, Ibrahim was a Muslim since her father was a Muslim. Even though Ibrahim explained that her mother was Christian and raised her in the Christian faith, she was considered to be Muslim because of her father's faith. Muslim women are not allowed to marry men outside the Islamic faith in Sudan (*BBC News*, 2014; Leins, 2014).

The news of the death sentence sparked an international protest, and diplomats, human rights groups, and members of the public protested the sentencing. In the end, a court overturned the death sentence, and Ibrahim was released from prison. She had given birth to her second child while being held in prison (Povoledo, 2014).

After being set free, Ibrahim, her husband, and their two children lived in the American Embassy in Sudan until her travel papers were approved for her to travel to the United States. After negotiations between Sudan, the Vatican, and Italy, the family was allowed to visit Italy for a few days before continuing on to the United States. While in Rome, Ibrahim and her family met with Pope Francis (*BBC News*, 2014; Leins, 2014), where they all received blessings from the Pope. According to Vatican spokesman, the Reverend Federico Lombardi, "The Pope thanked her for her witness to faith." He added that Pope Francis wanted the meeting to be a "gesture of support to all who suffer for their faith" (*BBC News*, 2014; Leins, 2014).

Ibrahim and her family have moved to her husband's home state of New Hampshire in the United States, where his family was looking forward to their arrival (*BBC News*, 2014; Leins, 2014).

Discussion Questions:

1. Do you believe that Meriam Ibrahim deserved the death sentence because she left Islam and married a Christian man? Please explain.
2. Do you believe it is appropriate for governments to decide what is morally correct on matters pertaining to religious freedoms? Please explain.
3. Do you believe that governments should have the power to impose the death penalty on citizens who are not behaving according to moral norms of the land? Why?
4. If countries have the right to impose the death penalty for morally objectionable behavior, where does this right end? Who gets to decide what it means to behave in a morally objectionable manner?

References

Abramson, J. (1975). *The invincible woman: Discrimination in the academic profession.* London: Jossey-Bass.

BBC News. (2014, August 1). Sudan 'apostasy' woman Meriam Ibrahim arrives in US. *BBC News.* Retrieved from http://www.bbc.com/news/world-us-canada-28596412

Beaver, W. (1995). Let's stop diversity training and start managing for diversity. *Industrial Management, 37,* 7–9.

Bell, M. P., Connerley, M. L., & Cocchiara, F. (2009). The case for mandatory diversity education. *Academy of Management Learning & Education, 8*(4), 597–609.

Bezrukova, K., Jehn, K. A., & Spell, C. S. (2012). Reviewing diversity training: Where we have been and where we should go. *Academy of Management Learning & Education, 11*(2), 207–227.

Bradford, D. L., & Cohen, A. R. (1984). *Managing for excellence.* New York: John Wiley & Sons.

Brewer, M. B., & Brown, R. J. (1998). Intergroup relations. In D. T. Gilbert, S. T. Fiske, & G. Lindzey (Eds.), *The handbook of social psychology* (4th ed., Vol. 2, pp. 554–594). New York: McGraw-Hill.

Briggs, T. E. (2002). *Diversity training: Intended and unintended consequences* (Unpublished doctoral dissertation). Northern Illinois University, DeKalb, IL.

Chrobot-Mason, D. (2004). Managing racial differences: The role of majority managers' ethnic identity development on minority employee perceptions of support. *Group & Organization Management, 29*(1), 5–31.

Chung, J., & Monroe, G. S. (2003). Exploring social desirability bias. *Journal of Business Ethics, 44*(4), 291–302.

Cox, T. (1994). *Cultural diversity in organizations: Theory, research, and practice*. San Francisco, CA: Berrett-Koehler.

Cox, T., & Blake, S. (1991). Managing cultural diversity: Implications for organizational competitiveness. *Academy of Management Executive, 5*(3), 45–56.

Dellasega, C. (2005). *Mean girls grown up: Adult women who are still queen bees, middle bees, and afraid-to-bees*. Hoboken, NJ: John Wiley & Sons.

Feagin, J. R., & O'Brien, E. (2003). *White men on race: Power, privilege, and the shaping of cultural consciousness*. Boston, MA: Beacon Press.

Galen, N., & Palmer, A. T. (1994, January 31). White, male, and worried. *Business Week*, 50–55.

Gilliland, S. W., & Gilliland, C. K. (2001). An organizational justice analysis of diversity training. In S. W. Gilliland, D. Steiner, & D. P. Skarlicki (Eds.), *Theoretical and cultural perspectives on organizational justice* (pp. 139–160). Greenwich: Information.

Gini, A. (2001). *My job myself: Work and the creation of the modern individual*. London: Routledge.

Gonzalez, J. A., & Denisi, A. S. (2009). Cross-level effects of demography and diversity climate on organizational attachment and firm effectiveness. *Journal of Organizational Behavior, 30*(1), 21–40.

Holladay, C. L., & Quinones, M. A. (2008). The influence of training focus and trainer characteristics on diversity training effectiveness. *Academy of Management Learning and Education, 7*, 343–354.

Holvino, E., Ferdman, B. M., & Merrill-Sands, D. (2004). Creating and sustaining diversity and inclusion in organizations: Strategies and approaches. In M. S. Stockdal & F. J. Crosby (Eds.), *The psychology and management of workplace diversity* (pp. 245–276). Malden, MA: Blackwell.

Jayne, M. E., & Dipboye, R. L. (2004). Leveraging diversity to improve business performance: Research findings and recommendations for organizations. *Human Resource Management, 43*(4), 409–424.

Kaiser, C. R., Major, B., Jurcevic, I., Dover, T. L., Brady, L. M., & Shapiro, J. R. (2013). Presumed fair: Ironic effects of organizational diversity structures. *Journal of Personality and Social Psychology, 104*(3), 504.

Kalev, A., Dobbin, F., & Kelly, E. (2006). Best practices or best guesses? Assessing the efficacy of corporate affirmative action and diversity policies. *American Sociological Review, 71*(4), 589–617.

Kalinoski, Z. T., Steele-Johnson, D., Peyton, E. J., Leas, K. A., Steinke, J., & Bowling, N. A. (2013). A meta-analytic evaluation of diversity training outcomes. *Journal of Organizational Behavior, 34*(8), 1076–1104.

Kaplan, D. M. (2006). Can diversity training discriminate? Backlash to lesbian, gay, and bisexual diversity initiatives. *Employee Responsibilities and Rights Journal, 18*(1), 61–72.

Kossek, E. E., & Zonia, S. C. (1993). Assessing diversity climate: A field study of reactions to employer efforts to promote diversity. *Journal of Organizational Behavior, 14*, 61–81.

Kulik, C. T., Pepper, M. B., Roberson, L., & Parker, S. K. (2007). The rich get richer: Predicting participation in voluntary diversity training. *Journal of Organizational Behavior, 28*(6), 753–769.

Kulik, C. T., & Roberson, L. (2008). Diversity initiative effectiveness: What organizations can (and cannot) expect from diversity recruitment, diversity training, and formal mentoring programs. In A. P. Brief (Ed.), *Diversity at work* (pp. 265–317). Cambridge: Cambridge University Press.

Lankau, M. J., Riordan, C. M., & Thomas, C. H. (2005). The effects of similarity and liking in formal relationships between mentors and protégés. *Journal of Vocational Behavior*, 67(2), 252–265.

Law, D. Y. (1998). *An evaluation of a cultural diversity training program* (Dissertation). Auburn University, Auburn, AL.

Leins, C. (2014, July 24). After death sentence in Sudan, Christian woman meets Pope. *US News*. Retrieved from http://www.usnews.com/news/newsgram/articles/2014/07/24/christian-woman-meriam-ibrahim-escapes-death-sentence-in-sudan-meets-pope

MacDonald, H. (1993, July). The diversity industry. *New Republic*, 2, 22–25.

Mann, J. (2017). Women Traveling in Saudi Arabia. *USA Today*. Retrieved from http://traveltips.usatoday.com/women-traveling-saudi-arabia-43269.html

McCombe, T. (2015, August 28). What to wear in Saudi Arabia as a business woman. LinkedIn. Retrieved from https://www.linkedin.com/pulse/what-wear-saudi-arabia-business-woman-tamara-mccombe

McDonald, M. L., & Westphal, J. D. (2013). Access denied: Low mentoring of women and minority first-time directors and its negative effects on appointments to additional boards. *Academy of Management Journal*, 56(4), 1169–1198.

McKay, P. F., Avery, D. R., Liao, H., & Morris, M. A. (2011). Does diversity climate lead to customer satisfaction? It depends on the service climate and business unit demography. *Organization Science*, 22, 788–803.

McKay, P. F., Avery, D. R., & Morris, M. A. (2008). Mean racial-ethnic differences in employee sales performance: The moderating role of diversity climate. *Personnel Psychology*, 61(2), 349–374.

McKay, P. F., Avery, D. R., & Morris, M. A. (2009). A tale of two climates: Diversity climate from subordinates' and managers' perspectives and their role in store unit sales performance. *Personnel Psychology*, 62, 767–791.

McKay, P. F., Avery, D. R., Tonidandel, S., Morris, M. A., Hernandez, M., & Hebl, M. R. (2007). Racial differences in employee retention: Are diversity climate perceptions the key? *Personnel Psychology*, 60(1), 35–62.

Mobley, M., & Payne, T. (1992). Backlash! The challenge to diversity training. *Training & Development*, 46, 45–53.

Mor Barak, M. E., Cherin, D., & Berkman, S. (1998). Organizational and personal dimensions in diversity climate. *Journal of Applied Behavior Science*, 34, 82–104.

Murray, K. (1993, August 1). The unfortunate side effects of diversity training. *New York Times*, Section 3, p. 5.Neville, H., & Furlong, M. (1994). The impact of participation in a cultural awareness program on the racial attitudes and social behaviors of first-year college students. *Journal of College Student Development*, 35, 371–377.

Noe, R. A. (1988). Women and mentoring: A review and research agenda. *Academy of Management Review*, 13(1), 65–78.

Pendry, L. F., Driscoll, D. M., & Field, S. C. (2007). Diversity training: Putting theory into practice. *Journal of Occupational and Organizational Psychology*, 80(1), 27–50.

Pettigrew, T. F., & Tropp, L. R. (2006). A meta-analytic test of intergroup contact theory. *Journal of Personality and Social Psychology*, 90, 751–783.

Pink Dot. (2017). About Pink Dot SG. Retrieved from http://pinkdot.sg/about-pink-dot/

Podsiadlowski, A., Gröschke, D., Kogler, M., Springer, C., & van der Zee, K. (2013). Managing a culturally diverse workforce: Diversity perspectives in organizations. *International Journal of Intercultural Relations*, 37, 159–175.

Povoledo, E. (2014, July 24). Spared Sudanese Christian woman meets Pope in Rome. *New York Times*. Retrieved from http://www.nytimes.com/2014/07/25/world/europe/sudan-christian-woman-spared-death-sentence-meets-pope-in-rome-.html?_r=0

Probst, T. M. (2003). Changing attitudes over time: Assessing the effectiveness of a workplace diversity course. *Teaching of Psychology, 30*, 236–239.

Pruegger, V. J., & Rogers, T. B. (1994). Cross-cultural sensitivity training: Methods and assessment. *International Journal of Intercultural Relations, 18*, 369–387.

Roberson, L., Kulik, C. T., & Pepper, M. B. (2001). Designing effective diversity training: Influence of group composition and trainee experience. *Journal of Organizational Behavior, 22*, 871–885.

Rynes, S., & Rosen, B. (1995). A field survey of factors affecting the adoption and perceived success of diversity training. *Personnel Psychology, 48*, 247–270.

Sanchez, J. I., & Medkik, N. (2004). The effects of diversity awareness training on differential treatment. *Group & Organization Management, 29*(4), 517–536.

Sharkey, J. (2015, February 2). Businesswomen navigate traditions in Saudi Arabia. *New York Times*. Retrieved from http://www.nytimes.com/2015/02/03/business/international/businesswomen-navigate-traditions-in-saudi-arabia.html?_r=0

Shen, R. (2016). Singapore's 'Pink Dot' LGBT Rights Rally Sees Record Turnout. *Huffington Post*. http://www.huffingtonpost.com/2015/06/13/singapore-pink-dot-gay-_n_7576136.html

Sherif, M. (1958). Superordinate goals in the reduction of intergroup conflict. *American Journal of Sociology, 63*, 349–356.

Shirts, R. G. (1977). *Bafá Bafá: A cross cultural simulation*. Del Mar, CA: Simulation Training Systems.

Staines, G., Travis, C., & Jayerante, T. E. (1973). The queen bee syndrome. *Psychology Today, 7*, 55–60.

Stevens, F. G., Plaut, V. C., & Sanchez-Burks, J. (2008). Unlocking the benefits of diversity all-inclusive multiculturalism and positive organizational change. *Journal of Applied Behavioral Science, 44*(1), 116–133.

Thomas, D. A., & Ely, R. J. (1996). Making differences matter: A new paradigm for managing diversity. *Harvard Business Review, 74*(5), 79.

Todd, A. R., Hanko, K., Galinsky, A. D., & Mussweiler, T. (2010). When focusing on differences leads to similar perspectives. *Psychological Science, 22*, 134–141.

Triana, M. D. C., García, M. F., & Colella, A. (2010). Managing diversity: How organizational efforts to support diversity moderate the effects of perceived racial discrimination on affective commitment. *Personnel Psychology, 63*(4), 817–843.

Triandis, H. C., Kurowski, L. L., & Gelfand, M. J. (1994). Workplace diversity. In H. C. Triandis, M. D. Dunnette, & L. M. Hough (Eds.), *Handbook of industrial and organizational psychology* (pp. 769–827). Palo Alto, CA: Consulting Psychologists Press.

U.S. Department of State. (2017). Saudi Arabia: Quick Facts. U.S. Passports & International Travel. Retrieved from https://travel.state.gov/content/passports/en/country/saudi-arabia.html

Vorauer, J. D., Gagnon, A., & Sasaki, S. J. (2009). Salient intergroup ideology and intergroup interaction. *Psychological Science, 20*(7), 838–845.

Wong, T. (2014, June 14). Singapore dilemma: When diversity policy meets local law. *BBC News*. Retrieved from http://www.bbc.com/news/world-asia-27584565

Wright, P., Ferris, S. P., Hiller, J. S., & Kroll, M. (1995). Competitiveness through management of diversity: Effects on stock price valuation. *Academy of Management Journal, 38*(1), 272–287.

sixteen
Conclusion

Diversity in organizations is increasing, and it presents many opportunities that the world's largest corporations are openly embracing. By 2050 there will be no majority racial group in the United States (Cárdenas, Ajinkya, & Léger, 2011), and according to a 2015 PricewaterhouseCoopers survey of 1,322 CEOs in 77 countries, "diversity and inclusion is no longer seen as a soft issue. It's now a core component of competitiveness—and most CEOs (77%) have, or intend to adopt a strategy that promotes it" (PricewaterhouseCoopers, 2015).

As nations and organizations become more diverse and both global diplomatic efforts and business practices advance with globalization of commerce, diversity and inclusion are more important than ever. Diverse teams and organizations have tremendous potential, and diverse teams are known to produce innovative solutions to complex problems. When diverse teams are managed well and value diversity, they can clearly excel.

Diversity can also present challenges such as differences of opinion, conflict, fear, and discrimination. When people fear change or simply do not see the value in change, perhaps feeling that they will be left behind as part of the change, they sometimes rely on practices and policies that have worked in the past to slow the pace of change. According to Betts (2016), this was recently observed with the Brexit vote, whereby the British voted to separate from the European Union. Betts (2016) explains that the vote split along "lines of age, education, class, and geography." People who did not see a benefit to globalization and immigration were more likely to vote to leave the European Union, which is why it is important to be mindful of how all groups are impacted by and can share in the benefit of globalization (Betts, 2016).

Despite the challenges of managing diversity and being inclusive, there are many recent examples of change whereby people have had opportunities they never would have dreamed possible in decades past. In 2016, London elected its first Muslim mayor, Sadiq Khan (*BBC News*, 2016). The U.S. military leadership has become more diverse as women and members of the LGBT community are being promoted to leadership positions. For example, Air Force general Lori Robinson became the first woman to lead a major military combatant command, including the United States Northern Command and the North American Aerospace Defense Command (Lamothe, 2016). Also, Eric Fanning was nominated by President Obama and confirmed by the U.S. Senate, becoming the first openly gay Army secretary in the United States (National Public Radio, 2016a). In Asian, Taiwan inaugurated President Tsai Ing-wen, its first female president (National Public Radio, 2016b). Finally, in 2016, Theresa May became the British prime minister (McKenzie & McLaughlin, 2016), and she is the second woman to hold this office, following the footsteps of Margaret Thatcher.

Part of embracing diversity also means acknowledging when one has not been inclusive in the past and celebrating those who led the way toward inclusion and civil rights. In 2016, the U.S. Treasury secretary announced that for the first time, U.S. currency will feature prominent leaders of the women's rights and civil rights movements as well as abolitionists who fought to end slavery. For example, Harriett Tubman, a former slave and abolitionist who helped rescue slaves in the late 1800s, will appear on the $20 bill. Also, five female leaders of the women's rights movement which culminated in the **19th Amendment to the Constitution** (ratified in 1920) granting women the right to vote will appear on the back of the $10 bill. These women are: Sojourner Truth, Lucretia Mott, Susan B. Anthony, Alice Paul, and Elizabeth Cady Stanton. The back of the $5 bill will feature Eleanor Roosevelt (former first lady of the United States and civil rights advocate), Reverend Dr. Martin Luther King Jr. (a prominent civil rights leader who delivered the famous "I Have a Dream Speech" referenced in Chapter 4), and Marian Anderson (an African-American classical singer who was denied access to perform in some prestigious venues because of her race) (Calmes, 2016). These changes help acknowledge the racism and sexism which have been present in United States history and honor those whose hard-fought battles paved the way for legal change and a more inclusive society.

Perhaps one of the most visible examples of a diverse team worldwide is the United Nations. Under the leadership of Secretary-General Ban Ki-moon of South Korea, this organization brings together a coalition of many nations worldwide to advocate for peace and human rights, including the dignity of the most poor and vulnerable people in the world. Although diplomatic efforts take time and do not always succeed, the persistent leadership of the United Nations over the past decades has applied political pressure and generated coalitions to shine light on problems, prevent or diminish abuse, build consensus around important global issues, and improve people's lives throughout the world.

These are but a few examples of what can be achieved through diversity in organizations.

References

BBC News. (2016, May 7). Elections: Labour's Sadiq Khan elected London mayor. Retrieved from http://www.bbc.com/news/election-2016-36232392

Betts, A. (2016). Why Brexit happened—and what to do next. *Ted Talks.* Retrieved from http://www.ted.com/talks/alexander_betts_why_brexit_happened_and_what_to_do_next

Calmes, J. (2016, April 20). Harriet Tubman ousts Andrew Jackson in change for a $20. *New York Times.* Retrieved from http://www.nytimes.com/2016/04/21/us/women-currency-treasury-harriet-tubman.html?_r=0

Cárdenas, V., Ajinkya, J., & Léger, D. G. (2011). Progress 2050. New ideas for a diverse American. Center for American Progress. Retrieved from https://cdn.americanprogress.org/wp-content/uploads/issues/2011/10/pdf/progress_2050.pdf

Lamothe, D. (2016, May 13). Air Force Gen. Lori Robinson becomes first woman ever to lead U.S. combatant command. *Washington Post.* Retrieved from https://www.washingtonpost.com/news/checkpoint/wp/2016/05/13/air-force-gen-lori-robinson-becomes-first-woman-ever-to-lead-u-s-combatant-command/

McKenzie, S., & McLaughlin, E. C. (2016, July 14). Theresa May becomes new British Prime Minister. *CNN.* Retrieved from http://www.cnn.com/2016/07/13/europe/theresa-may-david-cameron-british-prime-minister/

National Public Radio. (2016a, May 17). Senate confirms Eric Fanning, first openly gay leader of military service. Retrieved from http://www.npr.org/sections/thetwo-way/2016/05/17/478456199/senate-confirms-eric-fanning-first-openly-gay-leader-of-military-service

National Public Radio. (2016b, May 20). Taiwan inaugurates first female president. Retrieved from http://www.npr.org/sections/thetwo-way/2016/05/20/478813167/taiwan-inaugurates-first-female-president

PricewaterhouseCoopers. (2015). 18th annual global CEO survey. Retrieved from http://www.pwc.com/gx/en/ceo-agenda/ceosurvey/2015/download.html

Glossary

Access-and-legitimacy paradigm   a diversity management approach that accepts differences across demographic groups but considers diversity as a source of business opportunity.

Acculturation   is a broader term than assimilation and can include assimilation as well as resistance to change by both the dominant and non-dominant group and the creation of new cultural forms as the groups interact and blend.

Acts committed because of age and other reasons   as specified in the Age Discrimination Act of 2004, refers to discriminating against a person due to his or her age, due to the characteristics that generally pertain to individuals of that age, or on the basis of traits generally imputed to persons of a specific age group.

Active aging   is "the process for optimizing opportunities for health, participation, and security in order to enhance quality of life as people age. This definition includes continuing activity in the labour force" (European Network of Heads of PES, 2011, p. 2).

Active or problem-focused coping   emphasizes ways of resolving a particular problem; is an effective method to buffer the harmful effects of perceived discrimination.

Adaptive coping   represents ways of dealing with problems, including discrimination, in a way that buffers the harmful effects of the problem experienced for the individual.

Adverse impact   occurs when an organization uses a selection mechanism which inadvertently discriminates against members of protected classes, including women and racial minorities.

Affective learning refers to changes in attitudes toward diversity and changes in trainees' self-efficacy to perform the topics discussed in diversity training.

Affirmative action is a concept that is known throughout the world. It is also sometimes referred to as positive action. Affirmative action programs are typically aimed at historically disadvantaged groups that have been the target of discrimination. The aim of such programs is to rectify injustices and to restore balance.

Age Discrimination in Employment Act of 1967 (ADEA) is a U.S. law that forbids employment discrimination against employees 40 years of age or older.

Age discrimination, or ageism, is defined as treating people in a less desirable manner and denying them opportunities on the basis of their age.

Age harassment means to be treated in a way that is humiliating or offensive because of one's age group.

Age norms are informal expectations about the age groups that should occupy various jobs. The older, more experienced people should typically manage the younger, less experienced ones.

Age stereotypes are over-generalizations about individuals based on the age group to which they belong.

Age victimization means treating someone less favorably because he or she has either complained about age discrimination or has aided someone else in doing so.

AIDS stands for acquired immunodeficiency syndrome.

Allah is the name by which Muslims refer to God.

Ally is a heterosexual person or a cisgender person who supports the rights of the LGBT community.

Americans with Disabilities Act of 1990 (ADA) is a U.S. law that prohibits employment discrimination against individuals with a life-limiting disability. The law describes disabilities as conditions that limit major life functions such as walking, sitting, breathing, speaking, and thinking, among others.

Anti-Semitism is prejudice, hatred, and discrimination against Jews.

Asexual people have a sexual orientation characterized by a lack of sexual attraction or desire for a sexual partner.

Assimilation is the process of becoming more like the majority in the new host country.

Atheists do not believe in God.

Ātman is an inner self or soul in Hinduism.

Aversive racism theory explains that people have deep-seated prejudice but feel it is wrong to have and express such feelings about other groups.

Awareness training   attempts to enable employees to become aware of their stereotypes and processes underlying prejudice and discrimination. The goal is to bring about behavioral changes based on self-awareness.

Behavioral learning   refers to the development of trainees' skills as a result of diversity training.

Bhakti   means devotion to and love for a divinity.

Biases   are tendencies, inclinations, or feelings, particularly ones that are preconceived and lack reasoning; they are often implicitly, or subconsciously, driven.

Bible   is the name of the holy book for Christians.

Bisexual   refers to people who are attracted to individuals of both male and female sexes.

Bodhi   is a Buddhist term that means "awakening" and a state of enlightenment where one understands the nature of things.

Brahman   refers to a universal spirit in Hinduism.

Bridge employment   refers to workers who have retired from long-term positions but are still engaged in the workforce.

Brown v. the Board of Education of Topeka (1955)   is the Supreme Court case that banned the "separate but equal" educational system that existed in the United States.

Categorization-elaboration model   proposes that biases stemming from categorization effects that take place in a diverse team may impede groups in using informational resources. However, that same team diversity may introduce a process of group information elaboration, meaning that there is an information exchange, discussion, and integration of task-relevant information and perspectives which ultimately help the team perform better.

Caucasian   is often used to refer to White people in general. The definition of Caucasian refers to the inhabitants of Caucasus, a region of Southeastern Europe between the Black and Caspian Seas which is divided by the Caucasus Mountains. This includes a region roughly spanning from southern Russia (northern boundary) to Turkey (southern boundary) and the land in between those boundaries bounded by the Caspian Sea on the east and the Black Sea on the west. The term "Caucasian" is also broadly used to refer to people native to Europe, North Africa, and Southwest Asia, particularly people of European descent who have light skin pigment.

Cisgender   refers to people whose gender identity aligns with the gender assigned to them at birth.

Civil Rights Act of 1964   is major legislation in the United States which had an important and positive impact on increasing equal opportunity for various groups in society and in organizations.

Civil Rights Act of 1991   strengthened civil rights antidiscrimination legislation in the United States and provided the possibility of punitive damages (i.e., financial compensation paid as a penalty) for employees whose employers were found guilty of discriminating against them.

Cognitive learning   refers to the extent to which trainees acquire knowledge in diversity training.

Colorblind approach   is a diversity practice which attempts to ignore differences between groups.

Consumption   refers to the concern younger individuals have that older people may be using up more than their fair share of government and social resources.

Contact hypothesis   proposes that the more contact people from different groups have with one another over time, the more the tensions between those groups will subside as they begin to know and understand one another better.

Cook v. State of Rhode Island Department of Mental Health   is a landmark case in the United States where a court considered, for the first time, an obesity-related perceived discrimination claim covered under the Americans with Disabilities Act (ADA) or Rehabilitation Act of 1973 (RHA).

Correlation   is the linear relationship between two variables.

Cost argument   means that as organizations become more diverse, those that are able to integrate diversity more smoothly will realize cost advantages.

Creativity argument   suggests that a diversity of opinions in a decision-making process should de-emphasize conforming to norms of the past and should spur creativity.

Critical race theory   has several tenets. One is that racism in the United States is endemic and an ordinary occurrence of people of color because it is embedded in the fabric of American society. Another tenet is that race is a category that is socially constructed based on a contrived system of categorizing people according to observable characteristics. The theory also maintains that dominant groups within society can racialize people of other groups in different ways at different times. The theory further describes that progressive change around race will occur only when the interests of the powerful White majority happen to converge with those of the racially oppressed.

Deep-level diversity   refers to attributes that are not immediately observable such as attitudes, values, and personality.

Demobilization   is defined as discharging active combatants from the armed forces.

Dharma   refers to the idea that one must live in accordance with individual ethics, obligations, and one's place in the world and must perform the proper duties of one's particular caste.

Dhyana   is a Buddhist term that refers to a cultivated state of mind which leads to perfect awareness.

Direct discrimination   is where an employer treats someone less favorably than they do another person of a different demographic group (e.g., age).

Disability   is defined by the Americans with Disabilities Act as "a physical or mental impairment that substantially limits one or more major life activities, a person who has a history or record of such impairment, or a person who is perceived by others as having such an impairment."

Disarmament   is defined as collecting, controlling, and/or disposing of light and heavy weapons.

Discrimination   is to treat someone in a way that is less desirable from the way one would normally treat others because of their group membership.

Discrimination after a relationship has come to an end   means that an individual is treated less favorably or harassed because he or she has left the employer.

Discrimination-and-fairness paradigm   is a diversity management approach that is concerned with equal opportunity and fairness in recruitment for all demographic groups, observing legal and political guidelines. This paradigm is a color- and gender-blind approach that does not tolerate differences among groups.

Discrimination (Employment and Occupation) Convention, 1958 (No. 111)   prohibited discrimination on the basis of sexual orientation.

Discrimination for failing to carry out an age discriminatory instruction   is when people are treated less favorably for refusing to do something that would be against the age discrimination law. This is a tenet of the Australian 2004 Age Discrimination Act.

Disparate impact   happens when a selection method results in disproportionately ruling out some groups of candidates more so than others.

Disparate treatment   is a situation of blatant discrimination which shows intent to keep certain groups of people from joining or advancing within an organization.

Diversity   is defined as "the distribution of differences among the members of a unit with respect to a common attribute X" (Harrison & Klein, 2007, p. 1200). Diversity can be any difference between the members of a group on any given dimension. Diversity can be real, or it can be perceived by the members of the team. Diversity is a group characteristic that reflects the degree to which there are objective and/or subjective differences among group members.

Diversity as disparity   refers to differences in status or power. This could reflect the concentration of resources including status, pay, and the prestige of assignments among team members. It can create a situation where some team members feel more valued than others.

Diversity as separation   refers to differences on a particular attribute such as attitudes, beliefs, and values. Separation in a team will likely increase conflict, but it should also produce better decisions due to the increase in knowledge from various perspectives.

Diversity as variety   refers to differences in knowledge, life experience, and information among team members. Examples include different professional backgrounds, functional areas, and expertise.

Diversity climate   refers to "the degree to which a firm advocates fair human resource policies and socially integrates underrepresented employees" (McKay et al., 2008, p. 352), capturing the quality of diversity management.

Diversity management   is defined as "planning and implementing organizational systems and practices to manage people so that the potential advantages of diversity are maximized while its potential disadvantages are minimized" (Cox, 1994, p. 11). Diversity management includes not only attracting and retaining a diverse workforce but also fostering an inclusive environment so that employees, regardless of their backgrounds, can work together toward organizational objectives.

Diversity training   is defined as programs intended to facilitate positive intergroup interactions, reduce prejudice and discrimination, and enhance the skills, knowledge, and motivation of people to interact with diverse others.

Double jeopardy   represents the intersection of race and sex and the disadvantages that women of color can face because of both their sex and racial/ethnic group membership.

Dyadic   refers to the number two, and in this context, a relationship of two typically means a relationship between a supervisor and a subordinate.

Emotion-focused coping   involves eating or using alcohol or drugs to remove the immediate negative mood effects of stressors such as discrimination; however, it may lead to longer-term problems including addiction or obesity.

Employment Equality Act of 1998   is an Irish disability law which requires reasonable accommodations for the needs of disabled persons. The act explicitly states that "a person who has a disability shall not be regarded as other than fully competent to undertake, and fully capable of undertaking, any duties if, with the assistance of special treatment or facilities, such person would be fully competent to undertake, and be fully capable of undertaking, those duties" (ISB, 2016).

Employment Equity Act of 1998   is South Africa's disability law which requires modifications to the job or the working environment to enable a person from a designated group to participate and advance in employment.

Equal Pay Act   is a U.S. law that requires equal pay for men and women performing similar jobs.

Essential functions   of a job are the functions that are critical for the existence of the job, and applicants must be able to carry out these functions with or without accommodation to be considered qualified. This term is used in the Americans with Disabilities Act in the United States.

Ethnicity   refers to a social group that shares characteristics such as language, religion, and culture.

Executive Order 9066   is the 1942 executive order signed by President Roosevelt which required that all Americans of Japanese descent be moved into internment camps that were often located in remote, desert-like places of the United States, including Arizona. This executive order encompassed everyone who had at least one-eighth Japanese ancestry and accounted for over 90% of Japanese-Americans at the time.

Executive Order 11246 (Equal Employment Opportunity)   is a U.S. law enacted in 1965 which prohibits discrimination among federal contractors with contracts of more than $10,000. President Obama updated it in 2014 to include sexual orientation and gender identity in addition to the other categories previously covered (race, color, religion, sex, and national origin).

Executive Order 11478 (Equal Employment Opportunity in the Federal Government)   is a U.S. law enacted in 1998 which prohibits discrimination in federal civilian workplaces on the basis of sexual orientation but does not extend to other employers across the country. The law was updated in 2014 by President Obama to include both sexual orientation and gender identity instead of only sexual orientation.

Expectation-states theory   maintains that status hierarchy is formed among members of a group or organization and that the status hierarchy is driven by the interactants' expectations about the likely usefulness of each other person's contributions to their shared goals. These expectations are associated with the demographic characteristics of the people involved in the group.

Family responsibility discrimination   is discrimination that occurs on the basis of employee responsibilities to care for family members, such as their children, disabled family members, and elderly parents.

Faultlines   are hypothetical dividing lines which divide a group into subgroups based on the alignment of team members' attributes such as gender and race, and they are often characterized by their strength or how homogeneous these subgroups are.

Feminism   is a term which means individuals identify with being pro-women's rights and may also be engaged in women's rights activism.

Gay   is a term used to refer to men who are romantically/sexually attracted to other men.

Gender egalitarianism   is a society's beliefs about whether a person's gender should determine the roles he or she plays in the home, in business, and in the community. The less a society believes that gender should drive a person's roles, the more egalitarian the society.

Gender identity   refers to whether a person identifies as being of male or female gender.

Gendered race   is the notion that some racial groups tend to be associated with masculine or feminine traits.

Genetic information   refers to data about an individual's genetic tests or those of that individual's family members, in addition to information about the person's family medical history and manifestation of a disease or disorder in an individual's family members.

Glass ceiling   is the invisible but strong barrier which keeps women from ascending to the top layers of organizational management.

Glass cliff   theory predicts that women and minorities are more likely to be promoted to leadership positions in organizations that are having a crisis or are struggling and at risk of failure.

Glass escalator   effect is a phenomenon whereby men in traditionally female (pink-collar) occupations tend to get promoted more quickly than their equally qualified female peers.

Global Gender Gap Report for 2015   a report produced by the World Economic Forum which assesses opportunity and achievement of men and women in countries worldwide; shows inequities between men and women in almost every country.

Gurus   are masters of the Hindu faith.

Henotheistic   refers to religions that believe there is one ultimate god or goddess but that there are also many other deities which can be manifestations of the supreme god.

Henri Tajfel   is one of the most influential researchers in the study of group differences. He was instrumental in developing self-categorization/social categorization theory.

Heterosexism   is defined as attitudes or actions that stigmatize or belittle people who are not heterosexual.

Heterosexuality   refers to people whose primary attraction is to individuals of the opposite sex.

Highly job-related diversity   involves diversity attributes that refer to the knowledge, experience, education, and tenure needed for the task to be performed.

Hijra   refers to the Prophet Muhammad's emigration from Mecca to Medina.

Hispanic/Latino   refers to an ethnic group whose roots originate from Spanish-speaking countries, particularly those from Latin America. Hispanics/Latinos may be of any race.

HIV   stands for human immunodeficiency virus. HIV is the virus that causes AIDS.

Homophobia   is defined as "fear, hatred, or intolerance of lesbians and gay men or any behavior that falls outside of traditional gender roles" (Griffin & Harro, 1997, p. 146).

Homosexuality   refers to people whose primary attraction is to those of their same sex. According to the American Psychological Association, this is not a preferred term when referring to members of the LGBT community. One should use the correct term instead (e.g., gay, lesbian).

Human Rights Campaign   (HRC) is an organization that works for LGBT rights by documenting and maintaining extensive information on the current situation for members of the LGBT community, including injustices in employment or in society at large faced by members of the LGBT community.

Identity   represents one's sense of self; people may identify with being members of certain groups or having certain qualities or beliefs which shape who they are as a person.

Identity management strategies   (e.g., identity switching and identity redefinition) are short-term strategies that help individuals cope with discrimination.

ILO conventions No. 1 and No. 30   were held with the goal of reducing the negative impact of excessive work hours on worker lives.

ILO Forty Hour Week Convention No. 47   was held in 1935 to establish the possibility of a 40-hour week.

ILO Global Wage Report for 2014/2015   reported on the status of migrant workers, including unexplained differences in pay and the wage gaps between migrant workers and domestic workers. The ILO statisticians decompose wage gaps in two parts, explained portions and unexplained portions. The explained part takes into account experience, education, occupation, economic activity, location, and hours worked. The unexplained portion, or the wage penalty, is what remains after accounting for the explained portion.

ILO Maternity Protection Convention of 2000 (no. 183)   is the most recent convention where a major document was adopted for the benefit of working mothers and their children.

In the closet   refers to LGBT community members who conceal their sexual identity in order to avoid the stigma and discrimination that can come with identifying themselves as members of the LGBT community.

Inclusion   is a state whereby organizations welcome minority group members as well as majority group members and foster an environment that allows them to bring their full selves to work and both feel equal to others and have equal opportunity to excel and advance relative to others in the organization.

Incongruent   means opposite to something, particularly opposite to one's expectations based on the norms or stereotypes applied in that situation.

Indian Removal Act of 1830   is a U.S. law signed by President Andrew Jackson enforcing the relocation of several American Indian tribes, including the Cherokee, Muskogee, Seminole, Chickasaw, and Choctaw tribes, by force, to an area west of the Mississippi River designated Indian Territory.

Indirect discrimination   refers to using a practice which is applied to everyone but results in some groups having an advantage over others. For example, this term is used in the Australian Age Discrimination Law of 2004 and refers to instances when the discriminator imposes conditions, or requires practices that are not reasonable under the circumstances, or requires practices that are likely to disadvantage persons of some age groups relative to others.

Information-processing perspective   argues that any time there is task uncertainty, there is a greater amount of information which must be processed to accomplish a task and obtain good performance. A diverse workforce can help an organization meet information-processing demands and yield a competitive advantage by providing appropriate perspectives on cultural, institutional, and competitive environments.

In-group   refers to individuals who are similar to oneself.

Integrated Disarmament, Demobilization and Reintegration Standards (ILO, 2010)   are a plan developed by the United Nations to assist veterans after armed conflicts.

Intergroup bias   refers to attitudes or generalizations (often negative) which members of one group hold about members of another group.

International Labor Organization (ILO)   was established in 1919 as part of the Treaty of Versailles. It became a specialized agency of the United Nations in 1946. The ILO has 187 member countries as of the year 2016. The ILO brings together governments, employers, and worker representatives to set labor standards and create policies and programs to promote decent working conditions for men and women.

Intersectional invisibility   refers to individuals with multiple lower status identities being neglected because they are not prototypical of any of their identity groups.

Intersectionality   refers to an approach that simultaneously takes multiple categories of identity into account, such as gender, race, social class, and sexual orientation.

Intersex   is defined as a condition where a person is born with a sexual anatomy that does not fit the traditional definition of male or female.

Jihad   means an exertion or a struggle as one strives to realize the will of God, lead a life of virtue, and fulfill the mission of Islam.

Karma   is the notion of cause-and-effect, that good deeds eventually yield good consequences while bad deeds yield negative consequences.

Lack of fit model   is a common explanation for harsh reactions toward women who do not conform to their traditional gender role stereotypes. This theory predicts that people sense a mismatch between the target person's group stereotype and the person's actual behavior, which causes a reaction in the observer.

Learning-and-effectiveness   a diversity management paradigm which attempts to overcome the shortcomings of the discrimination-and-fairness paradigm and the access-and-legitimacy paradigm by promoting equal opportunity, acknowledging cultural differences, and recognizing the value in those differences. In doing so, firms would internalize differences among employees such that those firms would learn and grow because of employee diversity.

Lesbian   refers to women who are romantically/sexually attracted to other women.

Less job-related diversity   involves diversity attributes that refer to sex, race, age, and other characteristics which should not have any bearing on the task that is to be performed by the team.

LGBT   means lesbian, gay, bisexual, and transgender.

Major life activities   as described by the Americans with Disabilities Act include things such as walking, speaking, breathing, hearing, seeing, learning, working, and being able to take care of oneself, among many others.

Maldaptive coping   buffers the harmful effects of discrimination but may cause negative outcomes to the individual.

Marketing argument   suggests that diverse companies with a wealth of cultural information among employees will be able to better market their products in foreign markets as well as to domestic subgroups of the population.

Masculinity/femininity   refers to a cultural expectation of dominant gender role patterns such that men show more masculine behavior and women show more feminine behavior. In societies that value masculinity, men should be tough, assertive, and focused on material success, while women should be tender, modest, and concerned for quality of life. In countries where femininity is valued, both men and women are supposed to be tender, modest, and concerned with the quality of life.

Melting pot   is a metaphor to describe how a society develops, whereby people of different cultures, races, and religions are combined to create a diverse, multi-ethnic society.

Mental disability impairment   may include a psychological disorder, emotional or mental illnesses, and learning disabilities.

Meta-analysis   is a study that statistically aggregates the results of many other studies in order to estimate true population effects.

Migrant Workers (Supplementary Provisions) Convention of 1975 (No. 143) puts forth measures to combat illegal immigration as well as provisions for obligations to respect the human rights of migrant workers.

Migration for Employment Convention (Revised), 1949 (No. 97) requires members of ratifying states to facilitate international migration processes, provide free assistance and information for migrant workers, and prevent misleading propaganda related to immigration.

Minimum Age Convention of 1973 (No. 138) set a minimum employment age at 15 years (13 years for light work) and a minimum age of 18 years for hazardous work conditions (16 years under strict conditions).

Mobility impairment is associated with the loss of physical function, such as the inability to walk.

Modern racism theory and **modern sexism theory** are two theories which argue that people have deep-seated prejudice (on the basis of race and sex respectively) but nevertheless behave in socially desirable ways because they are aware that old-fashioned prejudice is socially unacceptable.

Monotheistic religions are those that believe in a single God.

Motivation to respond without prejudice is an internal motivation that some people have to respond without prejudice because they want to behave in a non-prejudiced way toward Black people and because they believe that using stereotypes against Black people is wrong.

Multiculturalism is a diversity practice that acknowledges and appreciates differences between different groups.

Muzafer Sherif is one of the most famous researchers to find social categorization effects. He developed realistic group conflict theory and found evidence that superordinate goals diminish intergroup conflict.

Nirvana is a state of liberation in which one's karma burns off and one is liberated from the cycle of life and death. The state of liberation is achieved after one has reached moral perfection.

Occupational Safety and Health (Dock Workers) Convention, 1979 (No. 152) makes provisions that stipulate safe access to the workplace, injury prevention training to employees, providing workers with protective equipment, maintaining adequate first aid equipment, and ensuring proper procedures are followed in case of an emergency.

Occupational segregation means there is an overrepresentation of women and minorities in the lowest paying jobs. Segregation occurs when members of one sex comprise 70% or more of an occupation.

Organizational citizenship behavior   is defined as discretionary behavior which is not part of one's formal job requirements but helps the functioning of the organization.

Out-group   refers to individuals who are dissimilar to oneself.

Passing (or to pass)   is a term used to refer to people who let others think they belong to a group when they in fact do not.

Personal value for diversity   is the belief that diverse viewpoints add value, that diversity is a business strategy, and that knowing more about diversity is helpful to make people more effective in their jobs.

Polytheistic   refers to religions that believe in multiple gods and goddesses.

Prajna   is a Buddhist term that means wisdom that results from moral and mental discipline and leads to nirvana.

Prejudice   is defined as an unfair negative attitude toward a social group or a person who is a member of that group.

Prime age   refers to an age group of employees who are the most preferred employees, specifically those between the ages of 25 and 35.

Privilege   refers to certain advantages the majority group experiences in daily life because society makes assumptions that their characteristics and/or their situation is the norm.

Problem-solving argument   explains that diverse teams should produce better decisions via a wider range of perspectives considered and a more thorough analysis of issues.

Prophet Muhammad   is God's messenger in the Islamic religion.

Queen bee syndrome   refers to women who have achieved success within the social structure and then endorse traditional sex roles and deny there is discrimination against women.

Queer   is a term that encompasses people who are gay, lesbian, bisexual, transgender, and intersex.

Qur'an   is the Muslim holy book in the Islamic religion.

Race   is a social category (as opposed to genetic or biological categories) of racial/ethnic background. This is consistent with race as defined by the U.S. government, which refers to social categories that encompass consideration of national origin and sociocultural groups.

Realistic group conflict theory   explains that there are scarce resources such as power, prestige, land, money, and other resources which create intergroup conflict.

Recategorization process   refers to accepting out-group individuals into one's in-group. This process may be achieved after the realization that there are commonalities among both parties.

Rehabilitation Act of 1973 (RHA)   is a U.S. law which prohibits employment discrimination against qualified individuals with disabilities by organizations that hold government contracts, receive federal grants, or are government agencies and departments.

Reincarnation   refers to the concept that a living being can begin a new life in a different body after death.

Reinsertion   is defined as the assistance offered to ex-combatants during the process of demobilization. Traditional reinsertion assistance covers the basic costs of food, clothes, medical services, and short-term training to help cover the basic needs of ex-combatants and their families. This reinsertion stage may last up to one year.

Reintegration   is a stage in the process of reintegrating soldiers into society where ex-combatants acquire civilian status and return to employment.

Relational demography theory   suggests that people compare their own demographic characteristics with those of their teammates to determine whether they are similar or different; those demographic similarities or differences then affect team communication, team processes, and team dynamics.

Religion   is defined as a set of beliefs about what people hold sacred. It is a way of seeing, behaving, and experiencing the world.

Reasonable accommodation   refers to an adjustment which an employer can make to enable a qualified person with a disability to perform the job without causing an undue hardship to the employer.

Resource-acquisition argument   proposes that companies with a good reputation for being inclusive and integrating diversity well will win the competition for the best talent.

Second shift   refers to all the extra work mothers do at home after they finish a full day of work for their employer.

Self-categorization theory or **social categorization theory**   maintains that people categorize themselves and others into in-groups (those who are similar to them) and out-groups (those who are different from them) based on surface-level characteristics (e.g., age, sex, and race). These categories then determine social inclusion/exclusion of others. Self-categorization theory has been termed the pessimistic view of diversity because demographic differences often have negative effects on group processes and outcomes.

Sexual orientation   refers to whom individuals are sexually/romantically attracted, and this could mean they are attracted to males, females, both, or neither.

Shramanas   are Buddhists who perform acts of austerity to achieve liberation and realize the essence of human life and consciousness.

Similarity-attraction hypothesis   states that people like others who are similar to themselves and gravitate toward those people. As a result, they generally have a better experience when they are with similar others.

Situational ambiguity   refers to a context that could have several root causes, thereby making it very difficult for the person on the receiving end of perceived discrimination to determine if or why the treatment occurred.

Skills training   in diversity training, this is designed to teach employees new skills that may be helpful in dealing with diversity issues such as communication and conflict management skills.

Social coping   is the act of reaching out to one's social support network for advice in order to resolve some matter that is causing one stress. Can be an effective method of reducing the effects of discrimination.

Social exchange   refers to a relationship between employees and their employers and is defined as confidence in the employer–employee relationship where if the employees work hard on behalf of the employer, the employer will reciprocate and provide benefits to the employees in the future.

Social support   refers to the network of people around individuals who can help them cope with life's challenges. Can be an effective method of reducing the effects of discrimination.

Social dominance theory   suggests that societies generate and sustain a trimorphic system (typically based on gender, age, and an arbitrary system of social values based on race, class, or religion) and that these systems are typically observed universally across the world. Additionally, the systems represent levels of social status.

Social dominance orientation   is defined as "the degree to which individuals desire and support a group-based hierarchy and the domination of 'inferior' groups by 'superior' groups" (Sidanius & Pratto, 1999, p. 48).

Social identity theory   describes the cognitive origins of group identification. Social identity is part of an individual's self-concept, and it derives from his/her knowledge of being a member of a social group. Because people typically attach a value or emotional meaning to the social groups to which they belong, there is a tendency to ascribe positive characteristics to those in the in-group and negative characteristics to those in the out-group.

Stained glass ceiling   is a term used to refer to the fact that women are often restricted to junior roles in the clergy compared to men.

Status construction theory   proposes that inequalities develop in the distribution of resources among the population. Levels of resources possessed becomes a meaningful distinction in the population such that people tend to develop sub-conscious associations about the level of resources, and potentially even the level of capabilities, of certain groups which are primed very quickly into the human mind when one sees members of various social groups.

Stereotypes   are defined as generalizations or beliefs about a particular group or its members which are unjustified because they reflect over-generalizations and factual errors as well as misattributions to other groups.

Sticky floor   is a situation where women tend to get stuck at the bottom of the organization (e.g., low pay, lower level positions).

Structured interviews   are interviews where interviewers ask the same questions of all candidates and evaluate the answers based on consistent, pre-determined criteria to provide a consistent interview experience and candidate evaluation.

Subconscious/implicit bias   is deeply embedded stereotypical information that can be stored in the human mind and triggered automatically from repeated expo-sure to stereotypes.

Succession   refers to older people making way for younger people to have politi-cal power and to determine how organizations and society should function.

Sunna   is a collection of the sayings, practices, and teachings of the Prophet Muhammad.

Superordinate goals   are goals that two different groups have in common which can reduce hostility and promote cooperation.

Surface-level diversity   refers to characteristics that are noticeable when you look at someone "on the surface." This includes things like sex, race, age, and weight.

Symbolic racism theory   maintains that prejudice against minority groups including African-Americans is driven by anti-Black emotions and political views.

Symbolic threat   refers to the majority group's concerns that immigrant groups will challenge their values or way of life.

System flexibility argument   states that companies adopting a multicultural approach to managing diversity will be less rigid and more fluid, which will allow them to better respond to environmental change.

Tanakh   is an acronym which refers to the division of the Bible of Judaism into the Torah (teachings), Nevi'im (books of the prophets, for example, Jeremiah, Eze-kiel, Amos, Hosea), and Ketuvim (writings, for example, First and Second Kings, Proverbs, Ecclesiastes, Job).

Theistic   is a term related to the belief in the existence of a god or multiple gods.

The Three Jewels, or The Three Refuges   are Buddha (the highest spiritual achievement that exists in humans), Dharma (the teachings of the Buddha which reveal the path to enlightenment), and Sangha (the community of those who have obtained enlightenment; used more broadly it refers to the community of Buddhist monks and nuns).

Threat rigidity   is a state of being where one feels threatened and therefore one's mental faculties narrow and one resorts to tried and tested ways of doing things to get by.

Title VII of the Civil Rights Act of 1964   is a major U.S. employment law which forbids employment discrimination on the basis of race, sex, religion, color, and national origin.

Tokenism   states that an individual whose demographic group comprises 15% or less of an organization's demographic will be highly visible and will have the potential to feel isolated or excluded.

Torah   is a holy book of Judaism. Also called the Pentateuch, it includes the first five books of the Hebrew Bible: Genesis, Exodus, Leviticus, Numbers, and Deuteronomy.

Transgender   refers to people who believe they were assigned the incorrect gender at birth. In other words, they were assigned to one gender at birth but identify as being of the other gender.

Transphobia   is the fear, hatred, or intolerance of transgender people.

Trinity   refers to the manifestation of God in three forms which are the Father, the Son, and the Holy Spirit.

Undue hardship   happens when an accommodation requires a significant expense or difficulty relative to the employer's size and financial resources. When this is the case in the United States, the employer does not have to provide the accommodation because it is not reasonable for them. They may instead consider providing a different accommodation which would not cause undue hardship if another alternative is available.

United Nations Convention on the Rights of Persons with Disabilities (CRPD),   adopted in 2006, "promotes the full integration of persons with disabilities in societies" (World Bank, 2015).

Value in diversity hypothesis   has been called the optimistic view of diversity. It proposes many ways in which diversity can create value for teams and how that value could overshadow any negative effects of team diversity, providing a competitive advantage.

Vietnam Era Veterans' Readjustment Assistance Act of 1974   is a U.S. law that was created to help veterans who served in a foreign war readjust to employment when they returned home.

White   is a term more commonly used in the United States both by researchers and by the U.S. government in its population reports to represent light-skinned people of primarily European descent.

Womanism   is a term that stems from work studying feminism. Womanism is defined as a commitment to fuse multiple identities and to combat multiple oppressions.

Work–family culture   is the shared assumptions, beliefs, and values about the extent to which an organization supports and values the integration of employees' work and family lives.

Worst Forms of Child Labor Convention of 1999 (No. 182)   defined a child as a person under the age of 18 and laid out rules which require the ratifying states to abolish the worst forms of child labor, including slavery, the sale or trafficking of children, debt bondage, forced labor, the use of children in armed conflicts, child prostitution or pornography, the use of children for trafficking drugs, and other activities that may be harmful to the health, safety, or morals of the child.

Yoga   refers to various practices through which humans can focus their bodily power to realize their true spiritual essence.

13th Amendment to the U.S. Constitution   was passed in 1864 and abolished slavery and involuntary servitude except as punishment for a crime. Slaves had been declared free by President Abraham Lincoln in the Emancipation Proclamation of 1863. This Constitutional Amendment formally abolished slavery across the United States in 1864.

19th Amendment to the U.S. Constitution   was ratified in 1920 and granted women the right to vote.

Bibliography

Cox, T. (1994). Cultural diversity in organizations: Theory, research, and practice. San Francisco, CA: Berrett-Koehler.

European Network of Heads of PES. (2011, December 8). Meeting the challenges of Europe's aging workforce: The Public Employment Service response. Issues paper adopted during the 29th meeting of European Heads of Public Employment Services, Warsaw.

Griffin, P., & Harro, B. (1997). Heterosexism curriculum design. In M. Adams, L. A. Bell, & P. Griffin (Eds.), Teaching for diversity and social justice: A sourcebook (pp. 141–169). New York: Routledge.

Harrison, D. A., & Klein, K. J. (2007). What's the difference? Diversity constructs as separation, variety, and disparity in organization. Academy of Management Review, 32, 1199–1228.

Irish Statute Book (ISB). (2016). Employment Equality Act, 1998. Government of Ireland. Retrieved from http://www.irishstatutebook.ie/eli/1998/act/21/enacted/en/print#sec2

McKay, P. F., Avery, D. R., & Morris, M. A. (2008). Mean racial-ethnic differences in employee sales performance: The moderating role of diversity climate. Personnel Psychology, 61(2), 349–374.

Sidanius, J., & Pratto, F. (1999). Social dominance: An intergroup theory of social hierarchy and oppression. Cambridge: Cambridge University Press.

World Bank. (2015). Overview. Retrieved from http://www.worldbank.org/en/topic/disability/overview

Index

Note: Page numbers in *italics* indicate figures and tables.